Jean-Luc Godard

Manchester University Press

FRENCH FILM DIRECTORS

DIANA HOLMES and ROBERT INGRAM *series editors*
DUDLEY ANDREW *series consultant*

Jean-Jacques Beineix PHIL POWRIE

Luc Besson SUSAN HAYWARD

Bertrand Blier SUE HARRIS

Robert Bresson KEITH READER

Leos Carax GARIN DOWD AND FERGUS DALEY

Claude Chabrol GUY AUSTIN

Claire Denis MARTINE BEUGNET

Marguerite Duras RENATE GÜNTHER

George Franju KATE INCE

Diane Kurys CARRIE TAR

Patrice Leconte LISA DOWNING

Louis Malle HUGO GREY

Georges Méliès ELIZABETH EZRA

Jean Renoir MARTIN O'SHAUGHNESSY

Coline Serreau BRIGITTE ROLLET

François Truffaut DIANA HOLMES AND ROBERT INGRAM

Agnès Varda ALISON SMITH

Jean-Luc Godard

Douglas Morrey

Manchester University Press
MANCHESTER AND NEW YORK

distributed exclusively in the USA by Palgrave

Published by Manchester University Press
Oxford Road, Manchester M13 9NR, UK
and Room 400, 175 Fifth Avenue, New York, NY 10010, USA
www.manchesteruniversitypress.co.uk

Distributed exclusively in the USA by
Palgrave, 175 Fifth Avenue, New York, NY 10010, USA

Distributed exclusively in Canada by
UBC Press, University of British Columbia, 2029 West Mall,
Vancouver, BC, Canada V6T 1Z2

British Library Cataloguing-in-Publication Data
A catalogue record for this book is available from the British Library

Library of Congress Cataloging-in-Publication Data applied for

ISBN 0 7190 6758 8 *hardback*
EAN 978 0 7190 6758 7
ISBN 0 7190 6759 6 *paperback*
EAN 978 0 7190 6759 4

First published 2005

14 13 12 11 10 09 08 07 10 9 8 7 6 5 4 3 2

Typeset in Scala with Meta display
by Koinonia, Manchester
Printed in Great Britain
by Bell & Bain Limited, Glasgow

For my father,
who introduced me to cinema,
to politics and to philosophy

Contents

List of plates

All stills reproduced courtesy of BFI Stills, Posters and Designs.

Every effort has been made to obtain permission to reproduce the images in the book. If any proper acknowledgement has not been made, copyright-holders are invited to contact the publisher.

Series editors' foreword

To an anglophone audience, the combination of the words 'French' and 'cinema' evokes a particular kind of film: elegant and wordy, sexy but serious – an image as dependent upon national stereotypes as is that of the crudely commercial Hollywood blockbuster, which is not to say that either image is without foundation. Over the past two decades, this generalised sense of a significant relationship between French identity and film has been explored in scholarly books and articles, and has entered the curriculum at university level and, in Britain, at A level. The study of film as art-form and (to a lesser extent) as industry, has become a popular and widespread element of French Studies, and French cinema has acquired an important place within Film Studies. Meanwhile, the growth in multiscreen and 'art-house' cinemas, together with the development of the video industry, has led to the greater availability of foreign-language films to an English-speaking audience. Responding to these developments, this series is designed for students and teachers seeking information and accessible but rigorous critical study of French cinema, and for the enthusiastic filmgoer who wants to know more.

The adoption of a director-based approach raises questions about auteurism. A series that categorises films not according to period or to genre (for example), but to the person who directed them, runs the risk of espousing a romantic view of film as the product of solitary inspiration. On this model, the critic's role might seem to be that of discovering continuities, revealing a necessarily coherent set of themes and motifs which correspond to the particular genius of the individual. This is not our aim: the auteur perspective on film, itself most clearly articulated in France in the early 1950s, will be interrogated in certain volumes of the series, and, throughout, the director will be treated as one highly significant element in a complex process of film production and reception which includes socio-economic and political determinants, the work of a large and highly skilled team of artists and technicians, the mechanisms of production and distribution, and the complex and multiply determined responses of spectators.

The work of some of the directors in the series is already well known outside France, that of others is less so – the aim is both to provide informative and original English-language studies of established figures, and to extend the range of French directors known to anglophone students of cinema. We intend the series to contribute to the promotion of the formal and informal study of French films, and to the pleasure of those who watch them.

DIANA HOLMES
ROBERT INGRAM

Acknowledgements

My thanks to the following for advice and encouragement, materials and hospitality: Steve Cannon, Paul Hatswell, Leslie Hill, Roland-François Lack, Chris Perriam, Phil Powrie, Keith Reader, Douglas Smith, Michael Temple, Ginette Vincendeau, Mike Witt.

1

Necessity or contingency: Godard as film critic, 1950–59

Little is known about Jean-Luc Godard's early life and, although the first authoritative biography of the director was published very recently (MacCabe 2003), the details of his youth remain somewhat sketchy. Godard was born in Paris in December 1930 to Swiss parents. His family were rich protestants, his father, Paul Godard, a doctor and his mother, Odile Monod, the daughter of a banker belonging to 'one of the most illustrious families in France' (MacCabe 2003: 5). Godard enjoyed a comfortable and cultured upbringing, acquiring a literary sensibility that would inflect the whole of his career in the cinema. His maternal grandfather was a friend of the poet and essayist Paul Valéry. Godard began to study anthropology at the Sorbonne, but dropped out, and the subsequent decade of his life was spent drifting between various occupations. It is this period of Godard's life in particular that has given rise to speculation, rumour and apocryphal stories. He avoided military service in both France and Switzerland and travelled in North and South America. Having distanced himself from his family, he survived on various little jobs, notably in Swiss television, but is also known to have resorted to petty theft on more than one occasion. Indeed, it was stealing from his own family that provoked a definitive rupture (Douin 1989: 12–13). But, if Godard's break with his family has frequently been stressed, MacCabe volunteers that this may have been the only way for Jean-Luc to 'separate himself from a too much loved and too seductive world' (MacCabe 2003: 4). The questionable nature of some of the tales surrounding the director's youth is reflected in Godard's own admission that, while working as *attaché de presse* for 20th Century-Fox in Paris, he amused himself by making up stories which would subsequently be reported as true in the press (Douin 1989: 17). What is certain is that, throughout the 1950s, Godard distinguished himself as a film critic, first in *La Gazette du cinéma*, then in the journal *Arts* and, most famously, in the hugely influential *Cahiers du cinéma*.

Along with other critics at *Cahiers du cinéma*, including Truffaut, Rivette, Chabrol and Rohmer, Godard's writing on film in the 1950s played an important role in shaping the canon of great film directors that would influence the development of both French and anglophone film studies. Godard was a particularly sensitive commentator on the new American cinema, two of his finest articles being devoted to Hitchcock (Godard 1998: 77–80; 101–8) with others extolling the virtues of Nicholas Ray and Anthony Mann. But Godard was also a firm supporter of those directors who were about to change the face of European cinema, most notably Ingmar Bergman in Sweden and, among his contemporaries in France, Chabrol, Truffaut, Franju and Rouch. Godard's writing on cinema is thoroughly infused with a literary sensibility, frequently offering comparisons between filmmakers and writers: Joseph L. Mankiewicz is compared to the Italian novelist Alberto Moravia (Godard 1998: 71) and *Strangers on a Train* (1951) likened to Goethe's *Faust* (Godard 1998: 79). This evocation of literary parallels needs to be understood in the context of the '*politique des auteurs*' propounded by *Cahiers du cinéma* in the 1950s. Filmmakers were routinely elevated to the status of great artists and thinkers, directors considered to be solely responsible for the style and meaning of a film. In Godard's determinedly romantic image, a director is as alone on the filmset as the writer before the blank page (Godard 1998: 129). But, if a certain polemical value is attached to these comparisons, the cinema, for Godard, is by no means a *literary* form. He is critical, for instance, of the films of Elia Kazan that are too beholden to theatrical and literary models (Godard 1998: 75–6). For Godard, cinema is not, first and foremost, a narrative form, but rather a new way of *seeing* (Godard 1998: 81). It is the attempt to define the specificity of cinema that led Godard to grapple, throughout his career as a critic, with the paradoxes of cinematic realism. As this question will remain central to Godard's work as a filmmaker, it is essential to gain some sense of the issues involved.

Readers who find Godard's films difficult or wilfully complicated may be surprised to learn that, as a critic, he frequently expressed his admiration for the simplest kind of cinematic realism. 'Le vrai cinéma', he wrote in 1950, 'consiste seulement à mettre quelques choses devant la caméra'[1] (74). As late as 1959 he opined: 'la première forme du talent aujourd'hui, au cinéma, c'est d'accorder plus d'importance à ce qui est devant la caméra qu'à la caméra elle-même ... Autrement dit, le fond

1 'True cinema consists simply in putting a few things in front of the camera.'

précède la forme, la conditionne'[2] (193–4). Cinema, Godard argued, was '[le] plus religieux des arts, puisqu'il place l'homme devant l'essence des choses'[3] (81). In these remarks, then, there is a rather surprising echo of André Bazin's evangelical rhetoric about cinema, a tendency to highlight the cinema's miraculous ability to *reveal* a world in mise-en-scène, rather than its capacity to *construct* a world through montage. The intriguing paradox of cinema which has fascinated Godard for over fifty years is its tendency to present the viewer *directly* with real life while at the same time suggesting that that life lies *elsewhere*. As he says of Mizoguchi, 'L'art de Kenji Mizoguchi est de prouver à la fois que "la vraie vie est ailleurs", et qu'elle est pourtant là, dans son étrange et radieuse beauté'[4] (124). The result is that those films that appear the most simple are often the most inexhaustible for the critic, such as Nicholas Ray's *Bitter Victory* (1957) which Godard called 'le plus direct et le plus secret des films, le plus fin et le plus grossier'[5] (121).

Yet elsewhere, Godard appears to contradict himself. On one hand, he says that cinema reveals the essence of things, but, on the other, he argues it is only the formal properties of films that confer this essential quality, this apparent necessity of the world on display. This is notably the function of montage: a skilful montage, argues Godard, 'métamorphosera le hasard en destin'[6] (92). It is also true of other cinematic techniques. Discussing the use of close-ups in Hitchcock's *The Wrong Man* (1956), Godard writes: 'La beauté de chacun de ces gros plans ... naît de l'intrusion du sentiment de la nécessité dans celui du futile, de l'essence dans l'existence'[7] (102). One can sense in these remarks the influence of André Malraux, whose work on the history of art would be plundered again by Godard some forty years later for his *Histoire(s) du cinéma* (1988–98). Godard borrows from Malraux a definition of art as 'ce par quoi les formes deviennent style'[8] (107), that is to say the means by which a series of specific technical choices come to represent an individual's *essential* expression.

If Godard believes in destiny, then, as he himself says of Hitchcock,

2 'The first form of talent in cinema today consists in granting more importance to what's in front of the camera than to the camera itself ... In other words, the content should precede, and determine, the form.'

3 'the most religious of arts, since it places man before the essence of things'.

4 'The art of Kenji Mizoguchi is to prove at once that "real life is elsewhere", and that it is nonetheless here, in all its strange and radiant beauty.'

5 'the most direct and the most secret of films, the most subtle and the most vulgar'.

6 'will transform chance into destiny'.

7 'The beauty of each of these close-ups is born from the intrusion of a sense of necessity in one of futility, of essence in existence.'

8 'that by which forms become style'

'Il y croit, le sourire aux lèvres' (89), he believes in it but with a smile, or a smirk on his face. Godard suggests that, in Hitchcock's films, the sense of fatality or necessity in the plot is often brought about through the most obvious or commonplace of cinematic effects. But this is the central paradox of cinema: it can only reveal the essential nature of things by showing their surface appearance, through superficial techniques. All of which suggests that there *is* no essence to things beyond that which *appears* to us through the evidence of the senses. If the essential nature of reality and the techniques which allow us to apprehend it are thus inseparable, then so too are the two poles of cinematic creation. In the debate between montage and mise en scène, Godard's position is clear: 'On ne sépare pas l'un de l'autre sans danger. Autant vouloir séparer le rythme de la mélodie'[9] (92). This consideration also leads Godard to conclude that, in the cinema, fiction and documentary are similarly inseparable. Even in the most artificially contrived film narrative, the *real world*, caught on film, will nonetheless make its presence felt; even the most rigorously factual documentary, by virtue of being organised through montage, partakes of fictional construction. The two forms are necessarily linked in cinema: 'Tous les grands films de fiction tendent au documentaire, comme tous les grands documentaires tendent à la fiction ... Et qui opte à fond pour l'un trouve *nécessairement* l'autre au bout du chemin'[10] (181–2). Godard will exploit this imbrication of fiction and documentary throughout his career in cinema and indeed it is one of the most frequently discussed aspects of his work among his early critics and commentators.

In the cinema, then, the question of whether the reality on display is *essential* or *constructed*, whether it is *necessary* or *contingent*, can be summed up with the following kind of childish logic: one says not 'il faut filmer ça parce que c'est beau, mais: c'est beau parce que je l'ai filmé comme ça'[11] (127). The problem of necessity and contingency is one of the oldest and most intractable in the history of philosophy, but also one of the most essential since it raises questions of the nature of time and causality and the possibility of human freedom. The question is how a situation that does not exist at one point in time can come to exist at a point in the future. How does a situation that exists only as a

9 'It is dangerous to try to separate one from the other. One might as well attempt to separate rhythm from melody.'

10 'All great fiction films tend towards the documentary just as all great documentaries tend towards fiction ... And whoever chooses one *necessarily* finds the other at the end of the road.'

11 'I must film that because it is beautiful, but: it is beautiful because I filmed it like that.'

possibility at one moment become a *reality* the next? Why are some possibilities realised and not others? This has given rise to a logical conundrum which states that, since something cannot exist and not exist at the same time, a possibility cannot emerge gradually but may only be realised *instantaneously*. But such would suggest that it was not a possibility at all but rather a *necessity*, in which case human will disappears. Worse, since the existing world has been shown not to be a consequence of the possible, it must logically be impossible! (Vuillemin 1984).

For the French philosopher Henri Bergson, this logical problem arises out of a confusion between time and space or, better, out of time considered in terms of space. Time considered in terms of an infinite series of discrete moments and experienced in terms of a succession of distinct states of consciousness is, in Bergson's analysis, simply time conceived as space, as an infinitely divisible expanse (Bergson 2001 [1889]: 68). This notion of an abstract homogeneous space is what allows us, as conscious subjects, to perform higher operations of reason like counting and abstraction. But our conception of time 'n'est que le fantôme de l'espace obsédant la conscience réfléchie'[12] (74). For Bergson, time, or rather *duration*, is not a quantity to be measured but an intensity to be experienced. The confusion of space and time affects questions of free will and determinism, necessity and contingency, because we tend to represent free subjects hesitating between two choices like forking paths, in other words a *spatialised* representation. If you take away this spatialisation, says Bergson, you are left with little more than the puerile truism that 'l'acte, une fois accompli, est accompli'[13] (137). The *possible* is simply abstracted retrospectively from the real which already exists. Bergson solves the problem of how possibilities are realised by talking instead about the virtual and the actual. Whereas the real appears in the image of the possible, eliminating thereby other possibilities, the actual does not resemble the virtuality that it incarnates. Actualisation proceeds not by the elimination of possibilities but by the *creation* of productive *difference* (Deleuze 1998 [1966]: 99–100). Time can be represented spatially, concludes Bergson, if we are talking about *spent* time ('le temps écoulé'), but not if we are talking about the time of *now*, flowing present time ('le temps qui s'écoule'), and it is precisely this latter which is the time of the free act (Bergson 2001 [1889]: 166). Duration is that

12 'is merely the phantom of that space with which reflective consciousness is obsessed'.

13 'the act, once it is accomplished, is accomplished'.

which is *other* and *multiple* without being *several*, without being *countable* or *divisible* (Deleuze 1998 [1966]: 35–6).

All this may seem rather abstract and distanced from the films of Jean-Luc Godard, but it is worth pointing out that, since cinema, more perhaps than any other form, is an art that exists in and is created from space and time (the literal recording of space *existing in time*), it is particularly well placed to address these questions. Indeed, Godard wrote in 1957, with implicit reference to Bergson, 'Les données immédiates de la conscience, Alfred Hitchcock, une fois de plus, prouve que le cinéma, mieux que la philosophie et le roman, est aujourd'hui capable de les montrer'[14] (Godard 1998: 104). Meanwhile, in *Alphaville* (1965), when asked about his religious beliefs, Lemmy Caution (Eddie Constantine) will reply 'Je crois aux données immédiates de la conscience'.[15] It is worth remembering, too, that Gilles Deleuze's famous and influential books on cinema repeatedly turn to Bergson for inspiration. In this book we will see how Godard's cinema explores some of the most fundamental philosophical questions – the nature of time and consciousness, the problem of language and the communication between subjects, the questions of causality and human freedom – through the recording, often in the simplest of ways, of space and time, space in time.

Naturally, it has not been possible to study all of Godard's films in this volume (the director's numerous short films, for instance, are not discussed herein). Nonetheless, I have sought to cover as many films as possible and, crucially, to give equal weight to each period of Godard's half-century in cinema. With the exception of the work of the 1980s, where the themes and methods employed are considered so similar as to allow the films to be taken as a unit, films are studied individually in order to help orient the reader within the otherwise bewildering range of influences and ideas that intersect in Godard's cinema. While determinedly pursuing the philosophical inclination of Godard's work, I have tried throughout to ground this theoretical interpretation in passages of close and concrete textual analysis to illustrate how the director's ideas take shape on the screen.

14 'Alfred Hitchcock proves, once again, that the cinema is today better placed than philosophy or the novel to show us the immediate givens of consciousness.'

15 'I believe in the immediate givens of consciousness.'

References

Bergson, H. (2001 [1889]), *Essai sur les données immédiates de la conscience*, Paris, PUF/Quadrige.

Deleuze, G. (1998 [1966]), *Le Bergsonisme*, Paris, PUF/Quadrige.

Douin, J.-L. (1989), *Jean-Luc Godard*, Paris, Rivages.

Godard, J.-L. (1998), *Jean-Luc Godard par Jean-Luc Godard, Tome 1: 1950–1984*, Paris, Cahiers du cinéma.

MacCabe, C. (2003), *Godard: A Portrait of the Artist at 70*, London, Bloomsbury.

Vuillemin, J. (1984), *Nécessité ou contingence: L'aporie de Diodore et les systèmes philosophiques*, Paris, Minuit.

2

Scenes from domestic life: 1960–65

À bout de souffle

From Godard's film criticism to his first feature, *À bout de souffle*, filmed in twenty-one days in 1959 and first released in March 1960, the transition was smooth. Godard once famously remarked that writing film criticism was, for him, already a kind of filmmaking: 'Écrire, c'était déjà faire du cinéma, car, entre écrire et tourner, il y a une différence quantitative, non qualitative'[1] (Godard 1998: 215). We will see later how *À bout de souffle* picks up some of the philosophical issues addressed in Godard's writing, but this debut feature represents a prolongation of Godard's criticism first and foremost through its proliferation of cinematic references, through the sheer joy with which it exhibits its cinephile culture. The film opens with a dedication to the Hollywood B-movie studio Monogram pictures before the title – huge capital letters filling the screen but with no further information on cast or crew – suggests a homage to, and a declaration of kinship with, the Orson Welles of *Citizen Kane* (1941) (Marie 1999: 53–4). Actual Parisian cinemas feature a number of times in the film as hiding places and *lieux de passage* and a young woman is seen selling copies of *Cahiers du cinéma* on the street. Above all, though, the film's narrative testifies to a deeply ingrained familiarity, an internalised identification with Hollywood genre cinema. *À bout de souffle* tells of a petty car thief Michel Poiccard (Jean-Paul Belmondo) who returns to Paris from the south of France in order to collect some money from an associate and try to persuade a young American student, Patricia Franchini (Jean Seberg), to leave with him for Italy. On the way back to Paris, however, he is stopped by the police and kills an officer, provoking a manhunt that will eventually lead to his death.

1 'Writing was already a kind of filmmaking because, between writing and filming, there is a quantitative, not a qualitative difference.'

Michel Poiccard clearly models himself on the heroes of American gangster films, most notably Humphrey Bogart, whose mannerism of wiping his thumb across his lip is appropriated by Michel. At one point, early in the film, Michel stops to look at a poster of Bogart (or 'Bogie' as Michel calls him) in *The Harder They Fall* (1956), and Godard briefly cuts the sound to give a particular intimacy to this personal communion between the two men. Indeed, this generic imitation in the film is so evident that *À bout de souffle* is not simply an imitation of film noir, but becomes instead a film *about* imitation, 'explicitly foregrounding and problematising the notion of imitation as such' (Smith 1993: 66). In this way, the serious tone of the original genre gives way to a much more playful atmosphere in Godard's film. Godard himself remarked that, although he thought he was making his own *Scarface*, it was only afterwards that he realised he had made *Alice in Wonderland* (Godard 1998: 219). The prologue sequence, in which Michel drives back to Paris, sets up this playful tone. Michel may be a gangster, but he is not a terribly convincing one (Cerisuelo 1989: 49; Smith 1993: 67) and, as David Sterritt points out, he ultimately comes across as rather childlike (Sterritt 1999: 48). In this opening sequence, he chatters away and sings to himself and plays with a gun he finds in the glove compartment of his stolen car, generally enjoying the sound of his own voice and the countryside he passes through. Yet, at the same time, the sequence constitutes a fairly classical narrative exposition since Michel's monologue reveals his character's motivations (to return to Paris to collect the money and persuade Patricia to leave for Italy), while the sudden murder of the policeman, unexpected even to Michel and disorientatingly filmed in a series of extreme close-ups and rapid cuts, installs the narrative tension that will be sustained until the end of the film.

This mixture of playfulness and reverent cinematic homage is also to be found in the film language that Godard employs in *À bout de souffle*. The film became famous for its use of jump-cuts, and it may be difficult for today's viewers, familiar with the ultra-rapid editing of music videos and advertising, to appreciate how disruptive this technique appeared to contemporary spectators. When a sudden cut to a different angle appears within the same scene without being motivated by a movement or a gaze, the image appears to give a little jump, an effect scrupulously avoided in classical continuity editing. The large number of jump-cuts in *À bout de souffle* arise from Godard's desire significantly to reduce the running time of the film without sacrificing whole scenes. The results can have a variety of elliptical and ironic functions, but most of all contribute to the dynamic rhythm and crackling energy of the film (Marie 1999: 73–4). In contrast to these very brief shots, Godard also uses a number of long takes, most notably of Michel and Patricia walking together in the streets of Paris, such as the shot on the Champs Elysées famously filmed with the camera in a post office trolley. As Michel Marie comments, these shots 'associent le couple dans une durée continue dont ils ne peuvent s'évader'[2] (Marie 1999: 75). Finally, Godard demonstrates his affection for film history by ending various scenes with an iris out, a technique which had fallen out of favour since the days of silent cinema. Godard uses this form of cinematic punctuation notably following Michel's communion with Bogart and after his own rather burlesque turn as a passer-by who identifies Michel from a picture in the paper and points him out to the police.

The playfulness of *À bout de souffle* is visible, too, in the lengthy central scene between Michel and Patricia in the latter's hotel room which, at twenty-four minutes long, constitutes by itself around one third of the whole film. This tendency to balance his generic action narratives with extraordinarily long sequences representing the domestic life of a couple is one that, as we shall see, characterises the whole of the first period of Godard's career. This is representative of what Serge Daney has identified as a general movement in European cinema between 1960 and 1980 away from stories of male heroes and towards 'un cinéma qui laisserait apparaître les femmes'[3] (Daney 1994: 114). The blueprint for most critical analyses of Godard's representation of women was provided in 1980 by Laura Mulvey and Colin MacCabe. They recognise Godard's importance in giving greater visibility to women in cinema and they appreciate, in later films, his examination of the commodification of sexuality within a capitalist economy. But Mulvey and MacCabe identify a significant problem in Godard's depiction of women: there is an automatic and simplistic equation, they argue, between women and sexuality; in other words, women in Godard's films are only ever portrayed *in terms of their sexuality* (MacCabe 1980: 85). Geneviève Sellier, picking up this argument, suggests that the long central sequence in *À bout de souffle* presents the stereotype of a woman who does not know what she wants (Patricia hesitates for a long time before finally sleeping with Michel) (Sellier 2001: 282). Implied in this argument is the criticism that, because women on film are presented from a masculine point of view, their desire tends to appear as an unknowable enigma. This is particularly true of the *femme fatale* in film noir, but Steve Smith, who analyses *À bout de souffle* in terms of film

2 'bring the couple together in a continuous duration from which they cannot escape'.

3 'a cinema which would make room for women'.

noir, gets into difficulty when he tries to assign Patricia to the category of *femme fatale* since, as he is forced to admit almost in spite of himself, 'sex is not ... the focus of prohibition and transgression in the film' (Smith 1993: 71).

On the contrary, what is most striking about the central scene in *À bout de souffle* is, once again, its *playfulness*. The sequence sees Michel repeatedly getting up and going back to bed, while Patricia is constantly dressing and undressing: she returns home in one dress, changes into shorts and a jersey, wears Michel's shirt after they make love and finally puts on another dress before going out. The pair play at hiding and revealing their faces (Michel with the bedsheets, Patricia with her hands in front of the mirror) and copy each other pulling faces before the mirror. They read to each other and listen to music, perform banal domestic chores, but above all *play games*. Patricia suggests a staring contest, betting Michel will look away before she does, while Michel playfully threatens to strangle Patricia if she does not smile before he counts to eight. All of which suggests that the sexuality and the gendered identities on display are not *fixed* at all, but are so many masks to put on and take off, so many performances to adopt and abandon. Michel plays the selfish and sulky child, the tough misogynistic gangster, but also the sensitive and sensuous lover; Patricia is the confident independent woman, the flirtatious *coquette* and the vulnerable *gamine*. The whole scene is one long, slow dance of mutual seduction, but one could argue that it is led, if at all, by Patricia, who sleeps with Michel but only when she is ready. And it should be pointed out that, while Patricia is dressed, as we have said, in a variety of outfits, Michel spends the whole sequence dressed only in his underwear (and occasionally his hat), his impressive torso on display throughout.

Michel's repeated attempts to telephone his associate during the scene serve to remind us of the generic narrative, but the urgency of Michel's flight from the police is forgotten as Godard fills the mid-section of his film with what is essentially dead time of the sort that would typically be expunged from classical narrative cinema. However, these long minutes spent with Michel and Patricia are vital in cementing the spectator's identification with the characters. As Michel Marie has demonstrated (1999: 85–6, 91–3), the sequence is constructed principally around long takes, which give the spectator a sense of evolving in real time with the characters, while the predominant framing in close-up allows for a rare sense of intimacy. If the playful qualities of *À bout de souffle* are doubtless largely responsible for the affection in which it is held by film lovers, there is also a more sombre side to the film – and its sense of passing time – which prevents it from becoming a mere frivolity. For a film which registers on screen and in the memory as so *vital*, it has a surprising preoccupation with death. Early in the film, Michel witnesses a fatal accident in the street and, later, tells Patricia about it. In Patricia's room, Michel tells a joke about a condemned man and, in a moment which seems to encapsulate the film's uncertain tone, asks, while playing with a teddy bear, 'Est-ce que tu penses à la mort quelquefois? Moi, j'y pense sans arrêt'.[4] Patricia admits she is afraid of getting old, a sentiment which finds an echo in lines from a Louis Aragon poem that Godard incongruously substitutes for the soundtrack of a western while Michel and Patricia hide out in a cinema: 'Au biseau des baisers/Les ans passent trop vite'.[5] Patricia also reads Michel the last line of William Faulkner's *Wild Palms*: 'Between grief and nothingness, I will take grief'. Meanwhile, Michel's expression of fatigue conveys a weariness with life itself: in Patricia's room, he says 'Je suis fatigué, je vais mourir'[6] while, at the end of the film, shortly before his death, he sighs, 'Je suis fatigué, j'ai envie de dormir'.[7]

There is doubtless a generic element to this preoccupation with death: these many references to death are so many premonitions which give a sense of fatality to Michel's death when it occurs at the end of the film. But there is perhaps more to be said about the treatment of death in this film. It might be tempting, initially, to give an existentialist interpretation: the morbid references are there to remind us that these characters are faced with stark choices which may ultimately lead to their death. As in the theatrical situations of Jean-Paul Sartre, this would then be a device with which to highlight human freedom and the necessity of taking responsibility for our choices. Both Michel and Patricia are faced with such difficult choices at the end of the film. Patricia must choose whether to run away with Michel and implicate herself in a life of crime, or give him up to the police and return to her career as a journalist. She chooses the latter. As a result, Michel must choose whether to run or to stay and face the consequences, and he too chooses the latter course of action. But there is still another approach we could take to death in Godard's film. The existentialist position implies a virile, stoical view of death as something which can give us greater knowledge of ourselves and our essential freedom. But, as Maurice Blanchot suggests, 'en cette mort véritable s'est bel et bien dérobée la mort sans vérité, ce qui en elle est irréductible au vrai, à tout dévoilement, ce qui jamais ne se révèle ni

4 'Do you ever think about death? I think about it all the time.'
5 'With the sharp cut of kisses/The years pass too quickly.'
6 'I'm tired, I'm going to die.'
7 'I'm tired, I want to sleep.'

ne se cache ni n'apparaît'[8] (Blanchot 1969: 50). This *other* death is of no *use* to us, it cannot be appropriated, understood or in any way *overcome*, for it is properly unknowable. It is that which haunts life without being, in any way, a part of life but without, either, being its opposite; it is, rather, that which is unthinkable from within life, that outside of thought which drives the process of thought itself.

Something of this sort would seem to be suggested by the conjunction of *looking* and *thinking* in *À bout de souffle*. Like most, and indeed perhaps all films, *À bout de souffle* is organised around a series of looks, but there is a rare degree of self-consciousness about the looking in this film, and also a sense of *futility* attached to it. On three separate occasions, Michel or Patricia, caught looking at the other, will say 'Rien: je te regarde'.[9] Patricia tells Michel, 'Je voudrais savoir ce qu'il y a derrière ton visage. Je regarde depuis dix minutes et je ne sais rien, rien, rien',[10] and later, 'On se regarde les yeux dans les yeux et ça sert à rien'.[11] Michel, meanwhile, seems preoccupied with the reflection in Patricia's eyes: 'Dès que tu as peur ou que tu es étonnée, tu as un drôle de reflet dans les yeux'[12] and, under the covers, says, 'C'est drôle, je vois mon reflet dans tes yeux'.[13] It is as if Michel and Patricia were looking for a kind of essential being in the other which isn't there, or rather which is nowhere *else* than in the superficial features they can see. Michel: 'Ton sourire, quand on le voit de profil, c'est ce que tu as de mieux. Ça, c'est toi'.[14] The *essence* of a person is to be found nowhere else than in their appearance, caught, as it were, unawares (as Maurice Blanchot puts it, this is 'ce que nous ne sommes autorisés à regarder qu'en nous en détournant'[15] (Blanchot 1969: 52)), as when Michel suddenly grasps Patricia's face in his hands and says 'Des fois tu as un visage de martien'.[16]

Thought is discussed in similar terms in *À bout de souffle*. Michel and Patricia talk about what they are thinking and discuss their desire to know what each other is thinking, but again there is a sense of futility to

8 'this veritable death has been sidestepped by a death without truth, by that which, in death, is irreducible to truth, by that which never reveals nor ever hides itself, nor ever appears'.

9 'Nothing: I was just looking at you'.

10 'I'd like to know what's behind your face. I've been looking for ten minutes and I know nothing, nothing, nothing'.

11 'We gaze into each other's eyes and it's completely useless'.

12 'Whenever you're scared or frightened, you have a funny glint in your eyes.'

13 'It's funny, I can see myself in your eyes.'

14 'Your smile, seen in profile, is your best feature. That's you.'

15 'what we can only see by turning away from it'.

16 'Sometimes you've got a face like a Martian.'

these questions. 'Tu ne sais pas à quoi je pense',[17] says Patricia, and Michel, 'Je t'aime, mais pas comme tu croies'.[18] Patricia complains 'Je voudrais penser à quelque chose et je n'arrive pas'[19] and, in a line which, as Jonathan Rosenbaum points out (1995: 20), Godard borrows from Ingmar Bergman's *Sommarlek* (1950), 'J'essaie de fermer mes yeux très fort pour que tout devienne noir. Mais je n'y arrive pas. C'est jamais complètement noir'.[20] Thought appears here not as something with a fixed and identifiable content or being, but as a *process* in a constant state of becoming. If you try to fix your mind on a single thought it appears impossible (if only because you are *also* conscious of the effort to concentrate on this one thought), and in this impossibility we glimpse precisely that unthinkable outside of thought which continues inexorably to drive thought forward.

These questions of the inexpressible, the unapproachable, are also raised in the film's treatment of language which has drawn much comment. Michel Marie has called *Àbout de souffle* 'a tragedy of language and of the impossibility of communication' (Marie 1990: 211). As David Wills points out, there is no 'pure' language in *À bout de souffle*, no transparent channel for communication: language is always mediated through various forms of translation (Wills 1998: 155). Naturally this is partly because Patricia is American and repeatedly has to ask Michel to explain the words he uses. But, at the beginning of the film, Michel also corrects the grammar of a *French* girlfriend, even though he himself talks almost entirely in slang, a kind of language within a language. Meanwhile, Michel and Patricia's misunderstanding is not only a function of their different nationalities, but more generally of the way in which they use language: as Marie suggests, Michel begins a kind of soliloquy in the film's opening sequence 'which Patricia's replies merely bounce off, without any real communication ever being established' (Marie 1990: 207). At the end of the film, Michel laments, 'Quand on parlait, tu parlais de toi et moi de moi. Alors, tu aurais dû parler de moi, et moi de toi'.[21] But the difficulty of communication is shown to be a necessary consequence of the slipperiness of language, its inability to fix definitive meanings. Patricia demonstrates this when she pronounces the phrase 'Of course' with three different intonations, implying

17 'You don't know what I'm thinking.'
18 'I love you, but not the way you think.'
19 'I want to think about something but I can't.'
20 'I'm trying to shut my eyes very tightly so that everything becomes dark. But I can't. It's never completely dark.'
21 'When we talked, you talked about you and I about me. But, you should have talked about me and I about you.'

three different meanings. The ease with which language can be detached from its referent is shown on two occasions in Patricia's room when she refuses Michel's compliments. When she denies that she is beautiful, Michel concedes 'Alors tu es laide' ('Then you're ugly'), though the sentence contains no less affection than the previous one. In exactly the same way, Michel replaces 'Gentille et douce Patricia' ('Sweet and gentle Patricia') with 'cruelle, idiote, sans cœur, lamentable, lâche, méprisable',[22] at which she smiles in agreement.

The problem of language in *À bout de souffle* reaches its conclusion in the final scene in which Patricia misunderstands, or mishears, Michel's dying words. Although this scene is frequently discussed, commentators have paid insufficient attention to the fact that Michel's line is *already* ambiguous for the spectator: exhaled with his dying breath, the line could be either 'C'est vraiment dégueulasse' or '*T'es* vraiment dégueulasse'[23] (Wills 1998: 160 n. 4). The policeman who has shot Michel in the back brutally cuts through this ambiguity as he repeats the line to Patricia: 'Il a dit "Vous êtes vraiment une dégueulasse"'.[24] In the final shot of the film, Patricia stares directly into the camera and asks, 'Qu'est-ce que c'est "dégueulasse"?' ('What does "dégueulasse" mean?') before wiping her thumb over her lip in an imitation of Michel's imitation of Bogart. It has been suggested that this look-to-camera implies an admission of guilt on Patricia's part and, as Charles Barr puts it, that her 'failure of verbal understanding stands for a failure of moral understanding' (in Cameron 1969: 16). I suggest it would be more precise to say that Patricia's final look testifies to the immense gulf between words (a word, for instance, like 'dégueulasse') and deeds, to the unbridgeable distance between Michel's last words and the irreducible event of his death. This look cannot be reduced to a single emotion like guilt but instead allows us to glimpse, on Patricia's 'Martian' features, an uncontainable *otherness*. This otherness is the terrible chasm that yawns between Patricia's desire, her actions and their consequences: the *difference* inherent in causality itself.

Le Mépris

Godard's most expensive film (largely thanks to the presence in a starring role of Brigitte Bardot), and one of his most successful, has also been written about more extensively than most. There are a number of

22 'cruel, stupid, heartless, pathetic, cowardly, hateful.'
23 Either 'This is really shitty' or '*You're* really shitty.'
24 'He said "You're a real shit".'

sensitive appraisals of *Le Mépris* (1963) in print, and I can hope to do little more here than summarise their conclusions. The film received a theatrical re-release in France in 1981 and, on this occasion, Alain Bergala admired its *airiness*, writing: 'Je ne vois que certains films de Dreyer ou d'Ozu pour être aussi aériens, déliés et musicaux'[25] (Bergala 1999: 15). As a result, Bergala suggests that the film seems somehow *out of time*, as though it could belong to any era of Godard's filmmaking, even to any era of cinema. This is perhaps also partly due to the imagery of classical mythology employed in the film and its timeless Mediterranean landscape. *Le Mépris*, adapted from a novel by Alberto Moravia, tells of Paul Javal (Michel Piccoli), a scriptwriter who is working on an adaptation of the *Odyssey* for the American producer Jeremy Prokosch (Jack Palance) and the German director Fritz Lang (playing himself). In the course of this project, his wife Camille (Bardot) falls out of love with him.

Despite its apparent timelessness, the film is closely related to others in Godard's first period by the presence of another lengthy domestic scene, in fact the longest of all at nearly thirty minutes. Once again, this scene constitutes a bravura demonstration of the creation of cinematic space. The sequence begins with a long take, the mobile camera following Paul and Camille as they move from room to room in their apartment, setting the table, running a bath and so on, a fluid, dynamic space gradually being created. The spectator's sense of the apartment is also created in offscreen space as Paul and Camille repeatedly call to each other from different rooms, an effect which serves to emphasise their separation and the increasing alienation of the couple – it provides, in Jean Narboni's words, a kind of 'montage dans le plan' ('editing within the shot') (Narboni 1964: 68). The discord between Paul and Camille is further stressed by the fact that they are repeatedly separated within the frame by doors, partition walls and objects of furniture (Marie 1995: 107). At the end of this long sequence, although Godard has the couple sat facing each other, his camera pans slowly back and forth between them past a white lampshade that suddenly appears unnaturally large. As Dave Kehr comments, the image suggests two people 'unable to inhabit the same frame but forced into the same shot' (Kehr 1997: 22). These techniques ultimately serve to create a domestic space that is at once familiar and strange: it is, as Harun Farocki notes, 'a nonunderstandable space' (Silverman and Farocki 1998: 43).

But this peculiar space is in the image of the characters who inhabit it, as their happy, comfortable relationship is slowly degenerating into tension and mutual mistrust. The whole apartment scene turns around

25 Bergala's adjectives are not easy to translate: 'I can think of only a few films by Dreyer and Ozu that are as light, as nimble, as musical'.

an argument that develops when Paul asks Camille why she is in a bad mood. This relates to an earlier scene in the film in which Paul unthinkingly encouraged Camille to ride alone in a car with the producer Prokosch. Although this scene seems innocent at the time, its importance is underscored later by repeated rapid flashbacks to it, but also, immediately after it, by a shot of a statue of the god Neptune: the camera pans slowly beneath the statue's outstretched arm, as though to suggest our subjugation to Neptune's divine will. *Le Mépris*, then, is another film about the problem of causality: specifically it depicts Paul's obsession with finding out when, why and how Camille's love turned to contempt. Alain Bergala has written better than most about this aspect of the film. He suggests that what Godard wanted to do in *Le Mépris* was to look at 'ce qui s'est passé dans un couple, non pendant des années (comme dans le cinéma des scénaristes) mais pendant un dixième de seconde ... invisible à l'œil nu',[26] he wants to show 'comment on peut passer en une fraction de seconde, entre deux plans, de la méprise au mépris'[27] (Bergala 1999: 19) (Bergala will use this same argument to describe Godard's filmmaking in the 1990s: see Chapter 9 of this volume.)

The argument between Paul and Camille arises, though, and ultimately leads to the destruction of the couple, precisely because Paul insists on going over this causal logic, obsessively trying to reconstruct a motive for Camille's contempt. It is not that there *is* no logic to Camille's feeling (as Dave Kehr comes close to suggesting when he says that her change of heart is 'beyond conscious thought' (Kehr 1997: 22)), rather that she takes this feeling as a starting point from which to reassess her relationship with Paul, whereas he takes it as an *end* point from which to work backwards to a cause. Godard seems ultimately more sympathetic to Camille's point of view here: in the notes which constitute his 'screenplay' for the film, he writes – employing once again a Bergsonian language – that he wants to show 'les sentiments dans leur *durée*, dans leur *évolution créatrice*'[28] (Godard 1998: 248). Bergala adds that Godard is more interested in showing than in explaining: 's'il se sert du cinéma pour montrer son expérience, ce n'est pas pour nous expliquer (comme dans le cinéma des scénaristes), mais bien pour comprendre en nous donnant à voir'[29] (Bergala 1999: 20).

26 'what has happened to a couple, not over several years (as in the cinema of scriptwriters), but in a tenth of a second, invisible to the naked eye'.

27 'how one can pass, in a fraction of a second, between two shots, from a misunderstanding to contempt'.

28 'feelings in their *duration*, in their *creative evolution*'.

29 'if he uses the cinema to show his experience, it is not in order to explain it to us (as in the cinema of scriptwriters) but rather to understand it by allowing us to see'.

Ultimately, then, it proves futile and destructive for Paul repeatedly to return to the reasons for Camille's change of heart, and certainly it seems pointless to try to circumscribe these reasons within *language*. The apartment scene continually demonstrates how the meaning of an utterance may be diverted or lost at the moment of its production. When Paul tells Camille that swear words don't suit her, Godard frames her in profile against a white wall as she pronounces 'avec une noblesse de tragédienne antique un chapelet de termes grossiers'[30] (Marie 1995: 115): 'Trou du cul, putain, merde, nom de Dieu, piège à con, saloperie, bordel'.[31] Camille's slow and deliberate intonation empties these words of their conventional meaning and makes them appear simply as strange, alien sounds, neither vulgar nor pretty. On another occasion, when Camille smiles at Paul, he asks if it's 'un sourire moqueur ou plein de tendresse':[32] 'plein de tendresse', she replies, in a voice dripping with sarcasm, such that the original intention of the smile is lost for good. Paul and Camille's difficulties in communicating relate to the problem of language more generally in *Le Mépris*. The preoccupation with translation that we noticed in *À bout de souffle* has here been generalised, as characters speak, between them, a mixture of French, English, German and Italian, necessitating another character, Francesca Vanini (Georgia Moll), to serve as interpreter between them all. The question of translation also affects the treatment of the *Odyssey*, as differing interpretations of Homer's epic are offered by Paul, Prokosch and Lang. As Kaja Silverman comments, 'The *Odyssey* is for all intents and purposes irrecoverable, disseminated into a cluster of competing translations' (Silverman and Farocki 1998: 32).

In the Judæo-Christian tradition, of course, the proliferation of languages is a sign of humankind's fall from grace and *Le Mépris*, with its preoccupation with an ancient world of gods, implies a nostalgia for an antediluvian world in which all language would be immediately clear and present to itself, with a perfect fit between words and things (a world, in other words, *before* language). Francesca and Fritz Lang, by virtue of their ability to speak all the languages in the film are, as Michel Marie remarks, on the side of the gods (Marie 1995: 79). This is demonstrated in their learned discussion of Hölderlin's poem 'Dichterberuf': Lang notes the way that Hölderlin altered the last line of the poem to change its sense: 'Ce n'est plus la présence de Dieu, c'est l'absence de Dieu qui rassure l'homme'.[33]

30 'with all the nobility of a classical actress, a string of vulgar terms'.

31 Swear words are notoriously difficult to translate: 'Arsehole, whore, shit, for Christ's sake, sucker, bitch, fuck'.

32 'a sarcastic smile or a tender one'.

33 'It's no longer the presence, but the absence of the God that reassures man.'

Elsewhere, Lang tells Paul that the world of Homer is a real world that is sufficient unto itself: 'la réalité se présente objectivement et dans une forme qui ne se décompose pas. Elle est ce qu'elle est, à prendre ou à laisser'.[34] Significantly, immediately following this speech, Prokosch asks Camille, 'Why don't you say anything?', to which she replies 'Je me tais parce que je n'ai rien à dire'.[35] As has already been intimated, while Paul gets tangled up in the knots of language trying to understand his wife's feelings, the presentation of Camille in Godard's film can often give the impression that she is somehow *beyond* language. At various points in the film, Camille is associated with the polyglot Lang and thereby with the language of the gods. In the apartment scene she is seen reading a book about Lang in the bath and, later, Lang recites a poem by Bertholt Brecht, whom he refers to as 'le pauvre BB'.[36] a formulation that also contains an obvious reference to Brigitte Bardot's own initials, at which Camille smiles knowingly. If Camille is further distanced from the language of men, it is because she is associated with nature: in Capri, she is at one with the Mediterranean landscape, swimming naked in the sea and sunbathing naked on the roof of Prokosch's villa, in contrast to Paul, who views the scenery through a picture window and Prokosch himself who, ironically, looks at it through a tiny postcard-sized window (Kehr 1997: 24).

There is, then, in *Le Mépris*, an undeniable equation of Camille with a kind of natural, *elemental* feminine sexuality. This is visible, too, in the apartment scene, where the centre of the frame is often taken up by a bronze statue of a woman, a further suggestion of the eternal feminine (at one point, Paul raps his knuckles against the statue's breasts and crotch immediately before slapping Camille in the face). In his notes on the film, Godard also compares Camille to that other figure of the eternal woman whose story he would film twenty years later, Carmen. Godard stipulates that Camille should be a brunette like Carmen (Godard 1998: 242), something he achieves in the film by having Bardot wear a dark wig in several scenes. In practice, however, this tends to work against the naturalising impulse, instead lending a degree of strangeness to Bardot's sexuality since it deliberately distorts her star persona which is so dependent on her being blonde. Finally, we should point out that the end of *Le Mépris*, in which Camille and Prokosch die together in a car crash, tends to appear as distinctly arbitrary and, as such, it is difficult not to conclude that Camille is being punished for her actions,

34 'reality is presented objectively and in a non-degraded form. It is what it is, take it or leave it.'

35 'I'm keeping quiet because I have nothing to say.'

36 'poor BB': 'BB', pronounced in French, sounds like 'bébé', baby.

and punished indeed for her *gender* which appears solely responsible for those actions. The sudden death at the end of *Le Mépris* has no generic or narrative motivation like Michel's death in *À bout de souffle*, but nor is it realistically motivated by milieu as in the death of Nana in *Vivre sa vie* (1962) (see Chapter 3).

The nostalgia that in *Le Mépris* is attached to the gods, to classical Greece (and, more generally, to the Mediterranean) and to *women*, is also notably attached to *cinema*, an attitude that will become increasingly important in Godard's work, culminating in his majestic *Histoire(s) du cinéma* (1988–98) (see Chapter 10). Although a self-conscious *love* of cinema has always been displayed in Godard's work, *Le Mépris* perhaps marks the first occasion on which the object of that love is seen to belong, almost irrevocably, to the *past*. The nostalgia seems particularly connected to an age in which cinema appeared all powerful, the studio system providing a formidable production line for this dream factory. This era of film history is enshrined in *Le Mépris*'s use of Rome's grand Cinecittà studios, already falling into ruin in 1963. 'Only yesterday there were kings here,' runs Jeremy Prokosch's opening line as he strides the length of the Cinemascope screen, 'and now they're going to build a Prisunic on this, my lost kingdom'. Francesca translates this statement somewhat loosely as: 'C'est la fin du cinéma' ('It's the end of cinema'). Although Prokosch is something of a cartoon villain in this film, an ambivalent respect for the era of great and powerful producers is one recurring feature of Godard's film historical reflection: in *Histoire(s) du cinéma*, he will compose portraits of the likes of Irving Thalberg, Howard Hughes and David O. Selznick. *Le Mépris* also finds Paul regretting the demise of United Artists, but above all the nostalgia for film history is *incarnated* in the figure of Fritz Lang who becomes, in Godard's own words, 'la conscience du cinéma' ('the conscience of cinema') (Godard 1998: 244). Paul recalls how Lang fled Nazi Germany rather than work producing propaganda for Goebbels and, as Dave Kehr suggests, this trajectory gives Lang a privileged position representing the best of 'European sophistication and American efficiency' (Kehr 1997: 21).

Finally, though, the nostalgia with which *Le Mépris* seems suffused, this apparent desire to return to some mythical origin of cinema, of womanhood, of European civilisation, is in a way undone by the film's final shot. Paul comes to say goodbye to Lang who, on the roof of Prokosch's villa, is preparing to shoot a scene for the *Odyssey*, 'le premier regard d'Ulysse quand il revoit sa patrie'.[37] We watch the filming of this shot and, as Lang's camera tracks Ulysses looking out to sea, Godard's

37 'Ulysses's first sight of his homeland'.

camera tracks along behind it and ultimately moves off left, away from Ulysses, to frame the empty sea and sky. The voice of Godard, playing Lang's assistant director, calls 'Silence' and is translated into Italian 'Silenzio', before the film ends. This remarkable shot, one of the most beautiful in all Godard, ultimately seems to make a mockery of the film's desire for a return to origins. At the moment when Ulysses is supposed to rediscover his homeland, his point of origin, it simply *is not there*, all we find is the vastness of the sea and sky, and *silence*. One can never locate an origin, Godard seems to suggest, much less return to it, for the origin is lost in that which comes after it, like the sea blending into the sky. Maurice Blanchot has said as much: 'C'est le propre de l'origine d'être toujours voilée par ce dont elle est l'origine'[38] (Blanchot 1955: 314): there is no way back from language, or from the dubious gift of consciousness.

Pierrot le fou

In a sense, *Pierrot le fou* (1965) appears as the culmination of this early series of films in Godard's cinema depicting the domestic life of couples. But, in another sense, it marks the beginning of a move beyond this domestic space. As Jill Forbes notes, *Pierrot le fou* is a transitional film in Godard's career, heralding 'the decade of rapid change that rendered the France of 1964 unrecognisable to that of 1974, and signalling the transition to a post-new wave aesthetic' (in Wills 2000: 108). At the beginning of the film, Ferdinand (Jean-Paul Belmondo) goes to a party with his wife but leaves early, offering a lift home to the babysitter, Marianne Renoir (Anna Karina), and spending the night with her. Godard gives us a scene in Marianne's flat the next morning which represents the last of the important domestic interiors from this stage of the filmmaker's career. The scene resembles the others we have seen in this chapter through its ingenious creation of space, its ludic qualities and its coded references to film genres, but it also marks a progression from those earlier films by its audacious combination of genres and by its radically non-linear montage.

The scene begins much like the others, a space of apparently everyday domesticity evoked in a long take with a mobile camera as Marianne prepares a breakfast to take to Ferdinand in bed. And yet, in the background of this shot, as though unremarked by Marianne, we see a dead body lying on a bed and a cluster of guns leaning against the wall.

38 'It is in the nature of the origin to be always concealed by that which it originates.'

Marianne takes Ferdinand his breakfast and breaks into song, not unlike Angela Récamier (Karina) in *Une femme est une femme* (1961). After this begins a voiceover in which the two characters, in urgent voices, speak in short, alternating phrases, Marianne's refrain 'Je t'expliquerai tout' ('I'll explain everything') implying that we are about to discover what happened to the dead man on the bed. A new long take then pans right from the dead man, past Ferdinand and Marianne, to show the same man, very much alive, entering the door. In other words, we have moved backwards in time *within the space of the same shot*, without any of the conventional signifiers of the flashback, without even a cut. The shot proceeds to show how the man was murdered while Marianne and Ferdinand's voiceover commentary continues as follows:

> MARIANNE: Une histoire ...
> FERDINAND: ... compliquée.
> MARIANNE: Partir en vitesse.
> FERDINAND: Sortir d'un mauvais rêve.
> MARIANNE: J'ai connu des gens.
> FERDINAND: La politique.
> MARIANNE: Une organisation.
> FERDINAND: S'en aller.
> MARIANNE: Du trafic d'armes.
> FERDINAND: En silence, en silence, en silence.[39]

This voiceover, then, suggests a generic narrative, but it is a narrative reduced to its most rudimentary and schematic elements: a vaguely evoked affair with arms dealers and the need to flee the scene as quickly as possible. As Marianne and Ferdinand leave the flat, Godard further confuses matters with a non-linear montage: one moment we see their car leaving the city, the next they are still on the roof of their building; a shot of Ferdinand getting into the car recurs twice, and so on. All this suggests that the scene is being presented from a subjective point of view: Michael Walker argues that the jumbled chronology and repetition gives the scene a nightmarish feel ('sortir d'un mauvais rêve', as Ferdinand puts it) (in Cameron 1969: 111), while Alain Bergala reads it as 'un événement déjà réélaboré par la mémoire en souvenir'[40] (Bergala 1999: 196).

So *Pierrot le fou* pays homage to generic film narratives, but only in the most fragmented, not to say tokenistic, of ways. Jill Forbes calls the film 'a brilliantly controlled exploration of different narrative genres' (in

39 'A complicated/story/Leave quickly/Come out of a bad dream/I knew some people/Politics/An organisation/Get out of here/The arms trade/In silence, in silence, in silence.'

40 'an event already redrawn in the memory'.

Wills 2000: 122) but, as Bergala points out, 'Godard ne se réfère pas vraiment à tel ou tel film précis, ses citations des genres prennent la forme d'une sémiographie, parfois même d'une pure et simple signalétique. Un gros plan déconnecté de revolver, par exemple, renvoie au film noir'[41] (Bergala 1999: 199). By the end of the film, such generic conventions as a rendez-vous in a forest and a shoot-out imply the culmination of the gangster narrative, even though by this stage it is barely clear what is going on. The other genre Godard makes use of in the film is the musical, although *Pierrot le fou* resembles a classical Hollywood musical even less than *Une femme est une femme* did. We have Marianne's song in the apartment, and another musical number later in the film with the couple dancing through a forest, Marianne singing about her 'ligne de chance'[42] while Ferdinand admires her 'ligne de hanches'.[43] Finally, the two genres are combined in the most unlikely of ways when the gang of arms dealers, who are using a dance troupe as cover, are seen practising their moves on the beach! On top of these generic indications, there are numerous cultural references in the film, covering everything and everyone from Velazquez to Samuel Fuller, from Balzac to Les Pieds Nickelés, Van Gogh and Picasso, Céline, Joyce, Lorca, Prévert, and so on.

Godard's cinema has always been highly referential. But what is perhaps new in *Pierrot le fou* is the sheer number of references Godard makes to *his own films*, be it through lines of dialogue, visual allusions or other means: Marc Cerisuelo calls it 'un festival d'auto-citations' ('a festival of self-citation') (1989: 111). Ferdinand and Marianne reveal that they have met before, five years ago, and, since both Belmondo and Karina have appeared in other films by Godard, it is tempting to imagine that, in *Pierrot le fou*, we are witnessing characters from *À bout de souffle* or *Une femme est une femme* five years down the line (Wills 2000: 50–1). Ferdinand's final line in this film is 'Après tout, je suis idiot', which echoes his opening line in *À bout de souffle*: 'Après tout, je suis con'.[44] Ferdinand talks about those days in which 'on commence à se regarder soi-même dans une glace et à douter de soi',[45] a line which recalls some of Bruno Forrestier's in *Le Petit Soldat* (1960). This film is further evoked by the form of torture employed by the gangsters, covering

41 'Godard does not really refer to specific films, his generic citations take the form of a semiography, sometimes even of a simple gesturing. A disconnected close-up of a revolver, for instance, refers to film noir.'
42 Her 'luck line' (i.e. on her palm).
43 The line of her hips.
44 Both mean 'After all, I'm being stupid'.
45 'you begin to look in the mirror and have doubts about yourself'.

Ferdinand's face with a cloth and soaking it with water (see Chapter 3). When Marianne returns to a subject she and Ferdinand have already argued about, he tells her not to start again: 'Je ne recommence pas, je continue',[46] she retorts, a line from *Une femme est une femme*. Ferdinand, who has no desire to go to a party with his wife, repeats 'J'y vais pas, j'y vais pas, j'y vais pas', just as Camille in *Le Mépris* told Paul 'J'irai pas, j'irai pas, j'irai pas'[47] in relation to Capri. The final shot of *Pierrot le fou*, of blue sky and calm sea, also recalls the end of *Le Mépris*. On a visit to a cinema, we see Ferdinand watching Godard's own short *Le Grand Escroc* (1963) starring Jean Seberg. The voiceover narration providing a fragmented summation of the plot is similar to a device used in *Bande à part* (1964). The presence of a Ford Galaxy and Ferdinand's observation that he is journeying 'jusqu'au bout de la nuit' ('to the end of night') recall *Alphaville* (1965). Other elements of *Pierrot le fou* will, in turn, be picked up in later films: a car accident in which the car is improbably balanced on its nose next to an incongruous fragment of bridge in the middle of nowhere looks forward to the anti-realist car wrecks of *Week-end* (1967) (see Chapter 4). Ultimately, then, the film threatens to create a closed circuit of self-referentiality, and Jill Forbes has suggested that *Pierrot* is 'a postmodern film before postmodernism was invented' (in Wills 2000: 122).

As we can see from the evidence of *Pierrot le fou*, when Godard refers to his own past, it is to a *cinematic* past, to the past as cinema. There is, in this film, a constant confusion of life with cinema and vice versa, a refusal to respect, or even to recognise, a boundary between the two. On their way to the Riviera, Ferdinand and Marianne stop at a roadside café and Godard interviews the customers found in this café. Framed in close-up, three people address the camera directly, giving biographical details of their date and place of birth and stating their current occupation. This appears to be an incursion of a purely documentary format into the film, but reality and cinema are confused here as one of the people interviewed is Laszlo Szabo, an actor who has appeared in other films by Godard (notably *Le Petit Soldat*), yet who gives his name as Laszlo Kovacs, the alias of Michel Poiccard in *À bout de souffle*. Meanwhile, an old man who clearly has been found by chance in this roadside café, gives his current occupation as 'figurant de cinéma' ('film extra'). In another scene, where Marianne and Ferdinand are driving in their stolen Ford Galaxy, Ferdinand turns round and speaks to the camera. 'A qui tu parles?' asks Marianne, and receives the logical

46 'I'm not starting again, I'm carrying on'.
47 'I won't go, I won't go, I won't go.'

response, 'Aux spectateurs'.[48] Later, when looking for Marianne, Ferdinand will ask a child, 'T'as pas vu une jeune femme, genre film d'Hollywood en Technicolor?'.[49]

If we find this interpenetration of life and cinema in *Pierrot le fou*, it is because, as we began to suggest in Chapter 1, for Godard there is no *essential* difference between the two. Cinema is made out of the very stuff of life itself. In an extraordinary text written for *Cahiers du cinéma* on the release of *Pierrot le fou*, Godard addressed this problem. The text reads almost as a stream of consciousness, Godard's allusions tumbling over one another as he struggles to describe the operation of cinema, all the while insisting precisely that its operation *evades* description. 'Difficile, on le voit, de parler de cinéma, l'art est aisé mais la critique impossible de ce sujet qui n'en est pas un, dont l'envers n'est pas l'endroit, qui se rapproche alors qu'il s'éloigne, toujours physiquement ne l'oublions pas'[50] (Godard 1998: 263). Cinema is about life, says Godard, is made out of life, and yet, when we try to describe or pinpoint life, it escapes our grasp. The proof is that, in trying to describe the *life* out of which cinema is made, Godard can find only *cinematic* references with which to evoke it: 'la vie se débat pire que le poisson de Nanouk, nous file entre les doigts comme le souvenir de Muriel dans Boulogne reconstruit, s'éclipse entre les images ...'[51] (262). So cinema is life, but life is cinema: one can only approach one, it seems, via the other and, with this movement, both recede from view and evade capture. One is reminded of the vanishing point of literature described by Maurice Blanchot in which words become reality (and hence disappear *as* words) just as reality becomes language (and hence disappears as reality) (Blanchot 1955: 44–5). The paradox is, if anything, all the stranger in cinema which composes with *real* bodies, *real* objects and *real* light: the film image is that obscure point of convergence where fantasy becomes reality and reality fantasy, where the unconscious desire of both filmmakers and spectators achieve a fleshy incarnation just as the recorded reality recedes behind a fictional representation.

48 'Who are you talking to? – The audience.'

49 'You haven't seen a young woman, like out of a Hollywood film in Technicolor?'

50 'We see how difficult it is to talk about cinema, the art is easy, but the criticism impossible, of this subject which isn't one, whose front is not the same as its back, which approaches even as it gets further away, and always physically, let's not forget.'

51 'life struggles even more than Nanook's fish, it runs through our fingers like Muriel's memories in the rebuilt Boulogne, escapes in between the images ...'. The films referred to here are Robert Flaherty's *Nanook of the North* (1922) and Alain Resnais's *Muriel* (1963). A recording of this text appears in *Histoire(s) du cinéma*.

More generally, *Pierrot le fou* demonstrates that life is *text*, that our experience is made up of the weaving together of a variety of discourses (hence Jill Forbes's labelling of the film as postmodern). A significant majority of lines in the film appear as citations, or approximate citations of generic film dialogue, literary texts, or advertising copy (in later films such as *Nouvelle Vague* (1990), it will become *literally* true that every line is a quotation (see Chapter 8)). At the party that Ferdinand attends at the beginning of the film, the guests speak in advertising slogans, for Oldsmobile cars and Printil deodorant, a condemnation of the emptiness of consumer society that looks forward to Godard's work later in the decade. Ferdinand himself asks a garage attendant to 'put a tiger in his tank'. As Barthélemy Amengual suggests, the tragedy of Godard's characters is that they are trapped in this logic of citation: 'Pierrot [i.e. Ferdinand] a beau chercher l'acte unique, l'originalité, la liberté singulière: l'auto à la mer, le suicide à la dynamite, c'est toujours du "à la manière de" (sinon de quelqu'un, à la manière d'un genre: surréalisme, dada, bande dessinée)'[52] (Amengual 1967: 163).

This is further demonstrated in the film's treatment of Vietnam, another recurring concern that points towards the committed film-making of the years to come. The first reference to Vietnam comes in a news broadcast on the car radio as Ferdinand drives Marianne home at night. The broadcast announces the deaths of 115 Vietnamese guerrillas and Marianne comments on how difficult it is to imagine the real lives of these men whose reality has been reduced in this mediation over the airwaves. At the end of the film, Ferdinand watches a newsreel about Vietnam in a cinema, a further conflation of the war with fiction, fantasy, spectacle. In between these two instances, Marianne and Ferdinand, short of cash, decide to act out the Vietnam war for a group of American sailors they meet at a port. The result is almost unbelievably crass, with matches used to make crude aeroplanes and suggest the burning jungle, while Ferdinand, dressed as a sea captain, brays the only words of American English he appears to know: 'Sure! Yeah! New York! Oh yes! Hollywood! Yes! Communist! Yes!'. Meanwhile, Marianne, with painted face and oriental costume, performs an approximation of East Asian vowel sounds, the escalating conflict signalled by the rising tone of voice of the two performers. Yet, with this overtly simplistic presentation, Godard perhaps manages to convey something of the jingoistic discourses which circulate in war itself. The American sailors are

52 'Try as he might to achieve a unique, original act, a singular freedom, when Pierrot [Ferdinand] drives the car into the sea or blows himself up, it's always "in the style of" (if not in the style of someone, in the style of a genre: surrealism, dada, the comic strip.'

certainly delighted with the performance, while Ferdinand and Marianne make their getaway, leaving 'Fidel' and 'Mao' chalked on the boardwalk.

But, if all this suggests a sophisticated argument about the imbrication of life and art, it is rather let down by the film's treatment of gender. As in *Le Mépris*, the heroine in this film will betray the hero and be killed at the end: Ferdinand shoots Marianne before painting his face blue, wrapping dynamite around his head and blowing himself up. But there is also a tendency, as in *Le Mépris*, to associate Marianne with nature, and with a concrete reality, while Ferdinand is associated with language and abstraction (he spends much of the film reading and writing). At one point, the couple list for each other the things they like. Marianne chooses 'les fleurs, les animaux, le bleu du ciel, le bruit de la musique'[53] whereas Ferdinand names 'l'ambition, l'espoir, le mouvement des choses, les accidents'.[54] Marianne's line 'Tu me parles avec des mots et je te regarde avec des sentiments'[55] would not have been out of place coming from Camille. Yet there is an inconsistency to this presentation of gender difference, the film seems unable to sustain this stereotypical association of woman with the concrete and man with the abstract. For if Marianne is associated with the simple life and Ferdinand with words and literature, then why is it *he* who wants to go and live frugally on an island? Asked what they'll do there, Ferdinand says 'On existera'. 'Oh là là, ça va pas être bien marrant!' complains Marianne, to which Ferdinand replies, 'C'est la vie!'.[56] Indeed, 'C'est la vie' becomes one of *Ferdinand*'s catchphrases, and it is Marianne who is bored on the island. She says, 'Allez, c'est fini le roman de Jules Verne, maintenant on recommence comme avant, un roman policier avec des voitures, des revolvers':[57] she appears to want a boys' own story of cars and guns. But later, Godard seeks to re-establish the same old gender division with two monologues to camera: Marianne says 'Ce que je veux, c'est vivre, et ça, il le comprendra jamais',[58] while Ferdinand muses on the impenetrable mystery of language: 'Quand Marianne dit "Il fait beau", à quoi elle pense? D'elle, je n'ai que cette apparence disant "Il fait beau"'.[59]

On one hand, then, *Pierrot le fou* suggests that art is life and that life is discourse, that language and reality are, in practice, inseparable. Yet, on

53 'flowers, animals, the blue sky, the sound of music'.
54 'ambition, hope, the movement of things, accidents'.
55 'You're talking to me with words and I'm looking at you with feelings.'
56 'We'll exist – That's not going to be a lot of fun – That's life!'
57 'That's enough of the Jules Verne novel, now let's go back to the crime novel with cars and guns.'
58 'What I want is to live and that's what he'll never understand.'
59 'When Marianne says "It's a nice day", what is she thinking? All I have is the appearance of her saying "It's a nice day".'

the plane of gender, the film attempts, unsuccessfully, to maintain a separation between these two domains, between the real and the representational. Ultimately, the only way out of this dilemma seems to be to join the two in an impossible totality. So, if in art, as in life, one can never quite grasp *life itself* nor *language itself*, the one inevitably disappearing into the other, *Pierrot le fou* aspires to a totality in which *both* can be held in their purity. Or, which perhaps amounts to the same thing, in which both are abolished. For this totality will be realised only through the deaths of Marianne and Ferdinand and the film's final suggestion of eternity, evoked through the image of sea and sky, and some lines from Rimbaud: 'Elle est retrouvée/Quoi?/L'éternité/C'est la mer allée/Avec le soleil'.[60] Arthur Rimbaud is an important presence in *Pierrot le fou*. The opening credits, in which the titles appear one letter at a time, in alphabetical order (so, beginning with a scattering of red A's across the screen) evoke Rimbaud's famous poem 'Voyelles' in which vowels were described in terms of colours. The association is strengthened by a poster seen later in the film in which coloured vowels are superimposed over a drawing of Rimbaud. It is notable that, at the end of the credits, all the letters disappear apart from a single blue O, which could thus also represent a zero, nothingness, and whose colour prefigures the film's final shot. If Rimbaud is an important model for the film, it is also because he is famous for having *abandoned* poetry at the age of 19, preferring *life itself*, and hence also death (Rimbaud died young after a brief career as a gun-runner, another trait echoed in Godard's film).

In a terrific article on the film, Marie-Claire Wuilleumier suggests that *Pierrot le fou* suffers precisely from its thirst for totality, from Godard's desire to show *everything*, the *whole* of life. At one point Ferdinand, for some reason impersonating the voice of Michel Simon, says: 'J'ai trouvé une idée de roman: raconter, non pas la vie des gens, mais *la vie*, la vie toute seule',[61] and, echoing Élie Faure's description of Velazquez which he had read at the beginning of the film, he adds, 'ce qu'il y a *entre* les gens et les choses, l'espace, les couleurs'.[62] But, says Wuilleumier, this proves impossible. One cannot control or hold on to life like this, for it possesses only itself: to want to grasp it is to want to stop time. And this is precisely what Ferdinand wants to do: he says towards the end of the film, 'Je voudrais que le temps s'arrête' ('I wish time would stop'). But this is only possible in death. Cinema, suggests

60 'It has been found again/What?/Eternity/It's the sea merged/With the sun.'

61 'I've thought of an idea for a novel: tell the story, not of people's lives, but of life itself.'

62 'that which exists *between* people and things, space, colours'.

Wuilleumier finally, can only search for poetry because, if it were ever to attain it, it would simply disappear. In *Pierrot le fou*, 'en cherchant pour la première fois à pénétrer dans cet *ailleurs*, le film en confirme, par son impuissance à le transmettre, l'impossibilité'[63] (Wuilleumier 1966: 304). To recall the conclusion of our discussion of *À bout de souffle* above, the essence of the real – call it the sacred, if you will – is to be found nowhere else than in the things we see, in the evidence of the senses, and yet somehow it only ever appears to us, we can only ever glimpse it, by turning away. It is across the privileged terrain of the couple, in the intimate domestic contact between two people who remain, somehow, complete strangers, that this anxiety of otherness is worked out in early Godard.

63 'while trying for the first time to penetrate this elsewhere, inasmuch as it is unable to transmit it, the film confirms its impossibility' (trans. in Wills 2000: 181).

References

Amengual, B. (1967), 'Jean-Luc Godard et la remise en cause de notre civilisation de l'image', *Études Cinématographiques*, 113–77.

Bergala, A. (1999), *Nul mieux que Godard*, Paris, Cahiers du cinéma.

Blanchot, M. (1955), *L'Espace littéraire*, Paris, Gallimard.

Blanchot, M. (1969), *L'Entretien infini*, Paris, Gallimard.

Cameron, I. (1969), *The Films of Jean-Luc Godard*, New York, Praeger.

Cerisuelo, M. (1989), *Jean-Luc Godard*, Paris, L'Herminier/Éditions des Quatre Vents.

Daney, S. (1994), *Persévérance: Entretien avec Serge Toubiana*, Paris, POL.

Godard, J.-L. (1998), *Jean-Luc Godard par Jean-Luc Godard, Tome 1: 1950–1984*, Paris, Cahiers du cinéma.

Kehr, D. (1997), 'Gods in the details: Godard's *Contempt*', *Film Comment*, 33, 5 (September/October), 18–24.

MacCabe, C. (1980), *Godard: Images, Sounds, Politics*, London, BFI/MacMillan.

Marie, M. (1990), '"It really makes you sick!": Jean-Luc Godard's *À bout de souffle* (1959)', in S. Hayward and G. Vincendeau (eds), *French Film: Texts and Contexts*, London and New York, Routledge, 201–15.

Marie, M. (1995), *Le Mépris: Jean-Luc Godard*, Paris, Nathan.

Marie, M. (1999), *À bout de souffle: Jean-Luc Godard*, Paris, Nathan.

Narboni, J. (1964), 'Ouvert et fermé', *Cahiers du cinéma*, 152 (February), 66–9.

Rosenbaum, J. (1995), *Placing Movies: The Practice of Film Criticism*, Berkeley, University of California Press.

Sellier, G. (2001), 'Représentations des rapports de sexe dans les premiers films de Jean-Luc Godard', in G. Delavaud, J.-P. Esquenazi and M.-F. Grange (eds), *Godard et le métier d'artiste*, Paris, L'Harmattan.

Silverman, K. and Farocki, H. (1998), *Speaking about Godard*, New York, New York University Press.

Smith, S. (1993), 'Godard and *film noir*: A reading of *À bout de souffle*', *Nottingham French Studies*, 32, 1 (spring), 65–73.

Sterritt, D. (1999), *The Films of Jean-Luc Godard: Seeing the Invisible*, Cambridge, Cambridge University Press.

Wills, D. (1998), 'The French remark: *Breathless* and cinematic citationality', in A. Horton and S. Y. McDougal (eds), *Play It Again, Sam: Retakes on Remakes*, Berkeley, University of California Press, 147–61.

Wills, D. (2000), *Jean-Luc Godard's Pierrot le fou*, Cambridge, Cambridge University Press.

Wuilleumier, M.-C. (1966), 'Pierrot le fou', *Esprit*, 346 (February), 302–4.

3

Outside: 1960–62

The separation of Godard's early career into two distinct categories of film is an artificial and a necessarily unsatisfactory gesture. The domestic scenes between couples that provided the focus for Chapter 2 recur in both of the films I will discuss here, even if they are slightly shorter than those to be found in *À bout de souffle* and *Le Mépris*. Meanwhile, as *Pierrot le fou* demonstrated, a burgeoning political conscience was also present in the films that are largely about relationships. The films I discuss in this chapter are characterised by an interest in political and social issues that would become more marked in Godard's cinema of the late 1960s: the Algerian war and prostitution. But, beyond their subject matter, perhaps the most significant factor linking these two films is a certain darkness of tone, a notably sombre mood. The films in Chapter 2 often had moments of sober reflection contained within their playful packages; the films in this chapter, on the contrary, have moments of playfulness that tend to be subordinated to the prevailing sense of darkness (the same could be said of *Les Carabiniers* (1963), *Bande à part* (1964) and *Alphaville* (1965)). Consider the opening line of *Le Petit Soldat* (1960): 'Pour moi le temps de l'action a passé, j'ai vieilli; celui de la réflexion commence'.[1] It is a rather incongruous line to find at the beginning of a film (it would seem more appropriate at the end), or indeed to place at the beginning of a career in cinema. Yet it announces the reflexive quality, the peculiar stillness that marks these films even in their moments of most apparent frivolity.

1 'For me the time of action is over, I have grown up; the time of reflection is beginning.'

Le Petit Soldat

Le Petit Soldat, made after *À bout de souffle* but banned from release until 1963, could, like Godard's first film, be looked upon as an existential drama. From a Sartrean position, the film's protagonist, Bruno Forestier (Michel Subor), might be described as a man acting in bad faith. Having deserted from the French army, Bruno is drifting in Geneva, working for the French secret military organisation the OAS. Yet, if he is linked to the OAS, it is not out of political conviction; indeed, Bruno does not seem to know why he is involved with them. In his voiceover commentary, he describes himself as 'un type sans idéal' ('a guy without ideals') and admits to being 'encore très con et très jeune' ('still very young and stupid'). Two things happen to Bruno in the course of the film which, were this a Sartrean play, would force him to confront his own mortality and the mortal consequences of his actions. First, the OAS orders Bruno to assassinate a Swiss radio announcer, Arthur Palivoda, with suspected links to the Algerian Liberation Front, the FLN; second, Bruno is captured and tortured for information by the FLN.

But, if these events do indeed place Bruno in touch with his own mortality (he certainly ruminates on questions of life and death in his voiceover and dialogue), crucially they do not help him to *make a decision* or to arrive at greater political conviction. The assassination attempt on Palivoda takes place in three stages: initially Bruno refuses to undertake the assignment; subsequently, when the OAS blackmail him by threatening to have him deported to France, Bruno attempts the assassination but finds himself unable to shoot at the crucial moment; finally, when the OAS blackmail him again by kidnapping the woman he has been seeing, Veronica Dreyer (Anna Karina), Bruno kills Palivoda. Ultimately, then, his action appears to be motivated more by his feelings for Veronica than by any political beliefs. Meanwhile, when Bruno is tortured by the FLN, he refuses to talk and undergoes a horrendous ordeal, yet it is never very clear *why* he will not talk. He decides, apparently almost arbitrarily, to remain silent, as though curious to see whether he will be able to hold out (he himself says, 'Je ne sais pas si je suis courageux, mais on va bien voir').[2] Eventually he becomes so weak and disorientated by the torture that he can no longer remember why he chose not to talk ('Pourquoi ne pas leur donner ce numéro de téléphone? Je ne savais même plus. Par dignité? Je ne savais même plus ce que ça voulait dire').[3] Yet still he remains silent.

2 'I don't know whether I'm brave or not, but we'll soon see.'

3 'Why not give them the phone number? I didn't even know any more. Out of dignity? I no longer even knew what the word meant.'

One of Bruno's problems in *Le Petit Soldat*, indeed perhaps his main problem, seems to be in trying to decide on what is important, or even what is *real*, what has the necessary gravity to lead to action. At the beginning of the film, he describes himself as 'cherchant ce qu'il y a d'important ici-bas'.[4] It is not that Bruno takes a frivolous attitude to life, but no one thing seems more important to him than anything else: there is a kind of flatness to his voiceover commentary, describing the weather, the city, his feelings for Veronica or his experience of torture all in the same tone of voice. If he has trouble taking a stand within the political situation, it seems to be partly because his view of that situation is always mediated in one way or another: either by the information he receives through the media (in newspapers or the radio broadcasts that provide a ubiquitous background crackle in the film), or, perhaps more importantly, through a series of references to an earlier generation, and an earlier political conflict. Bruno refers repeatedly to the 1930s and the Second World War, and particularly to artists and writers who displayed a political commitment in these contexts. He cites Louis Aragon, Jean Giraudoux, André Malraux, Robert Desnos, Georges Bernanos and Drieu la Rochelle, although it is notable that he makes no distinction between those who were committed on the left, like Malraux and Aragon, and those committed on the right, like Drieu. In a long speech delivered to Veronica at the end of the film, Bruno laments the demise of this generation and appears envious of their political conviction, complaining that his own generation is expected to act without conviction.

There is a general impression, then, in *Le Petit Soldat*, of a poor fit between the reality Bruno inhabits and reality as it exists in his head, or as it is spoken about by other people. In one extraordinary scene early in the film, Godard manages to convey something of this sense of uncertainty, anxiety or discomfort about reality. Bruno receives a message from an OAS contact telling him to catch a train to Nyon. He tells the friends he is with that he has to go to the station ('Il faut que j'aille à la gare'), but adds in voiceover: 'Ils ont cru que je disais "à la guerre"'.[5] Already, then, there is a sense that reality has slipped into the gap between these two words, that it is an uncertain, mobile thing for which language can only offer the most unsatisfactory of approximations. The same uncertainty even seems to characterise the weather in this scene: 'Allait-il faire beau, allait-il pleuvoir? Impossible à dire',[6] says Bruno. Once Bruno is on the train, Godard multiplies those instances in which there seems to be a poor fit, a disjunction between the reality

4 'searching for what's important in this world'.
5 'They thought I'd said "to the war" ["à la guerre"].'
6 'Was it going to be a nice day or was it going to rain? Impossible to say.'

Bruno inhabits and the language that labels and describes that reality. Bruno twice asks a fellow passenger for a light, but the man, with lit cigarette dangling from his lip, merely stares at him. Two men get on the train and tell a joke. It is a strange, and rather unfunny joke about a group of dullards who are fooled into thinking that 'intelligence' can be acquired by being hit over the head with a hammer. Whenever a joke is detached from its humour, its absurdity becomes all the more manifest, appearing as a vertiginously strange effect of language. This is a device that has been repeatedly used in Godard's films. Here, the sensation of discomfort is augmented because it is difficult to hear the joke properly: the speaker talks very fast, his words drowned out by the laughing and coughing of the two men, as well as the sound of the accelerating train.[7] The light in the train also serves to give the men a strange, and rather menacing appearance: they are generally filmed in heavy shadow, with the occasional shaft of bright light from the window cutting across their faces. Into this *mêlée* comes another voice which initially appears as a voiceover: a woman repeating 'Le gland et la citrouille, poésie de Jean de La Fontaine'.[8] A cut shows a woman holding a book and sitting near a child, suggesting that she is reading La Fontaine's fables to her son, and yet the repetition of the title in a monotonous tone of voice seems incompatible with such a situation. Just then, in an unlikely coincidence, the train happens to pass a station called Gland. The cumulative effect of this sequence is to generate a situation of tension and discomfort, the sense of a potentially imminent, though unidentified menace. It suggests further that the reality Bruno is having trouble identifying presents itself to us – is glimpsed in terror – in those moments where the sharp edges of experience seem to grind against each other (one is reminded of one of Ferdinand's lines in *Pierrot le fou*: 'Il y a trop d'événements à la fois'):[9] it is in the unbearable *noise* of experience that we approach the core of that which *is*.

More generally, we might say that, if Bruno is torn between two poles of experience – OAS and FLN, action and reflection, interior and exterior, noise and silence – the truth he seems to be looking for is to be found somewhere between the two. Not perhaps in their combination into a unity, but rather in the irreducible *gap* between them. This would appear to be the case in the scene in which Bruno telephones Veronica to tell her he must leave the city, but she is unable to talk openly to him because the FLN are in her room. To get around this problem, Bruno tells her, 'Dites des mensonges' ('Tell me lies'). Veronica replies: 'Je ne

7 The effect is increased for non-French speakers, since the joke is not subtitled.
8 '"The Acorn and the Pumpkin", a poem by Jean de La Fontaine.'
9 'There are too many events at once.'

suis pas triste que vous partiez. Je ne suis pas amoureuse de vous. Je ne vous rejoindrai pas au Brésil. Je ne vous embrasse pas tendrement'.[10] Here, it is in the disjunction of words and sentiments, in the awkward fit between the conventional meaning of these words and the emotion of the voice pronouncing them, that the truth appears.

The importance of this *space between* two terms is also shown in the film's location. Geneva is, as an early remark by Bruno makes clear, a city divided: 'un assez joli lac, le Léman, sépare la ville en deux'.[11] Moreover, Geneva seems almost to fall between France and Switzerland, too French to be truly Swiss, but too Swiss to be part of France. Switzerland, with regard to the Algerian war, was neutral territory, just as it had been in the Second World War, and the man Bruno is told to assassinate presents a radio show entitled 'Un neutre vous parle' ('a neutral voice speaks') (though in fact the suspicions of the OAS are confirmed when Palivoda is shown to be linked to the FLN). The notion of the *neutre* is a key concept for Maurice Blanchot and, although this linguistic coincidence may not justify such a *rapprochement* (Blanchot's *neutre* is usually translated as *neuter* rather than *neutral*, though the two words obviously have the same etymology), we might find further support for this move in a text on *Le Petit Soldat* written by Jean-Louis Comolli. Comolli suggests, but does not develop, a comparison with Blanchot in a review in which he argues that Godard's film 'mène ... la pensée jusqu'au bout d'elle-même' ('leads thought to its end') (Comolli 1963: 54). It is precisely this limit to thought, which we have already approached in our discussion of *À bout de souffle*, that Blanchot designates with the term *neutre*. If dialectics is the movement of thought that seeks to overcome the opposition between two poles by uniting them into a totality, the *neutre* designates the gap or gulf between those two poles that cannot be reduced, the irrecoverable *difference* that allows their identification as opposites in the first place. It is this *neutre*, also, which institutes the possibility of language, it is the unapproachable other against which language is enabled to signify. It is when experience degenerates to noise that we glimpse the *neutre*, the formless background that is precisely *not* a ground, the impossible condition of experience itself (Blanchot 1969: 66).

It is this that Bruno perhaps begins to understand over the course of

10 'I'm not sad that you're leaving. I'm not in love with you. I won't come and find you in Brazil. I don't send you a big kiss.' Jonathan Rosenbaum (1995: 23) finds a precedent for this scene in *Johnny Guitar* (Nicholas Ray, 1954) in which the sense is reversed: Joan Crawford pretends she has 'waited all these years' for Sterling Hayden to return and 'would have died' if he hadn't come back. Godard includes an auditory citation of this dialogue in *JLG/JLG* (1994) and *Histoire(s) du cinéma*.

11 'quite a pretty lake separates the city into two halves'.

Le Petit Soldat. Aside from the train journey to Nyon, two scenes appear crucial in this respect. The first is Bruno's first visit to Veronica's flat to photograph her. As Bruno tracks Veronica around the apartment taking her picture, he asks her a seemingly endless series of questions, claiming this will make his job easier: 'Je vais vous poser des questions, comme ça ce sera plus facile'.[12] He proceeds to ask her innocent questions like how long she has been in Geneva, where her parents are and whether she has a boyfriend, but also what she's thinking, whether she would be afraid to kill someone, if she believes in freedom and, repeatedly, why she looks so scared (the viewer might feel able to venture a response to this one!). Also, echoing Michel Poiccard, he asks: 'Est-ce que vous pensez à la mort quelquefois?'.[13] Blanchot suggests that, when somebody asks a lot of questions at once, as children often do, it becomes clear that 'toutes sont dirigées vers une seule, la question centrale ou la question de tout'[14] (Blanchot 1969: 13). This ultimate question, 'la question qui ne se pose pas'[15] (20), puts us in relation with the *neutre*, with that which makes all questions, and all thought, possible while always evading the question and refusing an answer. 'Le questionnement nous met en rapport avec cela qui se dérobe à toute question et excède tout pouvoir de questionner. Le questionnement est l'attrait même de ce détour'[16] (28). In the middle of his questioning, Bruno announces in voiceover: 'Elle m'a regardé d'un air angoissé et brusquement j'ai eu l'extraordinaire sensation de photographier la mort'.[17] If this is the case, it is surely because Bruno has glimpsed this *neutre*. As Blanchot says, our vision usually takes on a purely utilitarian character: in looking at things, we appropriate them, we assimilate them to our usual mode of understanding the world. But, when vision turns to *fascination*, as in the visual arts which represent a kind of *looking without object*, then we may suddenly be overwhelmed by the distance that separates us from things, the unbridgeable gulf between me and what I am looking at. As Blanchot puts it, 'la fascination se produit, lorsque, loin de saisir à distance, nous sommes saisis par la distance, investis par elle'[18] (41).

12 'I'll ask you some questions, that'll make it easier.'
13 'Do you ever think about death?'
14 'all are directed towards a single, central question, the question of everything'.
15 'the question that can't be asked'.
16 'Questioning brings us into relation with that which evades all questions and exceeds the power of all questioning. This represents the very attraction of questioning.'
17 'She looked at me with a worried expression and suddenly I had the extraordinary sensation that I was photographing death.'
18 'fascination is produced when, far from grasping something at a distance, that distance grasps hold of us, we are invested by it'.

The scene in Veronica's apartment finds a kind of terrible corollary in the scene where Bruno is tortured by the FLN. The scenes are linked by the way they are shot, mixing short edits with rapid pans and cuts to views from outside the building. They also share a sombre, serious mood granted largely by the measured tone of Bruno's voiceover. And both scenes create the sense of a domestic space, disconcertingly so in the torture scene where the use of the bathroom, the presence of a transistor radio and the jokes shared by the FLN in between sessions of torture lend the whole thing an eerie air of normalcy (Roud 1970: 40). But perhaps the scenes are most closely linked by an unexpected similarity in the situations. After all, Veronica had said of all Bruno's questions 'Je trouve que c'est comme si la police m'interroge',[19] and thus the comparison with the FLN's interrogation of Bruno is justified (Collet and Fargier 1974: 26). If questioning can ultimately lead us towards 'ce qui est autre que toute question'[20] (Blanchot 1969: 17), then so too can torture and Blanchot describes the way in which torture tends to reveal the *violence*, the necessary imbalance and imposition of will that inhabits all language. The true obscenity of torture, says Blanchot, is that it seeks to obtain a kind of *pure* language, the confession of a simple truth, all the while demonstrating the corruption and violence inherent to language, the power installed within dialogue (60–1).

Perhaps one of Godard's most remarkable achievements in *Le Petit Soldat* is in conveying some subjective sense of the experience of torture. There is a peculiar dilation of time in this sequence, such that it is difficult to say how long the torture has lasted. The repeated cuts outside to slow pans along the exterior of the building tend to imply ellipses and the passage of time and even, despite the appalling events, give a kind of tranquil regularity to the sequence. These shots imply the passing of at least a day and a night, but such temporal landmarks cease to have much meaning. Blanchot has written, too, about the deformation of time by suffering. Since in suffering we are divested of our power and possibility, he says, we lose our hold over time and become subject to another time, 'le temps comme autre, comme absence et neutralité': this is a 'temps sans événement, sans projet, sans possibilité'[21] (63). The miracle of *Le Petit Soldat* is in giving us access, briefly, to this time, in showing it to be situated somewhere beyond pain, beyond judgement, beyond thought. Indeed, in order not to feel the pain, Bruno tries to 'penser tellement vite qu'on ne pense plus à

19 'It's like I'm being interrogated by the police.'
20 'that which is other than all questions'.
21 'time as other, as absence and neutrality ... a time without event, without projects or possibility'.

rien'.[22] It is this terrible blankness of tone – in the image of the experience of torture itself which Bruno calls 'monotone et triste'[23] – that gives *Le Petit Soldat* its most extraordinary character, and it is this same tone that we will find in *Vivre sa vie*. It might be considered a kind of filmic equivalent of what Roland Barthes called 'l'écriture blanche', which he described as arising precisely out of the search for 'un troisième terme, terme neutre ou terme-zéro' between 'les deux termes d'une polarité'[24] (Barthes 1953: 59). In this way, said Barthes, we approach 'la fraîcheur première du discours, une écriture renaît à la place d'un langage indéfini'[25] (61).

Vivre sa vie

Vivre sa vie (1962), like *Le Petit Soldat*, appears, in places, to appropriate a kind of existentialist narrative form, only to move beyond it into something much stranger and more troubling. In *Vivre sa vie*, after Nana (Anna Karina) has just begun working as a prostitute, she meets a friend who has been working in the business rather longer and, in a café, delivers this lengthy speech:

> Moi, je crois qu'on est toujours responsable de ce qu'on fait, et libre. Je lève la main, je suis responsable. Je tourne la tête à droite, je suis responsable. Je suis malheureuse, je suis responsable. Je fume une cigarette, je suis responsable. Je ferme mes yeux, je suis responsable. J'oublie que je suis responsable, mais je le suis ... Après tout, tout est bon: il n'y a qu'à s'intéresser aux choses et les trouver belles. Un message, c'est un message; une assiette, c'est une assiette; les hommes sont les hommes, et la vie c'est la vie.[26]

This bespeaks a relatively simple and straightforward attitude to life in which everyone is responsible for their own happiness and all is right

22 'think so quickly you're no longer thinking of anything'.

23 'monotonous and sad'. We might point out that, if Claire Denis's appropriation of the character Bruno Forestier for her film *Beau travail* (1998) is justified, it is above all by the understanding she demonstrates of this *tone*.

24 'a third term, a neutral or zero-term between the two terms of a polarity'.

25 'the primal freshness of discourse, writing is reborn in the place of an undefined language'.

26 'I believe we're always responsible for what we do, and free. I raise my hand, I'm responsible. I turn my head to the right, I'm responsible. I'm unhappy, I'm responsible. I smoke a cigarette, I'm responsible. I close my eyes, I'm responsible. I may forget that I'm responsible, but I am ... After all, it's all good: you just have to take an interest in things to find them beautiful. A message is a message, a plate is a plate, people are people and life is life.'

with the world, things corresponding to themselves in perfect simplicity. But, as V. F. Perkins remarks, Nana speaks these lines in 'a tone of perfect complacency' (in Cameron 1969: 37) and David Sterritt adds that these 'repetitive, ritualistic phrases' have 'the sophistication of, say, a self-help manual or a greeting card' and that Nana appears above all to be trying to convince *herself* of her own freedom (Sterritt 1999: 78). Godard's film will repeatedly question Nana's discourse, first by showing that, even if things do correspond to themselves, our need to use language to name them installs an insuperable gap between us and them. As Nana says twice in the film: 'Plus on parle, plus les mots ne veulent rien dire'.[27] Second, the film will document Nana's slow decline into a world of prostitution in which, precisely, she has no control, she can exert little responsibility, she is not free.

Discussion of *Vivre sa vie* has tended to focus on Godard's use of techniques of distanciation inherited from Bertholt Brecht, which serve to disconnect the spectator from the fictional world in order to drive home a political message and stress the fact that artistic work itself belongs to a political history. Godard himself suggests that the division of his film into twelve 'tableaux' was intended to accentuate 'le côté théâtre, le côté Brecht' ('the theatrical, or Brechtian side') (Godard 1998: 221), and there are undoubtedly a number of techniques used to maintain a distance between the spectator and the fiction. The film's opening scene has become famous in this regard. Nana and her estranged husband Paul (André S. Labarthe) are having a conversation, sitting at the bar in a café. The scene is filmed, as conversations on film often are, with a mixture of two-shots and a shot-reverse shot formation, but Nana and Paul never turn around, keeping their backs to the camera throughout. This refusal to show the characters' faces tends to prevent identification, to prevent the spectator from entering fully into the fictional space. Harun Farocki has further commented on the use of 'pick-ups' in this scene, a device whereby an actor pronounces the same line at the end of one shot and the beginning of the next, one of these lines subsequently being eliminated at the editing stage (Silverman and Farocki 1998: 4). Godard deliberately leaves both lines in, stressing the artificial, constructed nature of the scene. 'Qu'est-ce que c'est que ce regard?' ('What's that look for?') asks Nana while the camera is on her, then, as it cuts to Paul, the line is repeated.

But, although Brecht's importance to Godard is beyond doubt and would become more marked later in the decade, I would like to suggest another model for *Vivre sa vie* from a surprisingly different source.

27 'The more we speak, the less words seem to mean.'

Robert Bresson, the famously austere Catholic filmmaker, may appear superficially very different to Godard, but the latter's recent work has revealed the extent of Bresson's influence over him. In *Histoire(s) du cinéma*, for example, Bresson appears as a far more important model for Godard's thinking on cinema than Brecht. And indeed, if Godard likens his twelve tableaux to a Brechtian device, other critics have compared it to the twelve stations of the cross, a more Bressonian idea (Beh 1976: 183). The kinship with Bresson can be felt in a number of ways in *Vivre sa vie*. First, we might point to the presence of Joan of Arc. Nana goes to a cinema to watch Carl Dreyer's *La Passion de Jeanne d'Arc* (1928) and Godard intercuts silent images from the film with close-ups of Nana, tears streaming down her face. By a striking coincidence, Bresson too was inspired by the story of Joan of Arc at this time: his *Procès de Jeanne d'Arc* was released only a few months after *Vivre sa vie* (in March 1963). This sense of a convergence of interests between Godard and Bresson is reinforced by Jean-Luc Douin's assertion that, during the filming of *Vivre sa vie*, Godard was obsessed with the idea of adapting Georges Bernanos's *Mouchette*, which Bresson would bring to the screen in 1966 (Douin 1989: 134).

But, beyond these coincidental links, there are a number of formal similarities between *Vivre sa vie* and Bresson's work. *Vivre sa vie* is probably the most austere of all Godard's films: there is a simplicity, a rigour, even a minimalism to the way many of its scenes are shot that resembles Bresson. There is a general tendency not to use more shots than are strictly necessary, and an overall limitation of focus in the film (with one or two exceptions which we will consider below). Godard tends to frame characters in medium shot, to move the camera only when they move, and to cut only when new information is introduced. A scene at Nana's apartment is exemplary here. A first shot shows Nana approaching the door to her courtyard, then abruptly changing her mind. A second shot reveals the reason for this hesitation: the presence of Nana's landlady. Finally, a third shot, with a high angle over the whole courtyard, shows Nana approach and ask for her key, pretend to leave, run back and attempt to gain access to the building before being blocked by the landlady's husband. In just three shots and the most minimal dialogue, Nana's economic trap has been made clear: unable to pay her rent, she will be driven first to theft and subsequently to prostitution.

Vivre sa vie also recalls Bresson in the film's ability to make us feel the real weight of things. This is partly because Godard uses natural light and sound in the film, the latter often picked up by a single microphone (Roud 1970: 74; Cannon 1996: 287), but it is also more than this. Godard, like Bresson, is a filmmaker who goes beyond realism: instead of showing us things as we recognise them from our everyday lives, he makes us see things as we have never seen them before, he makes ordinary objects appear alien. This is notable in Bresson's treatment of sound, as in Godard's. In the café scene at the beginning of the film, Nana and Paul eventually get up to go and play pinball, and we hear the sharp clacking of ball against flipper. Certainly there is a clarity, a precision to the sound here, but what is most remarkable is the way the silence beneath the sound, or rather *against which* it sounds, makes itself felt, something that Bresson too has always known how to achieve. 'Sois sûr d'avoir épuisé tout ce qui se communique par l'immobilité et le silence',[28] a line from Bresson's *Notes sur le cinématographe* (1975: 33), recurs in Godard's *Histoire(s) du cinéma* and *Éloge de l'amour* (2001). An analogous effect is achieved in the visual register when Bresson and Godard allow us to see objects – including bodies *as* objects – in all their strangeness. Harun Farocki cites a good example in *Vivre sa vie*: on Nana's first visit to the boulevards on which the prostitutes ply their trade, Godard gives us a slow pan along a white wall on which is written some graffiti which we can't quite read. As Farocki suggests, 'this is an image which somehow doesn't signify, an image which says only "wall" or "graffiti"' (Silverman and Farocki 1998: 14). This wall is not made to *mean* anything but rather presented to us in its irreducible otherness as a *thing*, a wall. Similar examples occur in the film with a bar of soap placed on a bedside table, and a man's back when he removes his shirt.

Another common feature of Bresson's films found in *Vivre sa vie* is the director's insistence on revealing what is going to happen before it does. Bresson strips away all conventional narrative suspense from his films by letting the audience know as early as possible the outcome of the film (in *Un condamné à mort s'est échappé* (*A Man Escaped*, 1956), as early as the title). The result is that a very *different* kind of suspense emerges, the spectator waiting not to see *what* will happen, but *how* events will become infused with the mysterious movement that leads to their inevitable conclusion. In this way, Bresson seeks to evoke the movement of divine grace. One might attribute a different motivation to Godard's adoption of this technique, for example showing how Nana is caught up in a causal chain of events that is beyond her control (although opinions will differ as to how far this really diverges from Bresson's intention). What is clear is that Godard too predicts the events of his film: each tableau is preceded by a title card announcing tersely what is going to happen, right down to the gunshots fired outside a café

28 'Make sure you have extracted all the meaning you can from stillness and silence.'

which, in other films, would be expected to surprise the viewer. There may be no title actually announcing Nana's death at the end of the film, but commentators have suggested that this death is foreseen in the earlier gunshots, in Nana's identification with Joan of Arc, in her early comment 'J'en ai marre, je veux mourir',[29] in the account she hears of Porthos's death in *Vingt ans après*, or in the quotation from Poe's 'Oval Portrait' (see below). As V. F. Perkins comments, Nana's death is made into a 'formal necessity' by the film (in Cameron 1969: 35).

What, then, are we to make of this stylistic resemblance to Bresson? How does this presentation affect our view of Nana? And how does she compare to some of Godard's other female characters? If there is a sense of necessity to Nana's death, is it because of some spurious equation between female sexuality and whoredom that requires Nana's punishment? I think not. The sense of predetermination that at times invests Godard's narrative does not reduce its realist impact or its political import, and those critics who claim that we are not told *why* Nana becomes a prostitute (Beh 1976: 181–2; Douin 1989: 135) have clearly not been watching the film closely enough. Nana asks several people at the beginning of the film if she can borrow money, she appears (as we saw) unable to pay her rent, and she eventually winds up before the police, having resorted to theft. Furthermore, Steve Cannon suggests that the film's scope is wide enough to imply that 'prostitution represents the basic condition of labour under capitalism' (Cannon 1996: 289), a point underscored by certain similarities between the scenes of Nana at work in a record shop and the later scenes of her prostitution. The parallel is in the client's anonymity and Nana's effacement, as Cannon suggests, but it is also in the slow pan along the shelves of records which equates to the tracking shots past whores on the street, themselves reduced to so much merchandise. Further, Nana's exchange with her bored co-workers in the shop prefigures similar scenes in the brothel.

But the grim unfolding of Nana's predicament, with seemingly little warmth reserved for the character, has led to criticism of Godard's film. Critics have lamented the apparent lack of interiority granted to Nana. As Steve Cannon puts it, she is 'an object to whom things happen rather than a conscious subject' (Cannon 1996: 286). But it is important not to lose sight of the cinema's constitutive difficulty in representing interiority: it can only ever suggest an interior world by filming the outside of things. As Godard remarks: 'Comment rendre le dedans? Eh bien, justement, en restant sagement dehors'[30] (Godard 1998: 229).

29 'I've had enough, I want to die.'
30 'How can we represent the inside? Precisely by remaining scrupulously outside.'

And, once again in *Vivre sa vie*, it is the uncomfortable fit between aspects of this *outside* that will suggest an interior world. Consider the scene in which Godard quotes lengthy sections of a report on the state of prostitution by one Marcel Sacotte. His stroke of genius, here, is to juxtapose these quotations with Nana's questions, as though she were receiving answers from her pimp Raoul (Sady Rebot) (and the juxtaposition of this scene with the one in which Nana agrees to work for Raoul reinforces this impression). The voiceover gives statistics about prostitution, describes a prostitute's typical day and details the legal position on the matter, but the rather haughty academic tone of the report sits oddly against Nana's naive and slightly timid questions. The voiceover strips all emotion away from the question of prostitution, just as some have suggested Godard's slightly clinical filmmaking does, yet Anna Karina's subtly nuanced performance manages to retain some emotion for her character. The result, finally, is all the more powerful because Nana's emotion appears lost and alone in a cold and empty world. The same effect is generated in a scene that shows Nana on her night off. Having missed a film showing, she retires with Raoul and his associates to a room above a bar. Nana puts on the jukebox and dances around the room, but the gleeful release of energy represented by this dance is viciously undermined by a point-of-view shot that shows the walls in which Nana is enclosed and the blackness of the night outside (Cannon 1996: 289). Similarly, when a friend of Raoul's tries to cheer Nana up by imitating a child inflating a balloon, Nana laughs, but the silence behind the laughter is deafening. This, perhaps, is what Godard means when he talks of his effort to 'extraire des plans de la nuit' ('extract shots from the night') (Godard 1998: 227).

The poor fit between the image Nana has of herself and the image appropriated by her pimps and johns is perhaps alluded to when, at the end of her interview with the police, she says 'Je est un autre',[31] another of Godard's references to Rimbaud (see Chapter 2 of this volume on *Pierrot le fou*). The line sounds rather incongruous coming from Nana, and it is certainly not something one would readily expect to say in a police station, so this is one of a handful of moments when the film's essentially realistic approach breaks down. Another is the scene towards the end where Nana meets the philosopher Brice Parain by chance in a café and engages him in conversation (Godard labels this scene somewhat patronisingly 'Nana fait de la philosophie sans le savoir').[32] This scene represents something like a theoretical summary of the

31 'I is another' or 'I is someone else'.
32 'Nana does philosophy without realising it.'

position occupied by Godard across his early films. Nana and Parain discuss language. Nana, lamenting the inadequacy of language to describe experience, asks 'Pourquoi faut-il toujours parler?'.[33] But Parain defends language, arguing that ultimately we have no choice: 'Il faut qu'on pense; pour penser, il faut parler'.[34] It is practically impossible to distinguish thought from the language we use to express thoughts, even if this implies a necessary detachment from life: 'On ne peut bien parler que quand on regarde la vie avec détachement'.[35] Words may never be entirely adequate, but they are the best we have. Such is the lesson of the German tradition in philosophy: 'On pense dans la vie avec les choses de la vie, il faut se débrouiller avec ça',[36] and, with practice, one becomes better at finding *le mot juste*.

The other scene in *Vivre sa vie* that diverges from the film's broadly realist aesthetic similarly finds Godard reflecting on the nature of his work in cinema. In the penultimate scene of the film, Nana is seen in a bedroom with a young man with whom she seems to have established a relationship. The man is reading from the complete works of Edgar Allan Poe, but his mouth is hidden behind the book and, in voiceover, it is *Godard's* voice we hear reading from 'The Oval Portrait'. In this story, an artist neglects his wife in favour of the portrait he is painting of her. He becomes engrossed in rendering as lifelike a portrait as possible until, finally, when he feels able to declare that the painting is 'la vie elle-même' ('life itself'), he finds that his wife is dead. The fact that Godard himself reads this text while lovingly framing Anna Karina's face in close-up is of capital significance since, as audiences at the time and since have been aware, the director was married to his leading actress. This scene appears, then, as a kind of *mea culpa* on the part of Godard, whose relationship with Karina was in difficulty at the time. Godard appears to blame himself for neglecting his wife in the pursuit of his art, for caring more about Karina's role in his films than in his life. Silverman and Farocki even suggest that this admission of guilt fans out to encompass the rest of the film, Godard implicitly comparing himself to Nana's pimps and clients who use her body for their own ends, just as he does in the cinema (Silverman and Farocki 1998: 28). It is a consequence of the cinema's proximity to life itself (as we discussed with regard to *Pierrot le fou* in Chapter 2) that it very easily gives rise to this kind of misuse. By allowing us to see the world anew, cinema can

33 'Why do we have to talk all the time?'
34 'We have to think, and to think we have to talk.'
35 'We can only really talk when we look at life with detachment.'
36 'In this life, we can only think using the things of this life, we have to manage with what we've got.'

play an important social and political role – indeed a revolutionary role, as we shall see – in shaping our relationship to the world. Yet at the same time, it can all too easily come to *replace* the world, to substitute for the world its addictive allure. There is no essential difference between these two different destinies of the cinema, these two different uses to which it may be put, for they both grow out of the medium's necessary proximity to the real. Godard will wrestle with this paradox at length in *Histoire(s) du cinéma*, which includes a discreet implication of his own neglect of Karina *via* cinema.

There is one final detail in *Vivre sa vie* that would seem to corroborate this reading. The film's last scene, in which Nana dies when caught in a shoot-out between Raoul and a rival pimp, has been discussed by critics, but few seem to have remarked upon an incidental detail here. On the way to the rendez-vous, the group pass a cinema where a queue is forming to see Truffaut's *Jules et Jim* (1961). Raoul's driver remarks: 'Le cinéma, c'est pas drôle. La semaine, on ne peut pas y aller, on travaille. Et le dimanche, il y a toujours la queue'.[37] This is, I would suggest, more than a light-hearted dig at Truffaut. The line has the authentic ring of Godard's films of the late 1960s and early 1970s in which he angrily dismantled the empty promises that the leisure economy makes to the working classes. The inclusion of this line in *Vivre sa vie*, even in the mouth of a no-good pimp, indicates Godard's desire, by this stage in his career, to use the cinema to document real difficulties, the real contradictions of real people's lives, and to move away from the kind of light romantic intrigues with which the Nouvelle Vague had become associated. *Vivre sa vie* marks the beginning of such a departure.

37 'The cinema's no fun. In the week, you can't go because you're working. And on Sundays, there's always a queue.'

References

Barthes, R. (1953), *Le Degré zéro de l'écriture*, Paris, Seuil.

Beh, S. H. (1976), '*Vivre sa vie*', in B. Nichols (ed.), *Movies and Methods: An Anthology*, Berkeley: University of California Press, 180–5.

Blanchot, M. (1969), *L'Entretien infini*, Paris, Gallimard.

Bresson, R. (1975), *Notes sur le cinématographe*, Paris, Gallimard.

Cameron, I. (1969), *The Films of Jean-Luc Godard*, New York, Praeger.

Cannon, S. (1996), 'Not a mere question of form: The hybrid realism of Godard's *Vivre sa vie*', *French Cultural Studies*, 6, 283–94.

Collet, J. and Fargier, J.-P. (1974), *Jean-Luc Godard*, Paris, Seghers.

Comolli, J.-L. (1963), 'La présence et l'absence', *Cahiers du cinéma*, 141 (March), 54–8.

Douin, J.-L. (1989), *Jean-Luc Godard*, Paris, Rivages.

Godard, J.-L. (1998), *Jean-Luc Godard par Jean-Luc Godard, Tome 1: 1950–1984*, Paris, Cahiers du cinéma.
Rosenbaum, J. (1995), *Placing Movies: The Practice of Film Criticism*, Berkeley, University of California Press.
Roud, R. (1970), *Jean-Luc Godard*, Bloomington, Indiana University Press.
Silverman, K. and Farocki, H. (1998), *Speaking about Godard*, New York, New York University Press.
Sterritt, D. (1999), *The Films of Jean-Luc Godard: Seeing the Invisible*, Cambridge, Cambridge University Press.

4

End of the beginning/beginning of the end: 1966–67

Masculin féminin

Masculin féminin (1966) is a film about young people in Paris in the winter of 1965–66. As commentators have noted (Douin 1989: 171; Haycock 1990), the film belongs to a brief trend for quasi-ethnographic documentaries about Paris established by *Chronique d'un été* (1961) and *Le Joli mai* (1963). Godard, who began to study anthropology at university, implies his desire to undertake an ethnographic survey when he remarks that 'nous vivons dans une société primitive'[1] and that Coca-Cola and General Motors are our totems (Godard 1998: 290). The documentary quality to *Masculin féminin* is highlighted by its subtitle, '15 faits précis' ('15 precise facts'), by its use of direct sound recording, and by the fact that the central protagonist, Paul (Jean-Pierre Léaud), works for a company that conducts opinion polls and spends much of the film asking people about their consumer habits, their political views, their social and sexual practices. The film is set between the first and second rounds of a presidential election, the first instance of the new constitutional law established by Charles de Gaulle whereby the French president is directly elected by the people. At one point in the film, we hear a radio broadcast by the Gaullist minister André Malraux (and tellingly, at this point, Godard shows a character playing with a toy guillotine, as though to signal the end of Gaullism). The film focuses on the young people who will be voting for the first time in this election, and Godard's treatment of these contemporary youths is marked by a certain ambivalence: on one hand, his characters display energy and optimism and a healthy political idealism; but, on the other, they are just as likely to be led into political complacency, or even apathy, by their overriding concerns with consumer items, popular culture and the opposite sex. This ambivalent attitude is neatly summed up in a title in

1 'we live in a primitive society'.

the film which was to become famous: Godard calls this generation 'les enfants de Marx et de Coca-Cola'.[2]

As the title suggests, *Masculin féminin* is principally concerned with the sexual relations of these young people. The opinion of young people is constantly surveyed with regard to their sexual behaviour, and in particular to their knowledge of contraception, from the new devices imported from America – the pill and the diaphragm – to the more 'traditional' methods of withdrawal or carefully selecting dates on which to have sex according to the female menstrual cycle. *Masculin féminin* captures a moment in French society before the pill had become widely available on prescription, but in which the discussion and use of contraceptive techniques was becoming generalised. The film tells the story of Paul's courtship of a young woman named Madeleine (Chantal Goya) who is attempting to forge a career as a popstar, and of the friends who gravitate around this central couple. Seemingly suffering from Madeleine's perceived rejection, Paul will commit suicide at the end of the film. But, despite this *dénouement*, the film's semi-ethnographic approach means that this love story is given a determinedly anti-romantic treatment. Characters rarely discuss their feelings for each other, but merely their physical attraction and their sexual habits. This is noticeable in a lengthy scene set in the bathroom of the magazine office where Madeleine works and where Paul tries to convince her to go out with him. When she asks what attracts him to her, Paul replies with a list of physical attributes: 'Les cheveux, les yeux, le nez, la bouche, les mains ...'.[3] Later he adds 'J'aime beaucoup votre style de poitrine',[4] and this discussion of physical types recurs frequently in the film. This scene depicts an attempted seduction and, as such, might be compared to the long hotel-room scene in *À bout de souffle*, yet it has none of the fun or playfulness of Godard's first feature. Jean-Pierre Léaud wears a resolutely glum expression throughout the scene and neither Paul nor Madeleine seem particularly optimistic about or interested in the prospect of a relationship with the other, but are merely going through the motions of a certain social ritual. Nor does the scene have any of the mobility and dynamism of *À bout de souffle*, comprised mostly of static close-ups of Paul framed against a wall and Madeleine combing her hair in the mirror. Meanwhile, the steely monochrome photography places *Masculin féminin* much closer to the grim realism of *Vivre sa vie* than to the wild romanticism of *Pierrot le fou*.

2 'the children of Marx and Coca-Cola'.
3 'Your hair, your eyes, your nose, your mouth, your hands ....'
4 'I really like your type of chest.'

Love is rarely mentioned in this world and, when it is, it is often summarily dismissed. Interviewing a young woman who has been elected 'Mademoiselle 19 ans' by a youth magazine, Paul asks her if she often falls in love: 'sûrement pas' ('certainly not'), she replies immediately. In the bathroom scene, when Madeleine asks Paul what he considers to be the centre of the world, he suggests 'l'amour' ('love'), which she finds a little odd. 'C'est marrant, moi j'aurais dit: moi'.[5] The description of love and sex in terms of purely external attributes, and the sense of the self as centre of the world, as a kind of inalienable point from which to perceive the world, betray the influence on *Masculin féminin* of the phenomenology associated with Sartre and Merleau-Ponty, philosophers frequently cited by Godard in interviews in this period. Both these writers argued that a person's character was not some mysterious essence that was slowly revealed over time, but was rather immediately present in a person's acts (Sartre 1943: 389–90). Merleau-Ponty challenged the idea that emotions could only really be understood by the individual experiencing them: instead he suggested that they could be studied in the form of behaviours since emotions did not in reality exist anywhere other than in the expressions, the gestures and the acts of individuals (Merleau-Ponty 1996 [1966]: 66–7). Merleau-Ponty was particularly prized by Godard because he had applied these ideas to the cinema. In a lecture delivered in 1945, but first anthologised in 1966, Merleau-Ponty suggested that the cinema was particularly well placed to illustrate this 'new psychology', since it showed, not people's thoughts, but their expressions and behaviour. He writes that 'le philosophe et le cinéaste ont en commun une certaine manière d'être, une certaine vue du monde qui est celle d'une génération'[6] (75), and this assertion appears on a title card in *Masculin féminin*.

But the apparently phenomenological approach in this ethnographic document about youth and sex in Paris at the end of 1965 is complicated by the gender imbalance in Godard's treatment of these young people. As noted above, Godard seems at once to admire his subjects' political energy and to point up the ease with which they are distracted by consumer items and pop culture. But this distinction between the good and bad aspects of youth is quite rigorously drawn along lines of gender. Paul and his friend Robert (Michel Debord) are actively involved with trade unions, engage in discussion about revolutionary politics, and participate in protests against the Vietnam war; meanwhile, the women

5 'It's funny, I would have said myself.'

6 'the philosopher and the filmmaker have in common a certain way of being, a certain view of the world which belongs to a generation'.

in the film are more likely to be found discussing boys and consumer items: Madeleine wants her record to be a success so that she can buy a Morris Cooper. This logic is taken to its limit when the women actually *become* consumer items: the interview with Mademoiselle 19 ans is introduced by a title as 'Dialogue avec un produit de consommation' ('Dialogue with a consumer product').

There are three long dialogues between a man and a woman in *Masculin féminin*: the first in the bathroom with Paul and Madeleine; the second this interview with Mademoiselle 19 ans; and the third a discussion between Robert and Madeleine's friend Catherine (Catherine–Isabelle Duport). In each of these dialogues, but particularly the latter two, the tone adopted towards the women is somewhere between condescension and open hostility. As Yosefa Loshitzky has observed, 'the use of the interview format, perhaps more so than any of Godard's other reflexive devices, expresses the power relationship between women and men' (1995: 167). Interrogated by young men, these women are all enclosed within a space from which they cannot easily escape: Madeleine is stuck by the wash basin in the bathroom; Mademoiselle 19 ans (real name Elsa) is sitting on a windowsill, backlit by the light from outside; and Catherine is trapped in the corner of a kitchen. There is a certain aggression to the men's questioning which delights in showing up the ignorance of the women. Mademoiselle 19 ans is asked what she considers to be the future of socialism, how she would define 'reactionary', whether she knows what the Popular Front was, and if she can identify where in the world wars are taking place. These questions are all justified by Paul's job with the opinion poll company, but a shrill laugh from the offscreen space of the magazine office repeatedly strays on to the soundtrack as though to comment upon Elsa's evasive and ill-informed responses. Meanwhile, Robert, who is not a pollster, similarly asks Catherine if she has ideas about democracy, and whether she takes an interest in what's going on around her. At the same time, though, he asks insistent questions about her sexual habits, and her stubborn reply of 'Ça ne vous regarde pas' ('That's none of your business'), repeated no less than eight times over the course of the scene, tends to portray Catherine as a guarded, sexually defensive figure, rather contemptuous of the working-class Robert. The overriding implication, then, is that all these women are hopelessly *superficial* when compared with the political awareness and emotional depth of the male characters (as we will see with regard to Paul in a moment). The fact that Madeleine spends almost the entire bathroom scene combing her hair reinforces this impression. And yet, as we have just seen, the phenomenology that Godard openly admires and endorses tends to dispel such simplistic surface/depth oppositions by arguing that the depths of the human 'soul' do not exist outside of the superficial characteristics that give us access to it.

Masculin féminin began life as a loose adaptation of stories by Guy de Maupassant including 'La Femme de Paul' (Douin 1989: 172) but, as Joel Haycock points out, 'the film has so little relation to them that the producer's contract for the stories' movie rights was voided' (Haycock 1990: 65). Haycock suggests that the film nonetheless maintains a certain kinship with the fictional tradition of naturalism with which Maupassant is associated (65). However, he does not take into account the specific story adapted by Godard: for 'La Femme de Paul' is not some simple realistic tale about sexual life in France, but is altogether hysterical in tone, characterised by paranoia and rampant misogyny. It tells the story of Paul's passionate love for Madeleine whom he discovers to be involved in a lesbian affair. After expressing his disgust for lesbians – 'on devrait les noyer comme des chiennes avec un pierre au cou'[7] (Maupassant 1973: 213) – he drowns *himself* in a river. *Masculin féminin* thus borrows from Maupassant the names of its central characters and the sense of an unrequited love leading to Paul's demise (see below). Joel Haycock also suggests that Godard's film retains hints of lesbianism (Haycock 1990: 54). Certainly, Madeleine shares a bed with her friend Elizabeth (Marlène Jobert) and with Paul at the same time, but this may be seen as an indication of poverty rather than of sexuality. However, there are other fleeting references which imply that *Masculin féminin* owes more to Maupassant than just the names of its characters. A shot from outside Madeleine's apartment at night shows the silhouettes of two women giggling together in what we may take to be the bathroom. Elsewhere, homosexuality appears to have been displaced from women to men when Paul surprises two men kissing in the toilet of a cinema. He writes 'À bas la République des Lâches'[8] on the door of the stall. More generally, we might say that something of Maupassant's paranoid misogyny filters through into the treatment of women in Godard's film, as shown in the hostile interview scenes. After Madeleine and Elizabeth dance together in a discotheque, Paul fumes: 'Moi, je trouve ça dégoûtant. Se montrer comme ça, ça m'agace!'.[9] Something of the hysteria of Maupassant perhaps shows up in the contradictions of the film between its phenomenological discourse and ethnographic detachment on the one hand, and its spiteful condemnation of superficiality on the other. As Joel Haycock points out, in the

7 'they ought to be drowned like dogs with a stone around the neck'.
8 'Down with the Republic of Cowards.'
9 'Well I think it's disgusting. Showing yourself off like that, it drives me mad!'

opening titles, the word 'Masculin' is decomposed into the three fragments 'Ma – scu – lin' whereas 'Féminin' appears whole. 'The film thus identifies the masculine term with breaking things down, with thinking, and the feminine term with "nothing", with woman as a thing in itself, inscrutable, unanalysable, and finally, with the end, *le néant*, and death' (Haycock 1990: 68–9). A brief exchange between Paul and Robert makes this clear:

> PAUL: Tu as remarqué que dans le mot 'masculin', il y a 'masque' et il y a 'cul'?
> ROBERT: Et dans le mot 'féminin'?
> PAUL: Il n'y a rien.[10]

The suicide that ends 'La Femme de Paul' also appears, disguised, in *Masculin féminin*. In the last scene of the film, which, again, is very reminiscent of *Vivre sa vie*, Madeleine and Catherine give depositions in a police station, during the course of which we learn that Paul has died after falling from an apartment window. The question of whether this was an accident or suicide is left open, but Haycock argues that Paul's death is necessitated by the internal contradictions of the film. Throughout his article, Haycock shows how Godard's attempt to produce an ethnographic document in *Masculin féminin* is repeatedly scuppered by the temptations of fiction: instead of a dispassionate survey of the state of sexual relations, Godard ends up filming a love story after all; instead of merely offering a cross-section of society, he presents us with individual characters. Just prior to the end of the film, in a long voiceover, Paul describes how he has become disillusioned by the process of surveying the opinions of the population; he realises that, far from revealing the current state of opinion, his questions betrayed it because they were based on a past ideology. Haycock reads this speech as Godard's own admission of failure in the project of producing an objective analysis of Paris in 1965, and he suggests that, if Paul dies in the subsequent scene (or rather, is eliminated in the space between the two scenes), it is because the film 'cannot support the contradiction of having the main character criticise the very premises of the fiction and then return to a fiction that continues to comply with those premises' (Haycock 1990: 70–1).

Yet there is also a degree of narrative justification for Paul's suicide (if that is what it is). Earlier, in the bathroom discussion with Madeleine regarding the centre of the world (which Paul had identified as 'love'), he remarked: 'On ne peut pas vivre, comme ça, sans tendresse. Il y a de

10 'Have you noticed that, in the word "masculine", there's "mask" and "*cul*" [sex]? – And in the word "feminine"? ... There isn't anything.'

quoi se flinguer'.[11] We might surmise, then, that Paul kills himself because he has not found this tenderness, an extraordinarily *romantic* death in what is otherwise presented as an objective, sociological film. Godard has evoked the nightmarish vision of a world without tenderness in his science-fiction film, *Alphaville* (1965), and *Masculin féminin* seems to share that film's bleak view of the future of sexual relations: at one point it is suggested that, in the future, sexual gratification will be provided by electronic gadgets. In this film about sex, tenderness is remarkable by its absence. The only time the word 'tendre' appears in relation to Madeleine, it is in the ironic context of a magazine article on the young popstar: reading aloud, Paul says 'Je ne savais pas que vous étiez "un petit être vif, social et tendre".'[12]

Theodor Adorno defined tenderness as an 'awareness of the possibility of relations without purpose', which he opposed to the 'pure functionality' of human relations in a capitalist economic system (Adorno 1974 [1951]: 40–1). With this in mind, we might identify *Masculin féminin* as the point of departure for an ongoing reflection in Godard's films on the relation of love and work: this vast and endlessly redefinable subject will preoccupy Godard for all the rest of his career, marking such diverse films as *Tout va bien* (1972), *Passion* (1981), *Nouvelle Vague* (1990) and *Éloge de l'amour* (2001). The theme may surface in a number of different guises, but central to it is a questioning of how alienated labour under capitalism has transformed our interpersonal relations and marked our social and sexual bodies. As Haycock notes, *Masculin féminin* is the first film in which Godard really showed people at work, a trait for which he would become famous in subsequent years (Haycock 1990: 59). If Paul's relationship with Madeleine fails, it is because she is more concerned with her career than she is with him, and Godard dramatises this conflict in a scene in the recording studio where Paul annoys Madeleine by hanging around and trying to interrupt the recording process. At one level, this may betray a sexist disapproval of women at work, but it is also part of a wider argument about the erosion of affective relations in a society driven principally by economic imperatives. *Masculin féminin* also contains discussions by Paul and Robert on the conditions of labour for unskilled workers in factories, the brutalising rhythms of the production line which, as Adorno argued, operate a virtual colonisation of the body (Adorno 1974 [1951]: 40); in Paul's words, 'Un ouvrier ne s'appartient plus'.[13] The notion of 'political

11 'You can't live like that, without any tenderness. It's enough to make you kill yourself.'
12 'I didn't know you were "a lively, sociable and tender little thing".'
13 'A worker no longer belongs to himself.'

filmmaking' in Godard's work needs to be understood on a much wider scale than his brief, if intense, involvement with Marxist–Leninist and Maoist politics in the late 1960s and early 1970s. It is, I suggest, precisely this attempt to understand interpersonal relations in the light of economic relations, the conflation of the public spaces of capitalist production and consumption and the private spaces of domestic and sexual interaction, it is the notions of love and work in their widest, and constantly evolving, sense that have given Godard's work a constant political significance. It is because it makes these concerns clearer than ever before that *Masculin féminin* is often taken as marking the beginning of what Colin MacCabe calls 'a series of explicitly political films which ended with [Godard's] withdrawal from the traditional cinema' (MacCabe 1980: 20).

La Chinoise

La Chinoise (1967) documents the activities of a group of young Maoist revolutionaries, centred around the apartment belonging to Véronique (Anne Wiazemsky)'s parents where they hold their meetings. The film would thus appear to mark the first evidence of Godard's interest in the political doctrine he would espouse in his radical post-1968 works, particularly those made with the Dziga Vertov Group (see Chapter 5). But, if Godard's commitment to revolutionary politics in the later films is not in doubt, there is some question as to how seriously we are to take *La Chinoise.* The Maoist cell, naming themselves 'la cellule Aden-Arabie' after a novel by Paul Nizan, are able to meet in the apartment because Véronique's bourgeois banker parents are away for the summer. There is, then, an irresistible sense of young people playing at politics and, at times, it is difficult to avoid the impression that Godard is making fun of his young charges. They get up in the morning and perform exercises on the balcony while reciting their Marxist-Leninist dogma, then set about lecturing to each other from the blackboard in what almost seems a parody of didactic political discourse. One member of the cell, Yvonne (Juliet Berto), was formerly a maid for Véronique's parents and, while the others listen to the lectures, Yvonne continues to polish shoes and clean windows, implying an ironic commentary on our heroes' rhetoric of class struggle.

The deliberations of the Aden-Arabie cell result in a plan to blow up university buildings and, when Véronique communicates this idea to the real-life writer and activist Francis Jeanson, he is horrified. He explains that his own defence of Algerian terrorists was motivated by the will of the Algerian people to emerge from colonial rule whereas Véronique's actions represent the will of only a handful of people. She protests that it does not matter that people do not yet think like them, because 'nous, on pense pour eux' ('we'll do the thinking for them'). When Véronique carries out the assassination of the revisionist Soviet Minister of Culture, Sholokov, she misreads the number of his hotel room upside down on the hotel register, and shoots the wrong man. At the end of the film, Véronique's sister returns and, disgusted at the Maoist graffiti on the walls, declares, 'Maman va être furieuse!' ('Mummy will be furious!'). Reviewing the film in the context of a thirty-year career retrospective of Godard's work in 1990, Iannis Katsahnias wrote: 'Et si *La Chinoise* n'était pas un pamphlet politique mais une comédie sur le rapport entre la mode et l'idéologie?'[14] (Katsahnias 1990: 118). Similarly, Dominique Noguez calls Godard a 'humorist', noting in the film 'un irrépressible goût du canular, de la farce à froid, et ces fusées subites d'une cocasse fausse naïveté'[15] (Noguez 1977: 147). If it is difficult to decide how serious Godard is being with regard to the characters in *La Chinoise*, it is because of what Noguez calls its 'imitation in the third degree': '"film en train de se faire" [this is the film's subtitle] sur l'imitation (l'*imythation*) en train de se faire d'une révolution en train de se faire'[16] (145).

The standard critical response to such questions would doubtless be that we are wrong to ask them in the first place. To ask whether Godard is being sympathetic or facetious towards the young Maoists is to partake of the bourgeois fallacy which presumes that a work of art provides a faithful representation of an externally existing reality. This ideologically determined conception of the work of art would be relentlessly challenged by Godard and his collaborators after 1968. But it is already clear, in *La Chinoise*, that the 'world' on screen is far from 'real'. As Jean-Louis Comolli comments with regard to the film, the image is not a *place* where people might live, but an *act* to be interpreted. 'This is an absolute image, sufficient to itself and not putting over any reality but its own' (in Cameron 1969: 156). The image does not *describe* a reality but *is* its own reality, *creates* its reality. As Kirilov (Lex de Bruijn), the shadowy Russian nihilist member of the cell who will kill himself at the end of the film, comments: 'L'art n'est pas le reflet du réel, mais le

14 'Perhaps *La Chinoise* is not a political pamphlet, but a comedy about the relationship between fashion and ideology?'

15 'an irrepressible taste for the hoax or practical joke, and these sudden bursts of a comical false naïvety'.

16 'a film in process about an imitation in process of a revolution in process'.

réel de ce reflet'.[17] The mise en scène of *La Chinoise* repeatedly refuses to establish the apartment as a realistic space in which we might identify with the characters. As Jacques Aumont comments, there is no depth of field to these images: shots are composed in two discrete planes, a figure in the foreground set against a background which is frequently a simple block of colour. The high incidence of frontal shots of the characters further contributes to this breakdown of realist perspectival space (Aumont 1982: 136). Comolli notes the use of 'stage lighting' which appears to come from in front of the screen, as though from theatre footlights or a film projector (in Cameron 1969: 155–6). But the anti-realism of *La Chinoise* is perhaps most striking in its use of colour. The apartment is marked by the presence, to the exclusion of practically all others, of the three primary colours red, yellow and blue. Nor do these colours mix with each other, but provide unified fields of colour: a blue wall, a red lampshade, a yellow sweater, the copies of Mao's *Little Red Book* that proliferate on the bookshelves. As Jacques Rancière points out, the frankness and incorruptibility of these primary colours 's'opposent aux dégradés de nuances et à la confusion de la "réalité", c'est-à-dire de la métaphore'[18] (Rancière 2001: 193). At the beginning of the film, we see written on the wall of the apartment a slogan that would become famous: 'Il faut confronter des idées vagues avec des images claires'.[19] Since form and content are inseparable in the work of art, since cinema creates its own reality, the best way to produce an effective political discourse in film is through the absolute clarity of the images and sounds (we will see the outcome of this philosophy in Godard's political cinema in Chapter 5).

La Chinoise is, after all, a film about the conditions of possibility of a *political art*. In interview, Godard complained of 'un fossé entre le cinéma et la politique' ('a gulf between cinema and politics'), arguing that those who knew about politics knew nothing of cinema, and vice versa (Godard 1998: 306). Godard, like his characters, is at the beginning of a lengthy reflection on the form that political art should take in the context of the ideological struggles of the late sixties. Véronique is critical of once-committed writers and thinkers like Sartre, Aragon and Malraux, who are no longer in touch with political reality, instead taking refuge from it in art history and literary criticism. Guillaume (Jean-Pierre Léaud), an actor, investigates various experimental theatre productions, his own self-criticism being performed

17 'Art is not the reflection of the real, but the reality of this reflection.'
18 'are opposed to the degraded nuances and the confusion of "reality", which is to say, of metaphor'.
19 'We must oppose vague ideas with clear images.'

when he invites people to pelt him with rotten vegetables. If *La Chinoise* at times appears confused or confusing, it is, suggests James Roy MacBean, because Godard too incorporates his own self-critique into the film: 'it is social thought and the critique of social thought, art and the critique of art' (MacBean 1968: 17). Francis Jeanson is also keen to indulge in 'cultural action', leaving Paris to bring theatre productions to working-class audiences in the provinces. However, as MacBean suggests, Jeanson's remarks perhaps conceal some of Godard's unease that 'the militant activists will never consider the artist's contribution bold enough or even of any real significance in the revolutionary struggle' (18). There is always a hint of self-interest in a revolutionary activity that can also help to develop an artistic career: the spectator notes that Jeanson is also hoping to profit from his time away from Paris in order to continue his writing (18).

Much of the inspiration for the ideas on political art, and for the demystifying of the fictional world on screen, comes from Brecht. At once point, Guillaume is seen wiping off the blackboard the names of scores of canonical writers until only Brecht remains. But Brecht's techniques of distanciation were developed for the theatre and, in what remains one of the most interesting responses to *La Chinoise*, Marie-Claire Ropars-Wuilleumier suggests that they may not work in quite the same way in the cinema. She argues that the consciousness that we are watching actors playing a role, instead of highlighting their situation within a concrete political reality, tends, in the cinema, to lead the spectator back to search for psychological depth in the character, as though to explain this role-playing. As a result, suggests Ropars-Wuilleumier, the game turns against the characters, and *La Chinoise* becomes, in spite of itself, a satire on young Marxist-Leninists (Ropars-Wuilleumier 1970: 149). I would suggest instead that this unavoidable search for psychological depth on the part of the spectator *combines* with inter- and extra-textual knowledge of the actors to produce a judgement of the characters. What seems undeniable in *La Chinoise* is that this judgement, like in *Masculin féminin,* is distributed along lines of gender: the male characters appear credible and command respect; the female characters are barely credible and held up for ridicule.

As in *Masculin féminin,* Godard repeatedly uses in *La Chinoise* the technique of the interview. The four main members of the Aden-Arabie cell are interviewed over the course of the film, and careful analysis of these interview scenes reveals the gender bias in the treatment of the characters. The first character to be interviewed is the actor, Guillaume. Framed against a wall decorated with photos of China, Guillaume responds to questions from Godard, offscreen, smiling as he says, 'Oui, je suis acteur' ('Yes, I am an actor'). He tells an anecdote about the political uses of theatre, describing how a Chinese student wrapped his head in bandages to draw the attention of the western media before revealing his uninjured face. For a true socialist theatre, says Guillaume, 'il faut de la sincérité ... *et de la violence!*',[20] clenching his fist and raising his voice at the end of the sentence. He stresses his sincerity, saying 'Vous croyez que je fais le clown parce que je suis en train d'être filmé ... Mais ce n'est pas parce qu'il y a une caméra devant moi ... Je suis sincère'.[21] Here we have a reverse shot showing the camera that is filming Guillaume.

In Guillaume's interview, then, it is difficult to draw a distinction between the reality onscreen and some external reality. There is no other reality than what we see in the image, and the reverse shot to the camera makes this clear. Meanwhile, when Guillaume talks about the need for sincerity and violence in revolutionary art, these qualities are clearly located *in his performance*, in the sincerity and the violence with which he pronounces this line. But if Guillaume is thus a credible and sympathetic character, it is partly because of the unproblematic equation between the character and the actor Jean-Pierre Léaud. Léaud was familiar to the audience of *La Chinoise* as the actor who played Antoine Doinel in Truffaut's *400 coups* (1959) and *Antoine et Colette* (1962), as well as from his roles in Godard's own *Masculin féminin* and *Made in USA* (1966). He would further prove his credentials with a series of roles in radical and experimental films over the coming years. There is thus a perfect fit between Léaud and his character, between image and reality, which makes it easy for Godard to show up the constructed nature of his film but which, at the same time, commands respect for the character of Guillaume.

The case of Henri is very different. He is played by Michel Semeniako, who had no other major film roles and is now known more as a photographer. But it is partly because he is an unknown face that Semeniako is convincing in the role of the working-class Henri. Henri is excluded from the cell for his 'revisionist' views and is subsequently interviewed over breakfast in his kitchen where, as Rancière comments, the down-to-earth decor and Henri's cloth cap give the weight of realism to his remarks (Rancière 2001: 190). And indeed, Henri often appears as an island of sense amidst the overheated discussions of the cell. He accuses Véronique of confusing politics with theatre; he objects to her plans for terrorist action; he points out that the French Communist

20 'You need sincerity ... *and violence!*'

21 'You think I'm playing the fool because I'm being filmed ... But it's not because there's a camera in front of me ... I'm sincere.'

Party (vilified by the Maoists) were the only group at the last elections who addressed the real conditions of workers rather than philosophical abstractions; yet he remains sensitive enough to artworks to condemn the Party's attack on *Johnny Guitar* (1954) purely on the grounds of its Americanness. Within the terms of the Maoists, Henri is undoubtedly a 'revisionist' but, particularly for the spectator of today, distanced from the internal ideological squabbles of the French left at this particular point in history, he is likely to come across as a dignified and reasonable character. As Marc Cerisuelo points out, his calm and common sense, together with his unjust vilification by the rest of the group, combine to give Henri 'le beau rôle' (Cerisuelo 1989: 133). And when, at the end of the film, he announces his intention to go and work as a chemist in East Germany, his commitment to socialism seems a lot firmer than that of his former comrades.

Henri is to be contrasted with the other working-class character in the film, Yvonne. Yvonne is interviewed in front of a plain blue wall on which is pinned a pamphlet about 'la paysanne française d'aujourd'hui' ('women in rural France today'). She explains that she comes from a village near Grenoble where she used to work on a farm. She came to Paris where she works as maid, supplementing her income with prostitution. Juliet Berto, in fact, really was born in Grenoble, although she is not entirely convincing in the role of this rural *ingénue*: although only really known from a small role in *2 ou 3 choses que je sais d'elle* (1966), Berto would subsequently work on post-1968 films with Godard and Jacques Rivette and, prior to her acting career, she had briefly been a singer. More important to the spectator's opinion of Yvonne, however, is the way she is treated by Godard. As she talks about her previous life on the farm, Godard inserts a couple of quite random shots of chickens clucking about a farmyard and cows grazing. Doubtless intended to show up the artificiality of this discourse, these shots instead tend to mock Yvonne and detract from the seriousness of her speech. By contrast, if the spare kitchen and the cloth cap gently poked fun at Henri, they did nothing to undermine the weight of reality contained in his words. Yvonne is often given lines that show up her stupidity. When Henri asks the group where 'just ideas' come from, she suggests: 'Elles tombent du ciel?' ('They fall from the sky?'). This is in fact part of a quotation from Chairman Mao which is divided between the group (it reappears in *Pravda* (1969)), but, by placing it in the mouth of Yvonne and greeting it with hoots of derision from the rest of the cell, Godard offers the character up for ridicule.

Godard would doubtless protest that this initial *naïveté* is necessary in order to show the character's progression, since Yvonne's political consciousness shows the most marked development over the course of the film (Godard 1998: 310). However, Véronique, despite starting on firmer intellectual ground, is similarly held up as a frequent figure of fun. Véronique is a philosophy student at Nanterre (as was Anne Wiazemsky in reality) whose political consciousness developed as a result of attending this university set (as it was at the time) among a shanty town of impoverished workers. Véronique is interviewed in front of a bookcase, as though to designate her intellectualism, and many of her ideas are evidently designed to raise a smile. For instance, she and her student comrades are keen to outlaw exams, in part because they are 'générateurs de névroses, d'angoisse et de frustration sexuelle'.[22] Wiazemsky, previously seen in Bresson's *Au hasard, Balthazar* (1966), makes an unlikely terrorist, and the farcical outcome of her assassination attempt has already been noted. Meanwhile, when Véronique tells Francis Jeanson of her desire to make students perform manual labour, she cites as an example a summer spent harvesting peaches with a friend near Avignon. At this point, a wash of strings, that Jacques Aumont refers to as 'Vivaldi-esque muzak' (Aumont 1982: 142), appears on the soundtrack as though to underscore Véronique's romantic delusions about manual labour.

Whereas the male figures are both convincing in their roles and come across as articulate exponents of sincerely held political views, the women in *La Chinoise* appear unconvincing and proffer comically inept or dangerously unthought-out opinions. If anyone is playing at politics in this bourgeois apartment, then, it is the women, whereas the men are entirely serious. Furthermore, in a film which seeks to challenge the pretensions of art to a 'truthful' representation of reality, the speech of Véronique and Yvonne betrays an uncritical belief in a metaphysical truth, at odds with the ludic performativity of Guillaume/Léaud's politics. Both Yvonne and Véronique discuss politics in terms of darkness and light: Yvonne complains that, when she was a maid in Passy, she worked all the time in darkness, 'tandis qu'ici ils discutent ... pour moi, c'est très clair'.[23] Véronique says, 'C'est parce que tout n'est pas très clair que je continue à étudier',[24] while her interview begins with a drawing taken from *Alice in Wonderland* of Alice peeling back a curtain to look behind it, suggesting that Véronique's political consciousness can be understood in terms of the *unveiling of a truth*. When asked to define Marxism-Leninism, Yvonne replies: 'Vous savez, quand le soleil se couche, il est tout rouge, et après il disparaît. Mais

22 'they generate neurosis, anxiety and sexual frustration'.
23 'whereas here they have discussions ... for me, everything's very clear'.
24 'It's because everything's not clear that I'm continuing to study.'

moi, dans mon cœur, le soleil ne se couche jamais'.[25] Combining the metaphysical value of clarity with a lyrical romanticism and an essentialist association of women and nature, this remark, perhaps more than any other, demonstrates how Godard's research into the possibilities of a political film form divorced from ideological preconceptions remained constrained by a latent sexism that would not be resolutely addressed until the 1970s.

2 ou 3 choses que je sais d'elle

There is a degree of uncertainty as to what the 'elle' in the title of Godard's *2 ou 3 choses que je sais d'elle* (1966) refers. The spectator may initially assume that the pronoun designates the central character, Juliette Janson, played by Marina Vlady. But the opening of the film complicates matters when, over a shot of Juliette/Vlady on the balcony of her apartment, Godard's whispered voiceover commentary, which intervenes throughout the film, says first 'Elle, c'est Marina Vlady', then 'Elle, c'est Juliette Janson',[26] before going on to describe the two women in identical terms. The trailer for the film had already installed this semantic uncertainty in the shifter 'elle'. It consisted simply of seventeen title cards which offered a variety of possible interpretations for this 'elle', from 'la région parisienne' to 'la prostitution', from 'la guerre du Vietnam' to 'la salle de bains que n'ont pas 70 pour cent des Français', from 'la circulation des idées' to 'la gestapo des structures'.[27] But it is not only the 'elle' of the title that is marked by uncertainty. Who, after all, is 'je'? Presumably Godard, but does Godard the filmmaker correspond to Godard the narrator? How can we be sure? Does 'je' refer to the spectator? And how many things are we going to learn about 'her', two or three? Thus, in the title of the film, all this uncertainty gravitates around the verb 'savoir', to know, and we will suggest that *2 ou 3 choses que je sais d'elle* is a film *about knowledge*, about the necessary uncertainty that inhabits knowledge, about the difficulty of knowing.

Like *Masculin féminin*, *2 ou 3 choses* can be seen as having, as its point of departure, a kind of ethnographic document about life in contemporary Paris. Godard devotes considerable attention to the construction

25 'You know when the sun goes down, it's all red and then it disappears. Well for me, in my heart, the sun never goes down.'

26 'She is Marina Vlady – She is Juliette Janson.'

27 [From] 'the Paris region' to 'prostitution', from 'the Vietnam war' to 'the bathroom that 70 per cent of French people don't have', from 'the circulation of ideas' to 'the gestapo of structures'.

of 'grands ensembles', large housing projects on the outskirts of the city where Juliette lives with her family. The film opens with the images and sounds of these construction sites while Godard's voiceover gives precise details about the government legislation permitting these developments and identifies the man, Paul Delouvrier, charged with overseeing them. (A sentence about Delouvrier's previous career in banking, which leads Godard to accuse the government of being led purely by the laws of capital, was censored prior to the film's release.) The film also discusses the consumer items and domestic appliances that have become the ultimate objects of desire for French citizens. Much of this detail is drawn from a report in the magazine *Le Nouvel Observateur*. One anecdote about how people unused to the luxury of hot running water tend to use it without moderation, thereby generating huge bills, is literalised in the rather broad comedy of a scene in which a metre reader surprises a young woman in her bath (Guzzetti 1981: 69–73). But the main inspiration for the film is the assertion, by this same magazine report, that young housewives in these 'grands ensembles' are turning to prostitution, not out of necessity, but precisely in order to pay for consumer items which, only a few years previously, would have been considered as luxuries. Godard's voiceover addresses this situation over a static shot of a young woman in a shopping centre: 'C'est toujours la même histoire: pas d'argent pour payer le loyer, ou alors pas de télévision. Ou alors une télévision, mais pas d'auto. Ou alors une machine à laver, mais pas de vacances'.[28] Alfred Guzzetti, noting that the woman in this shot is reflected in a window, suggests that it is a reference to Chris Marker's *Le Joli mai*, and that Godard's commentary corrects the poetic tone of Marker's film 'by insisting on the concrete commercial and sociological circumstances behind what we see' (73). The sense of the film as ethnographic document is reinforced, as in *Masculin féminin*, by the use of the interview format. In several locations (clothes shop, hairdresser's, playground), characters address the camera directly, reporting their name, age, preferred social activities, and so on.

The film then sets up various objects, various meanings for the 'elle' of the title, which the spectator expects to enter into his or her field of knowledge through the viewing experience: the Paris region, prostitution, consumer capitalism. But Godard repeatedly evokes knowledge as a *problem*, foregrounding the uncertain process by which things are known. Throughout the film, usually a propos of nothing, Juliette emits sentences describing how she knows things because she perceives them

28 'It's always the same story: no money to pay the rent, or no television. Or else a television, but no car. Or a washing machine but no holiday.'

to be the case. In her apartment, for instance, she declares, 'Je sens le tissu de la nappe contre ma main'.[29] In a clothes shop, she discusses colour (much of Juliette's speech in the film appears to be a dialogue with someone offscreen whom we cannot see or hear; in fact, she is responding to questions and cues provided by Godard that are, occasionally, just audible): 'Dans cette pièce, il y a du bleu, du rouge, du vert,' she says, 'Oui, j'en suis sûr'.[30] 'Mon chandail est bleu,' she continues and, after a brief exchange with a shop assistant, adds, 'Parce que je vois que c'est bleu'.[31] But finally she muses: 'Si on s'était trompé au départ et qu'on ait appelé le bleu, le vert ... Ce serait grave ...'.[32] Thus, from the confident description of things we can know with certainty, we pass to the troubling onset of doubt, where it suddenly seems difficult to be certain about anything. As Ludwig Wittgenstein has argued, the concept of 'knowing' tends to be equated with the concept of 'being certain', but certainty is always dependent on context-specific language games where there is an unspoken agreement about the meaning of words. The phrase 'I know' merely 'expresses the readiness to believe certain things' in the absence of any truly solid ground for certainty (Wittgenstein 1969: 42). In a line that would become famous, Juliette responds to her son's query about language with the definition, 'Le langage, c'est la maison dans laquelle l'homme habite'.[33] (The problem of how knowledge is shaped and complicated by its passage through language will be discussed further in *Le Gai Savoir* (1968); see Chapter 5.)

But, aside from the problem of language, *2 ou 3 choses que je sais d'elle* implies other reasons why it is difficult for us truly to know the world we inhabit at any given moment, and the first of these reasons is political. The film, as we have suggested, presents a critique of consumer capitalism, showing how the market economy creates a never-ending stream of merchandise whose rate of production always outstrips the average consumer's ability to pay for it. Thus the women who turn to prostitution to satisfy their spending needs might be seen as representative of a more general economic tendency; as in *Vivre sa vie*, it is possible to see prostitution in *2 ou 3 choses que je sais d'elle* as a metaphor for the general condition of the worker-consumer under an advanced system of industrial capitalism. This kind of critique was given a polemical voice in Guy Debord's book *La Société du Spectacle*, first

29 'I can feel the fabric of the tablecloth against my hand.'
30 'In this room there is blue, red and green. Yes, I'm sure of it.'
31 'My sweater is blue. Because I can see that it's blue.'
32 'But what if we were mistaken in the first place, and called blue green ... That would be serious.'
33 'Language is the house in which man lives.'

published in 1967. The Society of the Spectacle designated, for Debord, 'le moment où la marchandise est parvenue à *l'occupation totale* de la vie sociale'[34] (Debord 1992 [1967]: 39). The language of occupation, with its echo of French history, is by no means accidental, since Debord goes on to describe the serial logic of merchandise in terms of a Fascist dictatorship. Each new product must present itself as sovereign, as absolutely singular and thus absolutely desirable, yet, in order to satisfy the desire of the consumer, the product has to be mass produced such that, as soon as it enters into our possession, we recognise it for what it is: a vulgar, commonplace object. Thus we pass from one object to the next in pursuit of 'la terre promise de la consommation totale'[35] (63). 'Chaque *nouveau mensonge* de la publicité est aussi *l'aveu* de son mensonge précédent'[36] (65), says Debord, just as the toppling of a dictator reveals the illusory foundations of his absolute power. In *Made in USA* (1966), which Godard famously filmed at the same time as *2 ou 3 choses*, Paula Nelson (Anna Karina) at one point declares: 'Pour moi, la publicité, c'est une forme de fascisme'.[37]

What the logic of merchandise means, then, is that it is practically impossible for the consumer to live in the present moment. If it is difficult for us to know with certainty anything about a given moment in time, it is thus partly because our attention is always being directed towards the *next* moment: to the next major product launch, to next year's holiday, to next season's cultural highlights. The serial production of merchandise creates a linear, irreversible sense of time that always appears several steps ahead of those trying to *live* in it. As Debord puts it: 'la bourgeoisie a fait connaître et a imposé à la société un temps historique irréversible, mais lui en refuse l'*usage*'[38] (142). Within this logic, time itself becomes merchandise, becomes an object of consumption, it is sold in the form of package holidays and cultural subscriptions (the suburban brothel where Juliette works is decorated with a collection of tourism posters). In *2 ou 3 choses*, Godard represents this literal equation of time and money with a repeated close-up of the counter of a petrol pump turning, his voiceover pronouncing 'Il est seize heures quarante-cinq' ('It is 16:45'), just as the numbers on the counter reach 16FF45 (Guzzetti 1981: 225). The sense of fatigue generated by the hopeless effort to keep pace with the market economy

34 'the moment when merchandise has achieved the *total occupation* of social life'.
35 'the promised land of total consumption'.
36 'Each *new lie* of advertising is also the *admission* of its previous lie.'
37 'As far as I'm concerned, advertising is a form of Fascism.'
38 'the bourgeoisie introduced an irreversible, historical time which it imposed on society, while refusing to let it be *used*'.

is movingly evoked at the end of the film. Juliette and her husband Robert (Roger Montsoret) arrive home after their day's work and we witness the following exchange:

ROBERT: Ouf, on est arrivé!
JULIETTE: Arrivé où?
ROBERT: Chez nous.
JULIETTE: Et après, qu'est-ce qu'on va faire?
ROBERT: Dormir. Qu'est-ce qui te prend?
JULIETTE: Et après?
ROBERT: On se réveillera.
JULIETTE: Et après?
ROBERT: Pareil. On recommencera ... On travaillera, on mangera ...
JULIETTE: Et après?
ROBERT: Je ne sais pas ... Mourir.
JULIETTE: Et après?[39]

Following this exchange, Godard again inserts a shot of the petrol pump counter, with the numbers on zero before slowly starting to turn. Guzzetti argues that, given its syntagmatic placement within this sequence, this image signifies death and 'the afterlife', albeit with a heavy dose of irony (331). But we might suggest instead that this shot of the counter, while drawing a clear link between Juliette's existential fatigue and the logic of linear time defined by industrial capitalism, implies the need to *return to zero and start again*, to rethink a world in which life is so devalued as to be reduced to this stultifying cycle of work, eat, sleep, work. The last line of Godard's voiceover commentary makes this idea explicit, ending the film, like many others of this period, with a rallying call to a fresh start: 'J'ai tout oublié sauf que, puisqu'on me ramène à zéro, c'est de là qu'il faudra repartir'.[40]

If *2 ou 3 choses que je sais d'elle* is a film about knowledge, then, it explores the limits to knowledge and the possibilities for thought within a specific ideological system. This is not just a political inquiry, but a philosophical one. Gilles Deleuze has argued that, in the western philosophical tradition, knowledge and understanding tend to be conceived on the model of recognition, that is the assimilation of new information to pre-existing knowledge. That which is different cannot be identified in its difference, but only recognised to the extent that it can be

39 'Well, we made it! – Made it where? – Home. – And what are we going to do now? – What do you mean? Sleep. – And after that? – We'll wake up. – And after that? – The same. We'll start over again ... We'll go to work, we'll eat ... – And after that? – I don't know ... Die. – And after that?'

40 'I've forgotten everything except that, since I've been brought back to zero, it's from there that I'll have to start again.'

assimilated to the same. But this model of thought implies both a unified external object that is the same for all the senses, and a unified perceiving subject; and it is thought itself that is conceived as the highest human faculty that unites all the others. The trouble with this model of thought, says Deleuze, is that it is subordinated to a *doxa*, recognising only that which is already known, such that philosophy becomes indistinguishable from common sense (Deleuze 2000 [1968]: 174–6). Or, as Juliette puts it in *2 ou 3 choses*: 'rien n'est plus simple que de penser que telle ou telle chose va de soi'.[41] Following Plato, Deleuze distinguishes between things that do not trouble thought (objects of recognition), and things that *force* us to think. The latter are not objects of recognition, but the object of an *encounter*, they cannot be recognised but only *felt*. As Deleuze puts it, 'Ce n'est pas le donné, mais ce par quoi le donné est donné'[42] (182). Another line by Juliette, pronounced before leaving the clothes shop, makes this distinction clear: 'Oui, par exemple, quelque chose peut me faire pleurer, mais la cause des larmes ne se trouve pas intégrée à leurs traces sur mes joues. C'est-à-dire qu'on peut décrire tout ce qui se produit quand je fais quelque chose, sans indiquer pour autant ce qui fait que je le fais'.[43] Thought is *difficult*: it constantly runs up against its own limits, against the unthinkable, but it is precisely this incapacity within thought that forces it to keep thinking (191–2). When Flaubert talked about 'la bêtise' ('stupidity'), suggests Deleuze, he perhaps had an intuition of this generative incapacity of thought, 'à savoir qu'elle ne pense pas tant que rien ne la force'[44] (353). In *2 ou 3 choses*, Godard includes his own reference to Flaubertian *bêtise*, with two characters named Bouvard and Pécuchet after the anti-heroes of Flaubert's unfinished novel who, in seeking to acquire the sum of all knowledge, succeeded only in reproducing received ideas. Godard's Bouvard and Pécuchet sit at a desk piled high with books and read a handful of lines from tomes selected at random, mixing politics, literature and philosophy with the telephone book, a comment upon the fragmentation of knowledge by the culture industry.

In Deleuze's conception of thought, instead of the faculties being unified in the presence of an object of recognition, each faculty is brought into contact with its own limits, and communicates to the other

41 'nothing is more simple than thinking that such and such a thing goes without saying'.

42 'It is not the given, but that by which the given is given.'

43 'Yes, for instance, something might make me cry, but the cause of my tears is not contained within the trace they leave on my cheeks. In other words, you can describe everything that happens when I do something without being able to say how it is that I'm doing it.'

44 'that is to say that it doesn't think unless forced to do so'.

faculties only through the violence of this encounter (184). Learning is thus a violent process in which the points of our body are conjugated with the singular objects and experiences encountered through perception (214). Thought is not a simple, ordered process of recognition, but is a *messy* business, characterised by noise and interference. The detached, fragmentary non sequiturs that Juliette pronounces throughout *2 ou 3 choses* might be understood as an audibilisation of thought. The scene in the hairdresser's is illuminating in this regard. Juliette carries on a conversation with her manicurist while at the same time pronouncing apparently random, or unconnected, words and phrases, in a striking demonstration of the *noise* of thoughts:

> MARIANNE: Dis-donc, t'es vachement brune! Où tu as été?
> JULIETTE: En Russie.
> MARIANNE: Où?
> JULIETTE: Silence ... A Leningrad.
> MARIANNE: Ils sont gentils, les Russes?
> JULIETTE: Bonheur ... Oh, ils sont comme tout le monde.
> MARIANNE: Je te demande ça comme ça.
> JULIETTE: Mais ils sont sympathiques. Quelques bruits ...
> MARIANNE: Dis-donc, t'as revu les Duperret?
> JULIETTE: Oui, je les ai vus en passant gare Saint-Lazare. C'est vrai, d'autre part, qu'on ne se connaît jamais.
> MARIANNE: Il est cassé [*i.e. her fingernail*].
> JULIETTE: Robert ... Christophe ... Des cahiers bleus à spirales ...
> MARIANNE: Et toi, ça va?
> JULIETTE: Ça va. Ne pas être obligée de faire l'amour.
> MARIANNE: Tu sais, j'aime mieux ça que l'usine.
> JULIETTE: Moi non plus, j'aimerais pas travailler à l'usine.
> MARIANNE: Tes enfants? Tes enfants, ça va?
> JULIETTE: Ça va ... Ce que je dis avec des mots, n'est jamais ce que je dis. Ça va, mais ils ne sont pas sages, tu sais? J'attends, je regarde ...
> MARIANNE [*showing nail varnish*]: Je te mettrai celui-là.
> JULIETTE: Oui d'accord. Mes cheveux. [*Phone rings*] Le téléphone.[45]

45 'Gosh, you're really brown! Where have you been? – In Russia. – Whereabouts? – Silence ... In Leningrad. – What are the Russians like? – Happiness ... Oh, they're like everyone else. – I was just asking. – They're nice, though ... Some noises. – Tell me, have you seen the Duperrets again? – Yes, I saw them at Saint-Lazare station. On the other hand, it's true that we never really know each other. – It's broken. – Robert, Christophe ... Blue spiral notebooks ... – And how are you? – Fine ... Not be forced to make love ... – You know, I prefer this to working in the factory. – I wouldn't like to work in a factory either. – And your children, how are they? – Fine. What I say with words is never what I mean. Fine, but they're a bit naughty. I'm waiting, I'm watching ... – I'll give you this one. – OK. My hair ... The telephone.'

Here, then, Juliette's speech includes responses to Marianne's questions, vague impressions ('Happiness'), identification of some sense perceptions that are clearly recognised ('the telephone') and others that are not ('some noises'), images that pass through her mind ('blue spiral notebooks'), some thoughts that are clearly meant only for herself ('not be forced to make love') and others that could be directed to Marianne ('it's true that we never really know each other'). Thought emerges not as an ordered sequence, but as a chaotic jumble; it seems impossible to fix attention on one thought without another interrupting it. And this sense of chaos and interference constantly greets the spectator seeking knowledge through Godard's film. Rather than present us with images, sounds and ideas that can be immediately recognised and assimilated to our pre-existing categories of understanding, Godard forces us to confront the difficulty of making sense of the world, the violence which accompanies the process of learning. Often Godard will cut into an image or a sound that is not instantly recognisable and presents us with a pure, unassimilable difference. Such is the case with the sudden, intensely loud bursts of construction noise, or the extreme close-up on the paintwork of Juliette's red Mini as the light plays over it: this is not an image of a car, but of the pure difference of colour and light.

Difference has a tendency to be understood negatively, in terms of what it *is not*, but Deleuze argues that difference needs to be given a positive sense, needs to be considered as an *affirmation*, since it is only through the differential relations of heterogeneous elements that life exists at all (342–5). 'Il faut être attentif à l'ivresse de la vie',[46] says Ivanov, the fictional Nobel-prize-winning author seen in a café in *2 ou 3 choses*. The philosophy of recognition defines life negatively, separating elements off into neat little categories, until even life itself is defined by its opposition to death, being by its opposition to nothingness. 'Se définir en un seul mot?' says Juliette at the end of the film: 'Pas encore mort'.[47] To define life in this way is to deny it, whereas on the contrary, life results from the affirmation of difference; such is the lesson from Nietzsche prolonged in the philosophy of Deleuze and demonstrated by the Godard of *2 ou 3 choses*. Godard refuses an approach based in separation and negation, refuses to distinguish between that which is and is not suitable material for a film. 'On doit tout mettre dans un film'[48] was the title of a short article written for the release of *2 ou 3 choses* (Godard 1998: 295–6). 'Aucun événement n'est vécu par lui-même,' observes Juliette at

46 'We must remain attentive to the intoxication of life.'
47 'How would I define myself in one word? Not yet dead.'
48 'Everything should go into a film.'

one point, 'On découvre toujours qu'il est lié à ce qui l'entoure'.[49] Over the course of the film, Juliette becomes attuned to 'le sentiment de mes liens avec le monde',[50] illustrated by Godard by a 360° pan that starts from Juliette and returns to her via a tour of the 'grands ensembles' that she inhabits. It is this same sense of links to the world that leads Godard to represent the Vietnam war in the film by having Robert and another man listen to short-wave radio broadcasts, or by having a supposed Vietnam veteran act as a client for Juliette and Marianne, literally turning the prostitutes into merchandise by placing the flight bags of American airline companies over their heads. Prostitution in the 'grands ensembles' of Paris is linked to the Vietnam war via the all-pervasive law of capital in an American-led industrial economy. And, as Guzzetti points out, it is precisely because Vietnam is 'far away', that the war 'can be acted out only in the terms in which it is inscribed in reality – that is, in the radio, cartoon, and dishwashing soap that ... signify "Made in U.S.A."' (Guzzetti 1981: 53).

All of this might be illustrated by considering one of the most celebrated scenes in the film, in which Juliette goes to a café. The scene begins with a very classical kind of continuity editing, offscreen space, matches on action and shot/reverse-shot formations used to establish the realistic space of the café as Juliette enters and greets the barman and a friend she recognises. But, as Juliette approaches the bar, a young woman turns to address the camera directly, mentioning that she lives in the 'grands bâtiments' and comes to Paris twice a month. A shot of a young man, backlit against the window, now shows the provenance of the extremely loud and invasive noise of a pinball machine that has been heard on the soundtrack. Offscreen, a man who will shortly be identified as a pimp, draws attention to his new American shoes and a woman comments: 'C'est avec ça qu'ils marchent sur les pieds des Vietnamiens'.[51] But the main part of the scene begins with an establishing shot that shows three people sitting close, but not together: Juliette, her friend reading a magazine, and a young man smoking a cigarette. Here we have a close-up of the magazine being read by Juliette's friend, with its erotic drawings of young women, a cut to the woman reading, and a new shot of the magazine, as Godard comments: 'Voici comment Juliette, à 15 h 37, voyait remuer les pages de cet objet que, dans le langage journalistique, on nomme une revue. Et voilà comment, environ 150 images plus loin, une autre jeune femme, sa semblable, sa

49 'No event is experienced in isolation. You find that it is also linked to what surrounds it.'

50 'the sense of my links to the world'.

51 'That's how they walk all over the Vietnamese.'

sœur, voyait le même objet. Où est donc la vérité? De face ou de profil? Et d'abord, un objet, qu'est-ce que c'est?'[52] This commentary thus raises the problem of the identity of the object, asking if it is the same when seen from different angles, but complicates the matter by reminding us that these angles are produced within the logic of film editing (the 'real' time of 15:37 being doubled by the film time of 150 frames). Thus, if the discussion of objects implies the objectification of women by such cultural artefacts as this erotic magazine, Godard also seems to admit that a similar objectification occurs in the very process of filming which, as Guzzetti puts it, 'turns all subjects into objects' (133).

The scene continues with a series of shots of the three people sitting at this table, alternated with several increasingly large close-ups of a cup of coffee, which we assume to belong to the young man, despite the fact that we never actually see him in the same frame with the cup. The young man exchanges a number of glances with Juliette, although it is not clear whether this represents a failed commercial transaction between prostitute and client, or a genuine interest on the part of Juliette. Godard's commentary goes on to describe the difficulty of establishing relations within society and Guzzetti interprets this whole scene as a kind of meta-commentary on the filmmaking experience on the part of the director (he even suggests that this could be *Godard's* cup of coffee (135)). Godard, says Guzzetti, is here expressing the difficulty of situating his own subjectivity in relation to the fictional world he has created, which, once fixed on film, '*has* no mode but that of objectivity' (139). And the 'conclusion' that Godard seems to come up with – 'Il faut que j'écoute, il faut que je regarde autour de moi plus que jamais'[53] – 'though vague as a philosophical resolution, is precise as a response spoken by the persona of director in reference to the situation of the film' (139).

But, if this reading tends to imply a high degree of self-absorption on Godard's part, it fails to take account of the compelling nature of the *image* which, I would suggest, is more important to the spectator's interpretation of this scene than the dense and hurriedly whispered voiceover that is likely to go largely unregistered. Almost too rapidly to be discernible, a sugar cube is dropped into the coffee and, as it is stirred, we watch, transfixed, as bubbles rise to the surface of the liquid and gravitate towards one another. The image thereby provides a micro-

52 'This is how Juliette, at 15:37, watched the turning of the pages of what, in journalistic language, is called a magazine. And this is how, around 150 frames later, another young woman, her equal, her sister, saw the same object. Where, then, is the truth? Full face or in profile? And what's an object anyway?'

53 'I must listen, I must look around me more than ever.'

cosmic representation of the whole of experience in terms of differential forces which bring about the encounter of singularities: from the constitution of galaxies through the violent collision of bodies under the force of gravity to an image of thought as the product of singular encounters communicated through the perceptual faculties of the body. When Godard ends his commentary by announcing 'l'apparition de la conscience' ('the appearance of consciousness'), Guzzetti dismisses it as 'mystical' (145), but Deleuze's conception of consciousness is not so different. The repetition of an event or sensation, says Deleuze, produces a change in the mind that contemplates it, but the mind does not pre-exist the event, rather it is constituted through the repeated contemplation of the event (Deleuze 2000 [1968]: 96–100). More precisely, a scattered series of selves is generated by the contemplation of these repeated events, and is subsequently synthesised into a unified ego (129–31). All life, suggests Deleuze, can be understood as *contraction*, contraction of light and matter, contraction of experience and time. In turn, through the contraction of light on to celluloid in the process of filmmaking, the life that is played out in front of the camera becomes condensed and hardened into memory, an idea that will become crucial to Godard's historical work in the 1990s. In this sense, the action of filmmaking equates to the process of thought itself: the gathering together of discrete elements into a singular encounter before the camera, an encounter that is subsequently ordered in the memory (in montage) into a coherent form. If thought is a process in which a violent and unpredictable encounter becomes sanitised and reified into a familiar form, then so too the cinema takes the intoxicating movement of life itself and spins it into digestible, comprehensible chunks of image and sound. But just as a settled system of thought may be shaken and undone by the unexpected encounter with radical new data, so too the accustomed patterns of signification within chains of moving images may be blown open by the untapped signifying potential of images regarded anew: as when the universe appears without warning within the vertiginous close-up of a cup of coffee.

Week-end

The period 1966–7 marks a crucial transition in Godard's career from a commercial – if never conventional – cinema, to a radical committed cinema, formally audacious and politically incendiary. The films that we have studied in this chapter might be summarised as follows: they present the difficulty of knowing or approaching anything in isolation.

In other words, one cannot understand the sexual relations between young people without understanding the forces of consumer capitalism that shape their lives; but, by the same token, one cannot criticise consumer capitalism without recognising the sexual desires to which it appeals; nor can one understand a war (such as the one taking place in Vietnam) without situating it with regard to the wider violence operated by capitalism, and so on. As a result of the perspective developed over these films, the political situation appears so complicated and intractable that Godard is repeatedly led to call for a *return to zero*: we can only change society, Godard seems to say, by changing *everything*, by rethinking everything. *Week-end* (1967), Godard's last commercial film prior to his withdrawal from mainstream cinema in 1968, appears as the climax to this line of thinking.

Week-end pursues the critique of consumer culture begun in *2 ou 3 choses que je sais d'elle*, singling out the motor car for special attention. This is doubtless the aspect of the film that will be remembered by most viewers: the incredible eight-minute tracking shot of a traffic jam and the insane proliferation of stylised car wrecks by the side of the road. As in *2 ou 3 choses*, this is in part based on anecdotal evidence regarding consumer trends in French society: a response to the rise in traffic accidents occasioned by city-dwellers heading to the country for the weekend. At the beginning of the film, a character notes that there were seven dead at last weekend's pile-up in Evreux. But, over the course of the film, the car develops a symbolic importance that indicates the sovereignty of private property under consumer capitalism. As Kristin Ross points out, the car was at once 'the illustration and the motor' of the society of consumption, since it transported workers to work while also constituting an object of desire (Ross 1995: 39). But the car is a kind of ideal object since it provides a home away from home, combining the security of property with the adventure of displacement (Baudrillard 1968: 95). It thus comes as little surprise that the characters in *Week-end* display a pride of possession with regard to their cars that they never show, for instance, with regard to their spouse (Silverman and Farocki 1998: 84). *Week-end* shows people constantly fighting over cars: when Roland (Jean Yanne) and Corinne (Mireille Darc) leave their apartment, they bump into another car, prompting an argument that involves a tennis racquet, paint and a shotgun. Later, they attempt to steal a convertible Honda belonging to a young man (Jean-Pierre Léaud) who defends his prize with a spare tyre and jack handle like a knight of old. *Week-end* even anticipates the late twentieth-century crime of car-jacking when Roland and Corinne are held up by a man (Daniel Pomereulle) claiming to be the son of God and Alexandre Dumas!

Having left Paris, Roland and Corinne come across an enormous traffic jam and Godard's camera tracks slowly, interminably along the side of these vehicles as Roland forces his way past them. The relentless unfolding of this shot makes this traffic jam resemble the kind of conveyer belt of merchandise sometimes seen in television game shows (Silverman and Farocki 1998: 91) and, as Brian Henderson points out, the shot is matched in Godard's œuvre by a similar tracking shot along a car production line in *British Sounds* (1969) (Henderson 1976: 423). Meanwhile, David Sterritt notes the cacophony of car horns that sound throughout this scene, 'counterpointing the flatness of the image with a direct assault on the audience's eardrums, stamping the scene's immediacy on our bodies as we experience it' (Sterritt 1999: 97). The traffic jam is caused, of course, by a terrible car crash and, as Jane Arthurs and Iain Grant point out, the crash, in both its mechanical and financial manifestations, is an unpredictable event that reveals the *noise* within the system, crippling all communication, circulation and exchange (Arthurs and Grant 2002: 3). We might note, though, that, if this scene represents the logic of the car taken to its extreme, it also marks the point at which the private space of the car breaks down. With all these vehicles indefinitely stalled, people get out of their cars and the road returns to a social space, with drivers and passengers chatting, playing ball games, setting up a chessboard, and so on.

But if Godard is critical of car culture in *Week-end*, he also recognises our powerful *desire* for these objects of consumption. Indeed, Godard himself often displayed a certain car fetishism in his earlier films where, as Sterritt points out, the *meaning* of the car was closer to the ideals of liberation and flexibility promoted by manufacturers and advertisers (Sterritt 1999: 97). Think of the string of cars stolen by Michel Poiccard in *À bout de souffle*, Jeremy Prokosch's Alfa-Romeo in *Le Mépris*, Arthur (Claude Brasseur) and Franz (Sami Frey)'s Simca in *Bande à part*, the Ford Galaxies driven by both Lemmy Caution and Ferdinand/Pierrot, or even Juliette's red Mini in *2 ou 3 choses*. But, in *Week-end*, Godard seems to recognise a rather more troubling aspect to this fascination with cars. The crashes themselves, as Harun Farocki notes, are strikingly beautiful, like 'modernist sculptures' (Silverman and Farocki 1998: 84). Even the blaring horns can sound at times, as Pauline Kael so memorably put it, 'like trumpets in Purcell' (Kael 1970: 139). On more than one occasion, car crashes are associated with an expression of desire: both Roland and Corinne express the wish that the other would die in a road accident, and Corinne says the same about her parents. On one hand, of course, this serves as a condemnation of the greed and amorality of bourgeois culture (Roland and Corinne are on their way to murder her parents and claim the inheritance). On the other hand, it perhaps reflects a certain media fascination with car accidents, particularly those involving celebrities like Françoise Sagan or Albert Camus (Ross 1995: 27) (Roland drives a Facel, the same make of car in which Camus was killed). At the same time, though, I would suggest that Godard, in *Week-end*, gives us a glimpse of an erotics of the car crash of the same kind that would be explored by J. G. Ballard in his novel *Crash*. Ballard suggests that the relentless publicity about road accidents actually produces a *desire* for the crash, for an encounter with something that would appear more *real* than our everyday lives (Ballard 1995 [1973]: 39).

From this perspective, it is worth pointing out that the sexual experience described by Corinne in a long monologue at the beginning of the film *begins in a car*. This scene, introduced by a title reading 'ANAL/YSE', appears as a parody of both sexual narrative and psychoanalytic confession. Corinne, in her underwear, sits on the desk of a man, Paul, who is in fact her lover but here acts more like an analyst (at least until the end of the scene where he instructs Corinne: 'Viens m'exciter' ('Come and turn me on')). There is perhaps an anticipation, here, of Michel Foucault's critique of the injunction to speak about sex in western culture, a kind of enforced confession that accompanies the establishment of a scientific discourse about sex and the reinforcing of a normative sexuality (Foucault 1976). What is striking about the sequence in *Week-end* is the way it stubbornly refuses to allow the spectator to take any *pleasure* from this sexual narrative. The room is in near-darkness with only a faint light coming through the window, such that Corinne's undressed body is visible only in silhouette. The camera tracks slowly in and out from the characters, but for no apparent reason since, as Kaja Silverman comments, 'we never seem to get any closer to them' (Silverman and Farocki 1998: 86). A loud, unpleasant, dirge-like music appears on the soundtrack, drowning out Corinne's words. Ironically, this music cuts out whenever Corinne *stops* talking about sex, only to begin again as soon as she takes up the narrative. As the narrative progresses, the sexual acts described become increasingly bizarre: another woman sits in a saucer of milk while Corinne licks her genitalia; meanwhile an egg is placed between Corinne's buttocks until it breaks. But Corinne describes all this in the same impassive monotone, saying 'C'était pas désagréable, c'était assez terrible'.[54] The image of the milk and eggs is taken from the first two chapters of Georges Bataille's erotic novel *Histoire de l'œil*, first published under a pseudonym in 1928. The

54 'It wasn't unpleasant, it was pretty great.'

appeal to this novel, in which the narrator and his lovers repeatedly smear each other in their piss, shit, blood and sperm, would seem to be to an abject, unclean, unrecuperated sexuality, in which the true strangeness of desire appears ungovernable by any normative discourse. As Bataille writes: 'En général, on goûte les "plaisirs de la chair" à condition qu'ils soient fades ... La débauche que je connais souille non seulement mon corps et mes pensées mais tout ce que j'imagine devant elle et surtout l'univers étoilé'[55] (Bataille 2002: 63).

Week-end recognises, then, that consumer capitalism *engages our desire*: it must do so in order to continue to produce and sell merchandise. But at the same time there is a suggestion that capitalism is reluctant to recognise the true nature of desire, the untameable desire that threatens to overrun the system and cause its collapse. In his theoretical work, Bataille suggested that all living organisms and systems generate an excess of energy that needs to be expunged or expended if it is not to destroy that system. He identified ceremonial rituals in primitive societies like sacrifice or the potlatch tradition of the public destruction of wealth as serving this economic purpose. He argued that the individual accumulation of resources encouraged by capitalism was doomed to destruction since the status it confers is ultimately like an explosive charge waiting to go off (Bataille 1967). Something very similar is suggested in *Week-end*, where those items that would seem to signal the advancement of our civilisation, become instead markers of its decline. As Marie-Claire Ropars-Wuilleumier comments, *Week-end* documents 'un retour progressif à l'état sauvage, dont l'automobile sera à la fois le moyen et le signe'[56] (Ropars-Wuilleumier 1970: 153). Jean-Luc Douin suggests that the car wrecks in the film could be read as sacrifices (Douin 1989: 189), while a disorienting scene in which, with no preceding establishing shot, hands appear out of nowhere to pull Corinne's hair and strangle Roland, presents the car as the site of a regression to bestiality: Corinne and Roland respond by biting the hands and snarling like animals. *Week-end* suggests a return to a tribal society, as shown by the native American costumes worn by a boy in Paris and the hippy revolutionaries in the woods (although, as Harun Farocki notes, some of these latter look suspiciously as though they were dressed in Carnaby Street (Silverman and Farocki 1998: 106)). The primitivism of these revolutionaries is further implied by

55 'In general, one only enjoys the "pleasures of the flesh" on condition that they be tame ... The debauchery that I practise soils not only my body and my thoughts but everything I can imagine, and especially the starry skies.'

56 'a gradual return to a state of savagery, for which the automobile is at once the means and the sign'.

their warlike drumming and their indulgence in cannibalism. Picking up the imagery from Corinne's sexual monologue, a chef breaks eggs between a woman's legs before inserting a live fish into her vagina prior to cooking (all this tastefully offscreen, naturally).

What, then, are we to make of all this? Is Godard, in his disgust at industrial capitalism, advocating a return to primitive society? As in *La Chinoise*, we might ask how seriously we are to take any of this. Certainly *Week-end* is liberally dosed with black humour, from the slapstick fights over cars already mentioned, to the self-mocking distanciation devices, as when Roland complains: 'Ça fait chier, ce film, on ne rencontre que des abrutis'.[57] There is a caustic satire to scenes like the one in which, after Roland and Corinne crash their own car, Corinne emits an ear-piercing, blood-curdling scream that proves to be inspired by the loss of her Hermès handbag; no other human tragedy in the film solicits such a strong reaction. Silverman and Farocki admit that the film does, after all, provide 'a great deal of pleasure' (1998: 85); Sterritt recognises its carnivalesque qualities (1999: 122), while James Monaco describes it as 'very nearly a comedy' (1976: 198). But, if *Week-end* is very funny for an hour or so, it grows less so towards the end. It is perhaps the extraordinarily long and didactic political speeches delivered by two garbage men (see below) that marks the point where the spectator's patience runs out (Sterritt 1999: 113). Subsequently we run up against the cannibalistic horrors of the revolutionary tribe and are beaten into submission by their drums which, as Robin Wood notes, have 'a dehumanised quality, representing a stripping away of all *emotional* sensitivity to a purely nervous-physical level of experience' (in Cameron 1969: 171). As the leader of the revolutionaries (Jean-Pierre Kalfon) remarks: 'On ne peut dépasser l'horreur de la bourgeoisie que par plus d'horreur encore'.[58] *Week-end* closes on what many critics have seen as a vision of hell: Jean-Luc Douin calls it 'dantesque' (1989: 188); Silverman and Farocki describe it as 'a relic from the apocalypse' (1998: 84); Pauline Kael compares it to Bosch and Grünewald (1970: 142).

It might be tempting, then, to accuse Godard of nihilism in this despairing portrait of society. And indeed, his political certainties seem to have deserted him when he has a passer-by ask Roland: 'Vous préférez être baisé par Mao ou par Johnson?'[59] Though we might note that at this point, and shortly after Roland has unflinchingly allowed another passer-by to rape Corinne, Godard's camera moves off left away from Roland, as though to dissociate itself from this morally repugnant

57 'It's bloody annoying, this film, we only ever meet morons.'
58 'The horror of the bourgeoisie can only be overcome by even more horror.'
59 'Would you rather get screwed by Mao or by [Lyndon] Johnson?'

character (Silverman and Farocki 1998: 103). It would, I think, be more correct to say that Godard is seeking to present the world in an entirely new way that has nothing to do with social values whose foundation has been shown to be utterly untenable. Such would appear to be the sense of the scene in which Roland and Corinne come across two costumed characters, a woman (Blandine Jeanson) calling herself Emily Brontë but resembling Lewis Carroll's Alice, and a man (Yves Alfonso) dressed as Tom Thumb. Emily picks up a pebble, and the sudden cut to an extreme close-up of this object effects a dramatic change of scale that perhaps recalls Alice's experiments with size in Wonderland.[60] But the change in scale is also temporal: since the stone, as Emily points out, pre-dates humanity by millennia, it belongs to a *mineral* time that is quite unaffected by the ephemeral existence of man (Silverman and Farocki 1998: 101). Emily and Tom also speak in impenetrable riddles, presenting a knowledge that has no *value* for which it can be used or exchanged. Similarly, the political speeches by the garbage men outline a class-based interpretation of history drawn from Engels, but their repeated references to native American peoples infer the possibility of an entirely different history of civilisation to that promoted by the West.

More generally, we might talk of an aesthetic of incongruity that organises *Week-end*. This principle would seem to be behind the famous 'Action musicale' sequence in which a man brings a piano to a farmyard in order to instruct the residents about Mozart. As he plays a sonata and comments upon the music, Godard's camera completes two anti-clockwise 360° pans around the farmyard, before reversing direction for a clockwise pan. Despite the gentle satire on the French practice of 'cultural action' (see also the interview with Francis Jeanson in *La Chinoise*), there is no denying what Robin Wood (in Cameron 1969: 169) calls the 'formal elegance and symmetry' of this camera movement, which succeeds in bringing out the timeless beauty of the music, even if the pianist plays, by his own admission, 'un peu comme un cochon' ('a bit like a pig'). It should also be noted that the circular movement of the camera contrasts with the linear tracking shot along the traffic jam, thus opposing this peaceful scene to the cacophony of consumerism, but also perhaps suggesting a different temporality to the linear logic of merchandise (Silverman and Farocki 1998: 102). Iain Grant notes that, whereas primitive time was cyclical and primitive space flat, modern time is linear and modern space spherical. It is, in other words, as though time and space have reversed their positions. The result is that 'infinite space will afford no gain', and the only way to

60 I am indebted to one of my students, Jamie Richardson, for this observation.

defeat this limitation of space is through the accumulation of time by increased *speed*, 'revolutions per minute' (Grant 2002: 107–8).

Kaja Silverman notes the way that consumer capitalism is repeatedly associated with *waste* in *Week-end*. Recognising the serial logic of merchandise that we examined with Debord in *2 ou 3 choses*, Silverman argues that the appearance of each new product implies the degradation of the previous one into so much waste and, as the time allotted for the enjoyment of each new commodity becomes briefer and briefer, the entire system of value on which consumerism rests is revealed as so much shit (Silverman and Farocki 1998: 89–90). Such is ultimately the sense of all the anal imagery that Silverman and Farocki trace in *Week-end*, and which also highlights the influence of Bataille. Ultimately, then, it is not Godard who is nihilistic, but the value system of capitalism itself. This confusion over the sense of nihilism is frequently responsible for misreadings of Nietzsche, who is often labelled a nihilist despite criticising a tradition in western society and thought that attributes a value of nothingness to life by creating other, 'higher' values (God, money, truth) which have the effect of denying, or depreciating life (Deleuze 1967 [1962]: 169–70). Nietzsche, as we have seen, instead proposed an *affirmation* of life in its positive difference. The suggestions of cyclical time in *Week-end* perhaps owe something to Nietzsche's concept of eternal return, in which the being of the world is affirmed not in its stasis, not in its *truth*, but in its endless becoming, its ever-changing *appearance*. When Nietzsche wrote of a re-valuation of all existing values, he was not, as Deleuze comments, simply opposing to established values new ones that would subsequently become established in their turn. New values will remain new because they are of another order, characterised by their *difference*. The distinction is the same as that we saw in *2 ou 3 choses* between a thought that recognises identities and a thought that is forced to think its own difference, a thought that accepts other people's solutions to other people's problems and a thought that undoes and reorganises the terms of the problem. 'Qu'est-ce qu'une pensée qui ne fait de mal à personne?' asks Deleuze, 'ni à celui qui pense, ni aux autres?'[61] (Deleuze 2000 [1968]: 177).

The jarring violence of *Week-end*'s film form, its brutally confrontational style makes it, much like Bataille's *Histoire de l'œil*, an ultimately irrecuperable work, even in terms of cultural value (Silverman and Farocki (1998: 85) argue that the film has 'now-classic status', but the near-universal reaction of violent rejection by today's students would

61 'What kind of thought does no harm to anyone, neither to the one who thinks, nor to anyone else?'

suggest otherwise). In addition to Bataille, Godard cites another irrecuperable, uncommodifiable work in *Week-end*: the text recited by the drummer in the revolutionary camp is taken from Lautréamont's *Chants de Maldoror*, a uniquely horrific nightmare vision of humanity, much admired by the surrealists (Louis Aragon, interestingly enough, once suggested that there was no precedent for Godard except Lautréamont (quoted in Price 1997: 67)). In the passage cited, Lautréamont's narrator refuses the reader the comforting certainty that this terrible litany may constitute a swansong or, as James Monaco suggested of *Week-end*, some sort of 'farewell dirge' (Monaco 1976: 200): 'Ne croyez pas que je sois sur le point de mourir, car je ne suis pas encore un squelette, et la vieillesse n'est pas collée à mon front. Écartons en conséquence toute idée de comparaison avec le cygne, au moment où son existence s'envole, et ne voyez devant vous qu'un monstre, dont je suis heureux que vous ne puissiez pas apercevoir la figure; mais, moins horrible est-elle que son âme ...'. (Lautréamont 1970: 56).[62] If *Week-end* remains such a disturbing movie, if it has lost none of its power to shock and offend, it is because, as Robin Wood recognised at the time, and contrary to all those critics who have seen in it a vision of hell, *Week-end* has little to do with bourgeois Judæo-Christian myths of the end of world, instead 'it is simply about the end of *our* world' (in Cameron 1969: 169).

62 'Do not go thinking that I am about to die, for I am not yet a skeleton, nor is age pinned upon my forehead. Let us then avoid any thought of comparison to a swan at the moment where his existence departs him, and see before you nothing but a monster, whose face is happily concealed, though it be less horrible than his soul ....'

References

Adorno, T. (1974 [1951]), *Minima Moralia: Reflections from Damaged Life*, trans. by E. F. N. Jephcott, London, NLB.

Arthurs, J. and Grant, I. (2002), 'Introduction', in *Crash Cultures: Modernity, Mediation and the Material*, Bristol and Portland, OR, Intellect, 1–13.

Aumont, J. (1982), 'This is not a textual analysis (Godard's *La Chinoise*)', *Camera Obscura*, 8–10, 131–61.

Ballard, J. G. (1995 [1973]), *Crash*, London, Vintage.

Bataille, G. (1967), *La Part maudite*, Paris, Minuit.

Bataille, G. (2002), *Histoire de l'œil*, Paris, Gallimard.

Baudrillard, J. (1968), *Le Système des objets*, Paris, Gallimard.

Cameron, I. (1969), *The Films of Jean-Luc Godard*, New York, Praeger.

Cerisuelo, M. (1989), *Jean-Luc Godard*, Paris, L'Herminier/Éditions des Quatre Vents.

Debord, G. (1992 [1967]), *La Société du Spectacle*, Paris, Gallimard.

Deleuze, G. (1967 [1962]), *Nietzsche et la philosophie*, Paris, PUF.
Deleuze, G. (2000 [1968]), *Différence et répétition*, Paris, PUF.
Douin, J.-L. (1989), *Jean-Luc Godard*, Paris, Rivages.
Foucault, M. (1976), *Histoire de la sexualité, Vol I: La Volonté de savoir*, Paris, Gallimard.
Godard, J.-L. (1998), *Jean-Luc Godard par Jean-Luc Godard, Tome 1: 1950–1984*, Paris, Cahiers du cinéma.
Grant, I. (2002), 'Spirit in crashes: Animist machines and the powers of number', in J. Arthurs and I. Grant (eds), *Crash Cultures: Modernity, Mediation and the Material*, Bristol and Portland, OR, Intellect, 103–16.
Guzzetti, A. (1981), *Two or Three Things I Know about Her: Analysis of a Film by Godard*, Cambridge MA and London, Harvard University Press.
Haycock, J. (1990), 'The sign of the sociologist: Show and anti-show in Godard's *Masculin Féminin*', *Cinema Journal*, 29, 4, 51–74.
Henderson, B. (1976), 'Toward a non-bourgeois camera style', in B. Nichols (ed.), *Movies and Methods: An Anthology*, Berkeley, University of California Press.
Kael, P. (1970), *Going Steady*, London, Temple Smith.
Katsahnias, I. (1990), *'La Chinoise'*, *Cahiers du cinéma*, hors série, *Spécial Godard: Trente ans depuis*, 118.
Lautréamont, C. de (1970), *Œuvres complètes*, Paris, Gallimard.
Loshitzky, Y. (1995), *The Radical Faces of Godard and Bertolucci*, Detroit, Wayne State University Press.
MacBean, J. R. (1968), 'Politics and poetry in two recent films by Godard', *Film Quarterly*, 21, 4, 14–20.
MacCabe, C. (1980), *Godard: Images, Sounds, Politics*, London, BFI/MacMillan.
Maupassant, G. de (1973), *Boule de suif, La Maison Tellier*, Paris, Gallimard.
Merleau-Ponty, M. (1996 [1966]), *Sens et non-sens*, Paris, Gallimard.
Monaco, J. (1976), *The New Wave: Truffaut, Godard, Chabrol, Rohmer, Rivette*, New York, Oxford University Press.
Noguez, D. (1977), *Le Cinéma, autrement*, Paris, Union Générale d'Éditions.
Price, B. (1997), 'Plagiarizing the plagiarist: Godard meets the situationists', *Film Comment*, 33, 66–9.
Rancière, J. (2001), *La Fable cinématographique*, Paris, Seuil.
Ropars-Wuilleumier, M.-C. (1970), *L'Écran de la mémoire: Essai de lecture cinématographique*, Paris, Seuil.
Ross, K. (1995), *Fast Cars, Clean Bodies: Decolonization and the Reordering of French Culture*, Cambridge, MA and London, MIT Press.
Sartre, J.-P. (1943), *L'Être et le néant: Essai d'ontologie phénoménologique*, Paris, Gallimard.
Silverman, K. and Farocki, H. (1998), *Speaking about Godard*, New York, New York University Press.
Sterritt, D. (1999), *The Films of Jean-Luc Godard: Seeing the Invisible*, Cambridge, Cambridge University Press.
Wittgenstein, L. (1969), *On Certainty*, ed. by G. E. M. Anscombe and G. H. von Wright, trans. by Dennis Paul and G. E. M. Anscombe, Oxford, Basil Blackwell.

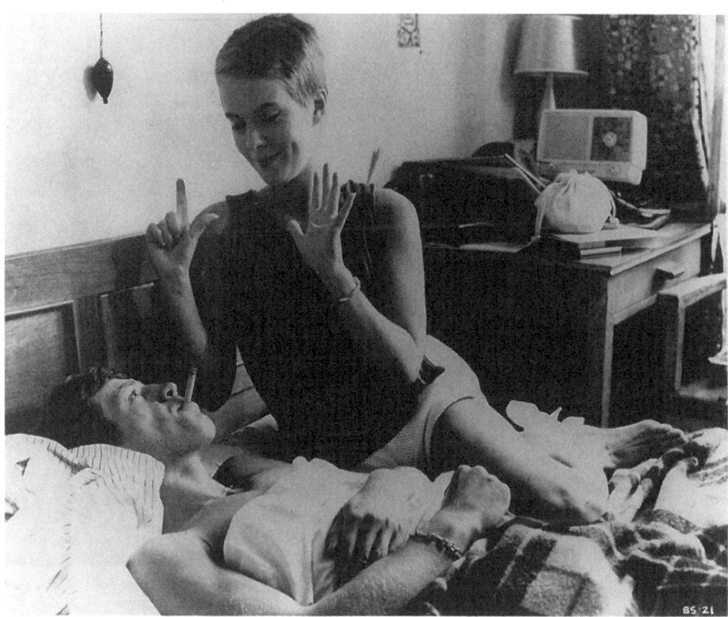

1 Michel and Patricia at play in *À bout de souffle*

2 Fighting over cars in *Week-end*

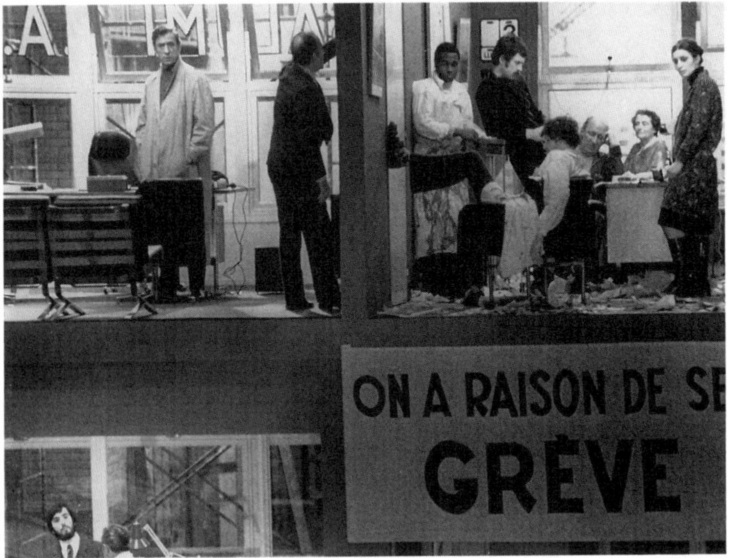

3 The Salumi sausage factory in *Tout va bien*

4 The violence of difference: *Sauve qui peut (la vie)*

5 Godard by the lake in *JLG/JLG: Autoportrait de décembre*

6 Edgar and Cécile in *Éloge de l' amour*

5

Schooling: 1968–72

Le Gai Savoir

Le Gai Savoir (1968) marks, within Godard's œuvre, the mythic *return to zero* that had been repeatedly called for over the preceding two years. If this is the case, it is doubtless largely because the film is articulated around the rupture represented by the student revolt and accompanying strikes and demonstrations associated with May 1968. Godard was involved in the events of May and contributed to the series of 'Ciné-tracts' – short, cheaply produced films which attempted to document strikes and demonstrations as they happened, and from the point of view of those involved. He also made *Un film comme les autres* (1968) which essentially consisted of a discussion between students and workers about their common stakes in the May uprising and the lessons they could learn from each other. *Le Gai Savoir* was shot in the studios of the Organisation de Radio et Télévision Française in December 1967 and January 1968, before being re-edited after the spring of 1968. The television studio provides a plain black background for the film against which two students, Émile Rousseau (Jean-Pierre Léaud) and Patricia Lumumba (Juliet Berto), named after the African revolutionary leader assassinated in 1961, come to study images and sounds. These students follow a three-stage (or three-'year') course of study: in the first instance they collect images and sounds; subsequently they criticise them; before finally constructing their own models of images and sounds. The rest of Godard's film is made up almost entirely of the found images and sounds that Patricia and Émile discuss. As Brian Price comments, this recycling of pre-existing materials constitutes in itself a political use of film: it returns to a more artisanal mode of production, doing away with the divisions of labour associated with commercial filmmaking; and it also challenges consumer culture's 'promise of the new' by suspending the production of images (Price 1997: 68) (Godard's use of found footage would become increasingly common in his subsequent career, as we shall see).

As the name of Léaud's character implies, *Le Gai Savoir* grew out of a project related to Rousseau's *Émile*, in which the Swiss writer suggested that it was possible to take a child as a blank slate upon which to imprint images of a simpler age and more natural life. But, as Robert Kolker and Madeleine Cottenet-Hage point out, if, for Rousseau, images precede ideas, for Godard, images *are* ideas, or at least they are already marked by ideology (Kolker and Cottenet-Hage 1987: 119). Patricia and Émile announce that they are going to proceed by *dissolving* images and sounds, the same way that one approaches problems in chemistry by dissolving solutions, or in politics by dissolving parliament. But it is not clear whether this will ever actually lead our students back to a state of absolute zero, or nothingness. In an exchange at the beginning of the film, Patricia and Émile address this concern directly:

> ÉMILE: On va repartir à zéro.
> PATRICIA: Non, avant de repartir, il faut y aller. On va retourner à zéro.
> ÉMILE: Et une fois qu'on y sera?
> PATRICIA: On regardera autour, voir s'il y a des traces ...[1]

The idea of 'traces' implies that it is never really possible to return to zero, never possible to step outside the fabric of language, culture and ideology that makes up a society. Instead, one can only ask *how* that culture is constructed, *who* that ideology serves, before proceeding to employ a *different* kind of language, to construct images and sounds *differently*.

Patricia and Émile, then, are studying images and sounds but, more specifically, they are studying the *relations between* images and sounds. For it is frequently this *combination* of image and sound that is most powerful in communicating ideology, particularly where the sound has the value of a linguistic message, as in television news for instance. As Roland Barthes has argued, the connotative message of discourse combines with the denotative message of the image to naturalise the latter, to fix the meaning of the image into a definite sense that is ideologically determined in advance (Barthes 1982: 41). As Patricia puts it: 'Dans chaque image, il faut savoir *qui parle*'.[2] And not only who is speaking, but *what they want*. This, as Deleuze points out, was also a key component of the methodology of Nietzsche (from whom Godard

1 'We'll start again from zero. – No, before starting again, we have to go back. We're going to return to zero. – And what will we do when we get there? – Look around, see if we can find traces ....'

2 'In every image, we need to know *who is speaking*.'

borrows the title of *Le Gai Savoir*): when faced with philosophers and scientists claiming to be engaged in the disinterested pursuit of truth, Nietzsche's response is always to ask *what they want*. Since 'Vouloir n'est pas un acte comme les autres'[3] (Deleuze 1967 [1962]: 88–9), this question tends to reveal the ideological underpinnings of apparently 'disinterested' enterprises. What Patricia and Émile discover is that certain associations between images and sounds are altogether forbidden within our society since they threaten to expose the ideological assumptions upon which it rests. Thus Godard presents various images and sounds as *missing*, that is to say censored because their combination would have provided a powerful indictment of western capitalism. For instance, over a silent image of a factory, Godard tells of a sound crew beaten up by the police for trying to record the sounds made by workers when locked into the relentless rhythms of their machines. Other image–sound combinations are telling in their apparent incongruity: for instance, when Godard has a little girl read a Foucauldian text about the birth of the clinic, the discomfort produced in the spectator speaks to our culture's reluctance, even in the wake of Freud, to recognise infantile sexuality.

The application of particular images or sounds in particular contexts is thus never natural but always ideologically determined, and the imposition of one image or sound over another always implies the exertion of power. A simple demonstration of this principle is presented by Patricia and Émile as a model of 'imperialist film' in the third 'year' of their course. Patricia, standing with her back to the camera, happily sings 'O – o – o – o – o – o' while Émile, standing behind her, places his hands around her throat and commands 'Aaaaa!'. Patricia's 'o's become increasingly uncertain before being gradually replaced altogether by 'a's. The fact that Patricia and Émile choose to make this demonstration using the simplest of sounds is typical of *Le Gai Savoir* in which it is repeatedly suggested that sound is even less familiar to us than images. As Émile remarks: 'L'image se mêle si intimement au son dont elle est l'image qu'elle a fini par usurper le rôle principal'.[4] The film thus frequently presents sounds detached from their expected visual accompaniment, and in many cases from any image at all, in order to encourage the spectator to pay attention to them *as sounds*. As Harun Farocki points out, although we do not see any footage of the events of May '68 in *Le Gai Savoir*, we *hear* a great deal of recordings, principally drawn from the student occupation of the Sorbonne (Silverman and

3 'Wanting is not an act like any other.'

4 'The image combines so closely with the sound that it represents that it has ended up usurping the principal role.'

Farocki 1998: 114). A very long passage at the end of the film presents nothing but a blank screen over which are alternated the speeches of student leaders with Godard's voiceover commentary. We presume we know what sound is, but as soon as we pursue the investigation, it is revealed as even more mysterious than the image. This is demonstrated when Patricia and Émile try, and fail, to repeat the intonation of a friend saying 'Oh oui!' As Émile comments, 'Ce son très simple, il est effroyablement compliqué à transmettre'.[5]

These singular qualities of the voice have meant that it is often attributed a transcendent value in the philosophy of language. Since, when I speak, I hear myself speaking as I produce the words, it is often assumed that the *meaning* of an utterance is immediately present in what I say, that it is somehow a *direct* expression of my true self. Thus speech is taken to enjoy a 'natural' relation to reality, unlike writing which is a secondary representation resting upon an arbitrary system of signs. This traditional view has been criticised by Jacques Derrida who argues that, on the contrary, any time I attempt to communicate something of my experience, that communication must necessarily pass through a physical mediation (sound, gesture, etc.) that compromises the purity of its meaning, establishing an irrecoverable distance between my intention and the reality of the signification (Derrida 1967: 41). The influence of Derrida's thought over Godard's film is clearly discernible, and at one point we see an image of the cover of Derrida's *De la grammatologie* (also published in 1967) with the word 'savoir' written over it in red. But, in line with the film's attempt to unite theory with practice (an ambition that testifies to Godard's continued Maoist inspiration), Patricia and Émile proceed to a very simple demonstration of Derrida's insight. 'Si on dit quelque chose, il faut le faire,'[6] says Émile. Having invited an old vagrant into the studio to perform various linguistic experiments, they record his voice and play it back to him. The look of startled confusion on his face is followed by a burst of laughter as he recognises his voice. But, in this moment's hesitation, we glimpse the *difference* that has inserted itself between the old man and his expression.

There is, then, no natural or true relation between language and the 'real' world. Language can only signify the real by virtue of its difference to that which it represents. And the same is true of images and sounds used to represent the real. To assume a natural link between image, sound and reality is to fall into the trap of self-evident truths, which always serve ideological interests. 'Nous n'acceptons plus aucune sorte

5 'This very simple sound proves incredibly difficult to convey.'
6 'If you say something, you should do it.'

de vérité évidente', reads a series of titles in *Le Gai Savoir*, 'Les vérités évidentes appartiennent à la philosophie bourgeoise'.[7] 'Vérités évidentes' is written over a drawing of a television set, flanked by two riot policemen, as though to suggest the ideological interests protected by such self-evident truths. Godard's commentary also insists that there is no such thing as 'neutral' science, reminding us that scientists collaborated with the regimes of Hitler and Stalin. 'Self-evident truths' play a crucial role in the constitution of bourgeois subjects in the western education system, as is demonstrated when Émile and Patricia analyse a classroom primer on the alphabet: under 'c', you will not find 'capitalism', 'culture', 'class' or 'combat', nor 'revolution' or 'repression' under 'r'. 'F' does not list 'fascism', but 'family' and '*fromage*', and the entry under '*faim*' ('hunger') reads 'J'ai faim quand je me mets à table'.[8] 'Et les enfants du tiers monde qui n'ont pas de table?!'[9] screams Émile.

As Patricia notes, when studying language, images and sounds, 'on étudie des rapports, des relations, des différences'.[10] Patricia demonstrates the detachment of language from truth, or from any natural relation to reality, by pronouncing patent falsehoods: 'J'ai 84 ans, je mesure 10 mètres ...',[11] thereby proving that signifiers can still *make sense* even in the absence of a referent that could act as guarantor of the veracity of that sense. They also investigate the signifying chain of language by playing word association games with a young boy and the old man mentioned earlier. As Harun Farocki notes, the little boy proves to be rather better at this game than the old man, who spends most of the time looking very confused (Silverman and Farocki 1998: 125). But what is perhaps most interesting about this sequence is the difficulty of deciding how genuine the experiment is. Patricia and Émile fire a series of words at the boy who replies, or so we assume, spontaneously. Some of these replies seem perfectly credible: 'crime–poignard', for instance, or 'voyage–train'.[12] Others seem extremely unlikely coming from the mouth of such a young boy: 'révolution–octobre', or even 'cinéma–lumière'.[13] But it is those associations that are undecidable that prove most interesting, since they demonstrate *our own ability* to draw inferences and make connections between apparently unrelated signifiers. For instance, when the boy responds to 'torture'

7 'We no longer accept any kind of self-evident truths. Self-evident truths belong to bourgeois philosophy.'
8 'I'm hungry when I come to the table.'
9 'What about the children in the third world who have no table?!'
10 'we study relationships, connections, differences'.
11 'I'm 84 years old, I'm 10 metres tall ....'
12 'crime–dagger, journey–train'.
13 'revolution–October, cinema–light'.

with 'tortue' ('tortoise'), is this a surrealist deactivation of the violence of torture on Godard's part, or is the boy merely responding to a word he doesn't really understand with another chosen for its phonetic proximity? When he responds to 'chinois' ('Chinese') with 'terre' ('earth'), is he merely demonstrating that he knows China is a country on the Earth, or is this an idealisation of Mao's return-to-earth agricultural policies? Similarly, when the boy responds to 'travail' ('work') with 'tigre' ('tiger'), and to 'communiste' with 'magicien', is Godard further propounding the transformative energy of communism via Mao's preferred imagery, or are these simply the kind of the images that a young boy has in his head?

The concerted effort to unite theory and practice in *Le Gai Savoir* is related, at the end of the film, to another binary pair, 'méthode' and 'sentiments', which Émile seeks to join together through the rather awkward word 'misotodiments'. This, he suggests, is what he has learned from studying images and sounds. We might understand by this the recognition that the production of images and sounds, like the production of language, cannot take place outside of a social and cultural space determined by ideology; but further that any utterance determined by ideology is also determined by *desire*: not just *who speaks*, but *what do they want*? The recognition that the political enters into the field of desire is implied by the frequent juxtaposition in the film of politically coded images (whether of repression or revolution) with erotic and pornographic images. This suggests, too, that political and economic oppression and sexual oppression go hand in hand. This idea is given clear expression in a scene from *One plus one* (1968), in which a character reads from Hitler's *Mein Kampf* while the camera pans over an array of pornographic magazine covers. This double criticism of the capitalist economy and the libidinal economy is further implied by the frequent citing, in the same breath, of Marx and Freud: on one image, reproduced in *Le Gai Savoir*, of a naked woman reclining on a beach, Godard has drawn an arrow to her head reading 'Freud' and an arrow to her crotch reading 'Marx'. This attempt to read Marx and Freud together was characteristic of a number of theorists of the late 1960s and early 1970s, such as Jean-François Lyotard or Deleuze and Guattari, whose intersection with Godard will be considered in the next chapter. For now, Godard's analysis remains limited to slogans – such as 'la liberté de la femme commence en son ventre'[14] – and provocative suggestions, for instance that the fear of a black revolution in the United States may be partly attributable to a sexual paranoia. Meanwhile, quoting Che

14 'a woman's freedom begins in the womb'.

Guevara, Godard writes across the image: 'Laissez-moi vous dire, au risque de paraître ridicule, qu'un révolutionnaire véritable est guidé par de grands sentiments d'amour'.[15]

It is perhaps the effusiveness of remarks such as this, the recognition that politics is built upon desire and emotion and thus need not be exempt from a sense of *fun*, that marks Godard's proximity to Nietzsche, whose title he borrows. As Nietzsche wrote in the preface to *The Gay Science*, his book was written after recovering from a long illness and was thus infused with a sense of gratitude and joy. He proceeds to argue that so-called 'serious' thought is merely a prop, or even a sedative for 'sick thinkers' (Nietzsche 2001 [1887]: 4). The *seriousness* of thought betrays an assumption that the life thereby approached and described is some sort of burden, whereas for Nietzsche, on the contrary, thought should be a source of laughter and joy at the *affirmation* of the world. As Kaja Silverman argues, the revolution to which *Le Gai Savoir* testifies is not only the social and political revolt of May '68, but also, and perhaps primarily, the revolution in French thought brought about by the works of Derrida, Deleuze, Foucault and Althusser in the mid- to late-1960s (Silverman and Farocki 1998: 113). The value of Godard's film is thus in providing a practical demonstration of some of the difficult and densely argued ideas in these texts and thereby revealing the joyful knowledge contained within. For the deconstruction of the bourgeois concept of truth, a process that unites all these authors, is rightly associated with a giddy sense of *liberation*. Where Derrida talks of the play of the signifier, Godard shows what he means by indulging in childish language games. The most revolutionary meaning of *Le Gai Savoir* is perhaps ultimately contained in Patricia's giggles as she claims to be 10 feet tall, or in the laughter with which the old man greets the recognition of his own voice: it is there that the hollow foundations of our culture ring with most resonance.

Pravda

Following the rupture of May '68, Godard began to make films collectively under the name of the Dziga Vertov Group, so-called after the great Soviet filmmaker, and in opposition to Sergei Eisenstein who was seen as tainted by his collaboration with the Stalinist regime (Godard 1998: 343). The membership of the Dziga Vertov Group fluctuated over the course of their films, but the core was formed by

15 'Allow me to say, at the risk of appearing ridiculous, that a true revolutionary is guided by great feelings of love.'

Godard and Jean-Pierre Gorin, a young militant keen to explore the possibilities of political filmmaking. This collaborative approach is bound up with a certain rejection of auteurism on Godard's part, which he considered to be incompatible with radical socialist politics: 'La notion d'auteur est une notion complètement réactionnaire,'[16] he declared in 1969 (Godard 1998: 335). The Dziga Vertov Group made a series of films financed by European television companies in Britain – *British Sounds* (1969) – Italy – *Luttes en Italie* (1969) – and West Germany – *Vladimir et Rosa* (1971) – each of which was subsequently rejected by the producer. From a certain perspective, as Steve Cannon points out, there is something a little perverse about this apparent refusal to make films *in France* during what was a time of real revolutionary ferment and political possibility (Cannon 1993: 77–8).

Pravda (1969), filmed in Czechoslovakia by Godard and Gorin with a Czech documentary team, but edited by Godard alone, is perhaps exemplary in this regard. In addition, it represents perhaps the most systematic application of the Dziga Vertov Group's Marxist-Leninist method and, as such, serves as a good demonstration of what are, today, generally considered to be the main failings of the Group. The film begins as a kind of travelogue. In voiceover, Vladimir (i.e. Lenin) describes a series of images for the benefit of Rosa (i.e. Luxemburg). At first, Vladimir invites Rosa to guess where these images were filmed: the billboard advertisements suggest we are in the West, but other elements, such as collectivised farms, reveal that this is a socialist country, even if the young people like the Beatles and the workers are allowed to grow their hair long – perhaps Yugoslavia? Eventually, the country is identified as Czechoslovakia and the images and voiceover continue to show us people at work in fields, factories and offices, together with Czech television footage, advertisements for large western companies and the tanks that watch over the people in the streets. In this early part of *Pravda*, the style is not dissimilar to Godard's earlier films, indeed at times it comes across as a kind of *2 or 3 Things I Know About Czechoslovakia*. In places, this reference appears to be quite deliberate, particularly in the repeated shots of a red Skoda which are not without recalling Juliette's red Mini from *2 ou 3 choses*. A frontal shot of the car approaching the camera, placed at a 45° angle, almost literally reproduces a shot from the earlier film.

But, if Godard thus refers to his own cinematic past, it is only in order to criticise it. This presentation of the concrete situation in Czechoslovakia, says Vladimir, is inadequate: this is *news*, but only in

16 'The notion of the author is a completely reactionary one'.

the sense defined by the *New York Times* or *Le Monde*. These images subsequently need to be re-edited along anti-revisionist lines in such a way as to show up the contradictions existing within this socialist society. Vladimir's voiceover thus proceeds to offer a commentary on the images we have just seen. He explains, for instance, that the red Skoda prominently displayed in the film was rented by the filmmakers from the Western company Hertz-Avis. Now, since the Skoda factories in Czechoslovakia are nationalised, this car theoretically belongs to the workers who built it, but Hertz and Avis rent cars for profit and this profit is certainly not distributed among the Czech workers. In other words, these workers are working for a western capitalist company: 'Le marché libre a besoin d'esclaves et les esclaves des pays révisionnistes sont mieux dressés que les autres'.[17] The film had also shown images of men at work in a munitions factory. Vladimir explains that the artillery from this factory will be delivered to North Vietnam for use against US fighter planes. However, this does not prevent the workers going out and buying models of the very planes they are building weapons to destroy. The workers are simply not told, says Vladimir, what they are building these weapons for, or where they will be used. 'Bref, le Parti demande aux travailleurs de saisir la production d'une main mais pas la révolution de l'autre.'[18] Just like workers in Paris, London or Madrid, those in Czechoslovakia have been refused what Vladimir calls 'le seul droit oublié par la déclaration des Droits de l'homme bourgeois: le droit au travail politique'.[19] When they are not building models of US fighter planes, says Vladimir, the workers from the munitions factory like to go to the cinema, where they watch films modelled precisely on the kind of reactionary movies produced in Hollywood, but no one *asked* the people whether this was the kind of film they wanted to see. Just as in the West, then, 'On arrive au peuple, on ne part pas de lui'.[20]

In the third section of the film, Rosa takes over the voiceover, explaining that, to these 'false' images, she is going to oppose 'true' sounds. Thus, over images of various revisionist institutions within Czech society, Rosa reads a text stipulating how these institutions should be run in a true socialist society. For instance, over images of the managerial offices in the Skoda plant and the first-class executive

17 'The free market needs slaves and the slaves of revisionist countries are better trained than the others.'

18 'In short, the Party asks workers to seize production with one hand but not revolution with the other.'

19 'the only right left out of the bourgeois declaration of human rights: the right to politically meaningful work'.

20 'They go to the people, they don't come from them.'

dining room, Rosa states that the managerial class must beware of privilege, refusing it wherever possible and sharing the life of the people, actively seeking the criticism of the people and modifying their practices accordingly. Over images of a university classroom with students taking notes from a professor's lecture, Rosa stipulates that students must be led by the proletariat: workers need to go into universities to encourage intellectuals to reject the bourgeois ideals of revisionism, while students and teachers should be sent to factories to take part in production. The idea of abstract knowledge that is somehow 'above class' is condemned: for everything taught, says Rosa, we must ask *for whom* and *against whom* it is taught. This section of *Pravda* thus has certain points in common with *Le Gai Savoir*: the deliberate disjunction created between sound and image and the questioning of who benefits from ideologically determined forms of knowledge. But, where *Le Gai Savoir* opened up a gap between image and sound in order to question the very possibility of some ahistorical truth inhabiting language or science, *Pravda* marks a step backward by re-inscribing sound and image with the metaphysical values of true and false: the images of the society on display are 'false', that is to say revisionist, ideological; whereas the sound (Rosa's voiceover) is 'true', that is Marxist-Leninist, which thereby equates to 'scientific' (*Cahiers du cinéma* editorial staff 1972: 36–7). The film, to be fair, recognises this failure, Vladimir interrupting Rosa to point out that they have acted dogmatically, that they are talking in slogans and that, for one step forward, they have taken two steps back.

Among all the images of Czech society in *Pravda*, a certain symbolism develops around the colour red. A close-up of a red rose recurs throughout the film, its first appearance coinciding with the first mention of 'the Czech and Slovak working class', thus identifying it as a symbol of that class. Subsequently the rose is intercut with images of cartoon crows taken from Czech television, themselves presented as a symbol for 'les fantômes de la Deuxième Internationale',[21] swooping down like vampires upon the Czech working class. Later, images of tanks and planes are juxtaposed with a shot of the rose crushed under foot to symbolise the martyrdom of the people. Elsewhere, during a sequence showing the trams in Bratislava, a red panel on the side of the tram briefly fills the screen as Vladimir describes 'des combats entre les différents rouges: le rouge qui vient de gauche et le rouge qui part à droite'.[22] As James Roy MacBean points out, the 'faded and blemished'

21 'the ghosts of the Second Internationale'.

22 'the struggles between different sorts of red: the red that comes from the left and the red that goes off towards the right'.

red of the tram perhaps signifies the revisionist socialism of Czechoslovakia, as it moves out of the frame to the right (MacBean 1972: 37). (The red of the tram filling the screen also recalls the extreme close-up on the paintwork of Juliette's Mini in *2 ou 3 choses que je sais d'elle.*) Red also signifies the blood of the oppressed and exploited workers and is filmed in a shot of red liquid disappearing down a plughole. Finally, a shot of a glass of red wine filled to overflowing signifies at once the privilege of the managerial class *and* the revolutionary power of the proletariat that cannot be contained by revisionist ideology. There is, then, a complex but coherent network of imagery in *Pravda* articulated around the colour red. But, within the strict Marxist-Leninist parameters that the film sets itself, this symbolism can only be seen as problematic. For instance, Andrew Britton, following the work of Rosemary Freeman on emblematic imagery, suggests that such images tend to imply 'one unified allegorical conception of the meaning of life', and that, originally, this was bound up with distinctly religious overtones (Britton 1976: 10–11). *Pravda* seems guilty of double standards where symbolism is concerned. Vladimir is critical of the way Czech students, when they occupied their university, flew the anarchist's black flag tainted with the bourgeois symbolism of mourning, rather than the red flag of revolution. But it is difficult to see how one symbol is more bourgeois than another if the notion of symbolism itself is to be criticised. Moreover, the shot of blood disappearing down a plughole would appear to be an allusion to Alfred Hitchcock's *Psycho* (1960) where a similar shot occurs in the famous shower scene. Despite Godard's often expressed admiration for Hitchcock, it is hard to imagine how a product of the Hollywood studio system such as *Psycho* could be considered as anything other than bourgeois by the dogma of Marxism-Leninism. Nor is this the only cinematic reference within the film. At the end of *Pravda,* we see a long, static wide shot showing workers leaving a factory, an image whose subject and whose framing inevitably recall the Lumière brothers' early film *Sortie d'usine.* This is, if anything, even more problematic than the Hitchcock citation, since the reference to Lumière tends to imply the cinema's capacity to *capture the real,* an ideological stance criticised in *Le Gai Savoir.*

If these criticisms of *Pravda* seem petty, they are nonetheless necessitated by the strict dialectical–materialist agenda that the film sets itself. The relentless onslaught of Marxist-Leninist analysis in *Pravda* can, at times, be exhausting, and this effect is clearly deliberate. When Rosa hesitates for a moment in her commentary, Vladimir berates her for it, instructing her not to leave too long between analyses to allow the revisionist images to take hold. As in *2 ou 3 choses que je sais d'elle,* the spectator often has a sense of being overwhelmed by the number of relations established between the elements of the society on display. However, whereas in *2 ou 3 choses*, Godard's voiceover commentary shared in this sense of bewilderment and impotence, in *Pravda* there is a certain mastery, a righteousness located in the voiceover and this has led to criticism of the film. Various defences for *Pravda*'s impenetrable form have been proposed: as the *Cahiers* critics argued, to say the film is too difficult, and in particular too difficult for a worker audience, 'revient à exiger des œuvres enfantins en présupposant l'abrutissement congénital du peuple'[23] (*Cahiers du cinéma* editorial staff 1972: 6). Meanwhile, James Roy MacBean argues that to ask whether 'workers' could 'understand' these films is to miss the point: they are not aimed at some vaguely identified 'mass' of workers, but at specific groups of committed militant activists (both workers and students) who can use the films to develop their revolutionary theory and practice. The films of the Dziga Vertov Group are not merchandise to be bought and sold or entertainment to be consumed and enjoyed, and should not be judged as such: they are political tools to be used in the service of the clearly stated goal of socialist revolution (MacBean 1972: 34).

Nonetheless, as Steve Cannon remarks, by targeting such a select audience, the Dziga Vertov Group missed a crucial political opportunity among a large section of the French population which, following May '68, would have been particularly open to revolutionary ideas. Instead, the films adopted a 'hectoring, sectarian tone which blocks off any real communication with the un-converted' (Cannon 1993: 80). As a result, far from developing the kind of open-ended, 'polyphonic' film form admired by the likes of Peter Wollen (Wollen 1985 [1972]), the films of the Dziga Vertov Group gave rise to a singularly *closed* form (Cannon 1993: 81). Indeed, Andrew Britton goes so far as to call the Group's *Vent d'est* (1969) 'one of the most repressive films ever made' (Britton 1976: 9)! Some of the most effective sequences in *Pravda* occur when the Marxist-Leninist commentary is kept to a minimum and the film simply shows the reality of life in the Czech socialist republic. For instance, there is one long, static shot of a man working on an industrial lathe in a factory where we simply watch the machine move backwards and forwards as the factory noise rings in the background. As James Monaco comments, this shot 'conveys very effectively the dehumanisation of industrial labour' (Monaco 1976: 228), the sheer oppressive boredom of factory work. But precisely this kind of illustration of real

23 'amounts to a demand for childish works which presuppose the congenital stupidity of the people'.

living and working conditions, which generates a visceral rather than an intellectual response from the spectator, is condemned by Godard as bourgeois: 'Tous les films bourgeois sont pour le vécu, l'émotion'[24] (Godard 1998: 338).

Although it is easy to criticise the films of the Dziga Vertov Group, it is perhaps only fair to acknowledge the bravery and commitment involved in making a film like *Pravda*. It is, frankly, difficult to imagine a respected western director of art cinema today going to make a film about the real conditions of labour in, say, the car factories of Eastern Europe or the sweatshops of South-East Asia and, moreover, a film that seeks not to excite the pity of a bourgeois western audience but to examine the concrete conditions of possibility of a socialist revolution. The fact remains, churlish as it may appear to say it, that *Pravda* is not a lot of fun. Godard, over this period of his career, repeatedly cited Chairman Mao's assertion that 'la révolution n'est pas un dîner de gala',[25] but the dour tone of *Pravda* is shown in the fact that the only laughter in the film is attributed to revisionists. 'Qui profite de ça? Qui se marre quand on lui dit qu'il n'y a pas d'art, pas de science au-dessus des classes? Qui rigole? Ceux qui ont trahi le marxisme: les révisionnistes'.[26] In addition, the revisionist students in the university classroom are shown laughing at the end of the sequence on the re-education of intellectuals (we are not permitted to share the joke). *Pravda* thus compares badly to films like *Week-end* and *Le Gai Savoir* where revolutionary fervour was seen to be a cause for joy and laughter. One of the Dziga Vertov Group films manages to preserve this sense of fun: *Vladimir et Rosa* is a ludic, carnivalesque restaging of the trial of the Chicago Eight, a group of revolutionaries charged with conspiracy to incite a riot for their organisation of a mass demonstration against the Vietnam War on the occasion of the Democratic National Convention in 1968. Refusing to recognise the legitimacy of the bourgeois court, the defendants blew kisses to the jury, brought a birthday cake into the courtroom and recommended the judge try LSD. Significantly, *Vladimir et Rosa* was dismissed at the time as 'by far the weakest' of the Dziga Vertov Group films (MacCabe 1980: 66), but, with hindsight, it is considerably more enjoyable than the Group's more didactic works. In *La Chinoise*, Jean-Pierre Léaud's character suggests that, over time, the roles of film pioneers Lumière and Méliès have been reversed: where

24 'All bourgeois films are in favour of lived experience and emotion.'
25 'revolution is no dinner party'.
26 'Who benefits from all this? Who has a good laugh when they are told there is no art, no science above class? Who chuckles away? Those who have betrayed Marxism: the revisionists.'

Lumière was considered to be documenting real life, he now looks like one of the last great French impressionists; where Méliès was considered a fantasist, his films of a journey to the moon and restaging of royal ceremonies now look like the real documents of twentieth-century history. MacBean, we might note, offers as a precedent for *Vladimir et Rosa* Méliès's reconstruction of the infamous Dreyfus trial (MacBean 1972: 42). Perhaps, over time, the value of the Dziga Vertov Group films has been similarly reversed: where *Pravda* reveals nothing so much as the self-absorbed didacticism of the Group's own discourse, it is the irreverent humour of *Vladimir et Rosa* that maintains a truly revolutionary energy.

Tout va bien

Tout va bien (1972), co-directed with Jean-Pierre Gorin, was Godard's first broadly commercial film since he turned his back on the mainstream film industry in 1968. As such, it surveys the progress made, both politically and cinematically since '68, and can even be considered as semi-autobiographical. Yves Montand plays Jacques, a filmmaker who began his career at the time of the Nouvelle Vague. In an interview scene he talks about his career. Already thoroughly disillusioned with the film industry prior to 1968, the events of May provided him with an excuse to abandon it altogether. When subsequently asked to adapt an American crime novel, he could not bring himself to do it. Jacques turned his hand to filming advertisements in order to pay the rent and enable himself to pursue other activities. In this willing capitulation to the capitalist economy, Jacques differs from Godard, but his proximity to the real-life filmmaker is recalled when he says, 'J'ai un projet de film politique sur la France qui traîne depuis trois ans'.[27] As we saw above, Godard himself had not made a film in France since 1968, and *Tout va bien* might be seen as the outcome of a long process of reflection on the events of May and their legacy. As Jacques says in the film, it is only now that the real extent of change (or otherwise) since '68 is becoming clear, it is only now that a distinction can be drawn between those who were determined to fight for social and political change, and those who were merely clowning around and have since returned to their status quo. Jacques, for his part, modestly identifies his own role in this situation: as a filmmaker, his task is to

27 'I've got a project for a political film about France that I've been trying to get made for three years.'

'trouver des formes nouvelles pour des contenus nouveaux'.[28] In interview, Godard stated that the reason all the Dziga Vertov Group films made for television companies were refused was not because of their political subject matter, but because the producers judged them to be 'uncinematic'. But, says Godard, this apparent aesthetic judgement was merely the way these state-affiliated TV stations expressed their political allegiance: 'Nous devons rompre avec cette vieille idée de la séparation de la forme et du fond qui appartient spécifiquement à l'idéologie bourgeoise'[29] (Godard 1998: 372).

Tout va bien, then, is an attempt to make a political film within the commercial film industry, and thereby to reach a wider audience than that targeted by the films of the Dziga Vertov Group. The film, with its international stars and elaborate sets, required a significant budget of 230 million francs, and, as Godard memorably put it, 'C'est le financement d'un cocktail Molotov par ceux qui vont le recevoir dans la figure'[30] (Godard 1998: 372). Aware that their film may appear tainted by the capitalist finance involved, Godard and Gorin are keen that the role of this money in the film should be made clear. This is demonstrated in the opening credits. After titles reading 'Mai 1968', 'Mai 1972' and 'France 1972', making clear the film's intention to trace the political progress of the country since '68, a male voiceover announces 'Je veux faire un film', to which a woman's voice replies 'Pour faire un film il faut de l'argent'.[31] Subsequently we cut to a close-up of a chequebook and a hand signs and tears off a series of cheques detailing the precise amount of money paid for the various elements of the film, everything from the screenplay and the photography to the studio and laboratory costs. The female voice advises that, if we have stars in the film, we can ask for more money, and the names of the stars, Yves Montand and Jane Fonda, appear on screen. However, the male voice notes that, in order for stars to accept a film, they require a story, and usually a love story. Here we see Montand and Fonda walking together in a park, each enumerating the parts of the other's body that they love, eliciting the response, 'Alors, tu m'aimes totalement?'.[32] This explicit reference to the dialogue from the beginning of *Le Mépris* is thus a direct allusion to another film in which Godard, working with a big budget and an international star, dispensed with the producer's expecta-

28 'to find new forms for new content'.

29 'We must break with this old idea of the separation of form and content which belongs specifically to bourgeois ideology.'

30 'It's like financing the Molotov cocktail that's going to be thrown in your face.'

31 'I want to make a film. – To make a film you need money.'

32 'You love me totally, then?'

tions of a traditional love story in a detached prologue before moving on to the film proper. The male and female voices go on to argue that, before telling a story about these characters, they need to be concretely situated, both geographically and historically. They thus posit a country (we see a relief map of France) before narrowing the focus to a city (Paris) and the apartment in which the characters live. Furthermore, they describe the different classes of people existing and acting around this central couple, and the conflicts existing between these classes: 'Il y aurait des paysans qui paysannent [over an image of a farmer milking a cow], des ouvriers qui ouvrièrent [over an image of a factory], et des bourgeois qui bourgeoisent [over a TV news broadcast discussing party politics]'.[33] In *Tout va bien*, then, Godard and Gorin are keen that their characters should not belong to some vague fictional world, but should be concretely situated with respect to the system of capitalist production in which the film itself is made. (It is worth pointing out that this technique of explicitly situating characters in their historical context has since become commonplace in mainstream cinema and, in the process, has been emptied of its political significance. Consider for instance Spike Jonze and Charlie Kaufman's *Adaptation* (2002) where the technique is taken to self-parodic extremes with a prologue which, in order to situate the film's protagonist, returns to *the beginning of time*.)

At the time of its release, *Tout va bien* was routinely compared to a film directed by Marin Karmitz entitled *Coup pour coup*, also released in 1972 and dealing with the same subject: the occupation of a factory and the sequestration of the managing director by the workers. As Pierre Baudry notes, *Tout va bien* often emerged badly from this comparison, judged as lacking generosity towards the workers it portrayed (Baudry 1972: 14–15). This was largely because *Coup pour coup*, unlike *Tout va bien*, used non-professional actors to play the workers and was thus considered more 'realistic', according to the ideological conception whereby truth is presumed to reside within reality, waiting only to be revealed (Groupe Lou Sin 1972: 8). *Tout va bien* is frequently deliberately anti-realistic, notably in its portrayal of the factory, for which Godard and Gorin had built a large two-storey set, open on one side rather like a theatre stage, thus enabling the camera to take in a cross-section of the whole factory. The Salumi sausage factory in *Tout va bien* is not supposed to be a realistic location but is deliberately set up as a metaphorical representation of the state of the political struggle in France in 1972 (Groupe Lou Sin 1972: 22–3). To this end, the film gives

33 'There would be farmers farming, workers working and a middle class middle-classing.'

voice to the various parties within this struggle: the striking workers, the managerial class and the Communist Party-affiliated trade union, the Confédération Générale du Travail (CGT). As such, the film makes many more political discourses available to the spectator than simply the hard-line Marxist-Leninist dogma of the Dziga Vertov Group films. Furthermore, these political discourses are generally filmed within an interview format which, by repeatedly designating the spectator as the absent addressee of the discourse, invites that spectator to situate him- or herself politically with respect to the opinions expressed (Groupe Lou Sin 1972: 20). In organising the film in this way, Godard and Gorin hoped it would provoke political discussion among spectators once they had left the cinema. Instead of providing a single 'correct' interpretation of the events on display, then, *Tout va bien* offers the terms for a debate which it invites the spectator to carry on beyond the confines of the film narrative. As Godard commented: 'Notre but est de diviser les gens et non de les réunir, à l'encontre de la télévision'[34] (Godard 1998: 375).

This is not to say that the treatment of the various parties in this political struggle is entirely even-handed. Much as in *Masculin féminin* or *La Chinoise*, which also deployed the interview format, the amount of sympathy allotted to each speaker can be determined by a close analysis of how each interview is filmed. The managing director of the factory, Marco Guidotti (Vittorio Caprioli) is interviewed sitting behind his desk, with a neon sign advertising the company name visible through the window behind him. As Margaret Atack comments, the familiarity of such signs from Hollywood genre cinema perhaps has the effect of Americanising this image of the capitalist (Atack 1999: 52–3). Guidotti is dismissive of the strikers, arguing that the class struggle belongs to the vocabulary of the nineteenth century and that 'le mot de révolution n'a plus de sens aujourd'hui'.[35] He describes the progress of capitalism, noting the increase in per capita income over the past twenty-five years and suggests that a healthy balance can be found between social democracy and market forces. But Guidotti, played by an Italian actor with a thick accent and rather stereotypically effusive body language, tends to come across as a comical figure. Indeed, Andrew Britton suggests that the 'tone of facile caricature' in this portrait of the factory boss is rather at odds with the complexity of the rest of the film (Britton 1976: 9).

The portrayal of the CGT representative (Jean Pignol) is more subtle. Admittedly, he appears flanked by two goons who are never permitted to speak, and at times he appears to be reading from a script, perhaps

34 'Our goal is not to unite people, like on television, but to divide them.'
35 'the word revolution no longer has any meaning today'.

implying his slavish adherence to the Communist Party line (Collet and Fargier 1974: 63). But he is given a sensible and serious speech in which he describes the monopolisation of the food industry by a handful of giant companies and complains that, over a period where food production has risen by 60 per cent and managerial salaries by 25 per cent, workers' salaries have seen no comparable increase. Nonetheless, he dismisses the occupation of the factory as 'un mauvais coup porté par une minorité',[36] saying it threatens to set back the cause of the union's global strategy. He also complains that the 'anarchists' involved in the strike are never to be found to help with the day-to-day work of the union. The portrait of this union delegate, unquestionably 'revisionist' by the standards of the Dziga Vertov Group, is nonetheless more balanced than that of *Coup pour coup* where his counterpart was seen emerging from his Citroën DS in a suit and tie, an image that, as the Groupe Lou Sin point out, tends to trivialise the struggle against revisionism (Groupe Lou Sin 1972: 22).

When the striking workers themselves are interviewed, rather than a simple frontal shot of the person speaking, we hear several voices commenting on the situation while the image often shows not the speaker but a group of his comrades listening. This thus tends to imply a more democratic, egalitarian organisation among the workers. The strikers condemn the union representative for talking only in figures, and for ignoring the wider context of their struggle: 'ils font comme s'il y avait l'usine et rien d'autre autour'.[37] This wider perspective is also provided by the women workers who complain not only about the sexual harassment they receive at the hands of their male colleagues, but of the additional work they are obliged to do at home after leaving the factory. In this interview, we do not even hear the woman who speaks; instead, her words are reported in voiceover by another woman, thus implying a solidarity between the workers. At the same time, though, one woman will interrupt another to disagree with her, demonstrating a certain openness to dialogue and exchange among this group that obviously has most sympathy from the filmmakers.

There is, then, in *Tout va bien*, a constant questioning of how best to represent this situation, the aspirations of the workers and the realities of the political struggle. In the film, Jane Fonda plays an American journalist, Susan DeWitt, who has come to the factory with her partner Jacques, initially in order to interview the managing director, and becomes caught up in the occupation. When Susan and Jacques are

36 'a bad idea brought about by a minority'.
37 'they act as if there was only the factory and nothing else outside it'.

released by the strikers, Susan agrees to write an article about the situation and the workers are keen to tell her about the conditions in the factory. Again, several people speak, some of whom are seen and others not and, as they describe the terrible smell, the back-breaking labour, the relentless rhythms and the sheer boredom of work in the factory, a series of cutaways show them at work. But another worker interrupts to protest that this description is inadequate, that they are, ultimately, talking about the factory in much the same terms as the CGT. The danger of this kind of discourse is that it will excite the *pity* of the listener, or the bourgeois reader, and nothing more. It is more important to describe the concrete struggle engaged in by the workers, to talk about the strike, occupation and sequestration of the director. 'C'est trop compliqué', decides the speaker, discouraged, 'je perds les pédales'.[38] Again, then, where the films of the Dziga Vertov Group refused to represent the realities of lived experience on the grounds that to do so was to target the pity of a bourgeois audience, *Tout va bien* recognises the importance of making space for such a representation while still acknowledging the dangers inherent in doing so, calling upon the spectator to bear witness to the necessary ideological choices involved in representing the class struggle.

The widening of the scope of *Tout va bien*, with regard to the films of the Dziga Vertov Group, is further visible in its representation of the relationship between Susan and Jacques. The tensions in this relationship come to a head in what Andrew Britton calls 'the scene towards which the whole film moves' (Britton 1976: 6). The scene takes place in the couple's apartment over breakfast. Jacques accuses Susan of sulking because he had wanted sex the previous night and she had not. Annoyed by this simplification of their relationship to a logic of 'cinéma, bouffe, baise' ('movies, eat, fuck'), Susan suggests that Jacques needs to think more carefully about the context of his sexual dissatisfaction. She accuses him of having only a single image of their relationship in his mind. At this point, we cut to a close-up of a black and white still photo of a woman's hand around an erect penis. In order to think about how *this* picture has changed, says Susan, she also requires a picture of both Jacques and herself *at work*. Here, cutaways show Jacques filming an advertisement in a studio and Susan recording an article for a radio broadcast. As Margaret Atack comments, Susan's argument constitutes a denunciation of Jacques's phallocentric view of their relationship, his definition of it exclusively in terms of his own

38 'It's too complicated, I get all mixed up.'

desires (Atack 1999: 62). But, just as Susan reminds Jacques of the context of capitalist production in which their relationship exists, Godard and Gorin do not allow the spectator to be drawn into the illusion that this is a 'real' couple, instead reminding us that this scene remains a filmic construction. This is achieved by bracketing the scene with shots that break the illusion established by continuity editing: as Susan sits down at the table, and again as Jacques stands up from it, the shot is repeated twice from different angles. As Andrew Britton comments, in addition to shattering the spatial continuity, these shots make the scene 'stand out in sharp relief' from the rest of the film (Britton 1976: 8). Furthermore, once Jacques has left the table, a maid appears in the frame to remove the tea tray. This further disorients the viewer since it imposes one of two interpretations, each of which undermines our identification with the couple: either this is simply a maid working on the filmset, thus calling our attention to the artifice of the scene; or Jacques and Susan *employ a maid* in their fictional world, in which case their credentials as political radicals are rather shaken. In any case, this scene highlights the considerable distance travelled by Godard since the many interior domestic scenes of his Nouvelle Vague period. It is very much Susan who leads this discussion, while Jacques appears inarticulate, emotionally, politically and linguistically. Furthermore, Andrew Britton points out the maturity in the presentation of this relationship. The film implies that Susan and Jacques's relationship may well be almost over, but that 'in no sense invalidates the relationship' (Britton 1976: 9). In *À bout de souffle, Le Petit Soldat, Le Mépris* and *Pierrot le fou*, the end of a relationship necessarily entailed the death of one or both of the partners. In *Tout va bien*, by contrast, it is simply the case that 'the developing maturity of the couple may require that their union should not be permanent' (9).

In the last major scene of *Tout va bien*, Susan travels to a hypermarket in Lille, where a group of activists are planning to stage an insurrectionary protest against consumer capitalism. The scene is filmed in one long tracking shot behind the checkouts at this enormous supermarket, Susan in the background taking notes as shoppers unload their trolleys on to the conveyer belt. Susan is aware that this article, like the one about the factory occupation, will be refused by her editors, since she wants to write not about the transformation of the urban landscape, but about 'ceux qui vendent et ceux qui achètent'.[39] At this point, the camera passes a Communist Party activist with a stall selling

39 'those who sell and those who buy'.

copies of the Party's manifesto entitled 'Changer de cap' ('Change direction'). The implication here, then, is that the discourse of the French Communist Party represents an ideology for sale, it represents so much merchandise within the marketplace of consumer capitalism. Describing the supermarket in voiceover, Susan notes the way that 'Tout le monde gueule dans ce théâtre, sauf le public',[40] concluding that 'en dehors de l'usine, c'est l'usine'.[41] As the voiceover cuts out and the ambient sound of the supermarket cuts back in louder than before, we see and hear what she means: the incessant rattle of the cash registers and the periodic interruption of the PA system create a cacophony comparable to that of the factory, while the gestures of the cashiers ringing up the merchandise, *but also those of the shoppers* lifting their goods from the trolley to the conveyer belt have the same mechanised, repetitive quality of factory labour. This scene is thus a powerful demonstration that one end (consumption) of the process of capitalist production is just as oppressive, just as alienating and, ultimately, *just as boring and unpleasant*, as the other (production). As the camera reaches the far right end of its track, a group of revolutionary activists stream into the supermarket and disperse among the aisles. The camera then follows these agitators back across the store where, after picking an argument with the Communist salesman, they pronounce that everything in the supermarket is free, encouraging shoppers to help themselves from the shelves before bundling them towards the exit. The camera tracks right again with the crowd to where the riot police are already arriving. 'Tout changer,' declares Susan's voiceover, 'mais par où commencer? *Par tous les bouts*!'.[42] If *Tout va bien* thus marks a significant progression over the dogmatic works of the Dziga Vertov Group, it is, on one hand, by demonstrating to French viewers the political implications of their familiar, everyday activities (a concern repeated throughout Godard's work in the 1970s); and, on the other hand, restoring to revolutionary politics a sense of *fun*, a sense of the giddy excitement that could, and should, accompany the destruction of the capitalist regime.

40 'everyone yells in this theatre, except the public'.
41 'outside the factory, it's still the factory'.
42 'Change everything. But where to begin? *Everywhere at once*!'

References

Atack, M. (1999), *May 68 in French Fiction and Film: Rethinking Society, Rethinking Representation*, Oxford, Oxford University Press.

Barthes, R. (1982), *L'Obvie et l'obtus: Essais critiques III*, Paris, Seuil.

Baudry, P. (1972), 'La critique et *Tout va bien*', *Cahiers du cinéma*, 240, 10–18.

Britton, A. (1976), 'Living historically: Two films by Jean-Luc Godard', *Framework*, 2, 1, 4–15.

Cahiers du cinéma editorial staff (1972), 'Le "groupe Dziga-Vertov" (2)', *Cahiers du cinéma*, 240, 4–9.

Cannon, S. (1993), 'Godard, the *Groupe Dziga Vertov* and the myth of "counter-cinema"', *Nottingham French Studies*, 32, 1, 74–83.

Collet, J. and Fargier, J.-P. (1974), *Jean-Luc Godard*, Paris, Seghers.

Deleuze, G. (1967 [1962]), *Nietzsche et la philosophie*, Paris, PUF.

Derrida, J. (1967), *La Voix et le phénomène: Introduction au problème du signe dans la phénoménologie de Husserl*, Paris, PUF.

Godard, J.-L. (1998), *Jean-Luc Godard par Jean-Luc Godard, Tome 1: 1950–1984*, Paris, Cahiers du cinéma.

Groupe Lou Sin (1972), 'Les luttes de classe en France: Deux films: *Coup pour coup, Tout va bien*', *Cahiers du cinéma*, 238–9, 5–24.

Kolker, R. P. and Cottenet-Hage, M. (1987), 'Godard's *Le Gai savoir*: A filmic Rousseau?', *Eighteenth-Century Life*, 11, 2, 117–22.

MacBean, J. R. (1972), 'Godard and the Dziga Vertov Group: Film and dialectics', *Film Quarterly*, 26, 1, 30–44.

MacCabe, C. (1980), *Godard: Images, Sounds, Politics*, London, MacMillan/BFI.

Monaco, J. (1976), *The New Wave: Truffaut, Godard, Chabrol, Rohmer, Rivette*, New York, Oxford University Press.

Nietzsche, F. (2001 [1887]), *The Gay Science*, trans. by Josefine Nauckhoff, Cambridge, Cambridge University Press.

Price, B. (1997), 'Plagiarizing the plagiarist: Godard meets the situationists', *Film Comment*, 33 (November–December), 66–9.

Silverman, K. and Farocki, H. (1998), *Speaking about Godard*, New York, New York University Press.

Wollen, P. (1985 [1972]), 'Godard and counter cinema: *Vent d'est*', in B. Nichols (ed.), *Movies and Methods, Vol. II*, Berkeley, University of California Press, 500–9.

6

Home movies: 1974–78

Ici et ailleurs

Like *Tout va bien*, *Ici et ailleurs* (1974) marks the transition between the strict Marxism-Leninism of the Dziga Vertov Group and the less idealistic politics of desire that Godard began to explore in the films made with Anne-Marie Miéville as the production company Sonimage. But, more than this, *Ici et ailleurs* sees the first tentative elaboration of ideas about history and its relationship to cinema, or, more broadly, to the image, that would be pursued and developed across the rest of Godard's career, to culminate in the massive *Histoire(s) du cinéma* project in the 1990s. *Ici et ailleurs* began life as a film by the Dziga Vertov Group. In 1970, Godard and Gorin were invited to Jordan to film the political struggle of the Palestine Liberation Organisation in their efforts to regain land occupied by Israel in the wake of the 1967 war. The film was to be called *Jusqu'à la victoire*, and the opening minutes of *Ici et ailleurs*, edited together from the original footage, give some sense of what the unfinished Dziga Vertov Group film might have looked like. The film begins, then, with images of the Palestinian revolutionaries preparing for and engaging in armed combat and taking part in political meetings and discussions. Meanwhile, a series of intertitles in French and Arabic present the Palestinian revolution as a kind of five-fold dialectic. The titles read: 'La volonté du peuple – La lutte armée – Le travail politique – La guerre prolongée – Jusqu'à la victoire'.[1] This dialectic is given a quasi-mathematical rigour by Godard's voiceover, which suggests that 'La volonté du peuple + la lutte armée = la guerre du peuple, + le travail politique = l'éducation du peuple, + la logique du peuple = la guerre prolongée',[2] all of which ultimately results in victory.

1 'The will of the people – Armed struggle – Political work – A prolonged war – Until victory.'

2 'The will of the people + armed struggle = the people's war, + political work = the education of the people, + the logic of the people = a prolonged war.'

'Et puis on est revenu en France,' comments Godard, 'et de ça on n'en revient pas encore', an untranslatable pun which essentially suggests that the filmmakers have not yet recovered from their return to France. The spectator is now presented with familiar images and sounds of France – a French family walking in the street and radio broadcasts discussing domestic politics – as Godard relates that, once returned to France, the filmmakers did not know what to do with their footage. This is principally because the idealised Palestinian revolution that they had filmed on the banks of the Jordan had since been overtaken by historical events. In September 1970, seeking to reassert their authority over the perceived Palestinian terrorists, the Jordanian army marched into Amman and slaughtered thousands of Palestinians, razing several refugee camps to the ground. As Godard remarks, in the time taken for the filmmakers to return to France and ponder over the montage of their film, 'ceci [images of Palestinian revolutionaries in training] est devenu cela [video images dated 'Amman, September 1970' showing dead Palestinians with horrific wounds]'.[3] As this disturbing juxtaposition of images continues, a series of flashing titles inform us that practically all of the 'actors' in the original film were killed in the massacre of September 1970: 'Le film a filmé les acteurs en danger de mort'.[4] The idea, borrowed from the likes of Jean Cocteau and Jean Epstein, that the cinema films death at work on the faces and in the bodies of actors, is one that Godard has repeated many times throughout his career; if this notion is generally associated with a frequent tone of poetic melancholy in Godard's work, in *Ici et ailleurs* it is given a far more troubling anchorage in a specific historical and political reality.

This historical reality, then, throws the film into crisis. How to continue with a film about the Palestinian revolution when its confident prediction of victory has been so comprehensively undermined by political reality? The failure of the Palestinian struggle in this sense shows up the failure of the film itself and leads Godard and Miéville to interrogate their methodology. The resulting discussion that forms the lengthy mid-section of *Ici et ailleurs* is probably one of the most abstract and difficult passages in all Godard, but, as I have already suggested, it is also one of the most essential for understanding the director's subsequent work. Picking up the mathematical imagery from the first part of the film, Godard suggests that 'on a dû faire des erreurs d'addition'.[5] Here we see a close-up of an adding machine and a hand appears to punch in sums using the figures 1789, 1968, 1936 and 1917.

3 'this had become that'.
4 'The film filmed the actors in danger of death.'
5 'We must have made a mistake in our calculations.'

With these key dates, Godard implies that the filmmakers were mistaken in trying to understand and interpret the Palestinian revolution according to western models like the French Revolution (1789), the Russian Revolution (1917), the Popular Front (1936) or May '68. Godard repeats 'Révolution française *et et et* révolution arabe'[6] over images and sounds of the Palestinians intercut with footage of May '68 in France, then, as a rather tacky insert of giant letters spelling 'ET' appears with lights flashing on and off and a dissonant electronic chord on the soundtrack, Godard proceeds to list a series of binary pairs: 'Ici *et* ailleurs, victoire *et* défaite, étranger *et* national, vite *et* lentement, partout *et* nulle part, être *et* avoir, espace *et* temps, question *et* réponse, entrée *et* sortie, ordre *et* désordre, intérieur *et* extérieur, noir *et* blanc, encore *et* déjà, rêve *et* réalité'.[7]

As Godard's intonation makes clear, the most important word in each of these pairs, and in the title of *Ici et ailleurs*, is 'et', *and*. In an influential article inspired by Godard and Miéville's first television series, *Six fois deux: Sur et sous la communication* (1976), but equally relevant to *Ici et ailleurs*, Gilles Deleuze remarked upon the importance of the conjunction 'and' to Godard. Deleuze notes that, whereas the opposition 'either/or' consigns things to a fixed identity, defining them in terms of what they are not, the conjunction 'and' marks the frontier between things as a line of flight that is continually crossed as one thing *becomes* another in the ongoing *process* of identification (Deleuze 1976: 11–12). Godard makes this clear as he announces a new set of terms separated by 'ou', over images of a French family watching television and French newspaper headlines describing in sensationalist terms the events surrounding the Palestinian struggle: 'Normal *ou* fou, tout *ou* rien, toujours *ou* jamais, homme *ou* femme, plus *ou* moins, vivre *ou* mourir, pauvre *ou* riche ... Trop simple et trop facile de diviser le monde en deux'.[8] As we saw in Chapter 4, Deleuze has been endlessly critical of a mode of thought that is based on the recognition of identities rather than the affirmation of difference. He suggests that this leads to a system of knowledge in which problems are assumed to arise naturally and to disappear once confronted with their solution, which can be conveniently assigned to the category of true or false (Deleuze 2000

6 'French revolution *and and and* Arab revolution.'

7 'Here *and* elsewhere, victory *and* defeat, foreign *and* national, quickly *and* slowly, everywhere *and* nowhere, to be *and* to have, space *and* time, question *and* answer, entrance *and* exit, order *and* disorder, interior *and* exterior, black *and* white, again *and* already, dream *and* reality.'

8 'Normal *or* mad, all *or* nothing, always *or* never, man *or* woman, more *or* less, live *or* die, poor *or* rich ... Too simple and too easy to divide the world in two.'

[1968]: 205). But, as Godard suggests when he intones 'question *et* réponse', the boundary between problems and solutions, questions and answers is not so clear-cut: the history of philosophy has repeatedly shown that, if a problem is formulated with sufficient care, it provides its own answer, whereas the most productive answer to a question often takes the form of another question. As Godard comments later in *Ici et ailleurs*, 'Ce n'est pas les réponses qui vont mal, mais les questions ... Et peut-être même il faudrait abandonner le système des questions et réponses et trouver autre chose'.[9]

If we say all this, it is largely as a warning to the reader and spectator not to expect simple answers to simple questions amidst the theoretical considerations that form the heart of *Ici et ailleurs*. Godard in the 1970s is doubtless addressing the same issues as French philosophers like Deleuze and his collaborator Félix Guattari, like Jean-François Lyotard and Michel Foucault: issues such as the nature of capitalism and its relation to desire, the epistemological systems underpinning our traditional understanding of these phenomena, and the possibilities for revolt within these complex and interrelated systems. But, where the above-named philosophers explore these issues in words, albeit with some attempt to resist the ideological constraints of academic discourse, Godard addresses them through a montage of images and sounds *and* through an extravagant, often intractable play with words. In places this allows for a more immediate apprehension of difficult arguments; but elsewhere it can lead to confusion and wilful obscurity. Consider a section from the middle of *Ici et ailleurs*: Godard asks 'Comment fonctionne le capital?' and a hand appears at a blackboard to explore this question, again in the form of a mathematical equation. 'Un pauvre + un zéro = un moins pauvre'[10] suggests Godard, and this process is repeated until the blackboard is covered with a single figure containing a one and multiple zeroes. Capital functions, then, by adding together zeroes, but these zeroes 'représentent des dizaines, des centaines, des milliers de vous et moi'.[11] What we are often unprepared to accept, however (and here Godard shows his French family watching TV again), is that this multiplication of zeroes represents our dreams (insert of a horrific image of a charred body from Amman, September 1970), and that 'puisque c'est des zéros, ça multiplie en même temps que ça annule. Et c'est à ce moment-là, à cet endroit-là, que nos espoirs

9 'It's not that there's something wrong with the answers, but rather with the questions ... And maybe we need to abandon the system of questions and answers and find something else.'

10 'How does capital function? A poor person + a zero = a less poor person.'

11 'represent dozens, hundreds, thousands of yous and mes'.

ont été réduits à zéro'.[12] Godard now seeks to illustrate this point with another equation: 'L'image d'un 17 + l'image d'un 36 ici = au mois de mai, l'image d'un 68', whereas 'L'image d'un 17 + l'image d'un 36 ailleurs = au mois de septembre, l'image d'un 70'.[13] There follows a montage in which an image from the Popular Front of 1936 is juxtaposed with an image of Hitler, whose voice we hear on the soundtrack, itself intercut with a Hebrew lament listing the names of Nazi death camps: Auschwitz, Maidanek, Treblinka. Footage of these same death camps, taken from a television documentary, is meanwhile edited together with images of death from Amman in 1970. This, comments Godard, is why 'les images du total n'auront rien à voir avec la totalité des images'[14] and why it is possible to live in poverty in one part of the world and be a millionaire elsewhere, even if only a millionaire *in images*.

What can all this possibly mean? Isn't Godard simply borrowing the language of mathematics to lend an appearance of rigour to a disjointed and largely meaningless association of ideas? Isn't he drawing rather flippantly on a pun between the word 'total', in the sense of a mathematical sum, and the totalitarianism implied in his images and sounds? Isn't he trivialising the problems of capitalism with all this talk of zeroes and being dangerously reductive when he compares Nazi Germany with the contemporary situation in the Middle East? And how dare he suggest that the massacre in Amman somehow represents our 'dreams'? Yosefa Loshitzky has been particularly critical of Godard's argument here, calling it 'simplistic and monstrous' (1995: 50), although Loshitzky's position at that time, as Lecturer at the Hebrew University in Jerusalem, should perhaps not be forgotten in this context. All these criticisms may be valid, but the faults in *Ici et ailleurs* arise as by-products of Godard's ongoing attempt to work out a complex argument about the image and its relation to history and how these function within the system of capitalism, a system that seeks at once to engage our desires and to enslave them, to release and to bind them. Still drawing on his mathematical imagery, Godard observes that, in the cinema, images do not *add up*: it is not possible to see the totality of images, to see them all together, but only in sequence, one after the other, as they pass before the beam of the projector. Godard illustrates this with five actors, each holding a still photograph representing one of the five points of the original dialectic of Palestinian revolution from

12 'since these are zeroes, they multiply at the same time as they cancel out. And it's then and there that our hopes are reduced to zero'.
13 'The image of 17 + the image of 36 here = in May, the image of 68, whereas the image of 17 plus the image of 36 elsewhere = in September, the image of 70.'
14 'the images of the total will have nothing to do with the totality of images'.

Jusqu'à la victoire. The actors file past a camera, each holding up their image in turn. In the cinema, then, 'une image vient remplacer l'autre, tout en en gardant plus ou moins le souvenir'.[15] As a result, the *space* that is represented in the image becomes translated into 'une sorte de sentiment qu'on a de l'espace, c'est-à-dire du temps'.[16]

Godard's explanation continues with more wordplay, this time around the word 'une chaîne', a chain or sequence, but also a factory production line: 'Le film, c'est-à-dire des images à la chaîne ... espace et temps enchaînés l'un à l'autre comme deux travailleurs à la chaîne où chacun est à la fois la copie et l'original de l'autre'.[17] With this image, then, Godard links the chain of images that is cinema to capitalist production. He goes on: 'Une chaîne consiste à ranger des souvenirs, à les enchaîner dans un certain ordre, qui fera que chacun trouvera sa place sur la chaîne, c'est-à-dire en fait retrouvera sa propre image'.[18] Since each film image that passes before the projector contains within it the memory of the previous image, we can say that the chain of the film strip consists of an organisation of memories. And it is in this way that Godard sees cinema as relating to history: just as, in the cinema, a string of singular images becomes, through the work of memory, a complete film, a whole narrative, so too the chain of singular events that constitutes our experience is synthesised in memory into the abstract flow of history. This is only possible, however, if we take the pure affirmation, the pure *difference* of the event and negate it, giving it a value whereby it can be determined in relation to other events with which it enters into circulation, taking on *meaning* only insofar as it is defined in opposition to other events, as that which it is not. This is precisely the law of *capital*, the way that objects are ascribed an exchange value in order to be circulated within the capitalist system. Things, and indeed people, can only enter the circuit of capital to the extent that their difference is denied in favour of a value which renders them comparable to all other elements within the system of exchange. This is why capital functions, according to Godard, by multiplying zeroes, an observation that he shares with Jean-François Lyotard who condemns the nihilism, the zero-thinking of capital (Lyotard 1974: 14).

15 'one image replaces another, even if it retains more or less the memory of the previous image'.
16 'a kind of impression that we have of space, that is to say of time'.
17 'The film, that is to say a chain of images ... space and time chained together like two workers on a production line [*à la chaîne*] where each is at once the copy and the original of the other.'
18 'A chain is constituted by organising memories, chaining them together in a certain order so that everyone can find his place in the chain, in other words, so that everyone can find his own image.'

Godard's suggestion seems to be that the events of history are given exchange value when they become *images*, because it is as images that these events are able to circulate within the system of capital. As he comments: 'Le monde entier, c'est trop pour une image. Non, c'est pas trop, dit le capitalisme international, et il fit toute sa fortune sur cette vérité'.[19] Within the system of global capitalism, there is nothing that cannot be captured as an image, given a value, circulated and exchanged. Godard illustrates this point in *Ici et ailleurs* by gradually multiplying a number of television screens on which a series of images play side by side, images of politics, war, sport, advertising. This proliferation of images coincides with our loss of influence over the reality of events: we have been, Godard suggests, 'remplacés peu à peu par des chaînes ininterrompues d'images, esclaves les unes des autres, chacune à sa place, comme chacun de nous à sa place dans la chaîne des événements sur laquelle nous avons perdu tout pouvoir'.[20] When Godard juxtaposes images of Nazi Germany with atrocities in the Middle East, as he frequently does in *Ici et ailleurs*, or when, at the end of the film, Miéville plays a lament for victims of the Shoah over images of the massacre in Amman and reminds us that, when Jewish prisoners in Nazi death camps had reached the final stages of physical weakness and degradation, their captors would refer to them as 'Muslims', the intention is double: on one hand, to point up the very real historical parallels between the Nazis' liquidation of the 'Jewish problem' and the terrible consequences of applying a similar rhetoric to the Palestinian struggle; but on the other hand, by insisting upon the irreducible *difference* between the two situations with jarring, often brutal juxtapositions, to show up the absurdity of a culture in which images have been devalued to such an extent that comparisons of this type are possible at all. Thus, when a critic such as Reynold Humphries brands Godard as reactionary for seeking to link causes and effects '*outside history*' (Humphries 1977: 23), he misses the point entirely. For this formulation implies that there is an *inside* to history and shows Humphries to be stuck in a dialectical conception of a history which can only unfold toward its natural end. The history that Godard begins to explore with *Ici et ailleurs* is not characterised by dialectics but by *catastrophe* (a view of history indebted to Walter Benjamin, whose influence will be explicitly acknowledged by Godard in the 1990s). History is seen as an accumulation, a pile-up of

19 'The whole world is too much for one image. No, it's not too much, says international capitalism, and all its fortune was built upon this truth.'
20 'replaced little by little by uninterrupted chains of images, slaves to each other and each one in its place, like each of us in our place in the chain of events over which we have lost all power'.

catastrophes that can only be smoothed into a linear sequence through a process of reductive, nihilistic thought.

If, as Godard suggests, the development in our culture of an economy of images coincides with our loss of influence over the real world, then the first step towards redressing this balance involves giving the powerless more control over *images*. As Serge Daney observes, the strange, almost magical operation of cinema, or of image-making more generally, consists of stealing images from people to exhibit them elsewhere, on 'une autre scène', another scene or stage: 'La vraie pornographie est là, dans ce changement de scène; c'est proprement, l'obscène'[21] (Daney 1976a: 38). The aim of Godard's political cinema in the 1970s, suggests Daney, is to return images to those from whom they have been stolen, or better yet to encourage them to produce their *own* images and sounds. This impulse is clear at the end of *Ici et ailleurs* when Godard and Miéville engage in a critical discussion of images of Palestinian revolutionaries taken from *Jusqu'à la victoire*. We see an image of a young girl reciting a poem of resistance against the backdrop of a ruined building and Miéville comments upon the theatrical nature of this decor which she suggests belongs to a very *French* revolutionary tradition that has been imposed on the Palestinians. We witness a group of Feddayin in a discussion which, in Godard's words, seeks to link theory and practice. But Miéville protests that they are talking in far more concrete terms about their relation with the earth: they discuss the digging of a trench, and their words translate literally as 'Quand la terre te défend, tu deviens son amant'.[22] We see an illiterate woman who, in her desire to participate in the Palestinian struggle, has agreed to repeat for the camera a revolutionary text. Miéville notes that, as the scene goes on, the woman looks increasingly bored and keen to return to other activities. Why ask a woman to repeat a text that she cannot read rather than ask her to speak for herself? In another scene, a pregnant woman expresses her joy at the thought that her unborn son will devote himself to the Palestinian revolution. But what's most interesting here, says Miéville, is not the image but the sound where, offscreen, we hear Godard's voice telling the woman to repeat her line and to adjust her scarf. In fact, this woman is not pregnant at all, but an actress who has been chosen to play a role because she is young and beautiful. This Godard never tells us and, as Miéville remarks, 'De ce genre de secret au fascisme, ça va vite'.[23]

21 'That's where the real pornography lies, in this change of scene; that, truly, is obscene.'
22 'When the earth protects you, you become her lover.'
23 'It's a small step from this kind of secret to fascism.'

In all of these examples, then, we see how the western filmmakers have attempted to impose their own agenda on the Palestinian revolution rather than allowing the Palestinians to speak for themselves and to set their own agenda, to exert control over their own images and sounds. This, ultimately, is why *Jusqu'à la victoire* was a failure and why it can only now exist as *Ici et ailleurs*, that is to say as an admission and a discussion of its own failure and as a theorisation of the wider modes of thinking underpinning that failure. As will have become clear from the preceding paragraph, it is the voice of Anne-Marie Miéville that repeatedly points out where *Jusqu'à la victoire* went wrong, those little decisions in the everyday process of producing the film which ran counter to its revolutionary aims. Godard's collaboration with Miéville in the 1970s is thus the occasion for a fruitful dialogue, providing a corrective to the dogmatic rhetoric of the Dziga Vertov Group films. However, as some critics have suggested, the decision to make Miéville's the dominant critical voice can itself be counter-productive at times. Daney has remarked upon the frequency with which female voices are endowed with a discourse of truth in radical Godard, from the 'Rosa' of *Pravda*, through Jane Fonda in *Tout va bien* to Miéville in *Ici et ailleurs*. The danger, he suggests, is that a new binary opposition is instituted, whereby the image (the eye) becomes the male domain and sound (the voice) is attributed to women (Daney 1976b: 40). This criticism has been taken up by Constance Penley who argues that the role of the female voice in these works risks making feminist discourse into 'a superior, authoritative truth' rather than 'a political theory and a set of strategies' and that, as a result, the only relation male spectators will be able to adopt towards such a voice is a masochistic one (Penley 1982: 51). As we shall see below in relation to *Numéro deux*, Godard's adoption of a feminist agenda has often made him more enemies than it has friends.

Numéro deux

Numéro deux (1975) begins with a lengthy prologue in which Godard, alone in a darkened studio, delivers a rambling monologue. Godard starts by recounting the career of a man whom he refers to as 'Machin', an all-purpose term in French to designate people or objects whose names one has forgotten. Finally, he announces: 'Il n'y a plus de Machin, il n'y a que des machines'.[24] And indeed, Godard is surrounded by machinery in this studio. He himself is barely visible in the darkness

24 'There is no more Machin, there are only machines.' In English susbtitles, 'Machin' tends to be rendered as 'Mac'.

in the top right-hand corner of the frame. The majority of the screen is taken up by a large video camera which films Godard as he speaks, the resulting image played back simultaneously on a television screen in the bottom right-hand corner of the frame. Godard appears here as a kind of cyborg entity, his organic body connected up to a circuit of machinery and electronic transmission through which the sound of his words and the image of his face are made available to the spectator. The studio, as he points out, is like a kind of factory in which he is at once the worker and the boss, and a part of the machinery. This preoccupation, from the outset, with factories and machines, in a film that goes on to observe the life of a family, and the role of sexuality within that family, tends to place *Numéro deux* under the sign of Deleuze and Guattari's major early-1970s work of philosophy and anti-psychiatry, *L'Anti-Œdipe*. In this book, Deleuze and Guattari suggest that sexuality needs to be understood in terms of what they call 'desiring machines'. This, they stress, is not merely a metaphor: desire, like all machines, works by plugging into and cutting off flows of energy: the anus cuts off the flow of excrement, the mouth cuts off the flow of breast milk, and so on. This flow of energy does not exist in the absolute but is only defined as a continuity to the extent that it is cut off by a machine. Thus machines do not exist in isolation, but only in connection to other machines, one plugging into, and cutting off, the flow produced by the other (Deleuze and Guattari 1972/73: 43–4). The problem with psychoanalysis, which becomes the subject of an extended critique in *L'Anti-Œdipe,* is that it constantly seeks to relate the sexuality of desiring machines back to the family; it assumes that everything the child encounters in this world of flows somehow represents or symbolises the parents as whole persons (54–5). When Godard, in his studio, mumbles 'J'étais malade longtemps, et ça m'a fait penser à l'usine',[25] he gives a sense, similar to that of Deleuze and Guattari, of the body as a factory in which a series of interconnected machines are in constant activity. He describes his hand as a machine that connects to the other machine that is the camera. He intuits a kind of language-machine when describing his taste for wordplay: 'un mot qui glisse sur le langage, ça indique des court-circuits, des interférences'.[26] Wordplay tends to be dismissed because it is not 'serious', notes Godard, and yet 'on s'en sert pour guérir des fois des maladies, donc c'est sérieux'.[27] Deleuze and Guattari, too, appreciate in Lacan's renewal of Freud, the image of the endless metonymic play of language to understand the flow of desire (46).

25 'I was ill for a long time and it made me think of a factory.'
26 'when a word slides across language, it can indicate short-circuits, interference'.
27 'it can be used to cure diseases sometimes, therefore it is serious'.

Subsequently, still in the studio, we see two television screens playing one above the other. The use of two screens within one is a repeated device in *Numéro deux*, and Harun Farocki suggests that it is likely to have been inspired by the technique of video editing which requires the editor to think two images simultaneously rather than sequentially (Silverman and Farocki 1998: 142). The images of the family in *Numéro deux* were shot on video before being reshot on 35mm; that is to say that the video images were filmed a second time as they played on monitors. As a result, the image we see frequently consists of two video screens of differing size surrounded by the blackness of the larger 35mm frame. This doubling of the image is just one of the many meanings implied in the film's title. One of the TV monitors in Godard's studio plays news reports about a workers' parade on 1 May and strikes organised by the CGT, while the other provides 'entertainment', including clips from a kung-fu film and pornography. This coupling of images is described in voiceover by Sandrine Battistella, who will play the wife and mother of *Numéro deux*'s family, as 'ce qui fait chier et ce qui fait plaisir'.[28]

Picking up a remark made by Godard earlier, Sandrine opines: 'Le plaisir, c'est pas simple. Je crois que c'est l'angoisse qui est simple, pas le plaisir. Je crois que c'est le chômage qui est simple, pas le plaisir. Je crois que, quand il y a du plaisir à être chômeur, alors c'est le fascisme qui s'installe'.[29] This link between pleasure, or desire, and oppression is also reminiscent of Deleuze and Guattari. They argue that, since the social sphere is immediately invested with desire, the role of this desire in social oppression needs to be taken into account: the most pressing question for a political philosophy is to understand how people can come, not merely to put up with their exploitation and enslavement, but actually to *want* it (Deleuze and Guattari 1972/73: 36–7). It is perfectly possible, and indeed quite common, to invest the social sphere with desire in a way that runs counter to the conscious interest of one's social class (305–6). 'Encore un film politique, alors?' continues Sandrine. 'Non, c'est pas de la politique, c'est du cul. Non, c'est pas du cul, c'est de la politique. Pourquoi tu demandes toujours ou bien, ou bien? Ça peut être les deux ensemble parfois'.[30]

28 'that which bores us [but literally: that which makes us shit] and that which gives us pleasure'.

29 'Pleasure is not simple. I think it's anxiety that is simple, not pleasure. I think it's unemployment that is simple, not pleasure. I think that, when there is pleasure in being unemployed, then fascism takes hold.'

30 'Another political film, then? No, it's not politics, it's porn. No, it's not porn, it's politics. Why are you always asking either one or the other? It can be both together sometimes.'

Like Deleuze and Guattari, then, *Numéro deux* insists that it can only talk about politics by talking about sexuality, and vice versa. *L'Anti-Œdipe* laments the way that psychoanalysis tends to reduce sexuality to the family's dirty little secret. For Deleuze and Guattari, it is simply absurd to claim the family as some kind of privileged theatre in which sexuality is played out, or even to argue that the family is a 'microcosm' of society. Rather, the family is bordered on all sides by society and these borders are repeatedly permeated and crossed by flows of desire which invest society as easily as they do the family (Deleuze and Guattari 1972/73: 115–16). Certainly, the Œdipus complex described by Freud may exist as one possible configuration of desire, but to make it into a general law is perverse and counter-productive. In *Numéro deux*, Godard constantly makes knowing allusions to Freud's phantasmatic ideas about the sexual secrets at the heart of the family, only to complicate matters by opening them up to the adjacent social sphere. For instance, the father of the family, Pierre (Pierre Oudry) raises the spectre of incest when he says of his children, 'Je ne les baise jamais, c'est interdit'.[31] But he goes on to reveal that sex with his wife, Sandrine, has become equally impossible, murmuring 'Merci, Patron' ('Thanks, Boss'). The film presents Pierre as being so worn down by his job at the factory where he tests sound-recording equipment that he can no longer achieve an erection. When Sandrine asks Pierre if they will make love that night and he replies only 'On verra' ('We'll see'), she sarcastically echoes his 'Merci, Patron', demonstrating her understanding of the social cause of his sexual dysfunction. Later, she suggests that, if they were rich, she would pay Pierre to sleep with her: if sex became a *job* for him, maybe he would be able to perform. This discussion illustrates Deleuze and Guattari's argument that, rather than the parents providing the models against which all subsequent relationships will be judged, society provides the models that condition our relation to our parents: the boss is not a substitute father, it is the father who is a substitute boss (Deleuze and Guattari 1972/73: 315–16).

The link between politics and sex is further suggested in a scene in which Sandrine goes to town to look for work. As she crosses a square, muttering 'Je cherche du travail' ('I'm looking for work'), she is approached by a neighbour who invites her to a meeting to discuss the treatment of women political prisoners in Chile. As Sandrine protests her lack of interest, a smaller screen appears alongside the first in which Sandrine is seen attempting to revive Pierre's limp penis with her mouth (although borrowing from the iconography of porn cinema, this

31 'I never fuck them, it's not allowed.'

image effectively defuses its erotic charge, not only through Pierre's obvious impotence, but also through the sheer *smallness* of the image which makes it quite difficult to see). The film invites us, then, to understand Sandrine's political apathy *in relation to* her sexual frustration, even as the pamphlet that Sandrine reads alerts her to the existence of other forms of oppression experienced by women in other parts of the world. Meanwhile, sexual and political desires are also united in the grandparents who share the home with Sandrine and her family. The grandmother (Rachel Stefanopoli) recites passages from a French translation of Germaine Greer's *Female Eunuch* while doing housework and while washing her naked body; the grandfather (Alexandre Rignault) sits naked behind a table as he tells tales of his adventures spreading the Communist word at the time of the Second International, his jokes about 'masturbating memories' pointing up the real investment of desire in this political work.

Desire in *L'Anti-Œdipe* is a question of connections, circuits and flows, and the same is true of *Numéro deux*. If desire is simply the free flow of energy between interacting desiring machines, then the repression of desire (which, for Deleuze and Guattari, is first and foremost *social*, and only secondarily familial) will result in a *blockage* somewhere in the system. This is the case in *Numéro deux* where Sandrine, weighed down by her responsibilities within the family and her sexual frustration, announces that she has been constipated for two weeks: 'J'ai l'impression que tout ce que je dis et tout ce que je fais, c'est de la merde. Tout ce qui devrait se passer dans le cul se passe ailleurs, et dans le cul, ça passe plus'.[32] It is clear that this constipation is a problem of *desire* when Sandrine relates it back to an incident when she came home loaded down with shopping: 'J'étais toujours chargée. Alors je décharge'.[33] In flashback here, Sandrine lies down on her bed to masturbate and, when, Pierre comes home, she asks to be left alone. The fact that Sandrine is relating this memory to her young son Nicolas again implies an Œdipal dimension to the scene: Nicolas enters the kitchen just as Pierre is leaving after an angry exchange with Sandrine and he tells his mother, 'C'est papa qui est méchant. Moi, je suis là'[34] before kissing her. But Sandrine's subsequent explanation makes clear that her constipation is not the symptom of some individual neurosis, but of *social* oppression: 'Un homme, on peut toujours le quitter, mais quand

32 'I feel like everything I say and everything I do is a load of shit. Everything that should be happening in the arse is happening somewhere else, and in the arse nothing's happening.'
33 'I was always loaded down. So I decided to unload.'
34 'Daddy's mean. I'm here now.'

c'est tout un système social qui vous viole …'.[35] Meanwhile, Sandrine's constipation is shown to belong to a logic of machines and flows by the parallel blockage in the toilet and by the malfunctioning washing machine.

But if desire is all about plugging into circuits, it need not have any relation to what we traditionally think of as sexual organs, nor does it necessitate the identification of an *object*. Indeed, Deleuze and Guattari stress that desire does not recognise whole persons, but only other desiring machines: 'La satisfaction du bricoleur quand il branche quelque chose sur une conduite électrique, quand il détourne une conduite d'eau, serait fort mal expliquée par un jeu de "papa–maman" ou par un plaisir de transgression'[36] (Deleuze and Guattari 1972/73: 13). In other words, desire is *also* in play when Pierre and Sandrine bicker over fixing the washing machine or painting the fence. One of *Numéro deux*'s most compelling depictions of the machinic nature of desire existing independently of genital sexuality is in its use of music. In one scene, Sandrine and her daughter Vanessa dance around the room to an Italian political song, their desire engaging at once with the abstract rhythms and melodies of the music *and* with its political content, as Sandrine explains the words to Vanessa. But their dancing and singing disturbs Nicolas, whose own desire is engaged in a more solitary pursuit of eating. As these desiring machines intersect and interrupt one another, Godard plays another song – Léo Ferré's 'La Solitude' – over the first, stemming its flow. In other scenes, the plugging into or switching off from the flow of music is made clear through the use of headphones, the music on the soundtrack cutting out as a character removes the earpieces. In this way, for instance, Sandrine plugs into the music to shut off the flow of Pierre's words as he yells at her.

But the film's most notorious example of the place of desire within the family comes in a scene in which Vanessa witnesses a sexual act between Pierre and Sandrine. Given the inclusive interpretation of desire elsewhere in *Numéro deux*, and the film's insistence on wider social influences over the family, it is disappointing that this scene has received such a literal and traditional reading from critics, who have seen it as a classic example of the Freudian 'primal scene' whereby the child is inducted into the world of adult sexuality through a traumatic encounter with the parents' lovemaking. Kaja Silverman, for instance,

35 'When it's one man, you can always leave him, but when it's a whole social system that rapes you … '.

36 'The satisfaction of a handyman when he plugs something into an electrical socket, or when he redirects a water main could hardly be explained away by a game of mummies and daddies or by a transgressive pleasure.'

comments: 'adult sexuality here invades an unprepared psyche, and the only possible defence is repression' (Silverman and Farocki 1998: 162). Pierre describes how, upon learning that Sandrine had slept with another man, 'J'ai eu envie de la violer' ('I felt like raping her'). Sandrine screamed when Pierre sodomised her and Vanessa witnessed the whole thing. Pierre's treatment of Sandrine is thus motivated by jealousy and, following a fairly classical psychoanalytic line of reasoning, Silverman and Farocki interpret his act of sodomy as a displacement of the latent homosexual desire he feels for the other man: 'by sodomising Sandrine, Pierre also seeks to situate himself sexually in relation to the man she slept with. Indeed, he seeks to use her as if she were his rival' (Silverman and Farocki 1998: 155). Silverman and Farocki see this reading as being supported by a later scene in which Pierre confesses that, in his fantasised sexual relations with Sandrine, 'elle, des fois, c'est l'homme, et moi la femme'[37] and his admission that he likes Sandrine to insert a finger in his anus during sex. But doesn't Pierre's ready awareness of the fluidity of their gender identifications during sex tend to undermine the patronising psychoanalytic revelation of his 'latent' homosexual desire? Jean-François Lyotard, in a work that goes even further than *L'Anti-Œdipe* in de-objectifying desire, argues that this psychoanalytic interpretation of jealousy is at once too simple and too complex. Jealousy, suggests Lyotard, is an inevitable and almost constant effect of desiring production: whenever desire invests a given surface, energy is withdrawn from the neighbouring surface which thereby becomes jealous. We need a conception of jealousy that is not simply anthropomorphic: 'La vulve est jalouse de la bouche bien baisée, la maîtresse l'est du livre qu'écrit son amant, l'homme de l'avenir du jeune homme, le soleil des volets clos derrière lesquels votre imagination se livre aux aventures de la lecture'[38] (Lyotard 1974: 53). Certainly, Pierre is jealous of both Sandrine and her lover, but he is also jealous of the washing machine that she won't let him operate (Sterritt notes that the scene with the washing machine follows immediately from the rape and that 'Sandrine's bent-over position echoes her posture when Pierre violated her' (Sterritt 1999: 149)). Sandrine, meanwhile, is deeply jealous of the factory that occupies Pierre's time all day and prevents him from making love to her at night.

But, even before we question the motivation for the scene, we might question *the nature of the scene itself.* Silverman and Farocki do not

37 'sometimes she's the man and I'm the woman'.

38 'The vulva is jealous of the well-fucked mouth, the mistress of the book that her lover is writing, the man is jealous of the younger man's future, the sun jealous of the shutters behind which your reading takes you on flights of the imagination.'

hesitate to qualify Pierre's act as 'anal rape' (Silverman and Farocki 1998: 162), yet Pierre notes that Sandrine 's'est laissée faire' ('she let me do it'). Even if we choose not to accept Pierre's account, we are forced to consider the possibility that Sandrine may have taken pleasure in this brutal treatment. Later, when Nicolas asks his mother about sex, Sandrine says 'des fois ça fait mal, mais j'aime ça quand-même'.[39] As we have already seen, Pierre is merely modelled on 'tout un système social' that is raping Sandrine, and it is far from excluded that she may desire the very conditions of her oppression. Furthermore, given the insistence with which critics have described the 'distanciation' techniques in Godard's cinema, the ways in which his films alert the spectator to their status *as films*, that is to say as constructed rather than naturally occurring realities, it is a little surprising to see Kaja Silverman refer to 'the image of Pierre anally penetrating Sandrine' (Silverman and Farocki 1998: 155). In fact it is nothing of the kind. In line with several other visual parodies of the forms of porn cinema in *Numéro deux*, the image is rather of Pierre positioned behind Sandrine, who is bent over a table. His movement as he 'penetrates' her is slow, awkward and highly stylised, far from the frenetic, violent activity we would expect from an act of rape. Meanwhile, an image of Vanessa is *superimposed* over the sexual act, raising a question about the reality of her presence in this scene. Nor should we ignore the disarming frankness of an *alternative* primal scene in *Numéro deux* where Nicolas and Vanessa are freely invited into their parents' bedroom to look at their naked bodies and be responsibly instructed about sex.

It is worth pointing out that, even in Freud's original formulation, the *status* of the primal scene is open to question, the event located somewhere between a *real* childhood experience that is neither understood nor assimilated and a *false*, falsely remembered or fantasised, experience later in life. As Laplanche and Pontalis comment, sexuality thus emerges in 'une dialectique entre le trop et le trop peu de l'excitation, le trop tôt et le trop tard de l'événement'[40] (Laplanche and Pontalis 1985: 27). The primal scene is thus indeterminable, unlocateable. And this is surely the point of its ambiguous presentation in *Numéro deux* where it is constructed by laying two images one over the other, and where it recurs throughout the film, appearing at the beginning, shortly after the prologue, and discussed on two separate occasions by Pierre, as though it had always already and never yet happened. Such might be the sense of Sandrine's 'Il y avait deux fois' in

39 'sometimes it hurts but I like it anyway'.

40 'a dialectic between too much and too little excitation, an event that occurs too early and too late'.

the prologue, a 'twice upon a time' opposed to the usual 'once upon a time': the primal scene only exists to the extent that it happened twice upon a time. Early in the film, Vanessa states: 'Des fois je trouve ça joli, Papa et Maman, des fois je trouve ça caca'.[41] Ultimately, the reason for all the twin images in *Numéro deux* must be to show that sexuality within the family is both pretty *and* poopy and *at the same time*, just as the film is at once a work of politics and porn.

Not all critics, however, have appreciated the omnipresence of these desiring machines in *Numéro deux* and some have detected a residual phallocentrism behind the appearance of polymorphous perversity. The loudest dissenting voice belongs to Thérèse Giraud who argues that the film is, in the image of its heroine, 'clos, rond, bouché' ('closed off, bloated, bunged up') (Giraud 1976: 22). The film is swollen up with sex and a sex that bears the mark of the phallus in its continued obsession with power and impotence. It is unable to imagine a female sexuality other than in the terms of a liberating ejaculation (Sandrine's 'unloading') which turns the woman's body into just another phallus (Giraud 1976: 23). Similarly, Silverman and Farocki remark that, if Pierre can imagine being a woman to Sandrine's man, or another man to Sandrine's man, he 'fails altogether to articulate the other possible transmutation implicit in this paradigm – that he be a woman to Sandrine's woman' (Silverman and Farocki 1998: 163). The sexual excesses of *Numéro deux* are finally very much of their time, in the image of *L'Anti-Œdipe* and *Économie libidinale* and their extravagant fantasies of a desire that permeates and pervades every inch of the social fabric. And, as Joseph Bristow comments, Deleuze and Guattari's imagery of 'plugs and sockets surely discloses more than a residual phallicism in their thought' (Bristow 1997: 131). The abiding memory of *Numéro deux*, though, remains a picture of polymorphous perversity, a world in which everything – washing machines, headphones, political pamphlets, arses, children, television, factories – is connected in the endless flow and counter-flow, blockage and release of desiring production.

France tour détour deux enfants

After *Six fois deux*, *France tour détour deux enfants* (1977–78) was Godard and Miéville's second attempt at making a television series. Consisting of twelve 26-minute episodes, *France tour* was conceived in order to be

41 'Sometimes I think Mummy and Daddy are pretty, sometimes I think they're poopy.'

broadcast, like any other television programme, one episode at a time during prime-time on France's second state TV channel, Antenne 2. As we shall see, the work's actual broadcast history proved rather different. Based around interviews with two children, Arnaud, aged 9, and Camille, 11, each of the twelve episodes follows the same format: alternating episodes for Arnaud and Camille, the programmes begin with footage of the child engaged in some everyday activity before an interlude in which a voiceover discusses the strange activities of 'les monstres', monsters who are actually the adults in Camille and Arnaud's world. The main body of each episode is taken up with a lengthy interview between Godard and the child, before a couple of 'presenters' (Albert Dray and Betty Berr) come in to discuss what has been said.

The series thus represents an altogether serious attempt to investigate the lives of children and their understanding of the world they inhabit. However, rather than take the usual condescending attitude towards children on television, where their partial understanding of the adult world is often the subject of humour, Godard asks a series of 'inappropriate' questions in order to try to approach his subjects from a position outside the received adult way of understanding the world, or, better, to determine the extent to which Arnaud and Camille have already been inducted *into* that system of knowledge. Naturally there is not room here to conduct a detailed analysis of Godard's questions, but we might suggest that his inappropriate interrogations fall particularly into two broad categories. He asks a series of questions related to economic matters: how much rent does Camille pay for her bedroom? Is her mother paid well to do the housework? Who owns the route that the children walk to get to school? Is it fair that they are not paid for their schoolwork? Second, Godard asks a series of questions related to ontological matters: is Camille sure that she exists? Does she have more than one existence? Would it be a catastrophe if there were no more light? When you return home from school, is the house still the right way up or is it upside down? Does the school ever change place? As Jérôme Prieur notes, Godard speaks with 'les mots de tous les jours mais combinés et vécus différemment'[42] (Prieur 1980: 372). Constance Penley suggests that 'the children are talked to like beings from another world to whom no one has ever spoken' (Penley 1982: 42). But it would be more accurate to say that it is Godard who appears to come from another world: *France tour détour* comes across, as the title of Prieur's essay has it, like the 'Premières impressions d'un nouveau monde' ('First impressions of a new world') (Prieur 1980: 367–6).

42 'everyday words but combined and experienced differently'.

Deleuze suggests that, in the questions he asks in his television series, Godard gives the impression of being a foreigner in his own language (Deleuze 1976: 6). But Godard, discussing the project in interview, seems perplexed by accusations of his provocative stance. He stresses the classical nature of his method: 'On est remonté jusqu'à Descartes, Aristote, systématiquement j'ai interrogé les deux gamins en disant: "Ou bien, ou bien"'[43] (Godard 1998: 404). The questions of *France tour détour* thus seek to explore the limits of the binary system of western thought, pointing up its contradictions and exposing the received ideas that underpin our culture. The two sets of examples we gave above offer a clear illustration of this process: by relentlessly asking about salaries and prices, Godard exposes the hypocrisy of a culture in which some forms of work are deemed worthy of payment and others not, but also raises the possibility of areas of activity that might escape the all-pervasive attribution of value within a capitalist economy. By posing his ontological conundrums, Godard reveals the extent to which our system of thought demands stable identities and excludes the possibility of *becoming other*. His questions about the school changing place or the house turning upside down may appear absurd, but as Deleuze points out: 'La porte de l'usine n'est pas la même, quand j'y entre, et puis quand j'en sors, et puis quand je passe devant, étant chômeur'[44] (Deleuze 1976: 11). It has been remarked that Godard's questions are far more interesting than the children's answers (Penley 1982: 38), and there is a danger that this process simply reproduces the condescension that Godard and Miéville sought to avoid. But, as the presenter Betty argues, this is only because no one else is asking these kind of questions: 'Avec nos questions, on a l'air de vouloir toujours le dernier mot, alors que c'est le premier qu'on veut. Et si le second ne vient pas souvent, c'est parce qu'on est trop seuls à faire ce genre de travail'.[45]

As the series seeks to document the real lives of children, *France tour* is naturally largely concerned with the experience of *school*. The series borrows its title from *Le Tour de la France par deux enfants*, a nineteenth-century pedagogical primer by one Georges Bruno which, as Constance Penley notes, is about the inculcation of patriotic sentiments in two

43 'We went right back to Descartes and Aristotle, I systematically questioned the two kids by saying "either this or that"'.

44 'The factory door is not the same when I go in as when I come out, or when I pass in front but am unemployed.'

45 'With our questions, we look as though we're always trying to have the last word, when actually it's the first word we're after. And if the second word rarely comes, it's because we're alone in doing this kind of work.'

children through an educational tour of the country (Penley 1982: 33). Gilles Delavaud adds that, not only was Bruno's work published exactly a century before *France tour détour* in 1877, it also provided the basis for the first major French television series, filmed in 1957 (Delavaud 2001: 124). Godard's intentions in his own *Tour* are, unsurprisingly, rather more subversive than those of the nineteenth-century pedagogue. Employing once again his taste for wordplay, Godard describes school as a site of '*class* struggle'; he compares the relationship between teacher and pupil to that between a boss and a worker, and, when Camille is given an assignment as punishment during a detention, he goes as far as to speak of 'travaux forcés' ('forced labour'). *France tour* shows us the humdrum reality of life in school as it has rarely been seen before or since on television. In the fourth episode, instead of an interview with Arnaud, the camera simply frames him at his desk in the classroom for twenty minutes and watches and listens as the lesson goes on. The effect is extraordinary, at once patently familiar and deeply strange, revealing the perverse regimentation and the overwhelming boredom of the school environment. In the sixth episode, Godard interviews Camille while her classmates shout in the playground and Godard, noting that one usually only cries out in pain, asks whether the children are responding to the pain of being in class. If such scenes appear strange, it is because, as is repeatedly pointed out, few adults ever see what goes on inside a school. As Betty remarks, having seen the footage of Arnaud in class, if this were her child she would feel 'intimidated', unsure whether she had made the right decision in sending him to school. Godard points out to Camille that schoolchildren are practically unique in *not being allowed visitors*: even in prison and in hospital one is allowed visitors. When he asks Camille if visitors are forbidden or simply choose not to come, she assumes the former. Asked if she would *like* to receive visitors in school, she replies yes.

School, in *France tour détour*, certainly does not come across as a very enjoyable experience. Betty notes how sad Camille looks when filmed on her way to school. The series repeatedly asks what function and *whose interests* school serves. Asked whether she would ever have had the idea of going to school if no one had told her to, Camille thinks not. She assumes that the point of school is for her to learn things, but Godard asks if what she learns will be of use to her or to other people. For instance, 'si tu apprends l'anglais, ça va servir à toi ou aux Anglais?'.[46] Ultimately, then, *France tour* analyses school as a tool of social control, serving the interests of the national and (as the example of English

46 'If you learn English, will that be of use to you or to the English?'

suggests) the international capitalist economy. As Penley remarks, 'what seems at first like an obsessive phenomenology' in Godard's questions about space and time 'is gradually revealed to be an interest in the institutional organisation of space and time and in the power of those spatial and temporal grids' (Penley 1982: 34). This concern, as Penley recognises, testifies to the influence of Michel Foucault's research into institutionalised forms of social discipline and control in his book *Surveiller et punir*. Foucault argues that the eighteenth century saw a rediscovery of the capabilities of the body and the elaboration of a series of techniques and procedures for creating the 'docile' bodies that would be of most use to society (Foucault 1975: 160). As Godard suggests, school ultimately works to produce 'de la main d'œuvre bon marché et docile' ('cheap and docile manual labour'). As Michael Witt points out, one of Foucault's key insights in *Surveiller et punir* is that 'disciplinary space is essentially cellular', and this applies not only to prisons, but to factories, schools, army barracks, hospitals and so on (Witt 2001: 184). Foucault writes of 'une codification qui quadrille au plus près le temps, l'espace, les mouvements'[47] (Foucault 1975: 161). This idea is picked up by Godard who notes that the little squares in French children's exercise books reflect not only the arrangement of desks in the classroom but also the grid according to which a city's streets are laid out. In places, *France tour*'s observation of the disciplinary regime in school is altogether frightening, as in the seventh episode where Godard films children being taught how to *march*. The lack of contextual information (is this physical education? a music lesson?) lends a sinister aspect to the children's bewildered expressions as the teacher barks orders at them. The series' preoccupation with ideas of copies and copying also resonates with these observations about discipline and control: Arnaud is shown working a roneo-printer and Camille has to copy out a sentence fifty times as punishment: 'Les copies conformes', muses Albert, with unmistakeably Godardian wordplay, 'les originaux qu'on déforme'.[48]

Constance Penley has suggested that, in seeking to document the form of social control exerted over children, *France tour détour* itself places contradictory demands on Arnaud and Camille. On one hand, says Penley, when responding to Godard's questions, 'the children's taciturnity and lack of spontaneity are used to demonstrate the completeness

47 'a codification that lays out time, space and movement according to little squares'.

48 It is difficult to render this pun in English: a 'copie conforme' is a copy certified accurate, but is phonetically identical to 'les copies qu'on forme', the copies that we (or they) are forming, as opposed to 'les originaux qu'on déforme', the originals we (or they) are *de*forming, distorting.

of their submission to capitalism's "programming"' (Penley 1982: 49); but, at the same time, the comparisons of children to other 'marginal' figures such as prisoners and factory workers tends to cast them as 'inherently or potentially radical', implying a facile romanticising of children (49–50). But it is not clear where Penley finds this radicalism, and her later condemnation of the series' 'easy nihilism' (52) tends to contradict her own argument. The more troubling implication of *France tour détour* is precisely that there is no such thing as inherent radicalism. As Jean-François Lyotard writes, we need to accept the disturbing reality that social control 'ne procède pas d'une erreur, d'une illusion, d'une méchanceté, d'un contre-principe, mais encore du désir. Que la mise en représentation est désir, que la mise en scène, en cage, en prison, en usine, en famille, la mise en boîte est désirée'[49] (Lyotard 1974: 20–1). It is in the nature of desire to seek at once its own dispersal, the destruction of all form, and its solidification into form; desire binds and assembles with one hand while undoing and scattering with the other. And there is no need to identify *different drives* to account for these activities (Freud's Eros and death drive), their *indiscernibility* is precisely what characterises desire (Lyotard 1974: 38). This is what accounts for the contradictions at the heart of capitalism. It is too simplistic to suggest that capitalism represses desire, or even that we desire our own repression. Capitalism, like desire, has two poles that are indiscernible in practice: one that seeks to bind capital (the accumulation and reproduction of wealth, the culture of saving, the regulatory function of banks), and another that seeks to disperse it (the politics of conquest and colonisation, the profligate culture of spending, the wasteful over-production) (Lyotard 1974: 265). Deleuze and Guattari note that, whereas earlier civilisations involved a strict control or *coding* of desire, capitalism proceeds via a *de*coding, or liberation of desire, even as it invents new forms of discipline and control to prevent the system from dispersing entirely (Deleuze and Guattari 1972/73: 306–7). Thus capitalism is constantly expanding through the displacement of its own internal limits (Deleuze and Guattari 1972/72: 292). According to Lyotard, capitalism expands by predicting, and thereby nullifying, the impact of future events. Hence the need for an effective policing of spontaneous movements. This is not just a phenomenon of totalitarian states, but a fundamental law of capitalism (Lyotard 1974: 253–6).

These conclusions may appear somewhat pessimistic, and this is doubtless what Penley means when she talks of *France tour détour*'s

49 'is not the result of a mistake, an illusion, a wickedness, or a counter-principle, but of desire. That the law of representation is desire, the enclosure within a theatre, a cage, a prison, a factory, a family, the boxing-in is desired'.

'easy nihilism'. But such accusations misconstrue the problem of nihilism as it appears in the work of Lyotard or Deleuze and Guattari. The real nihilism is that of a system that *denies difference*, that forecloses future events by attributing to them a value which will allow them to circulate as capital; a system that turns the amorphous desires of children into a series of 'copies conformes' to act as foot-soldiers in the army, cogs in the machine, money in the bank of capitalism. The goal of *France tour détour*, first and foremost, is simply to try and show this process at work. Second, Godard and Miéville's television series begins to search for elements that might resist appropriation by the system of capital. This occurs particularly in the use of slow, or more precisely, altered-motion sequences. The manipulation of tape speed to slow down, stagger, and decompose bodily movement is used in the footage of Arnaud and Camille that opens each episode, but also in the images of the 'monsters' going about their business, as well as other scenes such as that of a group of women jogging around a park or the busy kitchen of a café. Alain Bergala, whose descriptions of these sequences have been widely admired, notes that altered-motion is used by Godard and Miéville only for the most banal daily activities and also points out how dissimilar they are to the slow-motion used in advertisements or television coverage of sporting events (Bergala 1999: 32–3). Bergala suggests that these scenes give the sense of a slight temporal delay between the eye and the hand of the filmmakers, as we watch them *discover the images* only a moment before we do: 'il [*sic*] les redécouvre dans le même temps que d'une certaine façon elles lui échappent, comme si celui qui est en train de les regarder n'était plus tout à fait le même que celui qui les a prises'[50] (34). Bergala describes the *strangeness* of these images, which he attributes to the cold, machine-like vision of video, an ideal tool, perhaps, for filming children, or monsters: 'pas pour les comprendre ou les aimer, simplement pour les voir vraiment, sans empathie, dans leur irréductible étrangeté'[51] (36).

A number of commentators have suggested that these altered-motion sequences are descendents of the motion studies devised by early cinema pioneers like Étienne-Jules Marey and Eadweard Muybridge. Michael Witt, in particular, notes that, where Marey produced a sequence of photographs showing momentary stages in the production of movement, 'Video allows Miéville-Godard to rediscover and literally *animate*, Marey's spatial chrono-photographs through an injection of saccadic

50 'he rediscovers them just as, in a way, they escape his grasp, as though he who is looking at these images is not quite the same person as he who filmed them'.

51 'not in order to understand or to love them, but simply in order to see them properly, without empathy, in their irreducible strangeness'.

movement' (Witt 2001: 179). The aim, suggests Witt, is to 'reclaim cinema's scientific heritage in the age of television' (179–80). Indeed, this period sees the first of Godard's remarks on the medical uses of image-making technology, which would become more frequent as he pursued his research into film history. Godard's most common refrain is that the fortune of Kodak was made, not with family photos or feature films, but with X-rays (Godard 1998: 408). But the scientific application of cinema remains a somewhat ambivalent inheritance. As research by the likes of Jonathan Crary (1990) has shown, and as Godard implies in *Histoire(s) du cinéma*, the motion studies and optical devices of early cinema were part of the broader tendency identified by Foucault towards the categorisation and control of bodies and subjects. As Foucault stresses in *Surveiller et punir*, the 'discipline' he is describing is at once a discovery and a perfecting of the body's physical capabilities *and* a subjugation of the body to the demands of the state apparatus: the power of the body is released only to the extent that it is of use to society (Foucault 1975: 162). We might suggest, then, that *France tour détour* differs from the early scientific experiments in cinema in seeking a power in the body that is of no use to the capitalist economy, in detecting what Witt calls 'the fissures and disjunctions – sudden and mysterious points of corporal resistance – concealed beneath superficial homogeneity and continuity' (Witt 2001: 186). The way the wind catches Camille's hair as she runs to school, or the glimpse of disquiet behind the apparent insouciance as she chases around the schoolyard with her friends, suggest a dimension to experience that is beyond value, beyond ownership, beyond identity.

The strangeness of such moments creates an odd kind of existential vertigo, opens up a space of silence and stillness amidst the clamour and bustle of life as it is usually presented to us by television. Bergala notes this quality of emptiness in *France tour détour* (Bergala 1999: 37–8) and offers it as an explanation for the series' unhappy fate in the hands of television schedulers: instead of being broadcast one episode at a time in prime-time, *France tour* was shown in three blocks of four programmes at eleven o'clock on Friday night, and thus very strongly coded as a work of *auteur* cinema for a specialist, self-selecting audience (Witt 2001: 176). As Penley remarks, from the perspective of mainstream television, *France tour* depicts 'dead time' and activities that are 'neither newsworthy nor "now"' (Penley 1982: 43). It is instructive to compare the programmes with what today passes for 'reality TV', where already-artificial situations are carefully orchestrated and edited to generate the maximum drama. *France tour détour* revels in inactivity and is fascinated by boredom, as in the 20-minute shot of Arnaud at his schooldesk, or the corresponding example of Camille at the family dinner table. More precisely, at the same time as it opens up a space of stillness and silence amidst energetic behaviour, its prolonged focus on apparently monotonous activities ultimately creates a compelling sense of a *populated* boredom, inhabited not only by the most miniscule of gestures and looks, but by the unseen activities of power relations and desiring production. *France tour détour deux enfants* is a fascinating glimpse of what television *could be*: a powerful medium for the study of human interaction, capable of *showing us* the reality of our political lives with an immediacy and a subtlety that all the rhetoric of theory can only dream of; and perhaps its most abiding message is in showing us how far from that ideal we still remain.

References

Bergala, A. (1999), *Nul mieux que Godard*, Paris, Cahiers du cinéma.
Bristow, J. (1997), *Sexuality*, London and New York, Routledge.
Crary, J. (1990), *Techniques of the Observer: On Vision and Modernity in the Nineteenth Century*, Cambridge, MA, MIT Press.
Daney, S. (1976a), 'Le thérrorisé (pédagogie godardienne)', *Cahiers du cinéma*, 262–3, 32–9.
Daney, S. (1976b), 'Le son (Elle), L'image (Lui)/La voix (Elle), L'œil (Lui)', *Cahiers du cinéma*, 262–3, 40.
Delavaud, G. (2001), 'La place du spectateur', in G. Delavaud, J.-P. Esquenazi and M.-F. Grange (eds), *Godard et le métier d'artiste*, Paris, L'Harmattan, 121–38.
Deleuze, G. (1976), 'Trois questions sur *Six fois deux*: À propos de *Sur et sous la communication*', *Cahiers du cinéma*, 271, 5–12.
Deleuze, G. (2000 [1968]), *Différence et répétition*, Paris, PUF.
Deleuze, G. and Guattari, F. (1972/73), *L'Anti-Œdipe: Capitalisme et schizophrénie*, Paris, Minuit.
Foucault, M. (1975), *Surveiller et punir: Naissance de la prison*, Paris, Gallimard.
Giraud, T. (1976), 'Retour du même', *Cahiers du cinéma*, 262–3, 20–4.
Godard, J.-L. (1998), *Jean-Luc Godard par Jean-Luc Godard, Tome 1: 1950–1984*, Paris, Cahiers du cinéma.
Humphries, R. (1977), 'Godard – *Ici et ailleurs*: the ideology of the image', *Framework*, 11, 6, 22–4.
Laplanche, J. and Pontalis, J.-B. (1985), *Fantasme originaire, Fantasme des origines, Origines du fantasme*, Paris, Hachette.
Loshitzky, Y. (1995), *The Radical Faces of Godard and Bertolucci*, Detroit, Wayne State University Press.
Lyotard, J.-L. (1974), *Économie libidinale*, Paris, Minuit.
Penley, C. (1982), 'Les enfants de la patrie', *Camera Obscura*, 8–10, 33–58.
Prieur, J. (1980), *Nuits blanches: Essai sur le cinéma*, Paris: Gallimard.
Silverman, K. and Farocki, H. (1998), *Speaking about Godard*, New York, New York University Press.
Sterritt, D. (1999), *The Films of Jean-Luc Godard: Seeing the Invisible*, Cambridge, Cambridge University Press.

Witt, M. (2001), 'Going through the motions: Unconscious optics and corporal resistance in Miéville and Godard's *France/tour/détour/deux/enfants*', in A. Hughes and J. S. Williams (eds), *Gender and French Cinema*, Oxford and New York, Berg, 171–94.

7

Love and work: 1979–84

The series of films made by Godard in the early 1980s, following his return to features with *Sauve qui peut (la vie)* in 1979, are sometimes referred to collectively as Godard's 'cosmic period' (Moullet 1990: 108). These films have been grouped together in a variety of ways, but most commonly, following the example of Marc Cerisuelo (1989: 207–31), into a 'trilogy of the sublime' constituted by *Passion* (1981), *Prénom Carmen* (1983) and *Je vous salue Marie* (1984). Alain Bergala calls these three films 'une véritable trilogie, tant au niveau des thèmes que de l'esthétique'[1] (Bergala 1999: 26). However, Jean-Louis Leutrat has identified a different trilogy in *Sauve qui peut, Passion* and *Prénom Carmen*, 'trois films qui mettent en scène des cinéastes attelés à des projets impossibles'[2] (Leutrat 1990: 41), while Bergala recognises that *Sauve qui peut* 'porte en germe la trilogie à venir'[3] (Bergala 1999: 107). Ultimately, then, to the extent that one wishes to impose these rather arbitrary divisions within a body of work, it would perhaps be better to speak of a *quartet*, rather than a trilogy of films beginning with *Sauve qui peut (la vie)*, and in this chapter we will demonstrate the validity of Bergala's assertion regarding the thematic and aesthetic parallels between all *four* films. Indeed, Godard himself has remarked that these films are like four rungs on the same ladder (Godard 1998: 19). The films are in fact so close to one another in spirit that it is often tempting to see their fictional worlds as interchangeable, with characters and details overlapping between individual films, and this subsuming of individual identities to a larger, more indefinable entity is, as we shall see, a recurring characteristic of this period of Godard's work. To give just a few examples of echo and overlap between the films: both *Sauve qui peut* and *Passion* feature a character called Isabelle, played by Isabelle

1 'A veritable trilogy, as much in terms of themes as of aesthetics.'
2 'three films that portray filmmakers harnessed to an impossible project'.
3 'contains the seeds of the trilogy to come'.

Huppert, who could be taken as the same person; in *Passion*, we briefly see a young gendarme brought in to expel Isabelle from Michel (Michel Piccoli)'s factory and who bears more than a passing resemblance to Joseph (Jacques Bonaffé), the gendarme from *Prénom Carmen*; the petrol station at which Joseph and Carmen (Maruschka Detmers) stop on their flight from Paris is reminiscent of the one where Marie (Myriem Roussel) lives and receives a visit from the angel Gabriel (Philippe Lacoste) in *Je vous salue Marie*; Carmen's Joseph shares with his homologue in *Je vous salue Marie* not only a name, but a frustrating relationship with a woman who withholds the satisfaction of physical intimacy.

Given the extent to which this period has been presented as a new beginning for Godard (a sense reinforced by the director's own remarks in interviews, see for instance Godard 1998: 449), it is worth considering how much of a break with the past these films really represent. Many critics have pointed out similarities between individual films and earlier works in Godard's œuvre, but it would, I think, be wrong to overstate this continuity. As Luc Moullet puts it: 'Mais, dites-moi un peu, quel rapport y a-t-il entre *À bout de souffle* et *Passion*? Je n'en trouve guère'[4] (Moullet 1990: 104). André Dumas, on the other hand, suggests that the real mystery of this period is how Godard managed to transform himself from a hyperactive filmmaker to a contemplative one *without changing his style* (Dumas 1990: 90). Our own opinion is that, despite the continuity of certain thematic preoccupations and aesthetic strategies, *Sauve qui peut (la vie)* does indeed announce a significant shift in Godard's style, almost splitting his career into two halves: the films of this period see the development of an approach to narrative, character, dialogue and shot composition that will characterise all of Godard's major features throughout the 1980s and 1990s, up to and including *Éloge de l'amour* (2001).

Despite this stylistic rupture, which we will be describing in this chapter, one of the most prominent themes from this period is that favourite Godardian pairing of love and work, a preoccupation we noted in *Masculin féminin* and which was translated, in the video work of the 1970s, into a politics of desire. The features of the early 1980s constitute one of the high points of this theme in Godard's work with the key terms recurring frequently in the films themselves and in Godard's discussions of and around those films. Godard suggests that love and work have become irrevocably separated in our societies as a consequence of

4 'Tell me, what exactly is the link between *À bout de souffle* and *Passion*? I can't find any.'

the capitalist division between the time of work and the time of leisure, but that he feels unable to maintain this separation: 'je n'ai jamais pu travailler sans amour',[5] he declared in 1980 (Godard 1998: 456). These sentiments are echoed in *Passion* where the film director Jerzy (Jerzy Radziwilowicz) opines, 'Il faut travailler à aimer, ou bien aimer travailler'.[6] Meanwhile, Isabelle, noting that the physical reality of *work* seems to be forbidden from representation on screen in much the same way as the physical reality of *love*, suggests that 'le travail, c'est pareil que du plaisir: pas forcément la même vitesse, mais les mêmes gestes'.[7]

Behind these seemingly rather glib remarks lies a serious reflection about pornography which had gained a new prominence in the 1970s following the popularisation of porn cinema and the subsequent advent of video. Godard has always considered the development of film pornography to mark a significant defeat in the history of cinema since, in his view, mainstream filmmakers rapidly allowed the representation of sexuality to become monopolised (and thereby ghettoised) by porn cinema and subsequently shied away from any more artistic depiction of physical love (Godard 1998: 463). As he remarked at the time of *Je vous salue Marie*: 'C'est parce que [Catherine] Deneuve ne sait pas dire "je t'aime" qu'on fait un film porno qui ne sait pas le dire non plus'[8] (605). One of the most notorious scenes from this period of Godard's career is a grotesque parody of the mechanics of porn cinema in *Sauve qui peut (la vie)*. Isabelle, a prostitute, finds herself involved in a four-way orgy with two businessmen and another woman. The CEO (Roland Amstutz) sets up an elaborate sexual production line in which, every time his foot touches Christine's breast, she sucks Thierry's penis, whereupon he licks Isabelle's anus, who then kisses the CEO. 'L'image, ça va,' declares the boss, 'maintenant, on va faire le son',[9] and he instructs his charges to emit sounds – *aïe*!, *oh*!, *eh*! – at each stage of the circuit. This scene, of course, is far from erotic. If it is initially amusing, it soon ceases to be so (Bonitzer 1980: 6) since, as Jean-Pierre Oudart remarks (1980: 37), it begins to look less like group sex and more like some particularly perverse form of ritual torture. Rarely has the truly inhuman brutality of pornography been so scrupulously laid bare. Godard himself observed that, if this scene is so horrific, it is because 'il

5 'I've never been able to work without love.'
6 'We must work at loving, or love our work.'
7 'work is the same as pleasure: it may not be at the same speed, but it's the same gestures'.
8 'It's because Catherine Deneuve doesn't know how to say "I love you" that they make a porn film that doesn't know how to say it either.'
9 'That'll do for the image, now we'll get the sound.'

n'y a plus d'amour ni de travail'[10] (Godard 1998: 456). Godard went on to explain that, since this sex act consists of a cold, mechanical repetition, there is no *work* in the simple, thermodynamic sense of no generation of *heat*, no *energy*. This notion of energy, as we shall see, is central to an understanding of Godard's early 1980s films, to an appreciation of the way they *work*.

Image

How, then, are we to resist these brutalising, commodifying effects of the image? In the films of the early eighties, Godard is seeking nothing less than *a new way of seeing* (Jacques Aumont has referred to this period as 'un nouvel apprentissage du regard'[11] (Aumont 1989: 238)), a way of looking afresh at those things (bodies, nature) and those activities (love, work) that are at once most familiar and most profoundly unknown. How to look at bodies with love (and no longer simply lust or covetousness)? How to work at producing images with love (and no longer simply competence), how to love this work? These are the questions underpinning Godard's search for what Alain Bergala calls 'le visuel', a rare quality of the image in which a person or an object ceases to have a merely filmic existence and is remembered as having 'palpité un jour sur cette terre', belonging to 'cette planète et cette espèce qui sont tout aussi provisoirement les nôtres'[12] (Bergala 1999: 122). In *Sauve qui peut (la vie)*, this search for a new visual inspiration is conducted through an extension of the stop-motion editing pioneered in *France tour détour deux enfants*. The slowed, fragmented, decomposed movements are seen particularly in embraces between Paul (Jacques Dutronc) and Denise (Nathalie Baye) and, most famously, in shots of Denise cycling along a country road. In an account of these images, Thomas Albrecht suggested that they are free from the kind of self-analysis and self-criticism to which Godard's images of the radical 1960s and 1970s work were subjected and, as such, they reach the spectator without the same heavy discursive coding (Albrecht 1991: 62). Since the meaning of these images is not determined in advance or articulated in voiceover as in the Dziga Vertov Group films, the spectator is free to experience what Albrecht calls a '*jouissance* beyond predefined reception practice' (63). This is first and foremost a *bodily*, rather than an intellectual pleasure (66).

10 'There is no longer any love nor any work.'
11 'a new apprenticeship of the gaze', or perhaps 'a relearning of the look'.
12 'quivered once on this very earth, belonging to this planet and this species which, just as briefly, are ours too'.

But the clearest example of this problematic of filming the body and of looking with love is doubtless to be found in *Je vous salue Marie*. Hervé Le Roux suggests that the entire project of this film could be summed up by the question 'Comment filmer l'amour?' ('How to film love?') (Le Roux 1985: 13). This is most apparent in the scene where Joseph (Thierry Rode) asks to see Marie naked and repeatedly reaches out to touch her, saying 'Je t'aime', only to have Marie cry 'Non!' and the angel Gabriel emerge from nowhere to wrestle him to the ground. As Bergala points out in his analysis of this scene, Godard places a chair in the room so that its straight back is positioned directly between Joseph's gaze and Marie's body, but also between *our* gaze and the couple as though to symbolise the difficulty involved for all concerned (Joseph, spectator, director) in attaining a simple, unadorned view of this body in its real nakedness (Bergala 1999: 96, 102). It is only when Joseph approaches his hand to Marie's belly before withdrawing it and repeating 'Je t'aime', that she finally says 'Oui'. Joseph's lesson here (and, ideally, the spectator's too) is in how to approach a body with love but without treating it as a possession. As Colin Nettelbeck puts it, he learns that 'to say "I love you" is not about getting one's hands on, but about letting go' (Nettelbeck 2001: 91). This is an image of tenderness in the sense defined by Theodor Adorno: 'tenderness is nothing other than the awareness of the possibility of relations without purpose' (Adorno 1974 [1951]: 41). In this moment, Marie ceases to be an object for Joseph's sexual gratification, and her belly ceases to be simply the site of a reproduction, however miraculous: her body itself becomes the miracle, an infinitely strange object that requires no other justification than its own existence.

It is, as Bergala suggests (1999: 50), only after the distance travelled in this scene, that Godard can turn to the other most famous sequence in *Je vous salue Marie*, the stormy night during which Marie, through communion with the Holy Spirit, is made painfully aware of her own body. This sequence, in which a series of static shots of Marie struggling alone in her bed are intercut with shots of grasses blowing in the wind outside, does not present a continuous montage in narrative terms. David Sterritt notes a lack of continuity in Marie's apparel since she is sometimes naked and sometimes dressed in underwear (Sterritt 1999: 204), while the shifting patterns of light across her bedroom and the images of sun and moon outside suggest that some of these images belong to the day and others to the night, although there is no clear temporal progression. This is because, argues Bergala, Godard wishes for us to witness the difficulty of producing adequate images to capture the momentary beauty of a young woman's body or of grasses swaying in the wind without resorting to cliché. Godard is working here like a painter, sketching and discarding a series of unsatisfactory attempts at the image: 'Ce sont *des images essayées*. Godard ne les accumule pas, il les efface au fur et à mesure qu'il les produit. L'une chasse l'autre, comme s'il n'en trouvait aucune qui puisse être la bonne,'[13] (Bergala 1999: 51).

This multiplication of images of the body is matched, in this sequence but more generally throughout the films of the early eighties, by a multiplication of images of nature. This sudden proliferation of natural imagery, in the work of a filmmaker previously very much associated with the city of Paris, is in large part attributable to Godard's return to his native Switzerland, on the shores of Lake Geneva. This return to Switzerland is often seen as coinciding with Godard's effective retirement from political cinema, or even from socially aware film-making, his withdrawal into a kind of hermitic, self-imposed solitude. Laura Mulvey, for instance, argues that 'The last traces of analytical, politically radical Godard ... drained away somewhere between *Sauve qui peut* and *Passion*' (Mulvey 1996: 81). But remarks made by Godard in interview suggest that his new appreciation for nature need by no means exclude analytical or political thinking. Godard suggests that the beauty of the Swiss countryside cannot be divorced from the invisible but omnipresent circulation of finances in the country's economy: 'C'est un endroit où se trouvent côte à côte, à trois centimètres, tout l'argent de l'Esso Standard et un magnifique glacier [... et l'argent] finit par ressortir dans la nature, forcément, d'une drôle de façon'[14] (Godard 1998: 452). Just as he attempts to film bodies that are no longer enslaved by the possessive gaze of pornography, Godard seeks in nature that which might resist the contaminating influence of capital. So, in *Sauve qui peut (la vie)*, if the prostituting of nature by agribusiness is symbolised by a young woman who drops her trousers in front of a feeding trough in order that a cow might lick her arse, the magnificent opening shot of the sky and the tracking shots along lakeside trees portray a natural world that remains sublimely indifferent to the selfish demands of the human species. The repeated inserts of the sea in *Prénom Carmen*, the fields, flowers and the elusive play of light over water in *Je vous salue Marie* would seem to serve the same function. Ellen Draper

13 'These are *attempts at images*. Godard doesn't accumulate them, but erases them as he goes along, each one replacing the last, as though none of them were quite good enough.'

14 'It's a place where you find right next to each other, three centimetres apart, all the money of Esso Standard and a magnificent glacier [... and the money] ends up emerging in nature in a strange way.'

complains that no *people* figure in the shots of nature in *Je vous salue Marie,* they are 'devoid of psychological inflection, devoid of human scale', presenting a natural world that is 'cool, abstract' (Draper 1993: 68). But this, surely, is the point: precisely that these images present nature as it exists quite apart from humanity, with its own scale, its own rhythms that are not the same as ours. Discussing the stop-motion shots in *Sauve qui peut (la vie),* Godard complained about the imposition of a single, all-purpose rhythm governing all human activities: 'on donne un baiser au même rythme qu'on monte dans une voiture, ou qu'on achète une baguette de pain'.[15] His cinema, he added, could be defined as 'la recherche d'un autre rythme' ('the search for another rhythm') (Godard 1998: 461).

Music

The work of renewal with regard to the image undertaken in these films goes hand in hand, as always with Godard, with an innovative approach to sound and, most particularly in the early eighties films, to music. In making *Prénom Carmen,* Godard spoke of his desire to 'voir la musique ... d'essayer de voir ce qu'on entend et d'entendre ce que l'on voit'[16] (Godard 1998: 576). David Wills comments that, with *Prénom Carmen,* Godard pursues his long-term project to 'redress the primacy given the image' by highlighting 'the most dependent or repressed element of the film process, music' (Wills 1986: 41). Playing up the disjunction between sound and image, Godard, already in *Sauve qui peut (la vie),* sought to undermine spectatorial assumptions about diegetic and non-diegetic music. On several occasions in this film, characters enquire 'C'est quoi cette musique qu'on entend là?'[17] when the spectator can hear no music at all. Meanwhile music that is assumed to be non-diegetic is unexpectedly (and unrealistically) revealed as having a diegetic source: an opera aria plays over the opening scene of Paul in his hotel room which the spectator assumes to be an extra-diegetic embellishment or commentary until Paul bangs on the wall and tells his neighbour to keep it down. Elsewhere, a piece for accordion that accompanies shots of Denise cycling is revealed to stem from a man playing at the station. In the final scene, as an elegiac music greets Paul's death, his daughter Cécile (Cécile Tanner) walks unexpectedly past a full orchestra, with any

15 'we give someone a kiss with the same rhythm that we get into a car or that we buy a loaf of bread'.
16 'see music ... to try and see what we hear and hear what we see'.
17 'What's that music we can hear?'

realistic motivation for this apparition further challenged by the fact that the original music was electronic rather than string-based (Thompson 1988: 284).

Jacques Aumont has pointed out the paradox that music is most commonly found in Godard's work in the form of silence. That is to say that it is only by the sudden *cutting out* of musical accompaniment that it can cease to exist *as mere accompaniment* and become something more than a background that goes unnoticed (Aumont 1990: 46). Godard employs a great many canonical works by classical composers in the films of the early 1980s: Ravel, Dvořák, Fauré and Mozart in *Passion*; Beethoven in *Prénom Carmen*; Bach and Dvořák in *Je vous salue Marie*, but, as Petric and Bard comment, 'Whenever the music achieves a certain harmonic identity, it is precipitously cut off, causing an auditory shock that matches the already subverted narrative flow' (Petric and Bard 1993: 108). Rather than allow us to slip into a familiar approbatory response to these well-known works (which would equate to not really hearing them), Godard wants us to be startled by the miraculous emergence of this music. As Eva (Anne Gauthier) remarks in *Je vous salue Marie* while listening to a record by John Coltrane, 'Avec la musique je me demande souvent ... On s'émerveille qu'une nouvelle phrase arrive, mais après tout il pourrait ne rien y avoir ...'[18]

For an example of how Godard uses music in the construction of his early 1980s films, let us look in detail at a sequence from *Prénom Carmen*. Carmen and Joseph meet when Carmen's gang of outlaws attack a bank that Joseph is guarding. Godard intercuts this scene with rehearsals by the Prat string quartet as they 'attack' the difficult first movement of Beethoven's tenth string quartet (Op. 74). Rather than use the music of Bizet's opera for his version of *Carmen*, Godard has thus chosen Beethoven's late quartets and, as Amy Herzog (2002) points out, this music, unlike that of the opera (and much traditional film music), does not necessarily lend itself to dramatic situations: where the music of opera and film often develops specific motifs in association with characters or situations, the music of Beethoven's quartets comes with no such prior encoding. Nevertheless, it is the music that seems to dominate this sequence: the quartet does not illustrate or comment upon the action in the bank but *leads* that action. The attack on the bank does not begin until the quartet have launched into the music and one member's suggestion that their playing needs to be 'more violent' seems almost to motivate the escalation of hostilities inside the bank. In

18 'With music I often wonder ... You're amazed that a new phrase appears, but after all there could just be nothing ...'

the same way, Joseph and Carmen's romantic embrace after they have wrestled each other to the ground seems motivated less by realistic character psychology than by the changing mood of the music.

The music accounts not just for the overall progression of the sequence, but for the composition of individual shots. In compositional terms, *Prénom Carmen* is a film made up of frames bisected or otherwise carved up by horizontal, vertical and, particularly, diagonal lines. This is clear from the film's opening shot of the city (Paris) at night, in which an overground metro, lights in all its windows, crosses the frame horizontally from left to right, while a line of car lights moves diagonally down-screen from right to left. These visual motifs (crossing trains and lines of car lights) recur throughout the film, serving as a kind of regular punctuation, notably at the beginning of the bank robbery sequence in question. I suggest that these clean lines in Godard's visual composition are a response, partly to the harsh, angular sounds of many passages from Beethoven's late quartets, but also to the filming of the quartet, where the strings of the cello form a bright line up the centre of the screen while the violin bows cut it diagonally in two. This use of bold lines is also noticeable in the filming of the bank robbery. At the beginning of the sequence, a shot from inside the bank shows Joseph silhouetted in the doorway, the frame divided into three distinct stripes on either side of this central aperture. Within the bank, we have a shot taken through the cross-hatching of a glass-paned door. Carmen and Joseph's stand-off around a grand central staircase allows for a further geometric arc to divide the screen. Finally, the escape from the bank is shot from alongside the getaway car, with the diagonal edge of the windshield again bisecting the frame (this shot perhaps contains a homage to the getaway sequence from *Gun Crazy* (1949), especially if we remember that *Prénom Carmen* carries a dedication reading 'In memoriam small movies').

The rehearsals of the string quartet also lend to this sequence a logic of reprise. The players repeatedly stop and start again on a particularly difficult passage (which itself recurs several times throughout the first movement of Beethoven's quartet), discussing the trouble they are having with it. And, in the same way, Godard repeats shots and actions within the bank: Joseph advances cautiously down a corridor where customers lie on the ground and, after a brief insert of the quartet, we see (in a separate shot) Joseph advancing cautiously again down the very same corridor. Similarly, Carmen's entreaty to Joseph, 'Partons d'ici' ('Let's get out of here'), the kind of line that does not need repeating, is filmed twice. The effect, as Phil Powrie has observed, is that the realistic space and time of the bank sequence becomes highly confused, 'the time before the attack (customers reading) coincides with the time of the attack (customers being shot), as well as the time after the attack (the cleaner mopping up the blood)' (Powrie 1995: 66). Theodor Adorno has argued that the fragmentary style and the shrivelling of harmony in Beethoven's late work poses a challenge to individual identity: 'The music speaks the language of the archaic, of children, of savages and of God, but not of the individual' (Adorno 1998: 157). In this way, we might argue that the late style of Beethoven exerts a crucial influence over *Prénom Carmen* where individual psychology seems sacrificed to the pure physics of colliding bodies and the thermodynamics of energy exchange.

Grace

One of the more unexpected features of Godard's return to (relatively) mainstream cinema in the early eighties was his appeal to Christian imagery and biblical reference. The title of *Passion* seems to contain (among other things) a reference to the Passion of Christ, an idea apparently confirmed when Isabelle's first line in the film is 'Mon Dieu, pourquoi m'avez-vous abandonnée?'.[19] The film within the film being made by Jerzy (and also entitled *Passion*) involves the reconstruction of famous paintings, and the inclusion of El Greco's *Assumption of the Virgin* (1577) allows for a sublime visual gag in which Jerzy is seen wrestling, like Jacob, with his angel. *Je vous salue Marie* of course tells the story of the Annunciation and Immaculate Conception of Christ, and the closing scenes give a glimpse into the boyhood of Jesus who announces 'Je suis celui qui est' ('I am he who is') and declares that he must go and tend to his father's business. A number of critics have seen fit to disregard these religious echoes. Fredric Jameson confidently asserts that we can 'from the outset exclude the religious invocations' from a serious consideration of *Passion* (Jameson 1992: 177). Kevin Z. Moore suggests that it would be 'a misunderstanding' to construe *Je vous salue Marie* as 'a religious film' (Moore 1994: 18). Petric and Bard, rather more interestingly, argue that, since 'the diegetic world on screen [in *Je vous salue Marie*] becomes most incoherent' during those passages that most closely parallel the text of the Gospels, the spectator is right to be 'suspicious' (Petric and Bard 1992: 107). However, Alain Bergala has convincingly demonstrated that Godard's film is faithful to traditions of representing the Annunciation which stretch back to the Renaissance:

19 'My God, why have you forsaken me?'

where paintings of the Annunciation often featured a pillar or column separating Mary from the space of the angel, Godard keeps Marie and Gabriel rigorously apart through his montage, never showing them in the same frame and varying the angles from which they are shot (Bergala 1999: 156–60). Godard himself has remarked that, although *Passion* was not intended as a 'religious film', a number of otherwise rational members of the crew felt uncomfortable with the subject and distanced themselves from the production, 'comme si c'était un péché' ('as though it were a sin') (Godard 1998: 498–9). Meanwhile, the history of censorship and Christian fundamentalist protest that greeted the release of *Je vous salue Marie* in Europe and America is well known (for a comprehensive account, see Locke 1993).

Godard may not have an orthodox Christian faith, but this does not exclude the possibility that he might create spiritual or religious work, even if this may appear to some as a betrayal of the dialectical materialism of his Marxist-Leninist days. One of the key influences over Godard's religious (and, I would venture, also his political) thinking is Simone Weil, herself a highly unorthodox figure to whom Godard would pay an extended homage in *Éloge de l'amour*. In the 1930s, Weil gave up a job teaching philosophy in order to work in the Renault factories of Billancourt, before travelling to Spain to fight in the Civil War. Whilst fleeing the persecution of the Nazis she kept a written account of her spiritual development which was published in 1947 as *La Pesanteur et la grâce* and remains her best-known work (she died in England in 1943). Simone Weil is very much the model for the character of Isabelle in *Passion*, who is a militant in the Catholic Workers' Union and Godard has described his struggle to make Isabelle Huppert read Weil and talk to real women factory-workers in preparation for her role (Godard 1998: 505).

In *La Pesanteur et la grâce*, Weil outlines an eccentric but compelling theology that mixes Catholic dogma with inspiration drawn from Buddhist thought and her own experiences of working-class life and political struggle. Weil argues that a general law of human life, paralleled by the law of gravity, is that of a movement downward, such that those who suffer seek only to bring others down with them (Weil 1991 [1947]: 12). The only movement that escapes this trend is the *supernatural* movement of grace (18–19). But, says Weil, we only become aware of grace when we are at the lowest point of misery and suffering, for it is then that we encounter what is indisputably *real* about the world (20, 32). However, we can also attain, or approach, this state by renouncing desire or, better, by detaching desire from its object, that is renouncing the desire for *possession* (21–2). Thereby, we become dispossessed of illusory objects and are left only with the real. The energy released through this process (a desire without object) is grace (31, 45). This action implies also a renouncing of self, of ego (35–6), for it is only then that we may experience joy. Or rather, joy may be experienced in itself, for in this movement the self disappears as sovereign subject of any enjoyment: joy presupposes the superfluity of the self (41).

A number of the key points of this argument are already familiar from the work of Jean-Luc Godard: the detaching of desire, as energy, from its object was discussed in the previous chapter in relation to the seventies video work; the renouncing of self has begun to emerge as a clear motif across the 'cosmic' period of the early 1980s. In addition, Weil's argument about the value of suffering finds an echo in remarks made by Godard in interview: at the time of *Je vous salue Marie*, he declared, 'La souffrance, c'est la plus intime connaissance qu'on a de soi-même, au-delà de l'identité',[20] and he suggested that the cinema had a role to play as 'dépositaire de la souffrance'[21] (Godard 1998: 607–8). Lines spoken by Marie during the intimate spiritual communion in her bedroom also have a rather Weilian ring to them:

> Dieu est un vampire qui a voulu me souffrir en lui parce que je souffrais, et qu'il ne souffrait pas, et que ma douleur lui profitait ... Je suis la joie, celle qui est la joie et n'a plus à lutter contre elle, ni être tentée, mais à gagner une joie de plus. Je ne suis pas résignée, la résignation est triste. Comment se résigner à la volonté de Dieu? Est-ce qu'on se résigne à être aimé?[22]

Here, as in Weil, there is only *apparent* contradiction between suffering and joy: the one, in fact, permits the other. Alain Bergala, who has also noted the influence of Weil over this period of Godard's work, finds it too in certain ambiguous movements which seem to combine a downward and an upward motion, as though suggesting the possibility of grace amidst the laws of gravity. In the reproduction of the El Greco painting in *Passion*, a crane shot spirals upwards before returning to Earth, but the figures in the painting retain an unmistakeable upwards elevation (Bergala 1999: 113–14). Silverman and Farocki have pointed

20 'Suffering is the most intimate knowledge one can have of oneself, beyond identity.'

21 'depositary, or perhaps guardian of suffering'.

22 'God is a vampire who wanted me to suffer in him, because I was suffering and he was not, and my suffering was of profit to him ... I am joy, she who is joy and no longer has to fight it, nor be tempted, but gains a further joy. I am not resigned, resignation is sad. How could I be resigned to God's will? Does one resign oneself to being loved?'

out that there has been some debate among art historians as to whether this painting in fact represents the Assumption or the Annunciation: 'There is thus a certain undecidability in the original about whether the celestial is approaching the terrestrial, or the terrestrial the celestial' (Silverman and Farocki 1998: 194). Meanwhile, in *Je vous salue Marie*, the aeroplane which seems to bring the angel Gabriel and his young accomplice to Earth, because of the angle at which it is shot and the screen of branches through which it is seen, gives the disorientating impression of taking off even as it is landing (Bergala 1999: 93).

For Godard, this energy that, for Weil, is associated with grace, is manifested first and foremost in the form of *light*. Jean Douchet has noted, in *Passion*, but already in *Alphaville* (1965), the importance of light as a kind of pure energy, 'dont la seule raison d'être est d'être de l'énergie'[23] (Douchet 1990: 12). But Simone Weil talks in terms of light too. For instance, she claims to recognise only a single fault among humanity, 'ne pas avoir la capacité de se nourrir de lumière'[24] (Weil 1991 [1947]: 10), and, in an extraordinary passage with a distinctly Godardian flavour, she laments the fact that, in our earthly existence, seeing and eating are two separate operations: 'La béatitude éternelle est un état où regarder c'est manger'[25] (117). The importance of light as a kind of spiritual nourishment is clear in *Passion*. Godard described it as a film about 'des personnages qui ont besoin de lumière'[26] (Godard 1998: 498). And light often plays a leading role in the composition of images and the construction of sequences, much as music does in *Prénom Carmen*. This can be seen in the sequence in which Isabelle and her female colleagues hold a union meeting at her house. In this scene, Godard cuts back and forth between the individuals at the meeting while their discussion is heard in voiceover, but we never actually look at the person who is speaking. This device, which we have already seen used in Godard's filming of the female factory workers in *Tout va bien*, tends, as Kaja Silverman notes, to dispense with the suggestion that problems at work 'belong' to any one person: 'Here, there is no ownership, but rather a socialism of speech' (Silverman and Farocki 1998: 177). In *Passion*, though, it is particularly the lighting of the sequence that prevents us from identifying individual speakers with individual problems, since figures are frequently backlit or cast in heavy shadow so that their features are difficult to make out. Godard includes a little joke at our (or at his own?) expense here since, as Fredric Jameson points

23 'whose only reason to exist is as energy'.
24 'being incapable of nourishment by light'.
25 'Eternal beatitude is a state where looking equals eating.'
26 'characters who are in need of light'.

out, 'a deep male voice wanders across all these women's faces looking for a body' and, on closer inspection, is revealed as belonging to a transvestite (Jameson 1992: 178)! At times, though, the light and framing of these images serves almost to present the women workers as oil paintings (in keeping with the rapprochement between painting and cinema elsewhere in *Passion*), with the light giving an extraordinary clarity to the texture of skin, for instance, in a shot of a woman shielding her eyes from a bright light while much of her face remains in shadow, or in a static head-and-shoulders shot of Isabelle turned three-quarters facing the camera against a dappled blue background. Bergala notes the way that Godard's camera 'devient rêveuse, contemplative, et au lieu de s'intéresser à l'espace dramatique de cette discussion, se met à regarder les visages tout à fait singuliers de ces femmes ... pour eux-mêmes et non plus, comme dans n'importe quel autre film, par rapport aux enjeux de la discussion'[27] (Bergala 1999: 80).

The contrasting realms of light and darkness in many of Godard's images are doubtless inspired by the paintings he studied during the making of the film. *Passion* sees the first appearance in Godard's work of a quotation that would become ubiquitous across his late eighties and nineties films: 'Ce qui plonge dans la lumière est le retentissement de ce que submerge la nuit. Ce que submerge la nuit prolonge dans l'invisible ce qui plonge dans la lumière'.[28] The line is taken from a passage in Élie Faure's *Histoire de l'art* on Rembrandt (Faure 1987 [1921]: 101) which is quoted at considerable length in *Histoire(s) du cinéma*. These sentences, which I suspect are used more for their rich sonority than for their semantic profundity, refer, in their original context, to Rembrandt's use of light and shade in his late work. The first painting reproduced in *Passion* is Rembrandt's *Nightwatch* (1642) and the Dutch master's melancholic shadows would seem to cast their influence over other images in the film. In the sequence of the union meeting, the discussion is delayed as Isabelle's grandfather is occupying the table as he slowly finishes his supper. Lit only by a pool of light from a lamp directly over the table and otherwise surrounded by darkness, Godard gives us an effective image of the old man's solitude as he is hurried along and cajoled out of the way by the younger people (the sad fate of pensioners, here, is similar to that shown in *Numéro deux*).

27 'becomes dreamy, contemplative, and instead of concentrating on the dramatic space of this discussion, starts looking at the altogether singular faces of these women ... for themselves and no longer, as in any other film, in relation to the issues at stake in the discussion'.

28 'That which plunges into light is the repercussion of that which is submerged by night. That which is submerged by night prolongs in the invisible that which plunges into light.'

Light also plays a crucial role in motivating the editing between shots in this sequence. As Isabelle sits down at the table with her grandfather, she knocks the lamp and the next shot is a close-up of her face in the oscillating light and shadow of the swaying lamp (a favourite film noir effect already employed by Godard in *Alphaville*). Later, as Isabelle carries a lamp into the room, Godard cuts suddenly to a large spotlight on the set of Jerzy's movie and, without interrupting the downward movement of the camera, tilts to frame a third lamp in the reproduction of Goya's *3 de Mayo* (1814). Here, too, the reproduced painting appears to present a world of darkness pierced by powerful lines of light, as Godard's camera pans along the row of executioners, their rifle barrels glinting. When Jerzy aborts this particular take, it is inevitably because he is not happy with the light: 'La lumière ne va pas,' he complains, 'Elle ne *va* nulle part, elle ne vient de nulle part'.[29] In cinema as in painting, the light is only right when it is seen to *come from* somewhere: as Kaja Silverman comments, it exists only as 'transferral and transformation' (Silverman and Farocki 1998: 175).

Women

Notwithstanding their aesthetic originality, the films of Godard's cosmic period have come in for sustained criticism from feminist critics. The objections of these critics could be summarised in a series of points as follows:

1 Sexual relations between men and women in these films are routinely presented as the site of violence. We have already seen how the orgy scene in *Sauve qui peut (la vie)* resembles a form of torture, and one of the stop-motion sequences in the film shows Paul leaping without warning across a table and wrestling Denise to the ground. To Isabelle, who witnesses this scene, he explains: 'On a envie de se toucher, mais on n'y arrive qu'en se tapant dessus'.[30] In *Prénom Carmen* we have the impression that Carmen and Joseph are constantly colliding violently with each other, their affection expressed by slapping, grabbing, pulling, pushing. The same is often true of Joseph's relationship to Marie in *Je vous salue Marie*. As Raymond Bellour comments, in these films 'exaltation of women and aggression against women' seem to be 'indissolubly linked' (Bellour 1982: 120).

29 'The light is no good, [but literally: the light *doesn't go*]. It goes nowhere, it comes from nowhere.'

30 'We want to touch each other, but we can only manage it by hitting each other.'

2 Godard's films of this period repeatedly evoke the fantasy of father–daughter incest. In *Sauve qui peut*, Paul, watching his 12-year-old daughter at football training, asks the coach whether he ever feels like touching his own daughter or fucking her in the ass. In *Prénom Carmen*, intimations are made of a former incestuous relationship between Carmen and her uncle Jeannot, played by Godard himself. It is often suggested that the relationship between God and Marie in *Je vous salue Marie* is merely a displacement of this fantasy of father–daughter incest (see for instance Bergala 1999: 90).

3 These films reproduce the stereotypical division of women into the roles of either virgin or whore. Bergala points out that, in all of these films, the central male protagonist is torn between his desires for two women, 'l'une qui manifeste son désir à la face du monde, l'autre qui l'enfouit comme un secret indicible'[31] (107). Thus, Paul is torn between Denise and Isabelle, Jerzy between Hanna (Hanna Schygulla) and Isabelle; Joseph is torn between Carmen and Claire (Myriem Roussel) (just as, in Bizet's *Carmen*, don José wavers between Carmen and Micaëla), and the other Joseph between Juliette (Juliette Binoche) and Marie (although Eva has also been seen as a sexualised woman in opposition to Marie).

4 Women in these films are repeatedly associated with nature, implying some kind of natural or eternal feminine identity and sexuality. This is the sense attributed to the images of Denise cycling through the countryside in *Sauve qui peut* or to the shots of the sea which provide 'a metaphoric extension of Carmen' (Mulvey 1996: 88). It is most especially the case with the nature images in *Je vous salue Marie*. Laura Mulvey puts this argument most unambiguously when she states: 'Godard associates the cyclical with the sacred and the feminine, and inevitably it becomes a sign of renunciation of political desire, as a futile attempt to intervene in the designated course of existence' (Mulvey 1993: 47).

These films may devote a lot of space to the representation of women and the evocation of female desire, but, argues Constance Penley, they ultimately construct sexual difference as 'essential, absolute and irreconcilable to the point of violence' (Penley 1982: 18). Godard simply reverses the terms of traditional sexual representation such that 'femininity becomes the primary term of sexual difference and masculinity its other' (18). The only possible relation of masculinity to this femininity must then be a masochistic one. This masochism is particularly visible

31 'one who manifests her desire in the face of the world, the other who buries it like a shameful secret'.

in *Prénom Carmen,* and especially in the scene where Joseph follows Carmen into the shower with the intention of forcing himself upon her, but is unable to stimulate his limp member. When Carmen tells him 'Tu me dégoûtes', he can only reply 'Moi aussi'.[32] It is worth pointing out, however, that Phil Powrie has challenged this view of the necessarily masochistic position of the male spectator of these films. He suggests instead that *Prénom Carmen* oscillates between a construction of women as fetish-objects over which the male spectator may fantasise the exertion of power and control, and the concomitant defetishisation of women which implies a masochistic 'turning back on the self-as-female, always already castrated' (Powrie 1995: 71), the film being thus engaged in 'continuously constructing and deconstructing his [the male spectator's] position in relation to the fetish-object' (73). There is, in fact, a noticeable gender division in the reception of images of women in these films. The majority of female commentators tend to find these images exploitative, offensive, deliberately titillating for a male spectator; the majority of male commentators, on the other hand, see them as experimental, daringly *different* depictions of women. Rather than seeking to arbitrate between these two points of view, we should, I suggest, be open to the possibility that *both are true,* that is to say that women can and routinely do find these images offensive *as women,* even while men, who are used to the constant, aggressive interpellation of sexual images in the media, feel themselves to be *addressed differently* by Godard's films. Bergala remarks that women's bodies in Godard's films are only ever seen in one of three states: dressed, already naked, or *forced to undress.* Female undressing is never titillating in Godard but always clearly marked as the result of masculine aggression, in *Sauve qui peut,* for example, but already in *Les Carabiniers* (1963) or *Week-end* (Bergala 1999: 127–8). Bergala, who has made repeated reference to the distinction in these films between the arrangement of figures in the mise en scène and the angle from which Godard subsequently 'attacks' that arrangement with his camera, suggests that, if his sexual images are arranged from a rather uninventive, masculine point of view, at the moment of filming Godard tends to identify with a feminine point of view that frustrates the desire of the male spectator which it reveals to be 'un peu dérisoire' ('a little pathetic') (Bergala 1999: 133).

32 'You disgust me. – Me too.'

Nature

There is no doubt, then, that many criticisms of Godard's early 1980s films from a feminist standpoint are well founded, and I have no intention of attempting a point-by-point refutation of the complaints outlined above. I would, however, take issue on the question of Godard's nature imagery. Certainly, an association is developed in these films, and particularly in *Je vous salue Marie*, between these images of nature and images of women. The question is what *sense* are we to attach to this nature imagery? The feminist argument of Mulvey *et al.* implies that, by linking women to forms in the natural world, Godard seeks to fix them into a stable, preordained signification. My contention is that, if this discourse shows some understanding of the role of women in Godard's cinema, it displays an unfortunate misunderstanding of the role of *nature*. Godard draws a powerful symbolism from forms and forces existing in the natural world, but this symbolism has been the object of a reductive, one-dimensional reading by feminist critics. In *Je vous salue Marie*, for instance, Godard makes repeated use of circles which are frequently associated, through simple juxtaposition, with Marie: she is often seen holding a basketball; she wears a shirt sporting the number 10; she is intercut with a bright full moon ... Mulvey interprets these circles according to a logic of what she calls 'the hole and the zero': the gap or absence of the female genitals as they are represented in the male psyche. However, many of the circular figures in the film are without holes, suggesting instead the 'wholeness' of Marie's intact virginity and thus a disavowal of 'the psychologically threatening and physically disgusting "inside"' (Mulvey 1996: 85). This distinction between the full circle and the hole can then be mapped back on to the old virgin–whore dichotomy, with Marie's smooth belly representing a reproduction that is detached from female genital sexuality, while the film's infamous closing shot, an extreme close-up of Marie's gaping mouth after applying lipstick, returns her to the role of whore (Mulvey 1996: 93–4).

There are a number of problems with this analysis. Mulvey suggests that the associations of wholeness in the images of Marie's pregnancy imply a sublimation of female sexuality, a smooth, clean woman's body that must be considered 'in polar opposition to Carmen's sexualised body, which has to remain ultimately uncertain and unknowable' (Mulvey 1996: 93). But, if we consider carefully the images of Maruschka Detmers in *Prénom Carmen* and Myriem Roussel in *Je vous salue Marie*, it is difficult to see how Carmen is any more 'sexualised' than Marie. We see both women naked, but we do not see any *more* of Detmers' nakedness than of Roussel's (to put it bluntly: we do not see beyond her pubic hair). And Powrie has pointed out that, in the scene in which Carmen, naked from the waist down, has breakfast with Joseph, her body is actually defetishised by the sheer length and stability of the shot (Powrie 1995: 70). Problematic, too, is Mulvey's reading of the circular images of *Je vous salue Marie*: some of these images may invite associations with femininity, but that is only one of practically endless possibilities. Yes, the moon is traditionally associated with the feminine (and, as Harvey Cox notes, Godard's film thereby situates itself in relation to a much wider, pantheistic tradition (Cox 1993: 87)), but one of the most common round figures in the film is that of the *sun* (seen in countless glorious sunsets), which is more usually given masculine associations. David Sterritt concedes that a Freudian reading of the open-mouth-and-lipstick shot may well be 'the most obvious', but he rightly cautions that it would be 'regrettably simplistic' to reduce it to such an interpretation (Sterritt 1999: 216). Ellen Draper discusses a scene in *Le Livre de Marie*, the short film by Anne-Marie Miéville which is always appended to *Je vous salue Marie* as a condition of its distribution and exhibition. Marie (Rebecca Hampton) is being helped by her father (Bruno Cremer) with her geometry homework on triangles, and the pair discuss angles and intersections. Beyond the obvious associations of triangles (Œdipal triangle, Holy Trinity) and the vulgar interpretations of father and daughter's opposing angles (phallic, vaginal), Draper suggests that 'the symbolism of this scene is so widely applicable that it remains essentially obscure' (Draper 1993: 72). But in that case, how can it possibly be acceptable to impose a rigid interpretation on so basic a geometric figure as the *circle*? Stuart Cunningham and Ross Harley suggest that the image of the circle signifies not stasis, not fixed identity, but movement, *circulation* (Cunningham and Harley 1987: 73). Godard himself pointed out the universal significance of the circle when he said 'l'univers est courbe comme le ventre de toutes les mères'[33] (Godard 1998: 588). James Joyce said it too: 'Beauty: it curves. Curves are beauty' (Joyce 1968 [1922]): 176).

The implication, when feminist critics talk about nature in Godard's early-1980s films, is that it is something rather boring and predictable. I would be more inclined to agree with Petric and Bard when they write: 'In none of his other films has Godard associated a woman so *excitingly* with nature, especially with its energy and beauty, as he does in *Hail Mary*' (Petric and Bard 1993: 102, my emphasis). Nature in these films is *exciting*: above all, it *moves*. Godard:

33 'the universe is curved like the belly of every mother'.

> Que font les gens? Ils bougent. Les seules choses qui ne bougent pas, ce sont les objets que fabriquent les gens. Par contre, les objets que fabrique la nature bougent tout le temps. Cette table ne bouge pas, mais elle est sur la terre qui tourne. C'est tellement angoissant, une table qui ne bouge pas, que tous les deux ans il faut la changer de place. On passe son temps à ça.[34] (Godard 1998: 508)

Petric and Bard point out that, if the camera is static in the majority of Godard's shots of nature, it is the better to make us appreciate the movement within the frame, 'the perpetuity of natural phenomena' (Petric and Bard 1993: 110). Gilles Deleuze and Félix Guattari, in their 'sequel' to *L'Anti-Œdipe, Mille plateaux*, took issue with a view of nature couched in the logic of the copy where one becomes two, the binary logic of root and tree (Deleuze and Guattari 1980: 11). Such a conception could only describe a state of affairs assumed to be pre-existing, it is powerless to account for the dynamic *development* of nature (20). Deleuze and Guattari propose instead the concept of the rhizome, a view of nature modelled on the anarchic colonisation of a garden by weeds, on the spectacle of a pack of rats scrambling over each other, or on a colony of ants that continues to reconstitute itself even as it is exterminated (13, 16). The rhizome is a multiplicity, connecting to other multiplicities through lines of flight, and changing in nature as it does so (15–16). Any point on the rhizome can and will be connected to any other point so that it is not a linear form but has multiple points of entry (13, 20). Deleuze and Guattari suggest further that the work of art is not a copy or an image of the world, but forms a rhizome with it, connecting up at multiple points in a process of aparallel evolution (18).

I would like to suggest, then, not only that Godard's early 1980s work presents a rhizomatic view of the world, but further that the work itself constitutes a rhizome. This work does not present the spectator with a patient, logical, linear exposition of the world as in classical narrative cinema, but gives us instead what Luc Moullet calls 'une vision en coupe de l'univers' ('a cross-section of the universe') (Moullet 1990: 106). The world on screen is characterised by almost constant *movement*. André Dumas describes the rapidity with which characters move through the frame: 'Ils surgissent presque toujours par derrière un autre et ils disparaissent au moment même où l'on voudrait

34 'What do people do? They move. The only things that don't move are objects made by people. On the other hand, objects made by nature move all the time. This table doesn't move, but it's on the earth which is turning. A table that doesn't move is so disturbing that, every couple of years, you have to move it around. We spend all our time doing that.'

s'attarder avec eux'[35] (Dumas 1990: 89). Peter Wollen suggests that these films look rather like 'the pinball games Godard's characters love to play: people bouncing here and there, lights flashing, trajectories destined to run out of control' (Wollen 1983: 4). Part of this effect is due to the sheer proliferation of secondary characters, bit parts and extras, something which seems to affect, by contamination, the main protagonists: in his preparatory notes for *Passion*, Godard mused: 'lui [the character that would become Jerzy] serait un personage principal filmé de façon secondaire, et elles [Hanna and Isabelle] des personnages secondaires filmés de façon principale'[36] (Godard 1998: 485). Some viewers might complain that Godard's later films are unmemorable precisely because of this neglect of main characters in preference for the bustle and noise of myriad insignificant figures. Moullet recognises that 'Un Godard récent, c'est quelque chose dont on ne peut rien retenir'[37] (Moullet 1990: 106). But this refusal to allow his films or his characters to grow into stable and memorable monuments is clearly deliberate on Godard's part. Instead one remembers fleeting images, moments, and in particular phrases out of context, such as the repeated line from *Sauve qui peut*: 'La passion, c'est pas ça',[38] or the urgent injunction from *Passion*: 'Dis ta phrase!' ('Say your line!'). We remember the trains that cross in *Prénom Carmen* and the plane that lands in *Je vous salue Marie*. Deleuze and Guattari argue that the rhizome is more associated with short-term than long-term memory. Short-term memory does not necessarily imply a memory that elapses shortly after the event: 'elle peut être à distance, venir ou revenir longtemps après, mais toujours dans des conditions de discontinuité, de rupture et de multiplicité'[39] (Deleuze and Guattari 1980: 24). This is thus a cinema of the *instant*, perhaps that instant identified by Simone Weil in which, cut off from the past and the future, we are perfectly innocent (beyond good and evil, in Nietzschean terms), but an instant that is only gained through detachment from our desire (Weil 1991 [1947]: 47).

35 'They almost always emerge from behind another character and they disappear just at the moment when you'd like them to stick around.'

36 'he [Jerzy] would be a main character filmed like a secondary character, and they [Hanna and Isabelle] would be secondary characters filmed like main characters'.

37 'A recent Godard film is something from which one retains nothing.'

38 'That's not what passion is.'

39 'It can be at a distance, arriving or returning a long time afterwards, but always in conditions of discontinuity, of rupture and of multiplicity.'

Communication

Because this is a cinema of the instant, it has no beginning or end (because no *duration*), only a middle, and it is a characteristic of the rhizome that it may only be entered from the middle, because it is always *in* the middle (Deleuze and Guattari 1980: 34–7). Godard has spoken (in Steinebach 1984: 6) of the pointlessness of trying to find the beginning of a story, since one can always work further back, an idea that would become important in his historical work in the 1990s. When talking about himself in this period, Godard tends to characterise his identity by its in-betweenness, which stems partly from his sense of being situated between France and Switzerland (Godard 1998: 599). But he repeatedly refuses the idea of a stable individual identity, referring to himself as a 'réseau ambulant' ('walking network') (597) or saying he feels like a fraction in a world of whole numbers (464)! And from this unstable, incomplete sense of self, comes his definition of cinema as 'ce qu'il y a entre les choses' ('that which is between things') (580). He even described *Passion* as a film that takes place 'quelque part entre l'estomac et les poumons'[40] (484), these being two of the sites on the body where *love* might be located (i.e. as opposed to the heart). Verena Andermatt Conley has pointed out that, in a similar way, the canonical authors (writers, painters, musicians, filmmakers, philosophers) whom Godard quotes in these films, do not retain their original identity but are instead 'integrated into an impersonal network of forces' (Conley 1990: 72. We will consider this question at greater length in later chapters). Ultimately, Godard seems to suggest, individual identity does not exist at all, but only communication. 'Je crois que la seule chose qui existe au monde, c'est la communication. Je ne crois pas que j'existe, je ne crois pas que tu existes, je crois que nous sommes un mouvement matérialisé de mouvements, de formes qui passent entre nous'[41] (Godard 1998: 508). This view of the omnipresence, or omnipotence, of communication in the universe would also seem to be behind Godard's critiques of our communications society which he sees as replacing communication with the mere *appearance* of communication and information. He suggests that people's reluctance to speak to each other, for instance in the waiting room of a train station, implies a certain *fear* of information, at a time when the neighbouring news kiosk offers hundreds of titles and millions of pieces of information (in

40 'somewhere between the stomach and the lungs'.

41 'I believe that the only thing that exists in the world is communication. I don't believe that I exist, I don't believe that you exist, I believe that we are a movement materialised out of movements and forms that pass between us.'

Steinebach 1984: 7). 'C'est parce qu'on communique trop qu'on ne communique plus du tout,' he volunteers, 'Il faudrait faire moins d'images mais les faire mieux'[42] (Godard 1998: 586).

For an example of Godard's rhizomatic, cross-sectional approach to filmmaking, we might look at a section from near the beginning of *Sauve qui peut (la vie)*. In the film, Denise has given up her job at a television station in order to concentrate on her writing, but she considers various other kinds of employment to supplement her income. In the scene that interests us here, we see Denise preparing to write. Shot in front of an open window, with the bright morning light streaming in from outside, she lights a cigarette, sits on the windowsill and begins to write in a notebook, thinking aloud as she goes. This is, then, a fairly romantic, idealised image of the writer's leisurely lifestyle, but what Denise is writing describes more arduous manual labour and that which, within the worker, resists the oppression of this work. As Denise's thoughts continue in voiceover, the image cuts to her friend Piaget (Michel Cassagne) in a print works where, we soon discover, Denise has gone looking for work. A brief stop-motion sequence here shows a close-up of the man's hands arranging the letters on the printer and, as Denise's voiceover goes on, it becomes clear that it is in *movement* that she locates resistance: 'Cette maladresse, ce déplacement superflu, cette accélération soudaine, cette main qui s'y reprend à deux fois, cette grimace, ce décrochage, c'est la vie qui s'accroche. Tout ce qui, en chacun des hommes de la chaîne, hurle silencieusement "Je ne suis pas une machine"'.[43] No matter how much a body is colonised by the mechanised gestures of manual labour, it will always contain the potential for a random, unexpected movement that cannot be incorporated into the rationalised chain of reproduction.

As Denise and Piaget walk outside, he asks about the project she is writing: 'C'est ce qui m'a passionné dans votre lettre (– La passion, c'est pas ça, interjects Denise) ... En fait, décrire les choses secondaires, ça éclaire vachement les événements principaux. Montrer la vérité que le rôle secondaire est le principal'.[44] Here, then, it is a secondary character

42 'It's because we communicate too much that we no longer communicate at all ... We ought to make fewer images, but make them better.'

43 'This awkwardness, this superfluous shift, this sudden speeding-up, this hand that repeats the same action twice, this grimace, this switch-over, is life hanging on. Everything which, in each member of the production line, silently screams "I am not a machine".'

44 'That's what I was most passionate about when I read your letter (Denise: That's not what passion is). In fact, describing secondary things really helps to illuminate the main events. Show how the secondary role is, in truth, the most important.'

himself who expresses Godard's own sentiments regarding the importance of secondary characters in creating the impression of a vibrant, *living* world. And *Sauve qui peut* is full of such characters. As Denise and Piaget talk, the camera pans left to follow an incongruously overdressed woman who emerges from a neighbouring building and heads off down the street past a cow grazing on the verge. The woman, who reappears later in a bar, is coded as a prostitute and thus contributes to Godard's favoured theme of labour as prostitution, organised in particular around the character of Isabelle. But she is also inscribed within the film's consideration of nature, since her lurid fox-fur muffler, a particularly vile example of our exploitation of nature, is thrown into sharp relief by the magnificently impassive cow who continues munching at the grass as she passes.

Following some shots of Denise on her bicycle, including the accordion accompaniment that finds an unlikely diegetic source by the side of the road, and a stunning superimposition with a tractor ploughing a field, trailed by squawking, hungry birds, Denise arrives at the train station in Nyon. Here we find two bikers manhandling a woman and repeating the injunction 'Choisis!' while she insists, 'Non, je ne choisis pas!'.[45] This is one of the scenes that has led to the criticism that sexual difference in *Sauve qui peut* is always a site of violence, since it tends to be assumed that the woman is being asked to choose between the two men. However, there is nothing in the dialogue to specify what kind of choice is being made (or not made). As Denise watches, the men slap the woman around the face and the sequence switches briefly to slow-motion as her head jerks from side to side, returning to normal speed as, with blood running from the corner of her mouth, she determinedly repeats '*Je ne choisis pas*!'. What we have here is an image of resistance to any authority that would force us to choose, to fix our diverse movements and activities into stable, self-contained categories. This may apply to sexual choices, but why not also to choices about work: will Denise be a writer or a printer or an agricultural labourer? Will her activity constitute work or leisure? Must she choose between work and love? Is nature a source for us to exploit for our own comfort or a vast, self-organising system of which we are merely a small component part? As Pascal Bonitzer notes, Paul, in the film, is himself reluctant to choose between staying in his hotel suite or sharing a flat with Denise (Bonitzer 1980: 5). Nor should we forget the lesson learned from Guy Debord that we discussed in Chapter 4: choice is often only the alibi by which consumer capitalism effectively removes our

45 'Choose! – No, I won't!'

freedom. Rather than an image that closes off debate about sexual difference, this sequence presents one of the most open-ended and all-encompassing images of *resistance* in all of Godard's cinema.

While all this is going on, there is a lot of other activity in the square in front of the station. A racing car pulls up without explanation and a large American station wagon parks at a right-angle behind it. Trains pass quickly through the station. At the end of the sequence, a voice over a tannoy announces 'Environ vingt secondes' ('About twenty seconds'), leading us to suspect that there may be a film crew present, or perhaps that some kind of organised road race is beginning. Finally, the station wagon pulls off, followed by the racecar and one of the bikers. As Denise continues to pace up and down the station forecourt, another train hurtles noisily past in the foreground. Much of the sense of constant movement in this sequence (as elsewhere in Godard's films of this period) comes, then, from the proliferation of modes of transport: bicycle, tractor, racecar, motorbike, train ... characters are in constant motion. As Bonitzer puts it, they are 'toujours entre deux trains, deux lieux, deux corps, deux projets. De même l'image s'arrête, n'arrête pas vraiment, va s'arrêter, repart. Le sujet du film, c'est le mouvement, les mouvements'[46] (Bonitzer 1980: 5). When presenting *Sauve qui peut* in Avignon in 1980, Godard said of the image: 'c'est un moment de rencontre, c'est une gare où deux trains passent'[47] (Godard 1998: 463), which perhaps explains why this favourite Godardian image of a train (or two) rushing through a station became a constant in practically every Godard feature of the 1980s and 1990s. The significance of this (apparently) throwaway remark has also been noted by Michael Witt. Witt offers a conceptualisation of the image in Godard based on the theory of metaphor and suggests that all the different modes of transport in his films symbolise not just communication but the *transposition of sense* in the metaphor (the theory of metaphor speaks of the *vehicle* which conveys the sense) (Witt 2001: 27).

Science

The discourse of communication which Godard has held around these films, though it may at times appear flippant, has, in fact, some scientific grounding. Towards the end of *Sauve qui peut*, Denise and

46 'always in between two trains, two places, two bodies, two projects. In the same way, the image stops, doesn't really stop, goes to stop then sets off again. The subject of the film is movement, movements'.

47 'it's a momentary encounter, it's a station where two trains cross'.

Isabelle sit talking together in a car and Isabelle makes a rather cryptic comment about 'le cristal et la fumée, les deux visages de la mort'.[48] Isabelle claims to be referring to an English novel whose title she can't remember, but in fact this is a reference to a work by the theoretical biologist Henri Atlan entitled *Entre le cristal et la fumée* and published in France in 1979 (Godard quotes directly from this book on another occasion, in *JLG/JLG: Autoportrait de décembre* (1994)). Atlan is another writer who sees life as constituted first and foremost by *movement* and that any attempt to fix life-forms, either in the laboratory or in representation, leads life into one or other of two forms of death: the rigidity of crystal or the decomposition of smoke (Atlan 1979: 5). Atlan uses information theory to explain the organisation of life, arguing that a living system will only develop and change through the interference of *noise* from outside the system (44–51). The random errors generated by this noise may subsequently be integrated by the system such that they become 'des événements de l'histoire du système et de son processus d'organisation'[49] (57). Thierry Jousse, himself referencing Atlan, suggests that Godard's longstanding aesthetic preference for noise (pinball, car horns, construction, squawking birds, yelling passers-by, etc.) implies that noise is at the very foundation of communication: 'C'est le bruit qui informe, qui fait circuler, qui fait marcher le système. Car un système trop parfait est menacé de mort'[50] (Jousse 1990: 43). Alain Bergala has also suggested a kind of *visual* noise in Godard's films, particularly of this period: writing about *Passion*, he describes 'l'extraordinaire réseau de brouillages et de discordances calculées'[51] that Godard places between us and the images of a very pure beauty that we find in the film (such as the images of nature or the reproductions of paintings). Thus the film appears in the image of the shot where Isabelle, by a river, is seen through the dense branches of a tree. Other examples include the film crew wheeling cameras through the immaculately reproduced paintings, or Jerzy's assistant Laszlo (Laszlo Szabo) tapping insistently on the window as Jerzy shares an intimate moment with Isabelle (Bergala 1999: 39–40). But perhaps one of the most evocative examples of visual noise in this period is the shot of Joseph's hand against the restless static of a TV screen as he waits in his hotel room for Carmen to return and Tom Waits sings 'Ruby's Arms' in the background.

Henri Atlan is a rather unusual scientist in that his field of enquiry is

48 'crystal and smoke, the two faces of death'.

49 'events in the history of the system and of its process of organisation'.

50 'It is noise that informs and allows circulation, that drives the system. Because a system that is too perfect is threatened with death.'

51 'the extraordinary network of interference and calculated dissonance'.

much broader in scope than most of his contemporaries. A Hebrew scholar with a passionate stake in Jewish history and theology, he attempts to use his theoretical paradigm in an analysis of human societies (even totalitarian ones) as self-organising natural systems. This desire to use the acquisitions of science to think about society and culture much more widely is obviously one that is close to Godard's heart. We mentioned in the last chapter Godard's ideas about the scientific uses of cinema, and these ideas gather pace in his remarks around the early-1980s films. He considers it strange that the cinema, unlike other industries, doesn't devote a significant part of its budget to research and development (Godard 1998: 460). He discusses with perfect seriousness a proposal he made to the CNRS to use cinema to 'résoudre une fois pour toutes la question du cancer'[52] (463) (the CNRS never replied). He notes with regret that, although science employs *images*, both visual and verbal, all the time, scientists are reluctant to think critically about those images, assuming they have nothing to learn from cinema (606–7). This quasi-scientific approach to cinema is partly responsible for the fact that relatively little importance is ascribed to character psychology and emotion in the organisation of Godard's films. We might go so far as to say that Godard's cinema, from this period, tends to work against anthropocentrism, presenting human society as merely one living system, one system of *energy*, that intersects with others. Describing *Passion*, Godard suggested the characters could be considered 'comme des morceaux de fer traversant des courants magnétiques (des champs de force et de faiblesse). Et le film est l'histoire, la vision de cette traversée'[53] (Godard 1998: 485). This kind of basic magnetism is also implied by Carmen and Joseph's repeated puns around the phrases 'Tirez-vous, attirez-moi'.[54] Pascal Bonitzer describes the world of *Sauve qui peut* as a world without pity (Bonitzer 1980: 6), but this is only because humanity is granted no more importance than the rest of the natural world, or even than the vehicles that criss-cross the screen. At one point we hear Cécile discussing her homework which is about the migration of blackbirds. It is suggested that the shift in the blackbird's preferred habitat over the past two hundred years from the countryside to the city is a more significant colonisation than any of the human efforts of the same period, more significant because it testifies to a *cross-species* influence. In *Mille plateaux*, Deleuze and Guattari suggest similarly that we should conceive of a single 'mechanosphere'

52 'resolve once and for all the problem of cancer'.
53 'like iron filings crossing magnetic currents (fields of force and weakness). And the film is the story, the vision of this crossing'.
54 'Get out of here [literally: pull yourself away], attract me [pull me towards you]'.

encompassing all living things, all organisations, all fields of energy, since cultural or technological developments at one level may well provide the conditions for microbial or bacteriological development at another level (Deleuze and Guattari 1980: 89). The history of evolution is the history of these intersections between species, through the medium of viruses for instance (69–70).

These considerations about the nature and provenance of life receive considerable attention in *Je vous salue Marie*. In the film, the story of Marie and Joseph is to some extent paralleled by a subplot (though such traditional appellation seems inadequate given Godard's singular approach to narrative) involving an exiled professor of physics (Johan Meyssen) and the relationship he has with one his students, Eva. It is sometimes assumed that the scientific discourse and the spiritual parable in *Je vous salue Marie* are mutually excluding and that, if one is to be taken seriously, the other must be dismissed. I would argue instead that the film represents a serious attempt to think science and religion *together*, to consider how the two traditions might converge around the mystery of creation. We first encounter the professor giving a lecture where he expounds 'his' theory that life originated in outer space, showing a chart to illustrate how light is absorbed by extra-terrestrial bacteria. He goes on to suggest that life is not a random occurrence but has been *willed*, programmed. To illustrate this idea, he asks Eva to place her hands over another student's eyes who must then attempt to solve a Rubik's Cube. This would take several million years, he explains, but the time will be reduced to a couple of minutes if Eva directs his moves. As Eva calls 'Oui' and 'Non' to each of the student's turns of the cube, it sets up a situation that will be matched by the later scene in which Marie says 'Non' and 'Oui' to Joseph's attempted declarations of love. The compatibility of this scene with the film's sacred narrative is underscored by the use of Bach's *St Matthew Passion* on the soundtrack. As Charles Warren has commented, the music of Bach is singularly appropriate for this film since this 'unremittingly contrapuntal' work seems altogether mathematical in design, yet it is also given to 'unpredictable, even shocking' changes in direction (Warren 1993: 14–15).

Shortly afterwards, following the Annunciation scene, we find the professor and his students by the side of the lake. Here, too, they discuss the possibilities of inhuman intelligence of various kinds. One student describes an experiment to heat an ants' nest during the winter. His hypothesis was that, if the ants were prevented from hibernating, the time usually spent sleeping would be transformed into leisure time and the ants might start to be creative: 'J'avais pensé à la musique ...'.[55] he says hopefully. Meanwhile, the professor explains that his ideas about a higher intelligence programming life on earth were inspired by the artificial intelligence of computers. He also surmises that an inconceivably more developed human race millions of years in the future, having discovered some secret about the universe, might try somehow to transmit the message back to us. Again these considerations, admittedly far-fetched but nonetheless founded on rational grounds, are associated with the story of Marie and Joseph, but this time through a process of intercutting. The scene follows immediately from the Annunciation to Marie, with a beautiful match-on-action when a little skip in Marie's step is neatly correlated to a movement of one of the students on a rocky promontory out in the lake. As the professor and students talk, they are filmed through the branches of the trees by the side of the water (like Isabelle in *Passion*) and, in the parallel scene outside Marie's house, the foreground is also taken up with the budding branches of a tree. Petric and Bard have also pointed out the way that a shot of two birds of prey circling each other in the sky above the lake leads into images of Joseph's courtship of Marie, he prowling around her as she evades his grasp (Petric and Bard 1993: 104). The two narratives are further linked, though, because the professor's words, like Marie's experience of divine intervention, are linked to images of great natural beauty, of the *wonder* of creation: so we see the elusive play of light over the surface of the water, a pale sun setting behind the trees, its warm light bathing Eva's face in a golden glow.

The ideas expounded by the professor come, with a little creative reshaping on Godard's part, from a British cosmologist named Fred Hoyle, whose work Godard cites enthusiastically in interview (Godard 1998: 605). Hoyle is a well-respected scientist, but holds some views that diverge from the dominant trends of modern cosmology: he rejects, for instance, the hypothesis of a big bang at the beginning of the universe, preferring the notion of a 'steady-state universe'. In the late 1970s and early 1980s, Hoyle and his collaborators repeatedly proposed the idea that life on earth came from outer space. They argue that the conditions conducive to the origin of life were more likely to be found on comets than on the primeval planet earth and it is the earth's passage through clouds of evaporated cometary material that brought life (in the form of bacteria) to our planet (Hoyle and Wickramasinghe 1979: 158–9). They suggest, in addition, that the chance of a 'random shuffling' of amino acids producing the enzymes necessary for life is around 1 in

55 'I was thinking about music ....'

$10^{40\,000}$, and that the probability is 'vastly higher' that life was assembled by some form of intelligence (Hoyle and Wickramasinghe 1981: 129–30). In the rather eccentric conclusion to their book *Evolution from Space*, Hoyle and Wickramasinghe argue further that, since humanity has been able to produce an entity as intelligent as the silicon chip, we should not rule out the possibility that we ourselves were created by a higher intelligence. This sequence of intelligences could presumably go on indefinitely, somewhat as follows:

> ??? → ?? → ? → man → silicon chip → ? (Hoyle and Wickramasinghe 1981: 143)

Such a formulation must, admittedly, be taken with a pinch of salt, but the important point, and the one which Godard is making with *Je vous salue Marie*, is that ultimately science is at a loss to explain where the universe came from, how it came about, and what, if anything, preceded it. And the narratives it develops to answer these questions are, in many cases, just as fanciful as those of religion. What matters perhaps, finally, are precisely those questions with which the human mind, the power of thought runs up against its own limits and must turn to invention, to creation of its own in order to continue. David Sterritt, discussing *Je vous salue Marie* in relation to *Le Livre de Marie* which precedes it, suggests that Godard's film could be seen to emerge from the egg which Marie breaks, in close-up, at the end of Miéville's film. But, as Sterritt goes on to argue, 'This raises the fascinating question of what is to erupt from Mary's open mouth at the end of [Godard's] film' (Sterritt 1993: 58). Marie's open mouth, then, rather than providing a circular closure by returning her to the role of whore, signals, as Sterritt puts it elsewhere, 'an opening into mysteries greater than our everyday ways of thinking, knowing, and perceiving can coherently contain' (Sterritt 1999: 219). Nor is it simply a negative image for the zero or hole of female sexuality. As the angel Gabriel says, cryptically, at one point in the film: 'D'abord, un trou n'est pas un trou'.[56] This is another lesson Godard has learned from cosmology, with its study of black holes, and one seized upon by Deleuze and Guattari who note that a hole is not an absence of particles, but particles travelling faster than the speed of light, matter collapsed in on itself (Deleuze and Guattari 1980: 45). We need not take the ending of *Je vous salue Marie* as a negative image, nor as an ending at all, but rather as an opening into the unknown: *Le Livre de Marie* → *Je vous salue Marie* → ?

If love and work are connected, as Godard repeatedly insists, but

56 'First of all, a hole is not a hole.'

never more so than at this period of his career, it is perhaps because love – whether physical or spiritual love – involves *renouncing possession*, which ultimately amounts to renouncing the self. By the same token, the *work* of art – which is a labour of love – if it is truly to become art, must involve a similar renunciation, a dispossession, whereby it may testify to a life that escapes the confines of the artist's mind, suggesting an interconnecting network of energies of which human existence is only a part. It is this vast and unfamiliar scale that is touched by the work of Godard's cosmic period. Simone Weil envisaged a similar possibility when she wrote:

> *Littérature et morale*. Le mal imaginaire est romantique, varié, le mal réel morne, monotone, désertique, ennuyeux. Le bien imaginaire est ennuyeux; le bien réel est toujours nouveau, merveilleux, enivrant. Donc la 'littérature d'imagination' est ou ennuyeuse ou immorale (ou un mélange des deux). Elle n'échappe à cette alternative qu'en passant en quelque sorte, à force d'art, du côté de la realité – ce que le génie seul peut faire.[57] (Weil 1991 [1947]: 83)

57 '*Literature and morality*. Imaginary evil is romantic and varied, real evil is miserable, monotonous, barren, boring. Imaginary goodness is boring; real goodness is always new, marvellous, intoxicating. So the literature of imagination is either boring or immoral (or a mixture of the two). It can only escape from this alternative if, by the strength of its art, it goes the way of reality – and only genius is able to do that.'

References

Adorno, T. (1974 [1951]), *Minima Moralia: Reflections from Damaged Life*, trans. by E. F. N. Jephcott, London, NLB.

Adorno, T. (1998), *Beethoven: The Philosophy of Music: Fragments and Texts*, ed. by Rolf Tiedemann, trans. by Edmund Jephcott, Cambridge, Polity.

Albrecht, T. (1991), 'Sauve qui peut (l'image): reading for a double life', *Cinema Journal*, 30, 2, 61–73.

Atlan, H. (1979), *Entre le cristal et la fumée: Essai sur l'organisation du vivant*, Paris, Seuil.

Aumont, J. (1989), *L'Œil interminable: Cinéma et peinture*, Paris, Librairie Séguier.

Aumont, J. (1990), 'Lumière de la musique', *Cahiers du cinéma*, hors série, *Spécial Godard: Trente ans depuis*, 46–8.

Bellour, R. (1982), 'I am an image', *Camera Obscura*, 8–10, 117–22.

Bergala, A. (1999), *Nul mieux que Godard*, Paris, Cahiers du cinéma.

Bonitzer, P. (1980), 'Peur et commerce', *Cahiers du cinéma*, 316, 5–7.

Cerisuelo, M. (1989), *Jean-Luc Godard*, Paris, L'Herminier/Éditions des Quatre Vents.

Conley, V. A. (1990), 'A fraying of voices: Jean-Luc Godard's *Prénom Carmen*', *Esprit Créateur*, 30, 2, 68–80.

Cox, H. (1993), 'Mariology, or the feminine side of God', in M. Locke and C. Warren (eds), *Jean-Luc Godard's Hail Mary: Women and the Sacred in Film*, Carbondale and Edwardsville, Southern Illinois University Press, 86–9.

Cunningham, S. and Harley, R. (1987), 'The logic of the virgin mother: A discussion of "Hail Mary"', *Screen*, 28, 1, 62–76.

Deleuze, G. and Guattari, F. (1980), *Mille plateaux: Capitalisme et schizophrénie 2*, Paris, Minuit.

Douchet, J. (1990), 'Le théorème de Godard', *Cahiers du cinéma*, hors série, *Spécial Godard: Trente ans depuis*, 12–13.

Draper, E. (1993), 'An alternative to Godard's metaphysics: Cinematic presence in Miéville's *Le Livre de Marie*', in M. Locke and C. Warren (eds), *Jean-Luc Godard's Hail Mary: Women and the Sacred in Film*, Carbondale and Edwardsville, Southern Illinois University Press, 67–74.

Dumas, A. (1990), 'À bout de foi', *Cahiers du cinéma*, hors série, *Spécial Godard: Trente ans depuis*, 88–92.

Faure, E. (1987 [1921]), *Histoire de l'art: L'art moderne I*, Paris, Denoël.

Godard, J.-L. (1998), *Jean-Luc Godard par Jean-Luc Godard, Tome 1: 1950–1984*, Paris, Cahiers du cinéma.

Herzog, A. (2002), 'The dissonant refrains of Jean-Luc Godard's *Prénom Carmen*', paper presented at *The Carmen Conference*, University of Newcastle upon Tyne, 25–7 March.

Hoyle, F. and Wickramasinghe, C. (1979), *Diseases from Space*, London, J. M. Dent and Sons.

Hoyle, F. and Wickramasinghe, C. (1981), *Evolution from Space*, London, J. M. Dent and Sons.

Jameson, F. (1992), *The Geopolitical Aesthetic: Cinema and Space in the World System*, Bloomington and London, Indiana University Press and BFI.

Jousse, T. (1990), 'Godard à l'oreille', *Cahiers du cinéma*, hors série, *Spécial Godard: Trente ans depuis*, 40–3.

Joyce, J. (1968 [1922]), *Ulysses*, London, Penguin.

Le Roux, H. (1985), 'Le trou de la vierge, ou Marie telle que Jeannot la peint', *Cahiers du cinéma*, 367, 11–13.

Leutrat, J.-L. (1990), *Des traces qui nous ressemblent: Passion de Jean-Luc Godard*, Paris, Éditions Comp'act.

Locke, M. (1993), 'A history of the public controversy', in M. Locke and C. Warren (eds), *Jean-Luc Godard's Hail Mary: Women and the Sacred in Film*, Carbondale and Edwardsville, Southern Illinois University Press, 1–9.

Moore, K. Z. (1994), 'Reincarnating the radical: Godard's *Je vous salue Marie*', *Cinema Journal*, 34, 1, 18–30.

Moullet, L. (1990), 'Suivez le guide', *Cahiers du cinéma*, hors série, *Spécial Godard: Trente ans depuis*, 104–11.

Mulvey, L. (1993), 'Marie/Eve: Continuity and discontinuity in J.-L. Godard's iconography of women', in M. Locke and C. Warren (eds), *Jean-Luc Godard's Hail Mary: Women and the Sacred in Film*, Carbondale and Edwardsville, Southern Illinois University Press, 39–53.

Mulvey, L. (1996), *Fetishism and Curiosity*, Bloomington and London, Indiana University Press and BFI.

Nettelbeck, C. (2001), 'Trans-figurations: Verbal and visual *frissons* in France's millennial change', *Australian Journal of French Studies*, 39, 1, 86–101.

Oudart, J.-P. (1980), 'Lang, Eisenstein, Godard', *Cahiers du cinéma*, 317, 35–9.

Penley, C. (1982), 'Pornography, eroticism', *Camera Obscura*, 8–10, 13–18.

Petric, V. and Bard, G. (1993), 'Godard's vision of the new Eve', in M. Locke and C. Warren (eds), *Jean-Luc Godard's Hail Mary: Women and the Sacred in Film*, Carbondale and Edwardsville, Southern Illinois University Press, 98–114.

Powrie, P. (1995), 'Godard's *Prénom Carmen* (1984), masochism, and the male gaze', *Forum for Modern Language Studies*, 31, 1, 64–73.

Silverman, K. and Farocki, H. (1998), *Speaking about Godard*, New York, New York University Press.

Steinebach, S. (1984), 'Les signes du mal à vivre: Entretien avec Jean-Luc Godard', *L'Avant-scène cinéma*, 323–4, 4–11.

Sterritt, D. (1993), 'Miéville and Godard: From psychology to spirit', in M. Locke and C. Warren (eds), *Jean-Luc Godard's Hail Mary: Women and the Sacred in Film*, Carbondale and Edwardsville, Southern Illinois University Press, 54–60.

Sterritt, D. (1999), *The Films of Jean-Luc Godard: Seeing the Invisible*, Cambridge, Cambridge University Press.

Thompson, K. (1988), *Breaking the Glass Armor: Neoformalist Film Analysis*, Princeton, NJ, Princeton University Press.

Warren, C. (1993), 'Whim, God, and the screen', in M. Locke and C. Warren (eds), *Jean-Luc Godard's Hail Mary: Women and the Sacred in Film*, Carbondale and Edwardsville, Southern Illinois University Press, 10–26.

Weil, S. (1991 [1947]), *La Pesanteur et la grâce*, Paris, Plon.

Wills, D. (1986), 'Carmen: Sound/Effect', *Cinema Journal*, 25, 4, 33–43.

Witt, M. (2001), 'L'image selon Godard: théorie et pratique de l'image dans l'œuvre de Godard des années 70 à 90', in G. Delavaud, J.-P. Esquenazi and M.-F. Grange (eds), *Godard et le métier d'artiste*, Paris, L'Harmattan.

Wollen, P. (1983), '*Passion 1*', *Framework*, 21, 4.

8

Smiling with regret: 1984–90

The latter half of the 1980s probably constitutes the least well-known and the least liked period of Godard's entire career. The radical works of the Dziga Vertov Group may be rarely seen, and they may be unremittingly didactic, but they have been discussed at length with gravity and respect by critics. The films of the early 1990s, although they passed largely unnoticed on their initial release, have been eagerly rediscovered since the completion of *Histoire(s) du cinéma* in 1998. But the films of the late 1980s, in addition to being shunned by distributors and spectators, have long been overlooked by commentators on Godard's work, such that it is only now that they are beginning to be discussed at any length. In this chapter, I will consider why the films of this period have often attracted a negative response, looking at their claustrophobic settings and offputting themes of failure and regret. A consistent complaint develops across these films whereby Godard seems to argue that art, or even civilisation itself, have been consigned to the past. It is this discourse that has led to the characterisation of the director as a grumpy hermit, an image Godard willingly plays up to in his own roles in *Soigne ta droite* (1987) and *King Lear* (1987). Godard's practice in this period has also led critics to associate him with postmodernism, but, in the middle section of this chapter, I will argue that, even if Godard's citational aesthetic is in some senses postmodern, his films maintain a critical stance with regard to the post-industrial cultural economy. Finally I will show how Godard continues to search for images of resistance to this economic organisation, and finds them in images of the body (physical comedy and a new focus on hands) as well as elemental images of fire and water.

Plastic apocalypse: failure and fatigue in late 1980s Godard

Marc Cerisuelo has characterised this period in terms of what he calls 'le Grand Enfermement' (Cerisuelo 1989: 221), or the great shut-in. He notes that this tendency begins in *Prénom Carmen* with the lengthy sequence set in the Hotel Intercontinental, and continues in *Je vous salue Marie* with the scenes in Marie's bedroom. But it reaches its climax in *Détective* (1984), where the entire film takes place within the confines of the Hotel Concorde Saint-Lazare in Paris. Elements of this agoraphobia can also be found right up to *Nouvelle Vague* (1990) which is set within a large country house and its grounds. It is in *Détective*, though, that the sense of dingy rooms and stifled air is most striking. In this film, Claude Brasseur plays Émile, an airline pilot staying in the hotel during his passage through Paris with his wife, Françoise (Nathalie Baye). At one point, neglected by Émile, Françoise muses to herself, 'Au moins que je profite de Paris',[1] a line that resonates with a hollow irony since we never see her, or anyone else, leave the hotel during the course of the film. This sense of enclosure renders *Détective*, in the words of Jean-Luc Douin, 'un film désespéré, crépusculaire' ('a despairing, crepuscular film') (Douin 1989: 229). It is perhaps revealing that, interviewed on the film's release, Godard stated that he had always wanted to make a film of Jean-Paul Sartre's play *Huis clos*, in which three characters discover that hell is being confined to a room with each other (Godard 1998b: 78): something of this sense of entrapment and mutual resentment persists in *Détective*.

A sense of despair and disillusionment is further communicated by the fatigue that is displayed and expressed throughout the film by Émile but also by Jim (Johnny Hallyday), whose identity seems to be partly based on Conrad's *Lord Jim*, a novel about failure and regret that he carries with him everywhere (although it turns out he has never actually read it). This theme of fatigue has been interpreted, following remarks made by Godard himself, as a 'défaillance du mâle' (Godard 1998b: 79), or 'discomfiture of the male' (Powrie 1997: 99) in the wake of the gains made for women by the feminist movement. A particularly offensive and embarrassing example of this discomfiture comes in *Soigne ta droite* when Godard, in his role as the Idiot, addresses a woman at a flight desk as 'Mademoiselle'. 'Il n'y a plus de Mademoiselle,' she replies indignantly, 'Je suis manager de vol'. 'Ah bon,' continues Godard, '*manager* ou ménagère?'.[2] But the sense of irrelevance and destitution that

1 'At least I can make the most of Paris.'

2 This 'joke' is not really translatable: 'There are no more "Mademoiselles," says the woman, 'I am a flight manager'. 'Ménagère' means 'housewife'.

accompanies masculine identity in *Détective* is associated more widely with the identity of France and its declining importance on the world stage. At one point, the Prince, an ageing mafioso played by Alain Cuny, asks 'Comment est-ce que la France cherche encore à jouer un rôle principal puisque chaque Français est devenu un personnage secondaire?'[3] (we recognise the punning on principal and secondary roles from *Sauve qui peut (la vie)*).

The preoccupation with decline and decay, with the sense of an ending, affects other films of this period. *Soigne ta droite* seems particularly obsessed (even by Godard's standards!) with death. The film contains lengthy readings from two texts in particular, Hermann Broch's *Death of Virgil* in which the Latin poet spends a night of agony debating whether to burn the *Aeneid*, which he regards as a failure, his own tragic decline mirroring that of the Roman civilisation; and André Malraux's *Lazare*, the final volume of his memoirs, in which he relates his near-death experience while afflicted with a strange sleeping-sickness that saw him collapse without warning. *Soigne ta droite* also contains a discussion of regret, centred around Baudelaire's image of 'le regret souriant' ('smiling regret'), as analysed by Gaston Bachelard. Bachelard took this image to be representative of what he called the 'vertical instant' of poetry: a time in which ambivalent sentiments could co-exist without being reduced to antithesis, simultaneity or succession (Bachelard 1992 [1931]: 103–11). The theme of regret recurs in *Nouvelle Vague* where Elena (Domiziana Giordano) defines remorse as 'la conscience d'avoir payé un prix trop élevé pour un bénéfice quelconque'.[4] All of *Nouvelle Vague* takes place under the sign of memory: the large country house on the shores of Lake Geneva is similar to the one in which Godard grew up (Godard 1998b: 202) and, as Silverman and Farocki suggest (1998: 199), the film seems to come to us as though filtered through memory: 'Tout cela, ils avaient l'impression de l'avoir déjà vécu,'[5] says a voiceover at one point. Within this apparent context of personal and cultural decline, where so much emphasis is placed on memory, art itself, at this stage of Godard's career, begins to appear as a thing of the past. At least Godard seems to suggest that contemporary artistic production will never again attain the heights it once knew. In his comments around these films, Godard often appears nostalgic for the golden age of French cinema in the 1930s. He had hoped that the comings and goings in the hotel in *Détective* might achieve a similar

3 'How can France go on trying to play a major role, when all Frenchmen have become minor characters?'

4 'the awareness of having paid too high a price for an indifferent reward'.

5 'They had the impression that they had lived through all of this before.'

effect to Renoir's *La Règle du jeu* (1939) (Godard 1998b: 79). Complaining about what he sees as the laziness of today's actors, he cites, on more than one occasion, the commitment of Jean Gabin and Michèle Morgan in *Quai des brumes* (1938) (79 and 127). (Both of these films will have an important role to play in *Histoire(s) du cinéma.*)

King Lear, which contains elements of all the themes we have so far encountered – enclosure, fatigue, cultural decline, death, regret – might be taken as representative of this most unwelcoming period of Godard's cinema. It is representative, too, inasmuch as it was very rarely seen for at least a decade after its release, and came to be considered as a lost or invisible work. The idea of a version of *King Lear* directed by Godard was first discussed with Menahem Golan of Cannon Pictures at the Cannes film festival in 1986 with the intention that the completed product should be premiered at the festival the following year. Godard was granted a number of high-profile American stars – Norman Mailer, Woody Allen, Molly Ringwald, Burgess Meredith – but the production soon ran into difficulties. Typically, Godard writes these difficulties into the fabric of the film, which opens with a phone call from Golan expressing his concern that the movie would not be ready for the Cannes festival, followed by two separate takes of a scene between Norman Mailer and his daughter, over which Godard explains how Mailer abandoned the film following 'a ceremony of star behaviour'. A rough 'working copy' was indeed presented at Cannes in May 1987, although, when the final cut was revealed later that year, little of this roughness had been smoothed over (Benoît 1987). Cannon eventually gave the film a very limited release in the States, with Allen and Ringwald refusing to have their names used in publicity, but it received no official release in Europe (*King Lear* was released in France in 2002 in the wake of the interest in Godard inspired by *Histoire(s) du cinéma* and *Éloge de l'amour*). Vincent Canby of the *New York Times,* who has been one of the most outspoken critics of this period of Godard's filmmaking, called the end result 'sad and embarrassing' (quoted in Walworth 2002: 59). Godard's *Lear* is, unquestionably, a mess, although deliberately so, as we shall see. One of its most immediately offputting aspects is the dense soundtrack, in which three layers of voices will often compete with each other, themselves frequently drowned out by the screeching and squawking of birds and beasts. Two different versions of *King Lear* have been screened in France, one subtitled, the other in which Godard, in voiceover, translates all the dialogue as the film progresses. Naturally, this just adds to the confusion and cacophony, as when Lear (Burgess Meredith)'s punning line to the playwright William Shakespeare V (Peter Sellars), 'Are you trying to make a play for my girl?', has to be laboriously explained by Godard.

Godard's *Lear*, filmed once again on the banks of Lake Geneva, is set in some sort of post-apocalyptic future which Shakespeare V describes as existing 'after Chernobyl'. Shakespeare claims to be the only survivor of this nuclear holocaust (although plenty of other figures wander through the play), and takes it upon himself to 'recapture what had been lost', in particular the works of his ancestor. Shakespeare spends the rest of the film noting down lines from his playwright ancestor as they are spoken by other characters, most notably Lear (Meredith) and Cordelia (Ringwald). Again, then, *King Lear* presents art as a thing of the past, something lost to our culture that can only be rediscovered through a patient process of excavation. And again, cinema too is included in this category. Early in the film, Shakespeare muses (as though in place of Godard) on why *he* should have been chosen for this task, and he leafs through a series of portraits of other filmmakers who may have been adequate for the role. Significantly, with the exception of one (Jacques Rivette), all of these directors are dead or retired: Marcel Pagnol, François Truffaut, Georges Franju, Robert Bresson, Pier Paolo Pasolini, Fritz Lang, Josef von Sternberg, Jacques Tati, Jean Cocteau. In a similar way, Godard includes in his film, references to other great (and dead) directors who have adapted Shakespeare to the screen: we see an image of Orson Welles in *The Merchant of Venice* (1969) and hear an excerpt from the soundtrack of Grigori Kozintsev's Russian-language version of *King Lear* (1969).

Godard himself appears in *King Lear* as Professor Pluggy, an expert in 'visual signification' whom Shakespeare comes to question as part of his research. Pluggy, who appears with dreadlocks made of electrical cables and connector leads, is a deliberately self-mocking caricature of Godard. The character plays up to an image generated by the media of Godard as an eccentric hermit working away on impenetrable projects in his remote Swiss grotto. As Shakespeare V remarks, no one has seen Professor Pluggy for twenty years because he 'hates the outdoors and natural light' (this 'twenty years', we might note, is roughly equivalent to the time since Godard first abandoned mainstream film production after *Week-end*). Pluggy, when finally encountered, delivers cryptic, supposedly profound pronouncements on visual culture in a peculiar English accent which emerges out of the corner of his mouth making him look, as Laurent Benoît observes, a little like Popeye (Benoît 1987). When Shakespeare V asks searching questions – 'Just what are you aiming at, Professor?' – Pluggy responds with a loud fart, at which his assistant Virginia (Julie Delpy) announces, in hesitant English, 'When the professor farts, the mountains are trembling'.

All this is as ridiculous as it sounds, although what is perhaps most intriguing about Godard's self-portrait in *King Lear* is the way it spreads outward from Professor Pluggy to infect other figures in the film. There is a sense that Godard is designating himself with Lear's repeated line (read in voiceover) 'You must bear with me, I am old and foolish'. We have already seen how Shakespeare V's mission to recover lost art seems to mirror Godard's preoccupations in this period. Other critics have suggested that Godard's refusal to provide Cannon with the kind of film they want reflects Cordelia's refusal to tell her father what he wants to hear (Walworth 2002: 69–70, we will return to this point below), or that Pluggy/Godard resembles 'a Gloucester-like seer', a character from the play who is otherwise absent from the film (Robinson 1988: 21). But if all this suggests that *King Lear* is merely an excuse for Godard to make a film about himself, it nonetheless constitutes, in places, an intriguing study of Shakespeare's play (and 'A Study' is one of the film's many subtitles). Although the film's obsessive focus on Cordelia's silence, at the expense of the rest of the play's drama, may at first appear odd, Alan Walworth points out that Godard has correctly identified this scene as 'the initial hysterical impasse that precipitates the drama's ensuing crisis' (Walworth 2002: 62). Meanwhile, Jonathan Rosenbaum is right to praise Burgess Meredith's 'magnificent line readings' of Shakespeare's text (Rosenbaum 1995: 187): Meredith's extraordinary gravelly voice and his sensitivity to textual nuance must make his readings of speeches from the end of the play among the most successful elements of any adaptation of Shakespeare to the screen (the way Godard uses Meredith here is not dissimilar to Peter Greenaway's use of John Gielgud in *Prospero's Books* (1991)).

The mixture of deep seriousness and broad knockabout comedy that characterises *King Lear* and other films of this period can be seen in the sequence where Pluggy demonstrates the principle of montage to Shakespeare V. An apocalyptic tone is generated here, as elsewhere in the film, around a crisis of light, the sudden shift from blinding light to darkness. The sequence opens with a close-up of a photocopier, its bright light pulsing rhythmically on and off as the copier moves back and forth. Subsequently, we see an arrangement of toy dinosaurs unevenly lit by a rapidly shifting light bulb while, on the soundtrack, we hear a terrible animal shrieking whose provenance is difficult to determine: bird, insect, toad, monkey? When Shakespeare asks what all this means, he is told gravely 'The Last Judgement', while the voice of Virginia, off and apropos of nothing, cries 'Snakes!'. Also in this sequence we see an image of a lachrymose angel taken from Giotto's *Mourning of Christ* (*c.* 1305) and another painting illuminated by the naked flame of a cigarette lighter, an effect which tends to evoke the furthest origins of art in primitive cave paintings (more on this below).

When Shakespeare asks Pluggy what an image is, the Professor recites a poem by Pierre Reverdy. This poem, which is entitled 'L'Image' and was quoted by André Breton in his first surrealist manifesto, is one of the most frequently recurring citations in late Godard where it almost always appears as a demonstration and defence of the principles of montage. Godard's favourite line is as follows: 'Une image n'est pas forte parce qu'elle est brutale ou fantastique – mais parce que l'association des idées est lointaine et juste'.[6] Pluggy illustrates his reading by juxtaposing images on twin video screens in his editing studio. Two images of the famous shot from the beginning of Buñuel and Dalí's *Un chien andalou* (1928), in which an eyeball is sliced in close-up by a straight razor, are rapidly intercut with two reproductions of Fuseli's *Lady Macbeth Sleepwalking* (1784). These are then intercut with an image of Disney's Goofy. It is, frankly, a little difficult to grasp just what the 'association of ideas' is intended to be here. I would suggest that the idea uniting these heterogeneous images is, in fact, the violence of the image, although this violence is located elsewhere, as Reverdy's poem suggests, than in the brutality of the act represented. It is, on the one hand, the violence of the *cut*, literalized by Buñuel and Dalí, the irreducible ocular aggression by which cinema moves the spectator from one image to the next. But it is also the violence with which the image *replaces life*. Such would seem to be the significance of Fuseli's painting for Godard: Lady Macbeth wanders the halls of her castle, haunted by her crime, just as the image is haunted by the real which it must, in a sense, *put to death* in order to represent it (this argument is central to *Histoire(s) du cinéma*). The violence of cartoons would then be simply another displacement of this fundamental violence operated by the image.

But if all this implies a heavily theoretical and ultimately a moral discourse on the image, its seriousness is undone by Godard's absurd performance as Pluggy, the ridiculous accent and childish giggles with which he divulges such pearls of wisdom as 'Not tell: show' and 'Never know, always see'. Besides, the vision of the end of the world in this sequence, although rendered genuinely troubling by the din on the soundtrack, is really quite staggering in its ineptitude; later shots leave the spectator in no doubt as to the status of this apocalypse: it consists of a handful of cheap plastic dinosaurs arranged in a shoe box over which Godard waves a bare light bulb! Although we may congratulate the

6 'An image is not strong because it is brutal, or fantastic, but because the association of ideas is distant and true.'

director on his ingenuity at coming up with an image of Armageddon based on such frugal means, we are likely to find some difficulty in taking it seriously.

Casino capitalism: Godard and postmodernism

There has been some debate as to whether Godard should be labelled a postmodernist. David Sterritt, for instance, has called *King Lear* 'a postmodern pastiche', noting that it is 'extraordinarily self-reflexive even by Godard's high standard' (Sterritt 1999: 222). Armond White, meanwhile, suggests that Godard effected 'a transition from Sixties modernism to an even more controversial postmodernism in the Eighties. Whereas before he had made movies about movies, now he made movies and videos about that hyper-selfconsciousness itself' (White 1996: 26). Other critics have rejected the idea: Jacques Aumont insists that 'Il n'y a pas moins postmoderne que Godard',[7] arguing that his aesthetic project remains faithful to the ideals of modernism (Aumont 1999: 143). Of course, if this debate is to have any sense, we must first agree on what we understand by the term 'postmodern', a question that has itself become almost intractable. Jean-François Lyotard famously defined postmodernism as 'la crise des récits' ('the crisis of narrative'), a new incredulity with regard to the grand meta-narratives inherited from the Enlightenment: the perfectibility of humanity, the emancipation of the worker, the belief in progress, and so on (Lyotard 1979: 7). Dick Hebdige has summarised this position as follows: 'Postmodernity is modernity without the hopes and dreams which made it bearable' (in Rose 1991: 4). Some commentators have interpreted this situation as marking an end to history, or at least to ideological struggle: the triumphant recognition of liberal democracy as the best possible political system. Postmodernism is thus often associated, by commentators on the left, with an attitude of resignation or even *surrender* with regard to political questions (Eagleton 1996). We are entitled to ask whether this is the case with Godard, who was once so active in radical politics. Robert Stam, for instance, writing about *Nouvelle Vague*, argues that such politics have been 'bracketed' in Godard's late work, where the only radicalism is of an aesthetic nature (Stam 1991: 63) (we will address this question in greater detail in the following chapter). We have already noted, in the late-1980s films, a recurrent sense of *ending* (of art, of history, perhaps of politics) which might be characterised as typically

7 'No one is less postmodern than Godard.'

'postmodern'. But, as we saw with regard to *King Lear*, this eschatology frequently fails to convince: it is as though Godard adopts the form of an apocalyptic discourse without really believing, or making us believe, in its content, in its reality.

But this tendency to borrow *forms* without appropriating their meaning or ascribing to their morality is itself a characteristic of postmodernism. Fredric Jameson suggests that postmodernism differs from modernism in 'the emergence of a new kind of flatness or depthlessness, a new kind of superficiality in the most literal sense' (Jameson 1991: 9). Jameson associates this flatness with a loss of the unique or individual style in the artistic sphere, to be replaced by *pastiche*, a form of mimicry which has neither the satiric impulse of parody nor its belief in an original or normal language (that is to say, a language existing outside of that of the pastiche). With the collapse of style, the producers of culture thus have to turn to the past, to 'the imaginary museum of a now global culture', but this is not the past as 'referent', simply as a plurality of texts (Jameson 1991: 17–18).

We have already begun to see how Godard's films are made up of precisely such a 'plurality of texts'. Indeed, they always have been, ever since *À bout de souffle*. But Godard's quotation attains a new degree of intensity in the late 1980s. Godard claimed that not a single word of dialogue in *Détective* came from him (Godard 1998b: 78) and he made the same remark about *Nouvelle Vague* (200). His name does not appear in the credits to the latter film since, he argues, 'Ce n'est pas moi qui ai fait le film. Je n'en suis que l'organisateur conscient'[8] (201). But how are we to *read* the quotations in Godard's films? When he quotes a sentence from a novel or a work of philosophy, is he implicitly evoking the *whole* work, together with the author's cultural context and system of thought, as has been suggested by Antoine de Baecque (1990: 65)? Or is he merely isolating a single thought, image, or observation that pleases him or that fits into the associative schema of his film? Is he even quoting texts merely on the grounds of their agreeable aesthetic quality when read aloud? The truth is undoubtedly that Godard takes all of these approaches to quotation, and some of the texts in his films can be seen as more significant than others. Nonetheless, it is tempting to take the example of *Lord Jim* in *Détective* as representative of Godard's approach to intertextuality. In the film, Jim explains that he was given a copy of Conrad's novel thirty years ago with the advice that he could always open it at random to find inspiration in times of trouble. But he has never read a word of the text, because someone always interrupts him before he gets

8 'I didn't make the film. I'm only its conscious organiser.'

a chance to do so. There is, I would suggest, a further element of self-portraiture here from Godard, since he confesses that he has not actually read all the books he refers to, but only skimmed or dipped into them (Godard 1998b: 140). He also mentions a novel – Faulkner's *Absalom! Absalom!* – that he has been returning to for thirty years but has never managed to finish (128).

In addition to *Lord Jim, Détective* quotes from Shakespeare's *The Tempest.* One of the hotel detectives (Laurent Terzieff) is referred to as Uncle Prospero, and they are assisted in their machinations by a young woman named Arielle (Aurèle Doazan). The large pile of books in their room would also seem to be a nod to *The Tempest.* But the film also contains numerous references to Godard's own work: the male characters' repeated complaints that they are tired recall Michel Poiccard; the way all the 'A's of a title card appear before the other letters was used in *Pierrot le fou*; a telephone conversation in which Nathalie Baye says nothing but 'Oui' over and over again is something we have already seen in *Sauve qui peut (la vie)*; meanwhile, the solution to the murder, which involves misreading a hotel room number upside down from the ledger, is borrowed from *La Chinoise.*

Nouvelle Vague is very loosely based on Raymond Chandler's detective novel *The Long Goodbye*, although little is retained from the original aside from the question of a faked death, and the character of a blonde murderess. Alain Delon's character Roger/Richard Lennox combines elements of the novel's Terry Lennox and Roger Wade while Eileen Wade becomes Elena Torlato-Favrini, her surname taken from Joseph L. Mankiewicz's *Barefoot Contessa* (1954). In addition, *Nouvelle Vague* cites everyone and everything from the Sistine Chapel ceiling to *Les Dames du bois de Boulogne* (1945), from Friedrich Schiller to Dorothy Parker and Walter Brennan's refrain from *To Have and Have Not* (1945), 'Was you ever bit by a dead bee?'. As critics have noted, a major star such as Alain Delon merely becomes, in Godard's hands, another text to be quoted, 'a fragment of film history' alongside fragments of writing and music (Darke 1997: 35). As Ginette Vincendeau notes, 'His character's trajectory seems more motivated by references to Delon the star than by events in the (obscure) plot', with the pivotal drowning sequence(s) recalling similar watery deaths from *Plein soleil* (1960) and *La Piscine* (1969) (Vincendeau 2000: 181).

But does Godard have a way of treating these diverse texts that makes them, in a sense, his own, so that, rather than the random detritus of hundreds of years of civilisation, they come together to form a coherent work of art? Alain Bergala seems to suggest as much when he says that all of the texts quoted in *Soigne ta droite* 'finissent étrangement par former une seule voix, un discours tout à fait cohérent, une seule conscience'[9] (in Godard 1998b: 120). If this is the case, it is doubtless largely attributable to Godard's remarkable work with actors' voices, his sensitivity to the human voice, both in its materiality and its expressivity. We noted above Burgess Meredith's terrific readings of Shakespeare; similarly impressive are François Périer's voiceover readings of Hermann Broch in *Soigne ta droite* and the readings in *Nouvelle Vague* by Roland Amstutz, who plays the gardener, and Jacques Dacqmine (the CEO). Roland Amstutz, in interview, said that, on seeing *Nouvelle Vague*, he found his voice different to how it sounds in other films, 'plus grave, plus profonde, plus ancrée dans la terre'[10] (Amstutz 1990: 84), and he suggests that this earthiness to his voice cannot be divorced from the role as *gardener*. He tells how he worked on his voice with Godard, who gave clear instructions as to how to stand, 'bien planté sur le sol'[11] (85). Amstutz concludes: 'Avec Godard, on ne peut pas jouer comme on joue ailleurs. C'est autre chose ... C'est une autre façon de dire le texte, de le faire sien, d'en faire sa chose personnelle, de s'y impliquer'[12] (86). And indeed, there are certain quotations in late Godard which, by virtue of their repetition, and sometimes of their association with particular voices, become detached from their original source and seem to take on their own meaning, their own currency, their own *life* within the network of Godard's films: one thinks, for instance, of certain passages from Broch, of the Reverdy poem, or of the line from Saint Paul, 'L'image viendra au temps de la résurrection'.[13]

There is, then, a question of property at stake in Godard's practice of quotation. Godard takes a rather cavalier approach to intellectual property and certainly does not clear the copyright of all the works he quotes. (In 2004, Godard was taken to court by the publishing house Éditions du Seuil for quoting, in *King Lear*, from a book by Viviane Forrester without obtaining permission. The court ruled that *King Lear* could no longer be distributed unless an acknowledgement was made in the credits to Mme Forrester.) But Godard takes a similar attitude towards the quotation of his own work. He claims that, when asked by others for permission to quote his work, he replies 'Non seulement vous

9 'strangely end up forming a single voice, an altogether coherent discourse, a single consciousness'.

10 'deeper, more serious, more grounded'.

11 'planted solidly on the ground'.

12 'With Godard, you can't act the same way you would elsewhere. It's altogether different ... It's a different way of pronouncing the text, of making it one's own, one's personal possession, of implicating oneself within it.'

13 'The image will come at the time of the resurrection.'

avez le droit mais vous avez le devoir de le faire',[14] but requests that only his work and not his name be used; if the other party insists on using his name, he asks for the money he is owed to be paid to Amnesty International (Godard 1998b: 373–4). But this does not necessarily mean that art belongs to no one and can be appropriated at will. Marc Robinson has suggested that *King Lear* is, in a way, about this question of artistic property, just as Shakespeare's play is about the ownership and inheritance of Lear's kingdom. Godard does not attempt a 'faithful' adaptation of Shakespeare's play, because to do so would simply be to appropriate someone else's work. Instead, 'Godard's treatment argues for a new ethics of adaptation, one based on distance'. Shakespeare's *Lear* in a way accompanies Godard's, 'hovering alongside the film, untouched and silent', but its identity or authority is never usurped by Godard's work which ploughs its own, singular furrow. 'Like Cordelia, Godard does not want to respond to Shakespeare with the expected formula, repeating what one already knows' (Robinson 1988: 25).

The generalised use of quotation in Godard's late work might also illuminate his approach to genre. *Détective* partakes of perhaps the most popular genre in French cinema of the 1980s, the police thriller or *polar*. Phil Powrie, following Susan Hayward, suggests that, by this stage of its development, the French thriller had become 'ultra-codified', using generic cues as a kind of shorthand to establish character and narrative (Powrie 1997: 77). However, compared to a film like *La Balance* (1982), with its engrossing plot, its properly developed characters and its carefully nurtured sense of place, it is *Détective* that comes across as 'ultra-codified'. The scene in which Uncle Prospero grabs handfuls of *Série noire* thrillers and tosses them over his shoulder might be taken as an image of the film's conception: it is as though Godard threw a bunch of generic conventions in the air and filmed them where they landed (a strategy that actually recalls the 'action sculpture' in Godard's short *Montparnasse-Levallois* (1965), itself described as 'action-cinema'). The plot sees two former hotel detectives, Prospero and Isidore (Jean-Pierre Léaud), investigating the murder of a 'Prince' (this Prince is not the same as the mafioso known as the Prince, a confusion that Godard is pleased to encourage (Godard 1998b: 80)). Meanwhile, the boxing promoter Jim owes money both to Émile and Françoise and to the mafia, and there are whispers of match-fixing. The film contains a glorious pastiche of the gangster genre in a scene where Émile and Françoise receive a breakfast tray containing a dead white mouse, a coffee pot full of blood and a novel by the Sicilian author Leonardo Sciascia. There is also a flagrant

14 'You not only have the right, you have the duty to do so.'

red herring when Émile picks up a gun and Françoise cries, 'Arrête, tu ne vas tuer personne du tout! Sauf moi, peut-être, à la fin ... '[15] There are indeed murders at the end of the film, but neither Émile nor Françoise are involved.

An analysis of the scene in which Jim, Émile and Françoise meet in the hotel restaurant will demonstrate how Godard is able to employ generic conventions with confidence and affection, while also subverting those codes with other elements of mise en scène and performance. The scene begins with Jim sitting at a table in the restaurant, where he is joined first by Émile and then by Françoise. The scene is shot in a very classical, unobtrusive manner, mainly in medium close-ups with a pattern of shot/reverse-shot cuts from person to person, with one character frequently filmed over the shoulder of another. The sequence also follows a fairly classical development, beginning with an exchange between Jim and Émile in which these apparent adversaries swap nostalgic reminiscences. Jim tells of how he left home, wanting to see the world, and caught the train to Paris from Dijon: 'Il arrivait de Vienne ou Trieste à cette époque?'[16] 'Istanbul', remembers Émile. They recall the way a man used to walk along the train tapping the axles and we hear a hollow chiming on the soundtrack which we assume to be caused by Émile banging his knife against something on the table. Jim remembers too the man who walked through the train crying '*Aïlassé!*', which he subsequently identified as 'Chocolat glacé' (chocolate ice-cream). But Émile looks distracted and is rising to go and look for Françoise when Jim roughly grabs him by the collar and pulls him back into his seat. 'Faut pas se foutre de moi, hein?',[17] Émile warns the other man. This sudden eruption of violence into what had been a friendly exchange is typical of the way the thriller generates tension.

When Françoise arrives, the meeting gets down to business. As Émile remarks upon his wife's new dress, Jim announces that he has begun to pay the couple back the money he owes them. But Émile is not satisfied, protesting that he has barely begun to cover the interest on the interest on the interest on the interest. Meanwhile, Isidore, disguised as a waiter, comes to light the candle at their table. In a beautifully economical shot, Godard uses this prop to demonstrate the shifting power relations between the trio. In close-up, we see Françoise run her finger around the rim of the candle holder. When Émile approaches his own hand, Françoise withdraws hers and, when her husband places his hand over the candle, he burns himself and quickly pulls away. Jim's

15 'Stop it, you're not going to kill any one! Apart from me, maybe, in the end ... '
16 'At the time, it used to come all the way from Vienna or Trieste.'
17 'Don't bug me', offer the subtitles

hand now enters the frame and confidently cups the candle holder, while Françoise's finger discreetly caresses his hand. With this shot, the balance of power has shifted from Françoise and Émile to Françoise and Jim. Émile now notices the staff acting strangely and casting sideways glances in their direction. Jim mutters about 'des gens qu'il vaut mieux ne pas connaître'[18] and someone mentions the mafia. A cutaway shows Isidore talking to the girlfriend (Emmanuelle Seigner) of Tiger Jones, the boxer managed by Jim, implying some as-yet undisclosed conspiracy. Dialogue is generic but non-specific, Jim saying: 'Il y a des échéances que j'ai pas pu rembourser à la date précise ... À côté, les banques, c'est des anges'.[19] As Jim says that his deadline to pay off the mob is tomorrow, Émile taps his knife again to produce a hollow ring and announces gravely, 'Chocolat glacé', thus picking up the motif from earlier and giving a neat symmetry to the scene.

But, just as we saw in *King Lear*, this apparently tense and sober scene is undermined by comic elements, particularly associated with the performance of Jean-Pierre Léaud. It is here, at the beginning of the scene, that Jim explains how he has never been able to read *Lord Jim* since he is always interrupted, and, as though to prove the point, Isidore hurries across the room and sticks his head in between the two men to ask urgently, 'Un petit apéritif?'. The suspicion in which Isidore holds the other characters leads to an absurdly exaggerated performance of his role as waiter, as when he greets Françoise with another suggestively sardonic 'Un petit apéritif, *Madame*?'. The other waiters appear to be in on the secret since they too cast ostentatious glances over their shoulder at the trio, and, ignoring their queries about the *plat du jour*, aggressively yank the menus away from them ('Bon ben, trois sandwiches, alors!' concludes Jim). At one point, in the finest tradition of burlesque comedy, Isidore even collides with another waiter coming through the kitchen door, almost causing him to drop a pile of plates. In addition to all this tomfoolery, Émile's final 'chocolat glacé', although it makes structural sense within the scene, is, on reflection, a bizarre and meaningless thing to say: is Jim really supposed to feel threatened by this evocation of chocolate ice-cream?

In many ways, then, Godard's use of quotation in his late-1980s films is undeniably postmodern. But is this definition of postmodernism – as an aesthetic practice that plunders the past in its search for forms – too limited, or is it, on the contrary, too general? If we confine the discussion of postmodernism to questions of citation and pastiche, then

18 'people you're better off not knowing'.
19 'There are certain debts I couldn't pay off in time ... Next to them, the banks look like angels.'

the problem of Godard's relation to postmodernism becomes frankly uninteresting. As Terry Eagleton has suggested, if postmodernism becomes a catch-all term to define broad cultural phenomena, covering 'everything from punk rock to the death of metanarrative, fanzines to Foucault', then the question of whether one can be 'for' or 'against' it loses all sense (Eagleton 1996: 21–2). The first and most rigorous theorists of postmodernism gave the term a much more specific political–economic context. Fredric Jameson, for instance, is categorical: he argues that to talk about postmodern culture is to talk about multinational capitalism, to take a position on that culture is to adopt a political stance with regard to late capitalism (Jameson 1991: 3). This is because aesthetic production has today become thoroughly integrated into the system of commodity production, since, in the drive to produce fresh and novel commodities, aesthetic innovation has been assigned 'an increasingly essential structural function and position' within the world system of late capitalism (Jameson 1991: 4–5). David Harvey suggests that the mobilisation of fashion into mass markets, accelerating the pace of consumption and reducing the 'lifetime' of goods and services, may be responsible for the rapid capitalist penetration of so many sectors of cultural production since the 1960s (Harvey 1990: 285). The resulting culture of generalised disposability and instant obsolescence is perhaps also responsible for the diversification of values under postmodernism (Harvey 1990: 286). This gives rise to two, apparently contradictory, tendencies in the culture of management: on the one hand, a drive towards short-term profit-making and, on the other, 'the production of volatility', the 'manipulation of taste and opinion' through branding and marketing (Harvey 1990: 286–7). Adorno and Horkheimer, whose critique of the culture industry was first published in 1944 but seems more relevant than ever in the context of postmodernism, argue that this shaping of cultural opinion entails a loss of spontaneity: 'total planning takes precedence over the individual impulse, predetermining this impulse in turn, reducing it to the level of illusion' (Adorno 2001: 123). Cultural products of differing type and quality are produced for all sectors of society 'so that none may escape' (Adorno and Horkheimer 1997 [1944]: 123). The industry seeks to identify tastes and opinions that differ from the norm, the better to classify and contain them, and it incorporates deviation and chance into its planning to such an extent that 'chance and planning become one and the same thing' (Adorno and Horkheimer 1997 [1944]: 146). Jean-François Lyotard, too, described how the system of postmodern capitalism must work to bring the desires of individuals into line with its own in order to optimise its performativity (Lyotard 1979: 99–100).

As such, suggests Lyotard, the mode of operation of the system can best be described as 'terrorist' (103).

Remarks made by Godard in interview frequently reveal the extent of his sympathy with critics of postmodernism such as those cited above. Godard is endlessly critical of the culture industry. He repeatedly distinguishes between art and culture, arguing that the art of a symphony by Beethoven becomes culture when it is conducted by Herbert von Karajan or when it is distributed on CD by Sony, although it may become art once again in the ear of the listener (Godard 1998b: 251). This distinction between art and culture has become deeply unfashionable in the wake of cultural studies, with its unprecedented respect for popular culture and the very real pleasures it provides for audiences. But Adorno and Horkheimer refuse to be swayed by such arguments: they insist that 'The attitude of the public, which ostensibly and actually favours the system of the culture industry, is a part of the system and not an excuse for it' (Adorno and Horkheimer 1997 [1944]: 122). The ease with which criticism of the culture industry can be derided as ideology is merely a further demonstration of the power and terror that the industry wields (148). Meanwhile, pleasure all too often appears as an alternative to thought, it insists we 'forget suffering even where it is shown' and thereby becomes a kind of 'helplessness' (144). As Adorno has remarked, one falls too easily into the trap of accepting cultural categories 'as mere actualities', as a reflection of consumer desire rather than as the result of a complex historical and economic development (Adorno 2001: 130). Jameson suggests that there is a tendency to think of the postmodern capitalist economy as inconceivably, unmanageably large and complex, and hence, perhaps, beyond effective criticism, beyond all realistic possibility of change (Jameson 1991: 37). He goes on to argue that any cultural criticism or political art under postmodernism must make its goal the 'mapping' of this unimaginable social and economic space, to enable us 'to grasp our positioning as individual and collective subjects and regain a capacity to act and struggle which is at present neutralised by our spatial as well as our social confusion' (54).

It is my contention that Godard's films of the late 1980s and 1990s consistently seek to provide a critical representation of the system of multinational capitalism and the workings of the culture industry. Godard's political discourse in these films may not be so forthright and didactic as it was in the late 1960s and early 1970s, nor is it couched in the explicit rhetoric of socialism, but the director's increasingly frequent turn toward the past, which has been condemned in some quarters as an impotent nostalgia, is, I will argue, inseparable from a continued critique of the political and economic realities of the present. As a filmmaker who runs his own production company, Godard is nonetheless forced, at least to some extent, to work within the cultural marketplace in order to survive. And indeed, as Laurent Creton has remarked (2001: 320), Godard seems rather proud of the continued survival of his filmic enterprise, often preferring to discuss his role as producer, in interviews, rather than comment on the meaning of his art. The work of the late 1980s is dominated by a logic of the 'commande': commissions that Godard is obliged to accept in order to fund more personal projects. *Détective,* for instance, was a commission undertaken in order to finance the completion of *Je vous salue Marie. King Lear,* as we have seen, was the result of a deal struck with Cannon Films. In addition, during this period, Godard accepted commissions for commercial films from businesses outside the film industry: *Puissance de la parole* (1988) was made for France Télécom and *Le Rapport Darty* (1989) was intended to constitute a film of electronics retailer Darty's annual report (I have analysed elsewhere (Morrey 2005) how Godard deflects the commission in order to produce an eccentric interrogation of the theoretical bases of the capitalist economy).

But, if Godard is obliged to seek finance from the mainstream film industry and elsewhere, he is always attentive to the *waste* that occurs within the industry. When offered one million francs by clothing designers François and Marithé Girbaud to make a series of television commercials for their new jeans, Godard accepted the commission but told them that one million was far too much! *Jean-Luc Godard par Jean-Luc Godard* contains a series of letters written during the filming of *Détective* 'et non envoyées à leurs destinataires'[20] (Godard 1998b: 71–6). Two of these letters are to Godard's producers, in which he discusses the tendency of French films to go over budget. To director of production Christine Gozlan, Godard remarks that the filmmakers' proclivity for cutting corners in the hope of making a profit, but then going over budget anyway, can be compared to the way the countries of the North treat those of the South (71–2). To producer Alain Sarde, he suggests that the 30–40 per cent shortfall of the typical French production might be usefully juxtaposed to the corresponding over-production in European agriculture (73). These remarks may not stand up to rigorous economic scrutiny, but they testify to Godard's desire to see the economy of film finance within the wider context of global trade under multinational capitalism. Godard is always keen that the money financing a film should be *visible* (as was already made clear in *Le Mépris* and

20 'and never sent to their recipients'.

Tout va bien). This does not imply the need for glamour or expensive special effects as in Hollywood's prestige productions, indeed such deliberate display of capital is quite obscene: Adorno and Horkheimer are unanswerable when they write: 'The idea of "fully exploiting" available technical resources and the facilities for aesthetic mass consumption is part of the economic system which refuses to exploit resources to abolish hunger' (Adorno and Horkheimer 1997 [1944]: 139). Rather, Godard seeks to make visible the process of the commission itself, the process whereby a product is put together in exchange for money. *Soigne ta droite*, for instance, condenses this process to make it the narrative of the film: the Idiot (Godard) must conceive, produce and deliver a film for exhibition that very evening or, in other words, by the end of the film. The film thus takes the form of a commission that is somehow devoid of content (the film projected at the end of *Soigne ta droite* is, naturally, invisible), and thereby takes a satirical swipe at a purely market-driven industry.

Détective similarly lays bare the commission behind its existence: the film is 'about' the reunion of a group of French stars (who are clearly labelled as such: 'Johnny Hallyday: star' announce the titles) in a location (the hotel). Again, content (the generic narrative) appears as something of an afterthought. Godard stated: 'C'est un film complètement non préparé: des gens se rencontrent, n'ont rien à voir ensemble ni à faire'[21] (Godard 1998b: 79) and offered the following analogy: it is as though a group of actors were stranded on their way to the Cannes film festival and had to put on a production in order to pay for the last leg of the journey: 'C'est ce qui est arrivé' ('That's what happened') (79). The financial situation of the film is then built into the plot which, as we have seen, revolves around questions of debts to be repayed. Jim's surname, pointedly enough, is Fox-Warner, while the mafia hitman is known as 'le Comptable' ('the Accountant'). The culture industry, here, appears in the image of rigged boxing matches: as Tiger Jim's girlfriend tells him, 'Les matches sont truqués, c'est perdu d'avance'.[22] In a letter to Alain Cuny, Godard explains that this story of murder and corruption is to be related to 'les sanglants chiffres des entrées'[23] (Godard 1998b: 71).

The evocation of the mafia as a metaphor for the culture and entertainment industry figures prominently in *King Lear*. To begin with, the opening title places the film under the sign of the 'Cannon Group – Bahamas', a detail that tends to evoke dubious offshore investments,

21 'It's a completely unprepared film, a meeting of people who have nothing to do with each other.'
22 'The matches are fixed, you've already lost.'
23 'the bloody figures of the box office'.

and the subsequent phone call from Menahem Golan suggests the heavy-handed presence of the producer come to demand payment. As Iannis Katsahnias has noted, Godard's 'deal' with Cannon, supposedly signed on the back of a napkin, is itself like something out of a B-movie, 'le genre de contrat qu'on risque de payer très cher s'il n'est pas rempli'[24] (Katsahnias 1987: 19). In his only surviving scene in the film, Norman Mailer declares that he thinks 'the mafia is the only way to do *King Lear*' and renames the characters Don Learo, Don Gloucestro, and so on. Burgess Meredith then incarnates Don Learo and reminisces about his days with the gangsters Bugsy Siegel and Meyer Lansky. In particular, Learo dictates to Cordelia a text about how the Las Vegas casinos established by the mob have now been bought up by major entertainment conglomerates like M-G-M. 'Siegel's Flamingo is now the Las Vegas Hilton,' says Learo, 'All of America is now embracing our vision'. Coincidentally, David Harvey uses the terms 'casino capitalism' and the 'casino economy' to refer to the 'financial speculation and fictitious capital formation (much of it unbacked by any growth in real production)' of postmodern capitalism (Harvey 1990: 332). Jonathan Rosenbaum argues that the wilfully unprepossessing form of *King Lear* is motivated by hatred and disgust at this economy and that what fascinates Godard in Cordelia's silence is precisely 'the refusal to become a commodity, to function as an object'. The film, too, aspires to be 'ungraspable, intractable, uncomsumable', and, 'like Lear, we all wind up disinheriting it, much preferring the comfortable lies of a Goneril or a Regan' (Rosenbaum 1995: 189). Alan Walworth suggests that Godard's 'failure' to satisfy his contractual obligations is, in a way, a success, since 'he reaffirms his rebellious avant-garde status and thus gives the producers precisely the uncompromising "prestige" picture they at least in part desired' (Walworth 2002: 70). But this argument is even less convincing with regard to *King Lear* than it is with regard to *Week-end* (see Chapter 4): the hasty and embarrassed way in which Cannon withdrew the film from distribution speaks for itself (in the same way, Godard's unexpected upping of the stakes in *Le Rapport Darty* was not considered a witty postmodern wheeze by the company, but branded 'incomprehensible' and shelved indefinitely).

Nouvelle Vague is set among the world of precisely that 'financial speculation and fictitious capital formation' of which David Harvey speaks. Again, Godard quotes the *forms* of high finance – the luxury cars, references to *Business Week*, popular managerial slogans (see Creton 2001: 317), exchange rates (Elena is heard saying into her phone: 'You

24 'the kind of contract that will cost you very dearly if it is not fulfilled'.

go through Singapore, and *then* Bogotá, to end in Geneva, and then your dollar's worth ... ') – precisely in order to suggest that they are without substance. Silverman and Farocki make much of the fact that the film's characters belong to 'the new, working rich' (1998: 200), but what exactly is this work? We rarely see them do anything except chatter and talk into the telephone, and it is certainly not clear where their money comes from, nor what it is invested into. At one point, they take a tour of a factory, but nobody mentions what the factory is producing. Elsewhere, a painting (Goya's *Nude Maja* (1800)) is exchanged, but is the art market their business or just a hobby? In addition, the film's obsession with memory tends to consign all of this activity to the past. At one point, a voiceover read by the CEO (Jacques Dacqmine) muses:

> Bientôt, certaines formes de la vie sociale, des habitudes, des principes, des sentiments invétérés auront disparus. On peut tenir pour défunte la société où nous avons vécu. Si on l'évoque dans les siècles futurs, elle apparaîtra comme un instant charmant de l'histoire des hommes. On dira, 'C'était le temps où il y avait encore des riches et des pauvres, des forteresses à prendre, des degrés à gravir, des choses désirables assez bien défendues pour conserver leur attrait ... Le hasard était de la partie'.[25]

As Robert Stam comments, this depiction forces us to 'regard the alienated present from the imagined perspective of a distant future, just society ... Present power arrangements and hierarchies, it is suggested, are not necessarily permanent' (Stam 1991: 66).

Soigne ta droite includes another scene in which Godard makes a serious point by way of a comical situation. In the film, the comic actor Jacques Villeret, referred to throughout as 'l'Individu' ('the Individual'), incarnates a variety of different figures. In the scene in question he appears as a gardener at work by the side of a country road. A convertible Mercedes roadster pulls up as the driver asks the way to Paris and his passenger (Jane Birkin) recognises the gardener as 'la Fourmi' ('the Ant'). Fourmi greets the woman as 'la Cigale' ('the Cicada'). When Cigale asks Fourmi how he's doing, he replies 'Je *travaille*, je *travaille*, comme d'habitude'[26] and proceeds to wash their car with a watering can. Cigale, meanwhile, is travelling with her fiancé, heir to the fortunes

25 'Before long, certain forms of social life, customs, principles, deep-seated feelings will have disappeared. We can consider the society we have lived in to be over. When people talk about it in centuries to come, it will appear as a charming moment in human history. They'll say, "It was a time when there were still rich and poor people, still castles to attack and ladders to climb, when objects of desire were well enough guarded to maintain their appeal ... Chance was in the running".'

26 'I'm *working*, I'm *working* as usual.'

of TWA and Hennessy Cognac. They are on their way to get married in New York, but are stopping in Paris to buy clothes 'chez Dior' and to accompany the Brazilian ambassador to the opera. If they have time, they'll drop in to London to catch the Wimbledon final. Since they are going to Paris, Fourmi requests that they telephone Monsieur de la Fontaine, 'et dites-lui que je l'emmerde!'.[27] The characters in this sequence are borrowed from the first of Jean de la Fontaine's *Fables*, 'La Cigale et la Fourmi'. In this moral tale, the cicada, having spent all summer singing, has nothing to eat come the autumn and seeks a loan from the ant. But the ant refuses, declaring 'Eh bien! dansez maintenant'.[28] (La Fontaine 1966 [1668]: 51). The original fable, then, is a critique of the notion of credit, condemning instant gratification and the deferral of payment in favour of the dignity of labour with its material rewards. What Godard's scene seems to suggest is the way in which La Fontaine's moral has been overtaken by history, such that the cicada is now a part of the jet set, while the ant is still labouring by the side of the road. In the generalised climate of credit and deferred responsibility, suggests Godard, the dignity and integrity of honest labour has been lost.

But this is not the whole story, for this scene is sandwiched in between two others in which Godard films the rock band les Rita Mitsouko at work in the studio, scenes, in other words, where singing *is* presented as work. Here, then, Godard tries to show art as a process involving *labour* and not merely a commodity to be bought and sold. In interview, les Rita Mitsouko reveal how Godard was given a key to their studio and came and went as he pleased, such that they soon forgot that he was there (Rita Mitsouko 1995: 54). The result is an unusual sense of intimacy with these musicians in the process of composition. We watch as Catherine Ringer and Fred Chichin swap technical details, argue with each other, perfect bass lines and rehearse vocals. In addition, the band allowed Godard access to the master tapes of their album (*The No Comprendo*, 1986) and, in the finished film, he often mixes the final versions of songs together with their nascent forms on the soundtrack. In *One plus one* (1968), Godard filmed the Rolling Stones rehearsing 'Sympathy for the Devil', but refused to include the final version of the song in the film (when producer Iain Quarrier released a version of the film with the complete song, and re-titled it *Sympathy for the Devil*, Godard punched him in the face). In *Soigne ta droite*, Godard goes further in the process of fragmenting the music, frequently presenting

27 'and tell him to get stuffed'.
28 'Now you can dance!'

a vocal track or guitar track alone, while allowing the finished version of another song altogether to drift into the mix. In the scene before the Cigale and Fourmi, we witness the Rita Mitsouko laying down the guitar riff to their song 'C'est comme ça', and then adding vocals and bass to the playback. In the subsequent scene, they practise another song, 'Un soir un chien'. On the finished album, Ringer sings this track in an unusually high voice. Here, we see and hear her rehearse in her naturally much lower voice, but Godard mixes a later, higher version of the vocal over it. In places, we hear only Ringer's vocals, with the tinny sound emerging from her headphones; elsewhere we get the full playback, but the bass line and chorus to another track, 'Histoires d'A', drifts across the mix.

Despite, or because of, this fragmentation of the music, in this concerted attempt to resist commodification of the group's songs, these scenes attain moments of transcendent beauty in their filming of the alchemical process of artistic creation. Although they must have practised and perfected these tracks over numerous takes, Godard nonetheless captures moments where the music takes flight. The images of Catherine Ringer swaying and humming involuntarily to the rhythm of Chichin's guitar as it locks into a groove, or being transported by the emotion and power of her own voice are simply a joy to watch. There is a wonderful scene, too, at the end of the film, in which the band take a break in a café but Ringer, her body infected with the rhythms of the music, continues to drum her fingers restlessly on the table. Fred Chichin tells her to stop being so annoying, but Godard's camera has already caught the movement of his cigarette lighter, tapping unconsciously along to the beat.

Fire and water: resistance and redemption

Just as we saw in the previous two chapters, then, Godard, in the late 1980s is seeking forms that may resist the commodification operated by the culture industry and the capitalist economy and, just as in the earlier works, it is above all in the *body* that he finds those forms. In the example of les Rita Mitsouko above, it is in the extent to which music penetrates, infects or takes over the body (of the performer, of the listener) that it escapes the reification of the cultural commodity. After all, as Adorno reminds us, no matter how reified cultural categories become, they always refer back, in the last instance, to living subjects who ultimately retain the power to alter the function of the cultural institution (Adorno 2001: 130–1). It is, again, in the physicality of the body that Godard locates these living subjects. What is new in the work of the late 1980s is the frequency with which Godard explores these bodies through burlesque physical comedy, in figures such as Jean-Pierre Léaud's comical waiter in *Détective* or *King Lear*'s Professor Pluggy.

Nowhere is this comedy taken further than in *Soigne ta droite* which Serge Toubiana describes as being 'à la frontière entre Tati et Jerry Lewis'[29] (Toubiana 1987: 12). Jacques Villeret, who plays l'Individu, is a well-known comic actor in France and Godard films him in various unlikely positions, crawling across a table during an interview or miming a breast stroke while balanced on his belly at the top of a stepladder. In interview, Villeret compares comedy to manual labour, stressing the importance of timing and remarking that 'on n'a pas droit à l'erreur'[30] (Villeret 1987: 21). He also states that Godard's intention, at the outset, was to film *work*, although he recognises that this was achieved with greater success in the scenes of les Rita Mitsouko than in his own scenes (22). Godard too engages in physical comedy in *Soigne ta droite*, in his role as the Idiot. He states that he was keen to act in the film in order to establish a different kind of relationship with the film crew, but also 'Pour rendre mon corps moins intellectuel'[31] (Godard 1998b: 122). In the opening scenes, he mimics the experience of Wimbledon in the good old days compared with today and demonstrates his inability to get into a car. A chauffeur is waiting to drive the Idiot to the airport in a yellow Ferrari, but he walks dumbly up to the car and finds he can go no further. When the driver tells him to turn around and bend down, the Idiot takes him at his word and bunny-hops backwards in the direction of the car, only to push the door closed with his backside. Finally he opts to dive in through the open window of the door.

In his philosophical enquiry into laughter, Henri Bergson suggests that this kind of physical comedy relies on a sort of mechanical stiffness where one would expect to see the natural flexibility of the human body (Bergson 2002 [1940]: 8). In the scene with the Ferrari, it is the apparent inability of Godard's body to perform the habitual movements associated with getting into a car that creates the humour. Bergson goes on to suggest that this notion of stiffness or inflexibility (*raideur*) may be generalised to account for other comic situations: if a man falls down a hole because he is distracted, then it is because of an inflexibility in his thoughts; if a comical figure is defined by a vice (as in the comedies of classical French theatre), this constitutes an inflexibility of character (10–11). Bergson postulates that such stiffness, whether it be of mind,

29 'on the border between Tati and Jerry Lewis'.
30 'you're not allowed to make a mistake'.
31 'in order to make my body less intellectual'.

body or character, is worrying to society since it threatens the smooth operation of the social system. But, since society has experienced no material threat by this behaviour, it is not entitled to suppress it, and can only respond with the simple social gesture of laughter (15). Adorno and Horkheimer pick up on this argument and underline its rather sinister implications, what they see as the necessarily 'barbaric' character of laughter conceived in this way (Adorno and Horkheimer 1997 [1944]: 141).

This may go some way to explaining why the comedy in Godard's films rarely provokes uncontrollable belly laughs but an uneasy kind of laughter that is frequently cut short. Developing his argument, Bergson suggests that forms of social life that take on an unchanging, automatic character may become comical, as in the blind obedience to administrative rules in the face of logic (Bergson 2002 [1940]: 35) or a doctor or lawyer more concerned with the external posture of their profession than the exercise of their functions (41). Again, there is something eerie in such humour, as in Kafka where a nervous laughter is strangled by a sense of dread. Godard perhaps achieves something of this nature in his satirical portraits of the service industries that are the pride of the post-industrial West. Godard mocks these professions by citing their form – the costumes, the situations – but perverting the very notion of service. We have already discussed the restaurant scene in *Détective*, where Isidore's exaggerated politeness – 'Un petit apéritif, *Madame*?' – implies its opposite. This satire is taken further in *Soigne ta droite*, where a significant part of the film is taken up by a plane journey. Here, the uniforms and functions of the cabin crew are present and correct, but pretensions to politeness have all but disappeared. 'Allez, vite, y a pas que ça à faire!'[32] the staff grumble as they hurry the passengers aboard. When a woman claims to have lost her husband, the pilot smiles charmingly, 'On s'en fout, Comtesse' ('No one gives a toss, your Highness'). During the in-flight meal, soup is served from the captain's hat and the stewardess snaps 'Y en a pas' ('There isn't any') when a passenger requests a whisky. The pilot, meanwhile, leads the plane in a chorus of 'Je te salue, vieil océan', the same passage from Lautréamont chanted in *Week-end*, and apologises for falling asleep at the controls after forgetting to switch on the automatic pilot. At one point, he is seen reading a book entitled *Suicide, mode d'emploi* ('Suicide, a user's guide').

In Godard's exploration of the body in these films *hands* in particular are often singled out for representation. Some of Godard's most memorable compositions from this period are shots of hands. In *Soigne*

32 'Hurry up, we haven't got all day!'

ta droite, l'Individu is shown, in one scene, being accompanied on a train, presumably to prison (although it is not clear why). Godard films his hands, cuffed together and framed against the light from the train window. In *Nouvelle Vague*, Roger Lennox is almost run over by Elena. As she reaches down to help him up from the ground, Godard frames their hands in close-up against the rolling green fields in the background and the blue sky on the horizon. The image unmistakably evokes a detail from Michelangelo's fresco for the Sistine Chapel ceiling (1509–12), in which God creates Adam with a touch of his finger. This shot is the key to Godard's film. He himself has suggested that *Nouvelle Vague* can be reduced to three rhyming shots in which one person holds out their hand to another: 'Il n'y a rien d'autre' ('There is nothing else') (Godard 1998b: 203). As Kaja Silverman has written of the image of hands: 'This luminous moment stands altogether outside the psychodynamics of power. Since what is given is not owned, it cannot indebt or obligate. It is even unclear who has given, and who has received, this purest of all gifts' (Silverman and Farocki 1998: 202). Farocki adds that 'here the force of creation is human rather than divine love' (203), but I would not be so quick to dismiss the spiritual significance of the shot. It is not only the reference to Michelangelo, but also the dialogue uttered by the couple that is important here: 'Ô merveille qu'on puisse donner ce qu'on ne possède pas ... Doux miracle de nos mains vides'.[33] The line comes from Georges Bernanos's novel *Le Journal d'un curé de campagne*, by way of Robert Bresson's 1950 film version and, given the profound spiritual intent of both works, I would not deny Godard's image its own sacred ambition. In contrast to Farocki's interpretation, Godard's image would seem to suggest that human love is always already divine.

But this is not to deny that there is also a more prosaic sense to the imagery of hands in Godard's late work. Hands are associated with the dignity of manual labour, a dignity that Godard seeks to attach to the *work* of art. In the epilogue to *King Lear*, we see a close-up on Woody Allen's hands working at an editing table, bizarrely *sewing* strips of film together or splicing them with a safety pin. In voiceover, we hear a definition of montage that Godard attributes to Sacha Guitry: 'handling, in both hands, the present, the future, and the past'. The combination of a mystical manipulation of time with the simple work of the hands is typical of Godard's ambivalent characterisation of cinema. As Allen's hands continue to manipulate the celluloid, we see him remove his glasses and set them aside, a reminder of Godard's claim that he would

33 'What a marvel that we may give what we do not possess ... Oh sweet miracle of our empty hands.'

be more hindered in his work by the loss of his hands than by the loss of his eyes. In addition, hands tend to be associated, in Godard's work, with two keys texts: Jean-Paul Sartre's play *Les Mains sales* (1948) and Denis de Rougemont's polemic *Penser avec les mains* (1936), both of which use the central image of hands as a metaphor for the importance of taking historical responsibility for one's thought and action.

Hands are also frequently associated, in these films, with fire and water. In *Détective*, a close-up shows Julie Delpy and Stéphane Ferrara washing their hands together under a tap and we have already noted the way characters play with a candle in the restaurant. People often play with lighters in these films, Françoise using one to illuminate Jim's naked body with a pale orange glow during a love scene. In *King Lear*, Edgar (Leos Carax) lights a fire on the floor of Pluggy's room and he and Virginia dare each other to hold their hands over it, at one point clasping them together above the flames. The irresistible attraction of the flame, here as in *Détective*, seems to me further related to Godard's search for images and experiences that resist commodification. There is perhaps something about the irreducible material reality of *pain*, on contact with fire, that is irrecuperable, incorruptible. At the same time, of course, fire and water are *elemental*, immemorial, and imply a time scale and a rhythm that do not belong to capitalism, that do not belong to anyone.

Fire is central to *King Lear*. Following the opening evocations of the disastrous turn taken by the production, Godard announces, 'So anyway, I was fired'. But, he goes on, he took this as his cue to investigate the relationship between art and fire. This may just be a cheap pun, but the imagery of fire does indeed recur in the film's reflections on art. We have already noted the way paintings are often lit with a naked flame, a device that seems to suggest they are seen within the enveloping darkness of a prehistoric cave. The film thus implies some sort of primal relationship between art and fire stretching back to the dawn of humanity, as though the two discoveries were linked, both crucial developments in our evolution into conscious subjects. But if both fire and water are repeatedly used as metaphors for art and the artistic process, it is also because they are *ungraspable*. Both are necessary for life, both are potentially fatal, but both are ultimately uncontainable. And the same is true of art which cannot easily be contained within the form of a cultural commodity: music is not contained on the CD or on the paper score, but in the vibrations of the air which translate into the vibrations of the listener's body. A film is not simply its budget, nor the reunion of actors on a set; it is not the celluloid in the cans or even the passing of that celluloid in front of a projector: a film exists in some indeterminable space between a scene that really took place before a camera, and that same scene recast in the imagination of the spectator. Even a painting, where the art seems to coincide most simply with the object, is not immune to this ambiguity: as Maurice Blanchot has suggested, the physical support of the painting or statue that is susceptible to the ravages of time is not the same as the *image* that somehow exists outside of time (Blanchot 1971: 42).

Another of Godard's favourite quotations, repeated countless times in his films since the mid-1980s is taken from André Malraux: 'L'art est comme l'incendie: il naît de ce qu'il brûle'.[34] This implies a romantic, indeed an almost vampiric conception of art as an entity that feeds off the artist, but also feeds off the reality it represents. This was already the sense of Edgar Allan Poe's tale *The Oval Portrait*, quoted by Godard at the end of *Vivre sa vie*. For art to replace life, it must first of all *destroy* it, even if that life is subsequently reborn as cinema, as literature and so on. We might relate this to Godard's disarmingly honest remarks in interview regarding the ease with which cinema can take the place of life, not only for spectators but for filmmakers as well. He admits that, if his cinema has been consistently daring, it is partly because his life has not: 'tout ce que je n'ose pas faire dans la vie, dans le cinéma, j'ose le faire, je n'ai pas peur'[35] (Godard 1998a: 452).

The imagery of resurrection that proliferates in Godard's cinema from the mid-1980s onwards, although it may frequently borrow from Christian iconography, has, first and foremost, a *cinematic* meaning. The real world is put to death by cinema in order to be resurrected, through the miracle of montage, as art. We will explore the consequences of this argument, and the thinking behind it, in the last two chapters of this book. For now, let us take note of some of the images of resurrection that appear in Godard's late 1980s films. *Soigne ta droite* contains extensive readings from Malraux's *Lazare* which, as its title suggests, recounts the author's miraculous recovery from the near-death experience of his sleeping sickness. In *King Lear*, the death of Professor Pluggy is accompanied by reverse-photography shots in which a hand appears to re-attach the petals of a flower as Easter bells ring in the background. William Shakespeare V comments: 'Now I understood that Pluggy's sacrifice was not in vain. Now I understood, through his words, Saint Paul's words, that the image will appear in the time of resurrection'. What is most striking about this re-petalled flower, just as with the plastic apocalypse mentioned at the beginning of this chapter, is how artificial and frankly tacky it looks. There is something altogether

34 'Art is like fire: it is born from that which it burns.'
35 'everything that I daren't do in life, I dare to do it in cinema, I'm not afraid'.

barbaric about it, seemingly a deliberate demonstration of the principle that artistic beauty may only be obtained at the expense of natural beauty. As Alan Walworth comments, 'what is presented as a reversal of death, a resurrection, is actually predicated on a kind of murdering to dissect accomplished through the manipulation, and for the sake, of the visual image. But more significantly, this self-conscious effect only illustrates the inherent artifice of cinema' (Walworth 2002: 81).

Immediately prior to this scene, Godard films the waves lapping at the lakeshore where someone has placed a copy of Virginia Woolf's *The Waves*. This imagery is again associated with death at the end of the film. As Cordelia leads a white horse onto the beach (the 'pale horse of death', as Walworth points out (2002: 83)), a female voiceover reads from the last paragraph of *The Waves*, in which Woolf's narrator rides a 'proud horse' against death. Again, these deaths are associated with rebirth in and as cinema. Godard's voiceover comments that 'Il faut que quelqu'un apparaisse et disparaisse pour que le cinéma existe',[36] while Edgar remarks that Cordelia's death will 'accompany the dawn of our first image'. Here, Godard cuts briefly to a shot of the horse running on the beach, an image whose beauty is, in Marc Robinson's words, 'its own justification' (Robinson 1988: 22). If Godard privileges *waves* here, it is doubtless because their pattern – endlessly forming and expending themselves – gives a sense of the cycle of birth and death that is necessary in order to have any intuition of the process of being. Indeed, such is precisely their sense in Woolf's novel. Had we missed the point, a recitation of Shakespeare's Sonnet 60 by Woody Allen and Peter Sellars in the epilogue underlines it:

> Like as the waves make towards the pebbled shore
> So do our minutes hasten to their end
> Each changing place with that which goes before
> In sequent toil all forwards do contend.

Nouvelle Vague picks up this imagery of the wave, beginning with its title. Here, too, water is the site and the symbol of death and rebirth. Elena takes Roger Lennox out onto the lake and invites him to join her for a swim. When he protests that he doesn't know how, she pulls him into the water and watches him drown. But the crucial moments here, the moment where Elena's murderous intention is consummated as action, and the moment of Roger's death are both elided. As Elena holds out her hand and Paul Hindemith's *Mathis der Maler* symphony crescendoes on the soundtrack, we cut suddenly to a shot of the water

36 'Someone must appear and disappear in order for cinema to exist.'

and a big splash announces Roger's involuntary plunge. But the next shot shows Elena already out of the water and dripping on the boat as she calmly watches Lennox drown. We do not see the moment of death since Godard cuts away to the gardener whose apparently idle question 'quelles sont ces images?'[37] mingles with Roger's last gasps on the soundtrack. By the time we cut back, the low sun is glinting off the varnish of the boat, already back in harbour. It is, in other words, only in the montage, only in the editing together of sound and image, that this scene takes on its full significance.

In the latter half of *Nouvelle Vague*, Roger Lennox is miraculously resuscitated, or at least a double, calling himself Richard Lennox, takes his place. Richard exacts revenge on Elena by taking control of her corporation and, at the end of the film, he in turn takes her out on the lake. The same pattern of shots is repeated with the roles reversed, but there are important differences. The dramatic crescendo of Hindemith's symphony is replaced by the wild dissonance of his 1922 viola sonata and, as Elena desperately holds out her hand, Richard grabs it. This redemptive act redresses the balance between the couple, cancelling the debt that Lennox seemed to owe to Elena ever since she extended her hand to him at the beginning of the film. As they walk back through the garden, a crane shot looms magnificently above them and a voiceover tells how, despite their impression of having lived this scene before, they were more attentive to the *difference* between their acts in the present and those in the past. 'Ils se sentaient grands, immobiles, avec au-dessus d'eux le passé et le présent comme les vagues identiques d'un même océan'.[38] As Jean-Louis Leutrat has commented, 'Ebb and flow ... inform *Nouvelle Vague* where the same process, rather than arousing a feeling of weariness, brings with it the mystery of a rediscovery, or a reinvention' (Leutrat 1992: 32).

Nouvelle Vague, then, gives a sense of the cycle of life (the discussion and the images of the change of seasons in the garden adds to this impression), while suggesting that history need not repeat itself, that the past cannot be repeated or reborn without the inscription of some difference. In the last two chapters of this book, chronicling Godard's work over the 1990s, we will see how the reflection on the work of cinema, together with the imagery of resurrection and a persistent utopian politics become channelled into an overriding concern with history.

37 'what are these images?'.

38 'They felt themselves to be great, immobile, and above them were the past and the present, like identical waves on a single ocean.'

References

Adorno, T. (2001), *The Culture Industry: Selected Essays on Mass Culture*, London, New York, Routledge.

Adorno, T. and Horkheimer, M. (1997 [1944]), *Dialectic of Enlightenment*, trans. by John Cumming, London, New York, Verso.

Amstutz, R. (1990), 'Entretien', *Cahiers du cinéma*, hors série, *Spécial Godard: Trente ans depuis*, 84–6.

Aumont, J. (1999), *Amnésies: Fictions du cinéma d'après Jean-Luc Godard*, Paris, POL.

Bachelard, G. (1992 [1931]), *L'Intuition de l'instant*, Paris, Stock.

Baecque, A. de (1990), 'Le don du livre', *Cahiers du cinéma*, hors série, *Spécial Godard: Trente ans depuis*, 64–6.

Benoît, L. (1987), '*King Lear* de Jean-Luc Godard', *Le Journal des Cahiers*, 76, in *Cahiers du cinéma*, 399.

Bergson, H. (2002 [1940]), *Le Rire: Essai sur la signification du comique*, Paris, PUF/ Quadrige.

Blanchot, M. (1971), *L'Amitié*, Paris, Gallimard.

Cerisuelo, M. (1989), *Jean-Luc Godard*, Paris, L'Herminier/Éditions des Quatre Vents.

Creton, L. (2001), 'Godard et l'art stratégique de la redéfinition du métier', in G. Delavaud, J.-P. Esquenazi and M.-F. Grange (eds), *Godard et le métier d'artiste*, Paris, L'Harmattan, 315–34.

Darke, C. (1997), 'Hearing the invisible', *Sight and Sound*, 7, 9, 35.

Douin, J.-L. (1989), *Jean-Luc Godard*, Paris, Rivages.

Eagleton, T. (1996), *The Illusions of Postmodernism*, Oxford, Blackwell.

Godard, J.-L. (1998a), *Jean-Luc Godard par Jean-Luc Godard, Tome 1: 1950–1984*, Paris, Cahiers du cinéma.

Godard, J.-L. (1998b), *Jean-Luc Godard par Jean-Luc Godard, Tome 2: 1984–1998*, Paris, Cahiers du cinéma.

Harvey, D. (1990), *The Condition of Postmodernity: An Enquiry into the Origins of Cultural Change*, Cambridge, MA, Oxford, Blackwell.

Jameson, F. (1991), *Postmodernism, or, The Cultural Logic of Late Capitalism*, London, New York, Verso.

Katsahnias, I. (1987), 'Big trouble in little Switzerland (*King Lear*, de Jean-Luc Godard)', *Cahiers du cinéma*, 397, 19.

La Fontaine, J. de (1966 [1668]), *Fables*, Paris, Garnier-Flammarion.

Leutrat, J.-L. (1992), 'The declension', in R. Bellour and M. L. Bandy (eds), *Jean-Luc Godard: Son + image 1974–1991*, New York, MOMA, 23–33.

Lyotard, J.-F. (1979), *La Condition postmoderne: Rapport sur le savoir*, Paris, Minuit.

Morrey, D. (2005), 'An embarrassment of riches: Godard and the aesthetics of expenditure in *Le Rapport Darty*', in P. Crowley and P. Hegarty (eds), *Formless: Ways In and Out of Form*, Oxford and Bern: Peter Lang, 229–37.

Powrie, P. (1997), *French Cinema in the 1980s: Nostalgia and the Crisis of Masculinity*, Oxford, Clarendon Press.

Rita Mitsouko, les (1995), 'Entretien', *Cahiers du cinéma*, hors série, *Numéro Spécial Musique*, 53–5.

Robinson, M. (1988), 'Resurrected images: Godard's *King Lear*', *Performing Arts Journal*, 31, 20–5.

Rose, M. A. (1991), *The Post-modern and the Post-industrial: A Critical Analysis*, Cambridge, Cambridge University Press.

Rosenbaum, J. (1995), *Placing Movies: The Practice of Film Criticism*, Berkeley, University of California Press.

Silverman, K. and Farocki, H. (1998), *Speaking about Godard*, New York, New York University Press.

Stam, R. (1991), 'The lake, the trees', *Film Comment*, 27, 1, 63–6.
Sterritt, D. (1999), *The Films of Jean-Luc Godard: Seeing the Invisible*, Cambridge, Cambridge University Press.
Toubiana, S. (1987), 'Au-dessus du volcan', *Cahiers du cinéma*, 402, 11–12.
Villeret, J. (1987), 'Je ne sais pas si ce que je dis est vrai mais j'en suis sûr', *Cahiers du cinéma*, 402, 21–3.
Vincendeau, G. (2000), *Stars and Stardom in French Cinema*, London, New York, Continuum.
Walworth, A. (2002), 'Cinema *hysterica passio*: Voice and gaze in Jean-Luc Godard's *King Lear*', in L. S. Starks and C. Lehmann (eds), *The Reel Shakespeare: Alternative Cinema and Theory*, Madison, Teaneck, London, Fairleigh Dickinson University Press/Associated University Presses, 59–94.
White, A. (1996), 'Double helix: Jean-Luc Godard', *Film Comment*, 32, 26–30.

9

The sense of an ending: 1991–96

Allemagne neuf zéro

In the 1990s Godard's work was marked by a distinct turn towards the past, by a new concern for history. In part, this must be seen as a consequence of the director's ongoing work on the *Histoire(s) du cinéma* project, begun in the late 1980s. But the fascination with the past is also part of a much broader cultural and intellectual trend at this time, in France and elsewhere. If history has become so interesting to so many, some commentators have suggested, it is because history itself is at or nearing its end. The hypothesis of the end of history has been most famously asserted in recent times by Francis Fukuyama who identifies a 'liberal revolution', beginning with the fall of fascist and military dictatorships in southern Europe, South America and East Asia in the 1970s, and continuing in the 1980s with the thawing of the cold war, the break-up of the Soviet Union and the fall of the Berlin Wall. These regimes have all been ousted, argues Fukuyama, not by violent revolution, but by a crisis of legitimacy: leaders voluntarily liberalised their politics upon the realisation that 'democracy was the only legitimate source of authority in the modern world' (Fukuyama 1992: 21). For Fukuyama, then, liberal democracy emerges victorious from the ideological struggles of a global political history that is nearing its end. History will of course continue, but there will be no more of the bloody and embittered struggles over ideology that have characterised the last few millennia since 'we cannot picture to ourselves a world that is *essentially* different from the present one, and at the same time better' (Fukuyama 1992: 46).

Godard's *Allemagne neuf zéro* (1991) can be seen as a response to this kind of triumphalism surrounding the reunification of Berlin and the victory of western capitalist democracy. In the film, Eddie Constantine reprises his role as Lemmy Caution from *Alphaville*. In 1990, Lemmy is the last western spy in East Berlin, seemingly unaware of the end of the cold war, but he is discovered living behind a hairdressers' salon by a cinema researcher who encourages him to return to the West. Lemmy spends the film walking through East Berlin, past various sites of historical and cultural interest until he finally arrives in the commercialised West. *Allemagne neuf zéro* is indicative of the concerns of Godard's 1990s films, combining both a personal reflection upon the director's own cinematic past and wide-reaching excavation of European history which returns obsessively to the twentieth-century tragedy of the Second World War.

In general, the historical conjuncture of the late 1980s and early 1990s coincides not only with an increased public interest in history, but also with an unprecedented *production* of historiography. Pierre Nora has argued that this proliferation of historical works and public monuments is, paradoxically, the sign of a collective loss of memory: 'On ne parle tant de mémoire que parce qu'il n'y en a plus'[1] (Nora 1997 [1984]: 23). The institutions which were traditionally responsible for the transmission of public memory – church, school, family, state – have all been undermined in recent years, making memory into an increasingly private affair with each individual responsible for the preservation of his or her personal history (Nora 1997 [1984]: 34). In the face of this loss of memory, Nora identifies a fascination with what he calls 'lieux de mémoire' or spaces of memory: these are not necessarily physical places, but objects, monuments or traditions that crystallise historical meaning into a small number of signs (38).

The 1990s were of course a significant time, particularly in Europe, for the public commemoration of historical landmarks, with major events marking the bicentennial of the French Revolution and the fiftieth anniversary of V. E. Day, but also the centenary of cinema in 1995. Commemorations, as John Gillis points out, are always political in one way or another, since they tend to present as consensual events which in fact came about through intense ideological struggle (Gillis 1994: 5). In other words, commemorations are as much about forgetting as they are about remembering. This is a point made forcefully by Godard in his intervention around the centenary of cinema, *2 × 50 ans de cinéma français* (1995). In this film, Godard interviews Michel Piccoli in his role as Président de l'Association du Premier Siècle du Cinéma and asks why we feel the need to 'celebrate' cinema. He suggests that it may ultimately only be a way to assuage our guilt about an art form that has been neglected and forgotten and may soon cease to

1 'We only talk so much about memory because it no longer exists.'

exist altogether. Such tokenistic efforts as the screening of one minute per day of Lumière films in a twenty-four-hour television schedule serve only to confirm Godard's worst fears. In a move which is typical of Godard's conflation of film history with the history of the twentieth century, he compares our guilty acknowledgement of cinema's past with the commemoration of the Shoah: our need to build monuments and establish official Memorial Days for the exterminated Jews merely testifies to the extent to which they are already forgotten. If we really wanted to remember, says Godard, we could show Alain Resnais's *Nuit et brouillard* (1955) every evening on television with the message 'N'oubliez pas' ('Do not forget').

How, then, does Godard's historical work fit in to this overall trend for public acts of remembering? If Godard's films in this period explore the history of cinema through its relation to the wider history of Europe in the twentieth century, are they not in danger of becoming simple *lieux de mémoire* themselves, fixing history into a set of convenient meanings? Certainly, on his wander through Berlin in *Allemagne neuf zéro*, Lemmy Caution passes a number of sites that serve as reminders of Germany's role in the tragedy of the twentieth century, such as the bridge where Rosa Luxemburg was murdered. Jean-Louis Leutrat provides a useful explanation for the intertitle 'Topographie des terreurs' ('Topography of terrors') that appears in the film alongside a plaque commemorating the site of the Gestapo headquarters: 'Topographie des terreurs' was the name of an exhibition accompanying the archaeological excavation of the foundations of this building which had been demolished after the war. Leutrat points out that, in an earlier incarnation, the building had housed an ethnographic museum, such that, with a terrible irony, a space dedicated to the preservation of human diversity became devoted to its extermination (Leutrat 1994: 75–6).

But, if Godard evokes Germany's fascist past, he seems to warn against the commercialisation and commodification of Nazi history in a scene in which Lemmy encounters a flea market selling items retrieved from concentration camps. This scene is typical of the film's erratic appropriation of the past, since an evocation of Camp Dora leads into a quotation from Freud's famous case study of a patient by that name, while, when Lemmy picks up a paperback copy of Thomas Mann's *Lotte in Weimar*, the film lays claim to an artistic heritage based on intertextuality, cultural memory and strategic subversion. Mann's novel, written in exile in 1939, borrows the character of Charlotte Kestner from Goethe's *Sorrows of Young Werther* and exploits its early nineteenth-century setting to make a number of allegorical remarks about contemporary Europe, for instance inviting comparisons between Napoleon's occupation of Germany and another tyrannical leader's dreams of a united Europe in the twentieth century. In general, the wayward twists of memory and unpredictable cultural associations in *Allemagne neuf zéro* tend to militate against any notion of a monolithic German culture or identity, an idea whose murderous implications have been amply demonstrated. Instead, Godard seeks to present Berlin as a kind of crossing-space of cultural energies: for every great German evoked over the course of the film (Hegel, Rilke, Schiller, Beethoven) there is an Eastern European associated with Berlin (Kafka and Liszt), a Russian (Pushkin and Shostakovich), an Austrian (Musil and Freud) and even an Englishman (Christopher Isherwood).

An example of the unstable meaning of Godard's historical signifiers may be found in a sequence in which, having left the city of Berlin itself, Lemmy comes across a mammoth piece of earth-moving equipment grinding and clanking away in the East German countryside. This short scene is one of the most unforgettable and also perhaps one of the most mysterious in late Godard and, although it would be futile to attempt to pin down its meaning, it is worth considering its resonance at some length. The scene begins with a long shot of the great machine at work in a valley, before cutting first to a closer angle and then to a close-up of a page from the German text of Kafka's *Castle*. Lemmy approaches the machine and recites a text by Rilke: 'Les dragons de notre vie ne sont que des princesses qui attendent de nous voir beaux et courageux'.[2] He sits down and switches on a tape recorder concealed in his briefcase which plays an excerpt from the soundtrack of an earlier Lemmy Caution film with Constantine playing the dashing romantic lead. There approach a knight on horseback and a man driving an old Trabant. The knight, framed like don Quixote against a windmill, recites the lines from Rilke in German before Lemmy picks up the baton in French: 'Toutes les choses terrifiantes sont peut-être des choses sans secours qui attendent que nous les secourions',[3] before the knight and the Trabant ride off towards the giant machine. The glimpse of *Das Schloß* in this sequence encourages us to look on this machine as an image of the kind of inconceivably large and complex apparatus of power that Kafka imagined in his novels, and the rather anachronistic aspect of this huge and cumbersome machine in the age of the information-driven economy might lead us to take it as an image of the old East German administration. But the figure of the knight, aside from its reference to don Quixote, is based upon an engraving by Dürer entitled 'The Knight,

2 'The dragons in our lives are merely princesses who are waiting to see our beauty and courage.'

3 'All the terrifying things may merely be helpless things awaiting our help.'

Death and the Devil' (1513) which, in German Romanticism, became a kind of emblem of German national identity. The knight's charge at the machine, following Lemmy's question 'Which way is the West?', might therefore represent Germany's headlong rush towards an American technocratic capitalism. Meanwhile, the Rilke text comes from his *Letters to a Young Poet*. The passage quoted comes at the end of a long paragraph in which Rilke argues that we have no reason to fear or mistrust the world since it resembles us, 'if it has terrors, they are *our* terrors'; 'We must always trust in the difficult', says Rilke, give it a chance, welcome it, love it, in order to see its value, its beauty (Rilke 1984: 92). In the present context this could be read as an exhortation by Godard to accept the challenge of trying to read critically the current political consensus, just as it is a challenge to the viewer not to be daunted by this most difficult of Godard's late works.

It is, as I said, impossible to decide upon a final meaning for the scene. Jeffrey Skoller, in an article on *Allemagne neuf zéro* influenced by the philosophy of Deleuze and Guattari, suggests that the machine, which he identifies as a piece of strip-mining equipment, can be read as 'historicism itself': 'It tears away stratified layers of earth, each one a different period of time, keeping substratum that is of value to the needs of the historian and discarding the detritus that seems insignificant' (Skoller 1999: 40). This follows 'a model of history that is geological rather than chronological, in the sense that moments of time are sedimented and become strata' which coexist with the present (40). A connection might be made here with the work of the French historian Fernand Braudel whose distinction between different kinds, or different rates, of history has been influential over Godard's historical thought. Braudel is keen to stress that history does not happen at the speed of instantaneous news broadcasts and live satellite link-ups; it proceeds through the almost imperceptibly slow development of what he calls 'la longue durée', the gradual accretion of history as plurality. The appeal of this approach for Godard is perhaps to be found in the notion of resistance since, in his work on the history of France, Braudel suggests that a national identity is precisely that which resists the natural erosion operated by the passage of time and the accumulation of events (Braudel 1990: 19).

Godard's own resistance, in *Allemagne neuf zéro*, to producing fixed and easily intelligible images of Germany past and present, together with his sullen refusal to join the celebrations greeting reunification, imply a deep sense of suspicion at the kind of end-of-history discourse that was gathering around the capitalist triumph. This suspicion is shared by other critical commentators, notably Jacques Derrida, who writes of a sense of *déjà vu* at this 'end' of history, since the very same discourse was in common circulation after the Second World War, itself assumed to be the last great ideological struggle humanity would have to face. From such a historical perspective, pundits like Fukuyama can only appear strangely anachronistic, almost as though they were late for the end of history (Derrida 1993: 37–8). Derrida goes on to suggest that one is always, necessarily late for history: because history is constantly moving outside itself, or beyond itself, it can never coincide with itself and we can never catch up with it, so it can have no end. Godard too undermines the end-of-history discourse by comparing it to other, similar views from other eras, implying that history can have no single end, but only a series of false ends and re-beginnings. At the end of *Allemagne neuf zéro*, when Lemmy arrives in West Berlin, an Americanised city characterised by advertising hoardings, corporate logos and the featureless buildings of international finance, he reads from Oswald Spengler's pessimistic 1922 opus *The Decline of the West*. Spengler takes an organic view of culture which argues that, once a culture has fully expressed its own unique spirit, it begins to stagnate in a process of repetition without innovation and, eventually, dies. Godard quotes a passage from the end of Spengler's work which suggests that money, too, is subject to this same process: 'it fades as soon as it has thought its economic world to finality' (Spengler 1922: 507). Spengler has long since been discredited and largely forgotten as a historian, but Theodor Adorno has suggested that, in fact, he predicted many of the horrors that would befall Germany in subsequent decades, from the use of media to manipulate and pacify the people, to the degradation of democracy into dictatorship through the rule of the party (Adorno 1967: 51–72). Godard's appeal to Spengler is typical of his obsessive return to Europe's interwar years. At a time when the West has never been so powerful, prosperous or self-satisfied, Godard's continual evocations of the 1930s imply that it may actually stand on the brink of disaster. In *For Ever Mozart* (1996), Godard borrows from the Spanish writer Juan Goytisolo the idea that the 'cowardice and confusion' of the 1990s mirror that of the 1930s, with Europe's failure to prevent war in the Balkans offering a depressing repetition of the twentieth-century's worst mistakes.

But if Godard reminds us so incessantly of the 1930s and the war years, it is not only to make pessimistic predictions about our future, but also to remind us of a model of real political resistance. For instance, in a BMW showroom in West Berlin, Godard films a young couple named Hans and Sophie trying out the luxury cars, and Lemmy is prompted to remember Hans and Sophie Scholl, members of the

Weisse Rose student resistance movement executed by the Nazis in 1943. There is an appeal here to a political spirit that would resist the march of progress towards a free-market capitalism on the American model, an attempt to highlight the possibility of an alternative system of values in our consumer-driven culture. Godard's approach to history owes a considerable debt to Walter Benjamin, whose 'Theses on the Philosophy of History' he quotes, as we shall see, in *Hélas pour moi* (1993). Benjamin, whose text was written in 1940 shortly before he committed suicide while fleeing from the Nazis, is deeply suspicious of any history told by the victors, since it tends to leave out the suffering of the anonymous masses exploited by the victors, and without whom there would be no victory (Benjamin 2000 [1942]: 431–3). Benjamin argues that we have a duty to protect the memory of our ancestors, to preserve it from the rulers who would use it for their own ends (431). But, in order to perform this kind of historical work, we need to renounce the notion of history as linear progress through an empty, homogeneous time and make a dialectical leap into the now-time (*Jetztzeit*), the saturated present in which our ancestors lived. It is only in this deliberate cessation or blockage of time that we find the revolutionary possibility of combat for the oppressed past (438–42).

This critical conception of history seems to be shared by Godard who routinely challenges 'official' history, particularly as it is presented in images through the media. The media's privileging of certain images as more 'historical' than others necessarily entails the elimination or forgetting of other images, other people, other places. 'En quoi, par exemple, le jour de la chute du mur de Berlin est historique, alors que le jour d'avant ou d'après ne le serait pas? Qu'est-ce qu'on appelle "histoire"?'[4] (Godard 1998: 224). One of Godard's preferred refrains in this period is 'Joyeux non-anniversaire', or 'Happy unbirthday', a phrase attributed to Lewis Carroll and which enacts in a kind of shorthand the questioning of commemoration which was discussed at the beginning of this chapter. The phrase appears in *Allemagne neuf zéro* as a Mercedes drives over an old street sign reading 'Karl Marxstraße'. Godard shares, too, Benjamin's concern for the anonymous masses ignored by history and, although his historical work returns frequently to the lives and works of great artists, thinkers and politicians, it is regularly punctuated with newsreel footage of crowds, reminding us that history is not simply the preserve of individuals. What is striking is the extent to which all these crowd scenes end up resembling each other, regardless of their

4 'How is it that the day the Berlin Wall fell is historic but not the day before or the day after? What do we mean by "history"'?

context, suggesting a sort of common denominator of human suffering underlying all historical events and ridiculing the very notion of historical progress. There is one particularly disturbing example in *Allemagne neuf zéro* of a crowd of people reaching up with outstretched arms: it is difficult to tell whether these are fervent spectators declaring their support at a Nazi rally, or the starving prisoners of a Jewish ghetto clamouring for bread.

Godard's argument, throughout his historical work, is that the cinema is particularly well placed to perform the kind of dialectical leap between present and past that Benjamin describes thanks to its unique reliance on montage. Montage can literally bring an image of the past and an image of the present together in the kind of flash of recognition of which Benjamin writes (Benjamin 2000 [1942]: 430). In *The Old Place* (1998), a video essay co-directed with Anne-Marie Miéville, Godard offers a very basic demonstration of this principle by juxtaposing a painting of the Israelites' exodus from Egypt with a contemporary photograph of refugees fleeing Kosovo: in both images the principal mode of transport is a donkey. Here, the march of progress is halted and the undiminished suffering of humanity exposed. Godard represents the activity of film-editing several times in this period of his work, as we shall see shortly, and he talks about it with evident emotion:

> Au montage, on se sent enfin en sécurité ... Au montage ... on a physiquement un moment, comme un objet, comme ce cendrier. On a le présent, le passé et le futur. La maman n'a pas ça par rapport à son enfant, les amoureux ne l'ont pas par rapport à leur amour, et les politiques, vous le voyez d'après leurs visages, sont vraiment loin de l'avoir. (Godard 1998: 242)[5]

This kind of supernatural, almost holy sense of security granted by montage is similar to that provided by the cessation of linear time, which Benjamin describes as 'messianic' (Benjamin 2000 [1942]: 441). Benjamin's philosophy of history is deeply indebted to the Jewish theological tradition in which time is far from homogeneous, and certainly not empty since each moment may provide the gate through which the Messiah will enter (443). The messianic cessation of happening is based on the promise of the Last Judgement in which the whole of history will appear at once (429). If we believe in such a possibility, then it implies that the past has not *gone away*, but is in some sense *still there*, awaiting

5 'At the montage stage, you finally feel secure. In montage, you physically hold a moment, like an object, like this ashtray. You have the present, the past and the future. The mother doesn't have that security with regard to her child, lovers don't have it with regard to their love, and politicians, you can tell from their faces, are far from having it.'

judgement. Godard does not claim that montage provides such a judgement, only that it may serve as a preparation for judgement, it testifies to a desire for judgement (Godard 1998: 318). It is in this sense, too, that we may take seriously Godard's discourse of resurrection throughout this period. He repeatedly cites a phrase attributed to Saint Paul, 'L'image viendra au temps de la résurrection',[6] but it is important to remember that the image, for Godard, is a complex entity made, as in the Reverdy poem quoted so often, from the confrontation of two distinct realities. The image in this sense, then, is already montage and 'Pour moi, le montage est la résurrection de la vie'[7] (Godard 1998: 246). We will see further examples of this use of montage to save the memory of the past when we discuss *Histoire(s) du cinéma* in the next chapter.

JLG/JLG: Autoportrait de décembre

Of course, memory is not only a collective but an individual responsibility and Pierre Nora stresses that our era has seen an unprecedented production of personal historical accounts: memoirs, autobiographies, individual archival and genealogical research. In the early 1990s, the production company Gaumont requested an autobiography from Godard. Godard responded that he would not produce an autobiography, but instead a self-portrait, as in painting, 'chose qui me semble impensable à faire au cinéma, mais le cinéma est fait pour penser l'impensable'[8] (Godard 1998: 294). Gaumont requested a *Godard par Godard*, but the director preferred the title *JLG/JLG*, the bar giving the sense of reflection in a mirror, a common trait of the self-portrait in painting (Godard 1998: 300, 306). Michel Beaujour, who has discussed the notion of a literary self-portrait, suggests that, unlike the autobiography which follows a linear narrative from birth through to the present, the self-portrait gains its coherence from a series of relations and correspondences between homologous elements and is thus constructed according to principles of anachronic juxtaposition or montage (Beaujour 1980: 9). The self-portrait does not tell 'what I have done', but presents a snapshot addressing the question of 'who I am'. *JLG/JLG* does not tell the story of Godard's life, but presents an image of the director at a moment in time (hence the precise designation of the subtitle: 'Self-portrait in December' – the film was shot in the space of a

6 'The image will come at the time of resurrection.'
7 'For me, montage is the resurrection of life.'
8 'something that seems unthinkable in the cinema, but the cinema was made to think the unthinkable'.

single week (Godard 1998: 307)), engaging in such typical activities as working on films, walking by the lake and playing tennis.

JLG/JLG has been singled out for attack from those critics suspicious of Godard's late work. The film has been accused of wallowing in an indulgent nostalgia, a characteristic that some see as representative of the director's general withdrawal from social and political life at this time. Certainly *JLG/JLG* has a deep strain of melancholy to it, from David Darling's mournful cello which accompanies the opening shots to the pervasive blue light that suffuses practically the whole film (Jacques Aumont has referred to this as Godard's 'période bleue et grise', or 'blue-grey period' (Aumont 1996: 274)). In addition, the film presents Godard as a very lonely man, surrounded only by philistine film auditors, a blind editing assistant (of whom more later) and a nubile young cleaning woman (a rather obvious and objectionable fantasy-figure). Even Godard's staunchest supporters have been troubled by the way the director seems unable to relate to any living artists, instead carrying on a very personal dialogue with the dead (Bergala 1999: 62). When asked by the French radio station France Culture whom he would like to hear discussing his work, Godard was at a loss to find a name among anyone currently living (Godard 1998: 309). In one scene in *JLG/JLG*, the director walks beside the lake at twilight and, on the soundtrack, we hear snatches of dialogue from some of his most cherished films: *Adieu Philippine* (1962), *Au bord de la mer bleue* (1936), *Païsa* (1946) and *Johnny Guitar* (1954). Godard's solitude may be a populous one, as Deleuze pointed out (Deleuze 1976: 6), but it is populated by ghosts.

David Ipacki, who has mounted the most sustained attack on *JLG/JLG*, accuses the director of solipsism and autism (Ipacki 1995: 33), dismissing the film as 'le monologue pathétique d'un solitaire visiblement lassé par les conflits réels de la vie, et ceux, affabulés, des histoires imaginaires'[9] (36). Ipacki argues that Godard's retreat into the past, far from giving his work a historical dimension, in fact serves only to create a swollen, oppressive present with no possible opening to the future, just as the camera is 'privée d'horizon et sans aucune promesse d'extension'[10] (34). Again, this translates into a refusal of contemporary culture, a denial of the possibility that the cinema may still be able to produce great works of art. In *JLG/JLG*, this attitude is expressed in the same kind of art-versus-culture opposition that we discussed in the

9 'the pathetic monologue of a solitary man grown visibly weary from the real conflicts of life and the fantastical ones of the imagination'.

10 'deprived of a horizon and with no possibility of extension'.

previous chapter, Godard making such glibly provocative remarks as 'L'Europe a des souvenirs, l'Amérique a des T-shirts'.[11] This discourse finds its fullest expression in a sequence near the beginning of the film, in which Godard sits at a desk, backlit by a table lamp and thinks aloud as he writes: 'Il y a la culture, qui est de la règle, qui fait partie de la règle. Il y a l'exception, qui est de l'art, qui fait partie de l'art. Tous disent la règle: cigarettes, ordinateurs, T-shirts, télévision, tourisme, guerre. Personne ne dit l'exception.'[12] As thunder is heard on the soundtrack, we cut to an image of rough waves breaking on the lake and the opening chorus of Arvo Pärt's *Passio* begins. A page of Godard's notebook turns to reveal the handwritten word 'Ventôse'. We see a shot through a window to a house across the street bathed in blue light and Godard racks focus so that the frame of the window, in the form of a crucifix, is emphasised. As we cut to a shot of bare trees in the snow, Godard reads a text by Georges Bernanos that describes fear as 'la fille de Dieu' ('the daughter of God'): she may not be pretty, but she comes to us all on our deathbed. Mixed in with this is a snippet of dialogue from a film with Pierre Fresnay in which a woman repeatedly begs his pardon. We return to Godard at his desk who continues: 'Cela ne se dit pas. Cela s'écrit: Flaubert, Dostoïevski. Cela se compose: Gershwin, Mozart. Cela se peint: Cézanne, Vermeer. Cela s'enregistre: Antonioni, Vigo. Ou cela se vit, et c'est alors l'art de vivre: Srebrenica, Mostar, Sarajevo.'[13] A section from the third movement adagio of Beethoven's fifteenth string quartet is heard as Godard concludes: 'Il est de la règle que vouloir la mort de l'exception. Il est donc de la règle de l'Europe de la culture que d'organiser la mort de l'art de vivre qui fleurissait encore à nos pieds'.[14]

David Ipacki notes the way that Godard's critique of culture tends to evolve into 'un dépassement de l'art vers la religion'[15] (Ipacki 1995: 42), where art becomes associated with the sacred. This tendency is clear in this sequence with its use of Pärt's choral work based on Christ's Passion, the Christian implications of the window frame and the emphasis on

11 'Europe has memories, America has T-shirts.'

12 'There is culture, which is a question of rules, which is part of the rules. There is the exception, which is art, which is part of art. Everyone speaks the rules: cigarettes, computers, T-shirts, television, tourism, war. No one speaks of the exception.'

13 'It cannot be spoken. It can be written: Flaubert, Dostoyevsky. It can be composed: Gershwin, Mozart. It can be painted: Cézanne, Vermeer. It can be filmed: Antonioni, Vigo. Or it can be lived and thus it is called the art of living: Srebrenica, Mostar, Sarajevo.'

14 'It is part of the rules to want the death of the exception. It is thus the rule of European culture to organise the death of the art of living that was still flourishing at our feet.'

15 'a movement beyond art and towards religion'.

pardon. Jacques Aumont notes that, whereas in *Une femme mariée* (1964), *2 ou 3 choses que je sais d'elle* and *Prénom Carmen*, Godard exploited the radical dissonance of Beethoven's late quartets, here he quotes the most conventionally Romantic passage (the 'hymn of thanksgiving') from the fifteenth (Aumont 1996: 275–6). In addition, a certain self-pity is implied by the reference to a deathbed and the wintry imagery. Kevin Hayes notes that the evocation of the Revolutionary calendar in *JLG/JLG* recalls its earlier use in *Week-end* (Hayes 2002: 157), but he neglects to mention the transition from the summer months (Thermidor, Vendémiaire) in the earlier film to the winter (Ventôse, Frimaire, Pluviôse) in Godard's self-portrait. In his biography of the director, Colin MacCabe relates this melancholy tone to the death of Godard's elder sister in 1993 (MacCabe 2003: 17), but its appearance in the context of a 'self-portrait' tends also to imply the approaching end of *Godard's* life. In either case, however, the Christian imagery carries an implicit promise of resurrection. This is made explicit at the end of the film when Godard encounters an old woman reading Ovid in Latin and he translates: 'S'il y a quelque vérité dans la bouche des poètes, je vivrai'.[16] In other words, it is through his art that Godard will achieve immortality. Jacques Morice has been particularly critical of this ending, arguing that the language of sacrifice in the film implies a desire for sainthood or martyrdom on Godard's part. However, Morice goes on to suggest that this self-portrait is too abstract and cerebral to achieve such lofty aims: without the sufferings of the *flesh*, there can be no sense of the tortured soul and hence no sacrifice and no sainthood (Morice 1994: 17).

But, if Godard's body is largely absent from his self-portrait, it is precisely because he seeks to avoid the perils of self-mythologising by constantly questioning the possibility of self-representation. In the notes that constitute the 'screenplay' of the film, Godard muses on the difficulty of this project which essentially requires one to film the passage of time, 'mais on ne panoramique pas sur lui comme sur un cheval, ni même une étoile'[17] (Godard 1998: 286). In fact, *JLG/JLG* consists of a series of refusals and failed attempts at self-representation, just as it devotes less attention to Godard's films than to the films he *hasn't* made: 'La liste est longue' ('The list is long'), sighs the director. Marie-Françoise Grange notes that *JLG/JLG* resists the narrative impulse of autobiography: there is no particular relation between the actions presented, and certainly no sequential logic (Grange 2000: 100–1).

16 'If there is any truth in the mouths of poets, I shall live.'
17 'but you can't pan across it in the same way you would a horse, or even a star'.

Similarly, Nora Alter observes that, 'while the film never lapses into randomness, it never totally resolves itself either' (Alter 2000: 82). The main criterion of organisation in the film is not narrative, but the composition of individual shots and, as Grange points out, Godard's body is simply one element among others in the frame, claiming no representational priority over items of furniture, books, trees or anything else (Grange 2000: 102). In addition, Godard is almost never filmed frontally, instead shot from behind or in profile and concealed in semi- or complete darkness. We see his form silhouetted against a table lamp or walking in the murky half-light of dusk; he is filmed with his head in his hands or his face concealed by the brim of a hat.

This play on visibility and invisibility that characterises the representation of Godard's body is to be found elsewhere in the film, notably in the recurring theme of blindness. Godard quotes from Diderot's *Lettre sur les aveugles* and a paragraph from Wittgenstein's *On Certainty* which suggests that, if a blind man asked me if I had two hands, it should not be my eyes that I trust in giving a response. The theme is most fully exploited in a scene in which a blind woman applies to be Godard's assistant editor. This scene may be comical to begin with, a self-mocking reference to Godard's now famous remark – first made at the time of *Sauve qui peut (la vie)* – that losing his hands would hinder his filmmaking more than losing his eyes. But, as it continues, with the couple working together on the montage of *Hélas pour moi*, it becomes a moving tribute to the materiality, the sensuality of film, with the editor running the celluloid through her hands and exploring the editing table by touch. This latter image is accompanied by a reading from Merleau-Ponty's *Le Visible et l'invisible*, and Julie Dior notes that the philosopher's image of 'le visible enroulé sur le visible'[18] is literalised in a shot of a reel of film being wound (Dior 1997: 30).

There are other moments in the film where Godard pokes fun at his public image, such as the scene of a tennis match where he declares 'J'ai autant de plaisir à être passé qu'à ne pas être passé'[19] as his opponent scores a point with a well-judged passing shot. Throughout, Godard deliberately plays up to the notion of the eccentric hermit, exaggerating his 'autism' through incoherent mumbles and grumpy growls. As Marie-Françoise Grange points out, in the scenes with the auditors and the assistant editor, Godard is very much playing a role, 'génie visionnaire incompris et bien entendu ruiné'[20] (Grange 2000: 106), and the

18 'the visible wound around the visible'.
19 'I enjoy being passed/past as much as not being passed/past.'
20 'the visionary genius who is misunderstood and, naturally, bankrupt'.

(often rather wooden, perhaps deliberately so?) acting of his fellow players serves to underline a sense of Godard's identity as performance. Indeed, in the opening shots of the film, over a photograph of the director as a boy, Godard describes the assumption of identity as a process of learning a role by heart. Julie Dior suggests that Godard's being is only expressed as 'une fiction en cours, une mise en fiction du Je',[21] such that the film finally presents us with 'une circulation ou une variation continue des Je'[22] (Dior 1997: 26).

The representation of the self in the self-portrait is thus ultimately revealed to be impossible. As Grange argues, however much one tries to produce a unified, objective image of the self, one always ends up with 'l'absence, le double, l'autre'[23] (Grange 2000: 108). This is simply a necessary consequence of representation, of language: the personal dissolves into the impersonality of signs. Godard recognises as much when, at the end of *JLG/JLG*, he quotes from a text by Brice Parain, the philosopher who appeared in *Vivre sa vie*:

> Lorsqu'on s'exprime, on dit toujours plus qu'on ne veut puisqu'on croit exprimer l'individuel et qu'on dit l'universel. J'ai froid. C'est moi qui dit 'J'ai froid', mais ce n'est pas moi que l'on entend. J'ai disparu entre ces deux moments de ma parole. Il ne reste plus de moi que l'homme qui a froid, et cet homme appartient à tous.[24]

Our use of language to express ourselves thus reveals our dispossession and death. As Jacques Derrida points out, this is most immediately true of our own name. A person's name always survives, always has the possibility of surviving their death. Thus, even while a person is still alive, their name '*lui survit déjà* ... disant et portant sa mort chaque fois qu'il est prononcé'[25] (Derrida 1988: 63). And, once the person is dead, all we have left is the memory and the name, which suggests that the two are somehow intimately linked: the name is always already 'in memory of'.

Derrida goes on to argue that, when we know a friend is dead, we talk of them living on 'in us'. This being of the other 'in us' that occurs in grieving memory is not the resurrection of the other. Rather, it is

21 'a fiction in process, a fictionalising of the self'.
22 'a continual circulation or variation of 'I's'.
23 'absence, the double, the other'.
24 'When we express ourselves, we always say more than we mean to because we think we're expressing the individual whereas we are actually saying the universal. I am cold. It is I who says "I am cold", but it is not me that is heard. I have disappeared between these two instants of my speech. All that remains of me is the man who is cold, and this man belongs to everyone.'
25 'is already outliving them, announcing and bearing their death each time it is spoken'.

already the other who marks our relation to ourself: in other words, the grieving memory of the other is already a part of our subjectivity, as it were *before their death*. Because 'I' am never 'myself', never identical to myself, my self-reflection can never close on itself, it is made possible by the presence of the other in the self, that is to say by the possibility of the death of the other, the possibility of mourning. The terrible solitude I experience at the death of the other already constitutes my relationship to myself. The possibility of death (the death of the other and, hence, my own) has always already arrived, making possible this subjectivity itself. As Derrida puts it, 'nous arrivons à nous-mêmes par cette mémoire du deuil possible'[26] (Derrida 1988: 53). At the beginning of *JLG/JLG*, Godard gives expression to precisely this sentiment. Noting the distressed look on his face in the photo of himself as a child, Godard suggests that he inverted the normal order of things, experiencing grief before he had experienced death. The only possible conclusion is that 'j'étais en deuil de moi-même, mon propre et unique compagnon. Et je me doutais que l'âme avait trébuché sur le corps et qu'elle était repartie en oubliant de lui tendre la main'.[27]

We might argue, then, that the melancholy which has irritated critics in *JLG/JLG*, the sense of grief and loss, is not only constitutive of the self-portrait as such (Grange 2000: 107–8), but is more generally characteristic of the subject's existence in and through language. In this sense, Godard is far from exceptional: in the last line of the film, he describes himself as 'un homme, rien qu'un homme, et qui n'en vaut aucun, mais qu'aucuns ne valent'.[28] But again, Godard is not without a certain grim humour in the face of this common grief. One of the titles Godard writes in his notebook is 'Je suis une légende'. Behind the ironically immodest boast lies a reference to Richard Matheson's 1950s sci-fi novel, *I Am Legend*. This book is narrated by the last surviving member of the human race after a terrible plague has turned all his fellow humans into vampires. The reference is thus a sly gesture on the part of Godard to his sense of isolation as an artist working in a soulless, relentlessly commercial industry. Kevin Hayes points out that, like Matheson's (anti-)hero, 'Survival has become his work, and he has become so conditioned to it that he has redesigned his entire home as a fortress from outsiders' (Hayes 2002: 159). The twist to Matheson's novel, though, is that, in this new world order, the narrator ultimately

26 'we arrive at ourselves via this memory of a possible grief'.

27 'I was in mourning for myself, my one and only companion. And I suspected that the soul had stumbled over the body and continued on without offering it a helping hand.'

28 'a man, nothing but a man, no better than any other, but none better than he'.

realises that he is, in a sense, the vampire's vampire: it is he who has become legend. This brief reference is typical of the ambiguity and semantic density of the signs in Godard's self-portrait: it condenses a self-mocking acknowledgement of Godard's institutionalised solitude; it presents a wily rebuttal to those who would accuse Godard of high-cultural elitism; and, through its implicit appeal to the figure of the vampire, it offers a mournful conception of identity as a sort of necessary living-death.

Hélas pour moi

If Godard's films of the 1990s deal principally in the matters of history and memory, both public and private, political and cinematic, *Hélas pour moi* (1993) can be seen as an interrogation of the *material* of history, a questioning of the very notion of the *event* that repeatedly suggests the difficulty of locating or circumscribing this most basic component of history. The film, loosely based around the legend of Amphytrion, presents us with the following remarkable happening: in a small lakeside community, God descends to earth and assumes the form of one Simon Donnadieu (Gérard Depardieu), who is ostensibly away on a business trip, in order to spend the night with his wife, Rachel (Laurence Masliah). The event in question, then, is not only completely unexpected, but there is some doubt as to whether it ever happened at all.

The question facing Godard in *Hélas pour moi* is how to tell this story in such a way as to preserve its mystery: how to prevent the narrative falling into the traps of either banal reality or absurd fantasy. From its opening minutes, the film immediately sets about questioning the nature and status of narration: a title informs us that the film is 'based on a legend', while a voiceover relates the practice of storytelling to sacred ritual. We are told that our fathers' fathers' fathers, when faced with a difficult task, would retreat to a place deep in the forest, light a fire and say a prayer, and the task would be accomplished. Over the generations, we have forgotten how to light fires and how to say prayers, and we can no longer find the precise place in the forest, but we are still able to *tell the story*. Here, storytelling is related to the transmission of an ancient wisdom, much as it is in a text by Walter Benjamin which Godard quotes at various points in the 1990s (notably in *Allemagne neuf zéro*). Benjamin argues that the art of transmitting wisdom – that is to say knowledge rooted in experience – through storytelling has been lost (Benjamin 2000 [1936]: 115–17). The oral transmission of stories requires a profound assimilation of narrative, and the conditions for this reception (which Benjamin associates with artisanal labour) no longer exist (125–6). Such stories are not to be confused with information, which is only of value to the extent that it is new; the traditional tale may contain little that is novel, but its particular power is to offer material for further reflection and development, long after it has been told (124).

In *Hélas pour moi*, Godard aims to give his story a completely different status to the kind of information that is easily assimilated but quickly forgotten in the contemporary sphere of audiovisual media. It is because spectators have to work so hard to incorporate the story – perhaps seeing the film not two or three times but six or seven to appreciate it fully – that they necessarily develop a very personal relationship to the film, carrying elements of it around with them as long-time companions. In this sense, the spectator's surrogate, within the film, is the investigator Abraham Klimt (Bernard Verley) who comes to the lakeside town in search of the story. Initially, he seeks an audience with Simon and Rachel, saying 'On m'a dit qu'ils avaient peut-être une histoire à vendre'.[29] Over the course of the film, he will learn that the story in question is not the kind that can be bought and sold. Subsequent scenes present a confusing mixture of events dating from before and after the fateful night in the Donnadieus' house. We witness Klimt's ongoing investigation and Rachel's confession to the pastor, 'Il y a cinq jours, j'ai appris que la chair peut être triste'.[30] But we also see Simon's preparations for departure and the earlier investigations into human sexuality made by God (only ever seen as a shadow or filmed from his own point of view) and his messenger-assistant Max Mercure (Jean-Louis Loca).

All this would not be so difficult to follow if it wasn't for the extraordinarily complex shot composition that dominates *Hélas pour moi*. In an extension of the kind of multi-character swarms that we analysed in Chapter 7, hardly a shot goes by in the first half of *Hélas pour moi* without two or three figures crossing the frame in various directions, pulling the energy of the film and the attention of the spectator along divergent vectors. As Pascal Bonitzer argues, this principle of composition tends to prevent the film from coalescing into traditional scenes: 'ce sont des fragments à la fois plus et moins que des scènes, toujours quelque figure les traverse en diagonale qui n'appartient pas à la scène et rature celle-ci ... et la rend à l'inachevé'[31] (Bonitzer 1993: 11). Added to

29 'I was told they might have a story to sell.'
30 'Five days ago I learned the sadness of the flesh.'
31 'these fragments are at once more and less than scenes, there is always some figure crossing the scene diagonally who doesn't belong to it and who cancels it, rendering it unfinished'.

the sheer kinetic energy of these figures is the fact that they frequently greet each other or introduce themselves, and yet this information singularly fails to help spectators orient themselves. 'Monsieur, Monsieur, Mademoiselle', run the greetings, while characters introduce themselves by their functions, one man confusingly referring to himself as 'professeur de dessin, ou libraire' ('art teacher, or bookseller'). As Bonitzer says, we have little hope of identifying, or even counting what appear to be the 'innombrables habitants' ('innumerable inhabitants') of this small town (Bonitzer 1993: 10).

When Abraham Klimt interrogates some of these residents about what happened at the end of the afternoon on 28 February 1989, he receives a series of different responses. Several people remember an argument between Simon and Rachel over Simon's departure to Italy on business, but they disagree on the precise circumstances of the dispute. One person remembers Rachel sitting on the boardwalk by the lake, another thinks she swam up to them, a third pictures her wading through the water. The film, in turn, offers visual representations of all these possibilities. As Laetitia Fieschi-Vivet comments, 'the act of forgetting, memory's counterpart, interferes in the reconstruction ... The visual evidence is completely relativised by the mise en scène' (Fieschi-Vivet 2000: 195). We see Simon and Rachel talking together on a bench before Simon gets up and leaves. However, once we have witnessed the departure of Simon in his car, we return to Rachel on the bench with Simon still sitting beside her. As she turns towards him, he disappears in a brusque jump cut. Three more jump cuts, each associated with the thumping piano chord that has become a Godardian signature over this period, show the shadow of Simon walking out of the frame.

If the scene of Simon's departure is ambiguous, the scene in which the other Simon makes love to Rachel is mysterious almost to the point of invisibility. There is a lengthy sequence in the Donnadieus' house in which Rachel questions and resists this strange new Simon of whom she is rightly suspicious. God, having earlier complained to Max Mercure that the night on earth was too short, at one point calls up the light of day in order to prolong what is nevertheless still the night. Interspersed with this long scene are sections of a dialogue between Klimt and a young woman named Aude (Anny Romand) who seems to have witnessed more of the event than anyone else. Yet she expresses her doubt that an event of this nature can be *seen* at all: at one point she claims to have heard, rather than seen what happened, she asserts that there can be no image of it and, after a time, rests her head on Klimt's shoulder, sighing 'voir l'invisible est fatigant' ('seeing the invisible is exhausting'). The conversation between Rachel and Simon/God takes up this theme of invisibility, since he recounts the story of the astronomer Jan Oort's discovery of the missing mass, the invisible or 'dark' matter now thought to account for ninety per cent of the mass of the universe. This information is relayed over a black screen which fades gradually in to a shot of Rachel's naked lower body lit only by a sparkler. Subsequently, and as we see a shot of Klimt looking in (but in where? He was after all not present on the night in question) through a rainy window while he recites a French translation of Dylan Thomas's 'Do not go gently into that good night', the sexual act takes place. But it takes place, in Klimt's own words, 'au-delà des images et des histoires':[32] barely visible beneath a near-abstract shot of the rising sun reflected on the water of the lake, there is in fact the image of a hand stroking a penis. This is followed by an exceptionally rapid series of shots (Fieschi-Vivet counts twelve in two seconds: 201) in which the sun is intercut with images that are simply too dark and pass too rapidly to make out (but which Fieschi-Vivet identifies as copulating genitalia: 201). In other words, the event that is central to *Hélas pour moi*, the supposed sexual congress between a god and a mortal woman, occurs before we have had a chance to register it on anything other than a subliminal level. After all the preparation of Klimt's painstaking investigation, the event itself proves all but unlocatable, and the investigator leaves, disappointed.

Alain Bergala, who has written quite brilliantly about *Hélas pour moi*, argues that the key question of Godard's cinema is how to represent these essential points in time, these tiny events that may last only a fraction of a second (not so much the sexual act between Rachel and Simon/God, but her decision to go ahead with it; not so much God's night on earth, but the instant of his incarnation). Bergala suggests that one cannot approach such moments frontally without destroying them (Bergala 1999: 176). In fact, rather than trying to represent the fraction of time at all, 'il faudra la faire *revenir*'[33] (176), starting always from a new angle or approach, endlessly defining, or declining the moment so that it is never exactly present nor the simple return of a self-identical past. And Bergala suggests that we can tie this to Godard's ethics of cinema. If cinema failed to capture that single, crucial moment that was the Nazi death camps (an argument we will explore in the next chapter), then Godard sometimes gives the impression of working painstakingly through the history of cinema in search of the precise moment where the error was first committed (Bergala 1999: 180). But, at the same time, he has instigated a research for a new kind of image, an image-resurrection

32 'beyond images and stories'.
33 'you need to bring it back'.

or image-redemption that might compensate for the earlier fault; something that only becomes possible given a non-linear conception of time, where each present moment communicates with the past which it *corrects* as it reprises (180). We can see this, too, in the way Godard recalls the utterances of others in his films: their return is never exact, Godard's quotation always approximate, because it is only thanks to this slight difference that the sentence may be brought back to life (181).

Jacques Derrida, too, sees the possibility of a politics of the ghostly, the spectral (the *revenant*), which would amount to a politics of memory, of inheritance, and of generation. Derrida argues that a politics – a justice – must take into account those who are no longer or not yet here, those who are not *presently* living, already dead or not yet born (Derrida 1993: 15). (In Derrida's text, as in Bergala's, the spectre of Walter Benjamin is never far away. His 'Theses on the Philosophy of History' are quoted in *Hélas pour moi*, notably in an intertitle which reads 'Nous avons été attendus sur terre').[34] Derrida's *Spectres de Marx* grows out of the *Communist Party Manifesto*'s opening observation that Europe is haunted by a spectre, that is by the possible arrival of communism. Derrida argues that, 150 years later, we are still preoccupied by the spectre of communism, only now it seems to be *past*. But, says Derrida, the subtext to this discourse on the death of Marxism is an unspoken fear that it might return in the future. Because, he insists, 'Au fond, le spectre, c'est l'avenir, il est toujours à venir, il ne se présente que comme ce qui pourrait venir ou re-venir' (71).[35] Noting the distinct eschatological edge to a certain trend in historical thinking; deploring the continued conflicts caused by the three main messianic religions; and acknowledging the messianic element to Marxism itself, Derrida suggests that there may be something in all this that resists deconstruction: the structure of messianism, the promise of emancipation incorporates a domain much larger than that of monotheistic religions (102). The very concept of democracy exists in the form of a promise which partakes of this indeterminate, messianic hope, an openness towards 'l'événement qu'on ne saurait attendre *comme tel* … à l'événement comme l'étranger même'(111),[36] a limitless hospitality which would be the very condition of the event and of history itself.

Could we say that *Hélas pour moi* achieves something akin to this unconditional openness in relation to the mysterious event at its heart?

34 'Our arrival on earth has been expected.'

35 'Ultimately, the spectre is the future, it is always yet to come, it only ever presents itself as that which may yet come or come back.'

36 'the event that we cannot predict *as such*, the event as the foreign/the stranger itself'.

Godard, we might note, considered the film to be a failure, saying he had not had enough time to finish it to his satisfaction (Godard 1998: 272). But, as he himself suggests, the film becomes all the more interesting for having failed (276). Godard notes that, in most narrative cinema, spectators may forget individual scenes, but they have a vague memory of them as having set up the current scene (this is the pattern of classical narrative cinema where the logic of cause and effect between scenes is always transparent). In *Hélas pour moi*, on the other hand, 'On ne se souvient plus de rien' ('One no longer remembers anything') (276). What we have instead is the pure present of a shot that depends not on what came before but on what is going to come next and which we cannot know (276). In Godard's film, then, the present image does not predict and prepare the future, as in classical narrative cinema, but waits in suspense for it.

All these ideas are condensed in one particularly busy scene in the first half of the film that takes place in the café run by Simon and Rachel. The scene begins with an establishing shot of a couple sitting at a table, served by a waitress, and, in voiceover, Max Mercure advises his master to take up position in a corner to observe the humans. As the camera frames another set of tables, a young man reads aloud a text about certain phenomena which, however implausible and undemonstrable, may, by virtue of constituting an article of faith, approach the condition of being. At a different table, a man and a woman discuss another, unspecified couple in terms which range from the romantic to the pornographic. Off-screen, someone declares: 'Nous sommes incapables de nous libérer nous-mêmes, la chose ne fait aucun doute. Et nous appelons cela: démocratie',[37] a line taken from Robert Musil. We cut to a third angle where a group of four people sit in discussion. One man mentions that the *Communist Manifesto* was published in the same year as *Alice in Wonderland*, another that the idea of ascension pre-dates Christ by 2,000 years. A man walks diagonally right to left through the frame. It is pointed out that, during the Gulf war, no one thought to mention the Mesopotamian ziggurat – situated in what is now Iraq – great stone staircases for the gods, 'qu'ils puissent redescendre sur la terre'.[38] Rachel enters from the right and Simon from the left as someone orders a glass of red wine. 'Terminé, le rouge,' says Simon, 'même pour le dernier communiste de notre toute jeune Europe'.[39] In response, someone quotes the Spanish Republican José Bergamin: 'Avec les

37 'We are incapable of freeing ourselves, there's no doubt about it. And this is what we call democracy.'

38 'so that they may come back down to earth'.

39 'No more red, not even for the last communist in our oh so young Europe.'

communistes, j'irai jusqu'à la mort, et je ne ferai pas un pas de plus!'.[40] As the lights go out, the figures leave the frame in all different directions, while a young man heads over towards an arcade game that mechanically recites 'Quit talking and start chalking!'.

This dazzling scene doubtless represents all that Godard's critics find unbearable in his late work: the apparently random comings and goings of depthless characters, the sententious recitation of disjointed phrases (although this latter is ironically mocked by the mechanical injunction of the arcade game). But it testifies to the incredible condensation, or sedimentation of ideas in this work. Here, the political, the religious and the mythological are combined in a way that effectively suggests the desire for *deliverance* common to them all. More than this though, the scene operates a remarkable collapsing of time, covering in a couple of minutes a span of history that takes in ancient Mesopotamia and 2000 BC, nineteenth-century Europe, the Spanish Civil War, the Gulf crisis of 1991 and an as-yet unimaginable future. The trajectories of the myriad figures through the shot are so many lines of flight leading into and out from these diverse points in time, a time that has effectively been frozen in recognition of the common suffering and ageless desires of humanity. Throughout it all, God looks on, forgotten and disregarded but, as Max Mercure points out, nonetheless residing in each one of us.

40 'I'll follow the communists to death, and not a step further.'

References

Adorno, T. (1967), *Prisms*, trans. by Samuel and Shierry Weber, London, Neville Spearman.

Alter, N. M. (2000), 'Mourning, sound, and vision: Jean-Luc Godard's *JLG/JLG*', *Camera Obscura*, 44, 75–103.

Aumont, J. (1996), *À quoi pensent les films*, Paris, Séguier.

Beaujour, M. (1980), *Miroirs d'encre: Rhétorique de l'autoportrait*, Paris, Seuil.

Benjamin, W. (2000 [1936]), 'Le conteur', trans. by Maurice de Gandillac and Pierre Rusch, in *Œuvres III*, Paris, Gallimard, 114–51.

Benjamin, W. (2000 [1942]), 'Sur le concept d'histoire', trans. by Maurice de Gandillac and Pierre Rusch, in *Œuvres III*, Paris, Gallimard, 425–43.

Bergala, A. (1999), *Nul mieux que Godard*, Paris, Cahiers du cinéma.

Bonitzer, P. (1993), 'Dieu, Godard, le zapping', *Trafic*, 8, 5–12.

Braudel, F. (1990), *L'Identité de la France: Espace et Histoire*, Paris, Flammarion.

Deleuze, G. (1976), 'Trois questions sur *Six fois deux*: À propos de *Sur et sous la communication*', *Cahiers du cinéma*, 271, 5–12.

Derrida, J. (1988), *Mémoires: pour Paul de Man*, Paris, Galilée.

Derrida, J. (1993), *Spectres de Marx: l'État de la dette, le travail du deuil et la nouvelle Internationale*, Paris, Galilée.

Dior, J. (1997), 'À la poursuite du je: *JLG/JLG*', *Cinémathèque*, 12, 25–33.
Fieschi-Vivet, L. (2000), 'Investigation of a mystery: Cinema and the sacred in *Hélas pour moi*', in M. Temple and J. S. Williams (eds), *The Cinema Alone: Essays on the Work of Jean-Luc Godard 1985–2000*, Amsterdam, Amsterdam University Press, 189–206.
Fukuyama, F. (1992), *The End of History and the Last Man*, New York, Free Press.
Gillis, J. R. (1994), *Commemorations: The Politics of National Identity*, Princeton, Princeton University Press.
Godard, J.-L. (1998), *Jean-Luc Godard par Jean-Luc Godard, tome 2: 1984–1998*, Paris, Cahiers du cinéma.
Grange, M.-F. (2000), 'Images d'artiste', in G. Delavaud, J.-P. Esquenazi and M.-F. Grange (eds), *Godard et le métier d'artiste*, Paris, L'Harmattan.
Hayes, K. J. (2002), '*JLG/JLG – Autoportrait de décembre*: Reinscribing the book', *Quarterly Review of Film & Video*, 19, 155–64.
Ipacki, D. (1995), 'Le Verbe ressuscité et l'Image crucifiée: *JLG– JLG* de Jean-Luc Godard', *Cinémathèque*, 8, 33–42.
Leutrat, J.-L. (1994), 'Ah! les salauds!', *Cinémas*, 73–84.
MacCabe, C. (2003), *Godard: A Portrait of the Artist at 70*, London, Bloomsbury.
Morice, J. (1994), '4 × Godard', *Cahiers du cinéma*, 483, 17.
Nora, P. (1997 [1984]), 'Entre Mémoire et Histoire: La problématique des lieux', in *Les Lieux de Mémoire 1*, Paris, Quarto Gallimard, 23–43.
Rilke, R. M. (1984), *Letters to a Young Poet*, trans. by Stephen Mitchell, New York, Random House.
Skoller, J. (1999), 'Reinventing time, or the continuing adventures of Lemmy Caution in Godard's *Germany Year 90 Nine Zero*', *Film Quarterly*, 52, 3, 35–42.
Spengler, O. (1922), *The Decline of the West: Perspectives on World-History*, vol. 2, trans. by Charles Francis Atkinson, London, George Allen and Unwin.

10

Old man river: 1998–

Histoire(s) du cinéma

The autumn of 1998 saw the release in France of Godard's long-awaited *Histoire(s) du cinéma* project. The work, which was begun in 1988 and had been subject to a variety of advance reports, sneak previews and private viewings, was finally made available to the public as a set of four videotapes with a total running time of 265 minutes, accompanied by four art books, featuring images and text from the films, published by Gallimard. The complete *Histoire(s) du cinéma* was also screened on Canal Plus in France over eight weeks in the summer of 1999. The arrival of the *Histoire(s)* was the occasion for a revival of critical, public and academic interest in Godard, the release of the film coinciding with the publication of a new, two-volume edition of *Jean-Luc Godard par Jean-Luc Godard*, the invaluable sourcebook of texts and interviews. Since this date, Godard has been repeatedly honoured by academic publications, international conferences and reissues of some of his earlier features.

The *Histoire(s) du cinéma* project has a long history in Godard's career. The idea was originally mooted as a collaboration between Godard and Henri Langlois, founder and director of the Cinémathèque Française, in 1976. Following Langlois's death in 1977, however, Godard took his place delivering a series of lectures on film history at the Conservatoire d'Art Cinématographique in Montreal. The text of these lectures, largely improvised by Godard, was published as *Introduction à une véritable histoire du cinéma* (Godard 1980). Godard's method in these lectures was to project one of his own films in conjunction with another from film history and to use the resulting juxtaposition as the basis for his reflections. As such, he can be seen to have paid homage to Langlois, whose practice at the Cinémathèque was to project two or more films in an evening which, although they may have had no ostensible relation, would inspire unexpected connections in the minds of the spectators.

Something of this method may be seen to have survived in *Histoire(s) du cinéma*, which seeks to tell the (hi)story of cinema by editing together hundreds of images from film history. The vast majority of the material that constitutes the *Histoire(s)* is drawn from other sources: film clips and stills, reproductions of paintings and photographs, quotations from literature and philosophy and pieces of classical and popular music (in English, French, German, Italian and Spanish). The only original material filmed for the project tends to consist merely of readings from poetic texts by actors and actresses such as Julie Delpy, Sabine Azéma, Alain Cuny and Godard himself. All these elements are combined into an extraordinarily dense montage in which the sheer amount of information presented to the spectator can be quite overwhelming. As a typical, if hypothetical, example, two images might be superimposed over one another while a third flashes in and out in an iris; a short text may be written across these images while, on the soundtrack, film dialogue, a piece of music and Godard's voiceover commentary all compete for the spectator's attention. The unprecedented complexity of this montage means that we will be unable to describe in sufficient detail here even a single sequence from this epic film series that runs for four and a half hours.

But the incredible intricacy of this montage, as well as the sheer speed with which images flash in and out of it, is crucial to the film's impact. As Alain Bergala comments:

> La vitesse même de cette pensée en images produit des émotions dont on ne peut plus discerner si elles sont plastiques ou intellectuelles, mais l'impact de leur fulgurance visuelle est tel que ces seules collisions d'images peuvent faire venir les larmes aux yeux.[1] (Bergala 1999: 240)

As Bergala suggests, *Histoire(s) du cinéma* combines the intellectual pleasures associated with the recognition of Godard's sources and the reconstitution of his frequently surprising argument, together with the visceral pleasures provoked by the powerful rhythm and colliding forms of his montage. As Marie-José Mondzain has remarked, there is no particular erudition required to follow, and be impressed by, the *Histoire(s)* (Mondzain 1998: 94), and certainly the spectator need not be an expert in film history. Godard has made it clear that recognising the films cited

1 'The very speed of this thinking in images generates emotions in which it is difficult to distinguish the plastic from the intellectual, but their blazing visual impact is such that these collisions of images are capable of bringing tears to the eyes.'

is by no means a prerequisite to understanding the *Histoire(s)*, and indeed it would be disappointing if the response to the film descended to the level of playing spot-the-quotation (Godard 1998: 312). Godard's argument can still function if specific images are given a more general interpretation, as representing a particular national cinema, a particular film genre, a given era of film history or simply, in the broadest sense, *cinema itself*. This level of interpretation is inevitable given the varying degrees of expertise brought to the film by spectators and the sheer number of works alluded to by Godard. As Bernard Eisenschitz has commented, each spectator's path through the labyrinthine *Histoire(s) du cinéma* will differ according to the individual's competence and capacity for recognition, but also their emotional response to the film (Eisenschitz 1998: 54).

Histoire(s) du cinéma, then, is a history of cinema that is made of cinema, that is constructed from the images and sounds of cinema itself. As such, the history on display is very different to the kind you might find in a textbook. This is a mythical and very personal history of cinema which gives much consideration to the role of the medium within the wider history of art as well as in the political history of the twentieth century. Many elements of Godard's argument will be familiar from the kind of preoccupations we have discussed in earlier chapters of this book. Since to explain exactly *how* this argument is formulated through Godard's montage would require a book in itself, it will be easier to summarise it here before going on to consider some concrete examples of Godard's method. Godard argues that the cinema's greatest invention, its unique contribution to the history of art, was *montage*. But it is important to understand the breadth of meaning implied by Godard when he talks about montage. Michael Witt suggests that it needs to be defined as broadly as possible as 'a productive principle accompanying the combination or juxtaposition of two or more events, facts or objects across the arts' (Witt 2000a: 38). For Godard, montage marks the possibility of nothing less than a new form of critical thought, but this remarkable promise contained within the medium was systematically neglected by the cinema, which instead became enslaved to storytelling.

If montage facilitates new kinds of thinking, it is because it shares the fundamental operation of thought, that is combining discrete elements in new and productive ways. As Godard puts it, 'le cinéma est fait pour penser, puisqu'il est fait pour relier'[2] (Godard 1998: 426). *Histoire(s) du cinéma* makes much of the links between the early history

2 'the cinema is made for thinking, because it is made for bringing together'.

of cinema and developments in science and technology at the end of the nineteenth century, with episode 1B in particular reconstituting the cinema's birth amid the growth of transport and telecommunications technologies and the invention of psychiatry and psychoanalysis. Godard's film opens with a shot of James Stewart wielding a telephoto lens in *Rear Window* (1954) and an image of a magnifying glass from *Mr Arkadin* (1955), thus immediately inscribing the cinema within a lineage of visual technologies, of machines designed to help us see things differently and better (Witt 2000a: 45). (Colin MacCabe has suggested a possible biographical explanation for this obsession with optical devices, since Godard's doctor father wrote a thesis on ophthalmology (MacCabe 2003: 13).) The cinema is a scientific instrument, and should have been used, claims Godard in all seriousness, for curing diseases (Godard 1998: 423). It had the potential for treating physical and social maladies through what Witt calls 'the revelation of hitherto imperceptible physical realities and the injuries of social inequality' (Witt 2000a: 43). Instead, this radical potential of the new medium was soon contained within a narrow set of standardised forms, largely dictated by the imperative towards narrative, and mostly originating in Hollywood.

This failure to recognise or realise the potential of the nascent art form constitutes, for Godard, nothing less than an abdication of the cinema's historical and ethical responsibility. The cinema had the ability to show us our world in a new and revealing light, but people refused to see it (Godard 1998: 402). This is one of the more difficult and, as we shall see, controversial stages of Godard's argument. Because of the cinema's miraculous ability to record the real, and to record *more of the real* than was ever intended, Godard suggests that certain films foresaw the tragedy that was to befall the twentieth century. In the late 1930s, films like Renoir's *La Grande Illusion* (1937) and *La Règle du jeu* (1939) or Malraux's *Espoir* (1939) predicted the catastrophic violence of the Second World War, yet their warning was not heeded. Then, during the war itself, the cinema neglected its ethical duty to bear witness to the real when it failed to show the horrific reality of the Nazi death camps (and *Histoire(s) du cinéma* is littered with disturbing images, mostly from footage taken after the liberation of the camps, which serve as a reminder of how the cinema failed in its most urgent task).[3] *Histoire(s)*

3 Godard's insistence on *showing* the horrors of the Shoah as a means of remembering the catastrophe and educating spectators about it has led to criticism from Claude Lanzmann whose nine-hour documentary, *Shoah* (1985), is based precisely on the impossibility, and indeed the undesirability, of ever providing an accurate representation of the death camps. For an account of these arguments, see Saxton (2003).

du cinéma becomes, then, in the words of James Williams, 'a tragic narrative of waste and shame' (Williams 1999: 308): the cinema never recovers after this fundamental failure in its mission, and post-war film history is characterised by a gradual but ineluctable decline, with the few moments of inspiration – Italian Neo-realism, the French New Wave – unable to reverse the overall downturn. For Godard, then, cinema 'dies' at Auschwitz. But it is worth adding a few caveats to this rather simplistic statement. For a start, the failure to record the reality of the Shoah is responsible for only one in a series of deaths of cinema perceived by Godard. Michael Witt points to the loss of visual inventiveness occasioned by the arrival of sound cinema; the upheaval of May '68; and the gradual erosion of cinema by the cancer of television as other 'deaths' undergone by the medium (Witt 1999). In addition, it is a particular kind of cinema that can be seen to have 'died'. Films continue to be made, but what has been lost since the war is cinema in the sense of 'a buoyant film industry working to construct an immediate, relevant image of contemporary reality' (Witt 2000b: 31).

The notion that cinema has an inescapable *duty* to record reality is revealing of the kind of influences that have shaped Godard's film history. *Histoire(s) du cinéma* belongs to a tradition in art history, represented in particular by André Malraux (Temple 2000), that sees cinema as having inherited from painting this ethical responsibility towards the representation of the real. For Godard, cinema was the last representative of art as 'la morale de l'Occident' ('the morality of the West') (Godard 1998: 423). Art, from this rather Hegelian perspective, is a thing of the past (Aumont 1999: 145–50). But if cinema has a duty to record the real, it implies that the medium must be defined, not by montage as we saw above, but rather by the indexical relationship between the image and reality. Jacques Aumont suggests that montage is to the image what thought is to memory: in order to think, we must first be able to remember, we must be able to store traces, images, or ideas in the memory the better to combine them with each other in new ways. Similarly, montage works by reviving the memory of the real, by bringing out the reserve of sense contained within an image in order to place it in relation with another image (Aumont 1999: 18). In *Introduction à une véritable histoire du cinéma*, Godard expressed this relationship in terms of *impression* and *expression*: the filmmaker is only able to *express* him- or herself because reality has already *impressed* itself upon the film strip (Godard 1980: 63). In other words, *Histoire(s) du cinéma* presents an image of cinema as an art form that combines the miraculous mise en scène of the real with the creative capacities of montage. And this refusal to choose between montage and mise en scène, between fiction and documentary, the recognition that they are inevitably combined in the cinema is, as Michael Witt points out, 'a position held unswervingly by Godard from the 1950s to the present' (Witt 2000a: 44).

Nonetheless, the reverent discourse held in relation to the image in *Histoire(s) du cinéma*, the praise for its miraculous ability to bear witness to the real, has irked certain of Godard's critics. As in many of the director's films since the mid-1980s, the cinematic image in *Histoire(s)* is frequently discussed in terms of redemption and resurrection. If the cinema reneges on its ethical duty by failing to record the horrors of war, it is redeemed by Italian neo-realism's documenting of the post-war years. More generally, Godard often speaks of the image in terms of resurrection, repeating in the *Histoire(s)* the line attributed to Saint Paul: 'The Image will come at the time of resurrection'. It is not the resurrection of Christ that is implied here, but the resurrection of the real, the restoration to life, to presence, of something that has *passed* (Godard 1998: 430). In this sense, Godard's theory of cinema is compatible with the historiography of Walter Benjamin which, as we saw in Chapter 9, seeks to rescue the memory of past generations (Bergala 1999: 221–4). However, the potential political value of such an operation risks being lost in a kind of mystical awe before the wonders of the image. More than one critic has argued that the images of *Histoire(s) du cinéma*, divorced from their original context, are transformed into 'pure epiphanies', signifying nothing other than the essential mystery of cinematic creation (Forest 1998: 23; Williams 1999: 313). (Jacques Aumont, notably, disagrees, arguing that each image retains something of its original narrative charge (Aumont 1999: 96).)

For an example of how Godard's complex discourse on the cinema comes together into a single montage, we might look at an instance from *Histoire(s) du cinéma* that has already generated a certain amount of commentary. The first episode of *Histoire(s)* (1A) sets out the argument we have outlined above about the cinema's abandonment of its historical responsibility and its subsequent 'redemption'. The argument reaches a kind of rhetorical and visual climax as Godard reads the following text:

> On a oublié cette petite ville et ses murs blancs cerclés d'oliviers, mais on se souvient de Picasso, c'est-à-dire de Guernica. On a oublié Valentin Feldman, le jeune philosophe fusillé en '43, mais qui ne se souvient au moins d'un prisonnier, c'est-a-dire de Goya? Et si George Stevens n'avait utilisé le premier le premier film en seize en couleurs à Auschwitz et Ravensbrück, jamais sans doute le bonheur d'Elizabeth Taylor n'aurait trouvé une place au soleil.[4]

4 'We have forgotten this little town with its white walls surrounded by olive trees, but we remember Picasso, that is to say Guernica. We have forgotten Valentin

To illustrate this passage, Godard edits together footage of bombers and executions from the war with details of art works by Picasso and Goya. Then a horrific colour image of corpses stacked in the ovens at a Nazi extermination camp, taken from *D-Day to Berlin*, the film edited together out of George Stevens's war footage in 1985, dissolves in and out of shots of Elizabeth Taylor and Montgomery Clift sunbathing by a lake in *A Place in the Sun*, a melodrama directed by Stevens in 1951. Finally, Godard superimposes over these images a detail from Giotto's *Noli me tangere* (1304–6) in which Mary Magdalene, rotated through ninety degrees, appears as an angel reaching down to claim the young Elizabeth Taylor. At this point, Godard adapts the line from Georges Bernanos that appears at the spiritual centre of Robert Bresson's film of *Le Journal d'un curé de campagne* (1951) (and that was already used in *Nouvelle Vague*): 'Ô quelle merveille que de pouvoir regarder ce qu'on ne voit pas! Ô miracle de nos yeux aveugles!'[5]

This sequence has provoked what is probably the most sustained and serious criticism of *Histoire(s) du cinéma* from Jacques Rancière who argues that this particular montage is emblematic of Godard's entire project (Rancière 1998: 58). In addition to criticising the very narrow, Euro-centric view of film history presented in the *Histoire(s)* (58), Rancière accuses Godard's argument of being fundamentally incoherent. 'Le cinéma est coupable pour ne pas avoir filmé les camps en leur temps,' argues Godard, yet, at the same time, 'il est grand pour les avoir filmé avant leur temps,' and finally, 'il est coupable pour ne pas les avoir reconnus'[6] (59). This apparently contradictory argument betrays a quasi-religious *faith* in the image and its miraculous capacity to document the real. If the cinema should have been present to record the reality of the camps, it is because this presence to the real is the *essential nature* of the image (59). And furthermore, if such is the essential nature of the image, then, despite its historical betrayal of its duty, it must remain *essentially innocent*: 'Si le cinéma peut se reconnaître coupable ... c'est en effet que cette puissance de l'Image parle encore en lui, qu'il y a en

---

Feldman, the young philosopher executed in '43, but who can forget one prisoner at least, that is to say Goya? And if George Stevens hadn't been the first to use the first 16mm colour film at Auschwitz and Ravensbrück, Elizabeth Taylor's happiness would never have found a place in the sun.'

5 'Oh what a marvel to be able to look at what we cannot see! Oh the miracle of our blind eyes!' (The original line celebrates the ability to 'give what we do not possess', the miracle of our 'empty hands.')

6 'The cinema is guilty of not having filmed the camps at the time; it is great because it filmed them before their time; it is guilty because it failed to recognise them.'

elle quelque chose qui résiste à toute trahison'[7] (Rancière 2001: 230). This is precisely what appears to be suggested in the montage described above, where the angelic figure seems to trace a halo of light in which Elizabeth Taylor may be resurrected from among the dead whom Stevens had filmed in the Nazi camps a few years earlier (Rancière 1998: 61).

But we perhaps need to look a little more closely at what Godard is saying in this sequence. In particular, it is worth analysing the text that he speaks over these images. For, presented with these three successive examples, the spectator tends perhaps to amalgamate them into a single argument about art providing an immortal monument to the sufferings of history which are otherwise forgotten. And yet, on closer inspection, it proves difficult to maintain the analogy between the three examples. In the first, admittedly, Godard suggests that, if we remember the bombing of Guernica, it is largely thanks to Picasso's painting. But the second example is already more problematic: after all, there is no logical connection between Valentin Feldman and Goya, who died over one hundred years earlier. And, if Goya is chosen as an artist who communicates something of the experience of *imprisonment*, the argument is further complicated by the fact that this imprisonment, in Goya's case, is metaphorical, the isolation caused by his sudden deafness. There is already, then, a metaphorical slippage from a real historical event to an unrelated artistic corpus, and this conceptual instability continues in the example of George Stevens. We are not, in other words, authorised to think that *A Place in the Sun* could not have been made if Stevens had never filmed the Nazi camps, nor that Elizabeth Taylor is in any meaningful sense the resurrection of the victims of these camps: these are simply two heterogeneous examples linked by the chance presence of George Stevens. The only connection to be made is between the *unspeakable* horror of the Nazi crimes and that which remains *inexpressible* in the image.

As Alan Wright comments, Godard does not bring these two images together because they are in any way alike, but precisely because they are terribly different. The work of montage is 'to make visible the abysmal structure at the heart of cinematic representation, the absence that haunts every film image' (Wright 2000: 54). Godard has remarked that there is something 'sombre' about the happiness displayed in *A Place in the Sun* (Godard 1998: 172), and indeed, in the scene quoted by Godard, a shadow is cast over the lovers' embrace. For George Eastman (Montgomery Clift) has purchased this lakeside idyll with Angela

7 'If the cinema is able to recognise its own guilt ... it is because the power of the Image continues to speak through it, because there remains in it something that resists all betrayal.'

Vickers (Taylor) only at the expense of a betrayal of his pregnant fiancée (Shelley Winters), while Angela's recollection of a drowning that took place on the lake the previous year foreshadows the tragedy to come in the rest of the film. It is this death and destruction that hovers around the edges of the image that we cannot *see*, but which Godard makes visible through his montage, through the terrible gulf that yawns between the two images. The point is that, regardless of the narrative attached, the film image is *necessarily* bordered by death: for if it preserves from the ravages of time on one hand, on the other it demonstrates time at work, the transformation of matter in time, the work of death (Callahan 2000: 146). This is the sense of a quotation from Maurice Blanchot that appears in a privileged position at the end of *Histoire(s) du cinéma*'s last episode:

> Oui, l'image est bonheur, – mais près d'elle le néant séjourne ... l'image, capable de nier le néant, est aussi le regard du néant sur nous. Elle est légère, et il est immensément lourd. Elle brille, et il est l'épaisseur diffuse où rien ne se montre.[8] (Blanchot 1971: 50–1)

It is in the paradoxical nature of the image to comfort us against the approach of oblivion, while at the same time partaking of that oblivion.

Rancière complains that Godard's arguments in *Histoire(s) du cinéma* do not represent rigorous historical thought. But this is a different kind of thought altogether – Godard is *thinking in images* – and its processes and products need not be the same. We are not obliged to resort to Michael Witt's defence that Godard's statements in *Histoire(s)* are mere 'poetic formulae' (Witt 2000a: 48). After all, Godard has repeatedly made it plain over the past couple of decades that the cinema should be taken seriously as a mode of thinking, and he is unafraid to refer to himself as a philosopher or a scientist. But that does not mean that his methodology or the results of his enquiry need be identical to those of a philosopher or a scientist. Godard's method – which he has been perfecting for many years now – works by the unexpected bringing together of images, which in turn sparks off a process of thought in the observer. This is not only visible in Godard's films, but also in statements he makes in interviews. For instance, when Godard declares that the European Union remains a fallacy so long as the televisions across the continent broadcast bad American movies rather than bad Greek or Portuguese movies (Godard 1998: 251), he is thinking in images. This

8 Yes, the image is happiness, – but next to it resides the void ... the image, capable of denying the void, is also the gaze of the void upon us. The image is light, and the void is immensely heavy. The image shines, and the void is that diffuse density in which nothing may show itself.

may be a rather eccentric definition of European Union, yet it provides an instant and irrefutable illustration of how far from a united Europe we truly remain.

When presented with the criticism of a spectator of *Histoire(s) du cinéma* who accused Godard of being 'obscure', the director responded: 'Elle attend qu'on lui dise ce qu'elle sait. Alors que pour moi, l'art, c'est dire ce qu'on ne sait pas, montrer ce qu'on ne voit pas'[9] (Godard 1998: 410). This approach may frequently lead Godard to be a little slapdash with the facts (Aumont 1999: 20), but the value of his method lies elsewhere. Godard's montage works by soliciting an initial empathic response from spectators before inviting them to construct the meaning of a given association and proceed to judgement. Thus the shocking brutality or the seductive beauty of a juxtaposition awakens us to recognition, but we are obliged to search our own memories as to the provenance and meaning of these images or texts before proceeding to a kind of critical montage of our own in order to make sense of them.

We can demonstrate this process at work in another, longer example of Godard's historical montage. In chapter 3A of *Histoire(s) du cinéma*, Godard 'edits together' two train journeys which took place in 1942. The first was part of a promotional tour of German film studios undertaken by French film stars such as Danielle Darrieux, Viviane Romance, Albert Préjean, Suzy Delair and Junie Astor. Godard illustrates this piece of history with a celebrity newsreel depicting the stars' departure from Gare de l'Est, together with glamorous production stills of Darrieux, Romance and Delair and the ironic pomp and ceremony of a rendition of the opening bars of 'La Marseillaise'. All this razzmatazz suddenly gives way to a quiet, melancholy Schumann piano sonata, as a series of titles inform us that, in 'le train d'après' ('the following train'), was the young Jewish writer Irène Nemirovsky. 'Son train partait pour Auschwitz'.[10] Nemirovsky was a Russian émigrée writer who achieved a certain success with her novel *Le Bal*, which was filmed in 1931 with none other than Danielle Darrieux in the starring role. In 1942, having reached safety in the South of France, Nemirovsky made the unwise decision to return to Paris to retrieve a bracelet; she was arrested by the Nazis and deported to Auschwitz. As with the montage described earlier, it is coincidental factors that motivate the association in this sequence: there it was the presence of George Stevens at the liberation of the death camps and as director of *A Place in the Sun*; here it is Darrieux's role in the adaptation of Nemirovsky's novel, and the departure

9 'She expects to be told what she already knows. Whereas for me, art means saying what you don't know, showing what you can't see.'

10 'Her train was leaving for Auschwitz.'

of two trains from the Gare de l'Est. We are not dealing in causal logic: there is no suggestion that the French stars were somehow directly responsible for Nemirovsky's deportation and murder at Auschwitz. But by bringing together two such different train journeys, Godard seeks to show us, in this montage, precisely what Darrieux, Romance *et al.* refused to see: that the political regime to which they lent their support – however implicitly or unconsciously – was a regime guilty of mass murder, and that this *rapprochement* between the French cinema establishment and Nazi Germany was thus a failure to assume the necessary historical responsibility. The form of the montage serves to reinforce this point by contrasting the noise and excitement of the stars' departure with the stillness and sadness of the mute intertitles that reveal Nemirovsky's fate. The significance is clear: it was the stars' collaboration that gave them the right to such a clamorous voice at a time when so many, Nemirovsky included, were definitively reduced to silence.

But it is significant, too, that it should be *train* journeys that provide the focus of this sequence. For trains carry a certain symbolic weight within the associative networks of *Histoire(s) du cinéma*. We mentioned above how the *Histoire(s)* deal at some length with the birth of cinema amidst other nineteenth-century technologies, and the *train* has a crucial place in this history. Of course, the train has been associated with cinema since the Lumière brothers' *Arrivée d'un train en gare de la Ciotat* (1895) provided the nascent art form with the originary myth of frightened spectators fleeing from the oncoming train. Godard quotes this famous piece of film in *Histoire(s)* 1B along with other notable train films including Abel Gance's *La Roue* (1923) and Renoir's adaptation of Zola's *La Bête humaine* (1938). Trains were of particular interest to early filmmakers since they provided a perfect opportunity to demonstrate the cinema's capacity to capture movement and speed. But in addition, train travel transformed the way we see and experience the world, contributing to the development of an immobile spectator watching the world unfold through a window-like frame. The cinema, recognising this kinship, made the locomotive its first star (Aumont 1999: 124).

The sequence of crossing trains from *Histoire(s)* 3A serves to remind us, in other words, of the cinema's origins in the technology of the nineteenth century. This technology should have allowed the world to progress; instead it became enslaved to totalising ideologies and led to catastrophe. For Godard suggests that the politics of fascism and the mechanics of the Final Solution belong, in part, to the same techno-ideological nexus to which we owe the cinema, centred around an industrial capitalist economy that objectifies human beings even as it seeks, with quasi-scientific rigour, to complete its knowledge of those human beings and realise their perfectibility. Godard's history of the cinema returns obsessively to the Shoah: wherever we turn in the *Histoire(s)*, another image of the camps, another evocation of Nazi terror, another allusion to this war unlike any other seems to await us. The Shoah lies at the end of all the associative paths in *Histoire(s) du cinéma*, but it is also what drives the movement of association and montage: it is that which lies beyond the confines of thought, that outside of thought that propels thought inexhaustibly onward. It is Godard's achievement in the *Histoire(s)* to have shown this process at work in the art of montage: by making historical connections across time, Godard's montage serves, among other functions, to highlight historical injustice, but, by constantly and almost inevitably running up against the most *unpardonable* injustice, the desire for justice, necessarily frustrated, is forever rekindled and launches Godard into new and different historical considerations. It is ultimately as a warning against what must never be allowed to happen again that all of Godard's historical work in the cinema tends towards the unthinkable absence at the heart of the twentieth century.

Éloge de l'amour

Éloge de l'amour (2001) marked Godard's return to international prominence after a decade and a half of working on projects that rarely received significant distribution outside France. The film can be, and has been interpreted as the continuation of Godard's 1990s work in its preoccupation with history and memory. *Éloge* shares the concern of *Histoire(s) du cinéma* with the responsibility of cinema towards the memory of the twentieth century, and reflects, too, upon the role of memory within love relationships. In addition, the film inscribes the processes of memory into its narrative structure, the events of the second half taking place two years before those of the first. Although not wishing to dispute the film's proximity to the historical work (for which I have argued myself (Morrey 2003)), I intend to focus here on the extent to which *Éloge* actually marks itself off as *different* from the 1990s films, despite sharing many similar themes and using many of the same points of reference. As Isabelle McNeill has noted, this is 'a decidedly post-*Histoire(s)* film' (McNeill 2003: 115).

The main difference, it seems to me, from the 1990s films, is the extent to which history, in *Éloge de l'amour*, has become *cumbersome*. There was already a sense, in the earlier work, that the responsibility of history was a considerable burden, but it was a burden Godard seemed only too willing to assume. *Éloge*, on the other hand, appears marked by a degree of doubt as to the ultimate utility of so much historical reflection. *Éloge de l'amour* is a film *weighed down* by the presence of history. This is true on the level of the characters: Edgar (Bruno Putzulu) seems unable to forget Berthe (Cécile Camp), the young woman he met in Brittany two years earlier. He relentlessly pursues her with the aim of casting her in his artistic 'project', despite her continued, firm refusals. Indeed, we might suggest that, if Edgar seems unable to bring his project to fruition, it is because he is unable to get over this choice for his lead actress. On a wider level, too, the film shows us a nation – indeed a continent – that remains haunted by its past. Everywhere we turn there is some reminder of the tragedy of the twentieth century, as in the plaque that Edgar and Berthe see on a Paris bridge commemorating the killing of a *gardien de la paix* by 'the Germans'. But this history of conflict stretches much further back than the Second World War, Edgar at one point recalling the invasion of Gaul by Roman troops in 50 BC. As Europeans, we carry this history in our bodies. *Éloge de l'amour* contains two striking examples of the material trace of time and experience in the human subject: one is a recording of Paul Celan reading his poem 'Todesfuge' about the death camps, his fragile, wounded voice adding to the sense of a horror beyond expression. The other is the presence of the publisher Françoise Verny in the role of a former resistance fighter: clearly in very poor health, she is not spared the persistent gaze of Godard's camera as she struggles for breath, looking, in Charles Tesson's rather callous image, something like a beached whale (Tesson 2001: 38). The inordinate importance attached to the past is clearly demonstrated in the film's striking colour scheme. The first part of the film, taking place in Paris in the present, is filmed in black and white, which Godard in the *Histoire(s)* repeatedly referred to as the colours of memory and of mourning. The present, here, is so preoccupied with the past that it seems unable to take on a life of its own, as though it were already dead, already *past*. By contrast, the second part, taking place in the past, is filmed in the vivid colours of digital video, suggesting that the past is clearer, is more alive to us than the present.

If anything, then, the characters of *Éloge de l'amour* have *too much* memory. When Edgar tracks down Berthe two years after their first meeting, she tells him, 'Vous avez de la mémoire'. 'Oui, j'en ai, je crois,' he replies, 'J'en ai même trop'.[11] The dangers of becoming too fixated on

11 'You've got a good memory. – Yes, I think I have. Too good, even.'

the past were set out in a famous text by Friedrich Nietzsche. Nietzsche notes that 'it is possible to value the study of history to such a degree that life becomes stunted and degenerate' (Nietzsche 1983 [1874]: 59). There is a certain *fever* of history which involves becoming overwhelmed by the pressure of the past. On the contrary, it is forgetting, 'the capacity to feel *unhistorically*' that is the necessary precondition of happiness (62). More than this, though, it is the condition of all action: since, for Nietzsche, all action is necessarily selfish and will necessarily be offensive to someone, a heightened awareness of one's historical condition can only paralyse action: 'It requires a great deal of strength to be able to live and to forget the extent to which to live and to be unjust is one and the same thing' (76). Afraid of action, we settle for interiorising culture, thereby becoming 'walking encyclopaedias' (79) with a tendency towards irony, cynicism and stasis. Nietzsche does not, ultimately, advocate a complete dismissal of history. After all, an inability to think historically would imply an inability to make any relation to other living beings. But it is essential to be able to impose a limit, or a horizon, on this historical perspective if we are to act in the present: 'the unhistorical and the historical are necessary in equal measure for the health of an individual, of a people and of a culture' (63).

Éloge de l'amour seems painfully aware of the extent to which our obsession with the past threatens to block our progress in the future. This is suggested by the film's brief evocation of a stop on Paris's suburban tramway that has been named Drancy-Avenir. Ironically, the evocation of a 'future' in Drancy serves only to recall its shameful past, as the site of a Nazi holding camp for prisoners awaiting deportation. Similarly, a discussion of the crisis in Kosovo focuses on our apparent inability to learn from the lessons of the past. As the American journalist Mark Hunter puts it: 'Since the Second World War, how often have the victims been asked to live among the victimizers, without any acknowledgement of the facts by their authors, without judgement, without planning for the slightest reparation from the guilty party?' (for an analysis of this sequence, see Morrey 2003: 124).

If the weight of the past can hinder action in the present, then it also hinders creation, and *Éloge de l'amour* at times appears so preoccupied with *images of the past* that the creation of new images comes to seem a virtual impossibility. This may be the sense of the blank pages of a book through which Edgar leafs at intervals throughout the film: the difficulty of creating new works of art when one is all too aware of those that have gone before. This would be another explanation for Edgar's apparent inability to get his project off the ground (despite financial backing from a wealthy benefactor). Godard's film is haunted by other images from the history of cinema. In particular, as reviewers were quick to point out, the first part of the film, with scenes centred around cafés and cinemas in Montparnasse and the *quartier latin*, inevitably recalls the location shooting of Godard's Nouvelle Vague films. Indeed, Charles Tesson goes as far as to suggest that the constant recalling of both the Occupied Paris and the New Wave Paris ultimately implies an audacious conclusion: 'ce n'est pas De Gaulle qui a libéré Paris mais bien la Nouvelle Vague'[12] (Tesson 2001: 39). How to film Paris today in the light of such an illustrious past? Individual films and filmmakers creep constantly into view: Robert Bresson is present in posters advertising a revival of *Pickpocket* (1959) as well as in the ubiquitous quotations from his *Notes sur le cinématographe*. A scene by the river with a barge drifting past cannot fail to evoke *L'Atalante* (1934). The glimpse of a café named L'Odessa inevitably brings to mind *Battleship Potemkin* (1925). There is also one particularly striking example of what we might call, following Deleuze (1985: 66–7), a memory-image. An early treatment of the screenplay for *Éloge* shows that Godard had planned to include a sequence at a swimming pool in which the young lovers Perceval and Églantine split up. At one point, Églantine was to pull nervously at her necklace and its pearls would drop into the water (Godard 1998: 465). In the finished film, this scene exists only in the form of a rehearsal in which Edgar directs his two young actors and Églantine (Audrey Klebaner) *mimes* the action of pulling at her necklace. However, for the spectator who has followed Godard's work in the 1990s, this scene necessarily recalls an image from a Russian film by Boris Barnet entitled (in French) *Au bord de la mer bleue* (1936), and which Godard quoted in *Les Enfants jouent à la Russie* (1993), in *Histoire(s) du cinéma* and in *De l'origine du XXI*[e] *siècle* (2000). There is a sense in which Godard, after such a lengthy absorption in film history, has become so infused with *past images* (and images of the past) that images in the present can only act as ghosts of those that have gone before.

It is in this way that *Éloge de l'amour* evinces a somewhat paradoxical *refusal* of image-making. In interviews around the film, Godard repeatedly noted how cheap, lightweight video cameras lead people to believe that anyone can make movies, but he complained that these budding filmmakers are more inclined to look at the video screen than at what they are filming (Godard 2001a: 62; 2001b: 57). 'Ce qui compte, ce n'est pas ce que l'on voit dans l'écran de contrôle de la petite caméra, c'est ce qu'on ne voit pas. Une chose qu'on ne voit pas, il faut y croire, la

12 'it wasn't De Gaulle who liberated Paris, but the New Wave'.

vouloir ...'[13] (Godard 2001b: 57). The film's provocative condemnation of Hollywood movie-making (see Morrey 2003: 122) seems to me to rest on the implication that these are *films without images* (just as the Americans are a nation without a history), precisely because the Americans have no idea how to look at the world. *Éloge de l'amour* underlines the difficulty of making images by refusing to provide us with those that we expect. The images of Edgar and Berthe's relationship, of Monsieur and Madame Bayard's resistance activities, of Edgar's work of art, in short of all those elements that make up the narrative, are definitively *absent* from the film (Morrey 2003: 127). Berthe/Cécile Camp, who, in a more traditional film, might be described as the 'lead actress' or the 'love interest' is consistently hidden from view, filmed from behind, concealed behind her hair, backlit to appear in silhouette and so on, never becoming the kind of erotic object that is the fate of so many women on screen (Morrey 2003: 126–7). When Godard does create images of startling beauty, they are fleeting and detached from the main plot, as though the director were afraid that their power would dissolve upon contact with narrative. Hence we glimpse an itinerant magician making a cigarette levitate in a Montparnasse café; a rollerblader performing solitary tricks in an arcade; a rapidly and confusingly edited gathering of young people on a tennis court; a shot of a speedometer in a moving car at night that flickers and jerks, in the words of Jacques Drillon, 'comme une pulsion'[14] (in Godard 2001a: 62).

In order further to illustrate the weight of the past in *Éloge de l'amour*, I would like to compare two matching scenes, one from the first half and one from the second half of the film (for another comparison based on the same principle, see Morrey 2003: 124–5). The first scene takes place in the apartment of Rosenthal (Claude Baignères), Edgar's benefactor. Various hints might encourage us to see this character as a kind of surrogate for Godard. Rosenthal is an art collector and begins this sequence by comparing two paintings placed side by side, a practice that recalls André Malraux's approach to art history as well as Godard's theory of montage. Rosenthal also shares Godard's discourse on rights and responsibility, implying a 'devoir' rather than 'droits d'auteur'[15] when he suggests that the Louvre is stealing works of art from the public: 'le directeur du Louvre ne veut plus simplement protéger *la*

13 'What counts is not what you see in the little camera's control screen, but what you don't see. If you can't see something, you have to believe in it, you have to want it ... .'
14 'like a [psychic] drive'.
15 'Droits d'auteur' means copyright, but literally: 'rights of the author'. Godard tends to replace it with 'devoir d'auteur': 'responsibility of the author'.

Victoire de Samothrace, il veut être l'*auteur* de cette protection'.[16] But this surrogate-Godard also appears burdened by the oppressive weight of the past. He talks about 'ce sentiment d'être hier qui décourage';[17] he notes the way we laugh about 1900 even though our own age is just as ridiculous. Rosenthal's apartment, with its antique furniture, certainly seems to belong to another age, and a cutaway shows us, hunched in a chair in profile to the camera, the gaunt and rangy figure of Rosenthal's assistant Philippe (Philippe Loyrette), looking like an escapee from a German Expressionist film. In addition, we discover that Rosenthal is inhabiting the apartment in which Henri Langlois began his collection of films which would one day become the Cinémathèque Française. Rosenthal explains to a friend how, as a youth, he had been in love with Edgar's mother at a time when her family was being persecuted by the Nazis. With Edgar's parents now dead (his father in a car crash, his mother from suicide), Rosenthal feels a kind of responsibility towards the young man. But this responsibility to a memory of the past extends beyond the characters to infect the city itself. A shot outside shows an American flag fluttering in the breeze (on a neighbouring building? We are in the diplomatic quarter of the city) as though to imply that American cultural imperialism is the legacy of Paris's historic debt to the USA. Rosenthal's French-Vietnamese maid remarks: 'Les Américains sont partout, n'est-ce pas Monsieur? Qui se souvient de la résistance du Vietnam?'.[18] Over this scene drifts the voice of Kevin Spacey in *American Beauty* (1999), although no *image* from the film is made visible. Elsewhere in the sequence, a beautiful shot shows the light shining off the still and silent keys of a grand piano as a piano *plays* on the soundtrack. It is an image, much like that of Edgar's empty book, of the impossibility of art in a world so overloaded with cultural memory.

This scene is matched, in the second half of *Éloge de l'amour*, by the scene (or pair of scenes) in which Edgar meets Berthe's grandfather, the former resistance fighter Monsieur Bayard (Jean Davy). The scene takes place in a similarly old-fashioned salon with Bayard hunched on a chair in much the same posture as Philippe earlier. Like Rosenthal, Bayard reminisces about the past, his time in the Resistance, his wife and granddaughter, all illustrated by photos that Godard cuts into the dialogue. Bayard's difficulty in moving beyond the past is illustrated in the second of the two scenes in which he reads from a text by Jean-Paul

16 'the director of the Louvre is no longer content to protect *La Victoire de Samothrace*, he wants to be the *author* of that protection [i.e. to own the rights to it]'.

17 'this discouraging feeling of being yesterday'.

18 'The Americans are everywhere, aren't they Sir? Who remembers the Vietnamese resistance?'

Sartre entitled 'La fin de la guerre'. 'Aujourd'hui, 20 août '45', reads Bayard, 'dans ce Paris désert et affamé, la guerre a pris fin, la Paix n'a pas commencé'[19] (Sartre 1945: 164). In this article, Sartre highlights the difference between official history, decreed by men sitting behind desks, and *lived* history, in which the line between war and peace is indistinct, if it exists at all. He also expresses the disappointment of a nation emerging from the war to discover that France now only has a minor role on the world stage and the new terror looming in the future as the spectre of nuclear annihilation: 'Nous voilà pourtant revenu à l'An Mil, chaque matin nous serons à la veille de la fin des temps'[20] (Sartre 1945: 166). This reference to the Millennium of course resonates with the *other* millennium celebrated around the time of *Éloge de l'amour*, just as Rosenthal's evocation of 1900 reminded us of our own new century. If, for Sartre, the end of the Second World War seemed to mark a strange step *backwards*, then for Godard, our emergence from the twentieth century appears equally inauspicious, still struggling as we are to shake off the legacy of that century's conflicts. And, as in the earlier sequence, the burden of the past translates into the difficulty of creating new images. This scene is in fact the occasion on which Edgar first lays eyes on Berthe and it contains the *only* image in the whole film in which we get a good look at her face. Offscreen, we hear Berthe enter the room and ask her grandfather about a videocassette. After she leaves, Monsieur Bayard asks Edgar to close the door. As Edgar walks towards the glass door, we see Berthe standing outside, her yellow coat matched by the glow of the winter sun as it sinks low in the late-afternoon sky. Her gaze is cast down towards the ground and, as Edgar greets her, she looks up briefly before moving rapidly out of the frame. As with some of the other examples we have seen, Godard appears to suggest that an image of such beauty can only exist *for an instant* if it is not to be lost forever in a reifying process of signification that would destroy its radical innocence.

It is in these two scenes also that one of the key themes of *Éloge de l'amour* is raised. At the end of the sequence in Rosenthal's apartment, Edgar arrives and discusses his project with his benefactor. Edgar stresses that, in addition to the four moments of love, his project must contain the three ages of man: youth, adulthood and old age. But it is the central category that appears problematic: Edgar notes that, if you pass a youth or an old person on the street, you identify them essentially *as*

19 'Today, 20 August 1945, in a deserted and starving Paris, the war has ended, but Peace has not yet begun.'

20 'Yet here we are returned to the Millennium: every morning we will be at the eve of the end of time.'

young or old, whereas one would never say 'There's an adult'. Adults always require some kind of (hi)story to explain who they are. This theme is taken up in the later scene where Bayard suggests that the Resistance has known its youth and its old age, but never 'l'âge adulte'. Edgar is forced to agree with him (and so this is presumably where he gets the idea in the first place): 'Un adulte, ça n'existe pas'.[21] Charles Tesson has put forward the argument that Edgar's project about love is in fact something of a red herring in *Éloge de l'amour,* a kind of mourning for a screenplay that Godard never filmed, and in fact it is this notion of the non-existent adult that becomes 'le leitmotiv secret du film'[22] (Tesson 2001: 38). If adults *don't exist,* I suggest, it is because, paradoxically, they are too closely bound up with the movement of history. Adults are defined by their work, be it the work that drives the economy or the work that drives the population, the work of parenting. As Godard explains, 'Il faut ajouter son rôle (emploi) dans la société pour définir l'adulte'[23] (Godard 1998: 469). Hence also the complete erasure from society of those who have no work with which to define themselves: one aspect of *Éloge* that has survived the various mutations of the script is the desire to show the homeless on the streets of Paris. Young and old people exist to some extent outside time, or at least in a different relationship to time. Young people project themselves into the future in an effort to define an identity; old people reminisce about the past in an attempt to interpret who they have been. Adults live in the present, that is to say a *point* in time that does not exist, since it is continually slipping away to be replaced by another present. It is in this invisible present that a life exhausts itself. Berthe is a perfect example of an adult who doesn't exist, primarily because she has *no time.* It is practically impossible, in watching *Éloge de l'amour,* to determine how many different jobs Berthe has. Edgar and Philippe initially look for her in a café in Montparnasse where she may be waitressing, before finding her in railyards to the north of the city where she works as a cleaner. From there she goes directly to clean offices at the place d'Italie. But she also works in a bookshop and her grandfather mentions something about her working for a legal practice. There is certainly no time for her to take on a role in Edgar's production. When he insists that she must have at least one day off, Berthe announces that she must drive her son to Dijon that day. If Berthe is invisible in *Éloge de l'amour,* it is not only because of Godard's anxiety about image-making, but also, as McNeill

21 'There's no such thing as an adult.'
22 'the secret leitmotiv of the film.'
23 'You have to add their role (their job) within society in order to define an adult.'

points out, due to her disillusionment and overwork (McNeill 2003: 118). This enigmatic theme of the missing adult can thus be inscribed within a political tradition in Godard's work which may be traced at least as far back as *2 ou 3 choses que je sais d'elle* and which laments those lives lost in the thankless support of a capitalist economy, all those individuals obliged, in Berthe's image, to enter life through 'l'entrée de service' ('the back door').

This paradox whereby the adult does not exist precisely as a result of being *within history* might be seen as central to the work of art itself. In a commentary on Nietzsche's *Birth of Tragedy*, Leo Bersani defines art as the attempt to give figuration to a being or a process that, in its oneness, necessarily refuses figuration (Nietzsche calls this oneness Dionysus; we might call it history). The heroes of Greek tragedy are 'symbolic appearances' of Dionysus, despite the fact that its oneness implies not their transcendence but their annihilation (Bersani 1990: 93–4). The Dionysian impulse may be countered by the Apollonian, which is 'the impulse to save consciousness from the nonidentity ... of an always potential oneness of being' (95). But the Apollonian is not to be confused with 'character' in the traditional sense of subjectivity: rather this is a kind of experience of '*pure demarcation*' from the oneness of being that is never allowed to take on an individual identity (96) since the individual is that which 'dies at the moment of being defined' (99). It is these 'risks of appearance and disappearance' (101) that are at stake in the work of art, then, and, I would suggest, in Edgar's project (and, by extension, Godard's) in *Éloge de l'amour*. Auditioning the actress who will play Églantine, Edgar asks: 'Est-ce que vous avez compris que ce n'est pas l'histoire d'Églantine, mais un moment de l'histoire – la Grande Histoire – qui passe à travers Églantine?'.[24] Later, with Berthe, Edgar complains that people often say 'Ça, c'est une autre histoire. Mais on ne la dit jamais, cette autre histoire. Peut-être parce qu'il faut la dire autrement'.[25] This is precisely the (hi)story that Edgar is interested in: 'Pas votre histoire, ni la mienne. Quoi qu'il arrive, la nôtre. Même si on ne se connaît pas'.[26]

This, it seems to me, is also the sense of a quotation from Jean Anouilh that appears in the latter half of the film. The quotation, taken from Anouilh's modern retelling of *Antigone*, is delivered by the chorus in the play:

24 'Have you understood that this is not the story of Églantine but a moment of history that passes through Églantine?'

25 'That's another story. But no one ever tells this other story. Perhaps because you have to tell it in a different way.'

26 'Not your (hi)story or mine but, whatever happens, *ours*, even if we don't know each other.'

> C'est facile la tragédie. On est tranquille. Ça roule tout seul. La mort, le désespoir, la trahison sont là tout prêts, et les éclats, et les orages, et les silences, tous les silences. C'est propre, la tragédie, c'est reposant, c'est sûr ... D'abord, on est entre soi. On est tous innocents en somme. Parce qu'on sait qu'il n'y a plus d'espoir, le triste espoir; qu'on est pris, qu'on est enfin pris.[27] (arranged from Anouilh 1986: 62–3)

Isabelle McNeill places this view of tragedy on a level with Hollywood cinema in its attempt 'to recuperate the past in a redemptive narrative': tragedy in this sense may be sad, but it is 'perfectly comprehensible, in no way disturbing to a sense of the order of things' (McNeill 2003: 117). I would be tempted to give a more positive reading of this reference to tragedy, and to see it as quite consciously post-Nietzschean. For this is the goal of *Éloge de l'amour*, to depict these characters only to the extent that they can be individuated from the imperious movement of history that flows through them and in which they are caught up. This sense of being *caught* in history is an ambiguous one: in the original text by Anouilh, one is caught 'comme un rat, avec tout le ciel sur son dos'[28] (Anouilh 1986: 63). By omitting the end of this sentence and having the lines read by Berthe in a calm, even tone over an image of waves washing against rocks, Godard conveys instead the sense of being caught in a welcoming hand, there is a feeling of *security* to this enclosure within history. It is significant that Anouilh's words should belong to the chorus of his play, since Nietzsche identifies the chorus as representatives of the Dionysian in Greek tragedy, and principally responsible for communicating 'an overwhelming feeling of unity', a 'metaphysical comfort' to the unfolding of the tragedy (Nietzsche 1995 [1872]: 22).

This sense of the necessity of history's movement (not of its outcome, but of its *continuation*) returns us, ultimately, to the preoccupation with necessity and contingency that we detected in Godard's critical writing back at the start of this book. When Godard talks of a form – or a style, for this is where form *becomes* style – that appears necessary, he means a form in which the impersonal movement of history makes itself felt, beyond any mere authorial signature. In an interview at the time of *Éloge*, Godard declared: 'La forme ressentie comme une nécessité, on la trouve encore; elle est le fait d'individualités qui sont traversées par ce qu'il y a eu de bien dans le cinéma depuis

27 'Tragedy is simple. You're at ease. It works all by itself. Death, despair and betrayal are close by, and storm and commotion and silence, all those silences. Tragedy is clean, it's restful, it's secure. In the first place, we're among ourselves. We're all innocent, in the end. Because we know that there is no longer any hope, sad hope, that we're caught, caught at last.'

28 'like a rat, with all of heaven on one's back'.

Lumière, qu'elles connaissent ou pas l'histoire ... La forme, c'est ce qui reste, sans parler, sans pouvoir dire ce qu'on a fait. Sans commentaire'[29] (Godard 2001b: 52).

Ultimately, too, this must be the sense of love in *Éloge de l'amour*, inasmuch as love remains in the film even after it has been all but erased from the screenplay. As I have argued, following the quotation from Bataille that appears in the film (Morrey 2003: 128), love is that which grants us the possibility to see totality, to see the oneness of history, but only at the expense of our individual identity. For through, or across, or in between the object of our affections – be it a human being or a film – what we really love, each time, is the movement of life itself.

29 'Form experienced as a necessity can still be found; it is the fact of individualities through whom has passed all that has been good in the cinema since Lumière, whether or not they are aware of the history ... Form is that which remains, without speaking, even though you can't say what you've done. Without comment.'

References

Anouilh, J. (1986), *Antigone*, London, Nelson.

Aumont, J. (1999), *Amnésies: Fictions du cinéma d'après Jean-Luc Godard*, Paris, POL.

Bergala, A. (1999), *Nul mieux que Godard*, Paris, Cahiers du cinéma.

Bersani, L. (1990), *The Culture of Redemption*, Cambridge, MA and London, Harvard University Press.

Blanchot, M. (1971), *L'Amitié*, Paris, Gallimard.

Callahan, V. (2000), 'The evidence and uncertainty of silent film in *Histoire(s) du cinéma*', in M. Temple and J. S. Williams (eds), *The Cinema Alone: Essays on the Work of Jean-Luc Godard 1985–2000*, Amsterdam, Amsterdam University Press, 141–57.

Deleuze, G. (1985), *Cinéma 2: L'Image-temps*, Paris, Minuit.

Eisenschitz, B. (1998), 'Une machine à montrer l'invisible', *Cahiers du cinéma*, 529, 52–6.

Forest, P. (1998), 'La rose dans la poussière de l'acier', *Art Press*, hors série, *Le Siècle de Jean-Luc Godard: Guide pour 'Histoire(s) du cinéma'*, 13–26.

Godard, J.-L. (1980), *Introduction à une véritable histoire du cinéma*, Paris, Albatros.

Godard, J.-L. (1998), *Jean-Luc Godard par Jean-Luc Godard, Tome 2: 1984–1998*, Paris, Cahiers du cinéma.

Godard, J.-L. (2001a), 'Je serai content si mon film est un peu vu ...', *Le Nouvel Observateur*, 10–16 May, 62–3.

Godard, J.-L. (2001b), 'Je reviens en arrière mais je vais de l'avant', *Télérama*, 2679 (16 May), 52–7.

MacCabe, C. (2003), *Godard: A Portrait of the Artist at 70*, London, Bloomsbury.

McNeill, I. (2003), 'Phrases, monuments and ruins: Melancholy history in *Éloge de l'amour* (2001)', *Studies in French Cinema*, 3, 2, 111–20.

Mondzain, M.-J. (1998), 'Histoire et passion', *Art Press*, hors série, *Le Siècle de Jean-Luc Godard: Guide pour 'Histoire(s) du cinéma'*, 91–7.

Morrey, D. (2003), 'History of resistance/resistance of history: Godard's *Éloge de l'amour* (2001)', *Studies in French Cinema*, 3, 2, 120–30.

Nietzsche, F. (1983 [1874]), *Untimely Meditations*, trans. by R. S. Hollingdale, Cambridge, Cambridge University Press.

Nietzsche, F. (1995 [1872]), *The Birth of Tragedy*, New York: Dover Publications.

Rancière, J. (1998), 'La Sainte et l'héritière: À propos des *Histoire(s) du cinéma*', *Cahiers du cinéma*, 537, 58–61.

Rancière, J. (2001), *La Fable cinématographique*, Paris, Seuil.

Sartre, J.-P. (1945), 'La fin de la guerre', *Les Temps Modernes* (October), 163–7.

Saxton, L. (2003), 'Anamnésis: Godard/Lanzmann', *Trafic*, 47.

Temple, M. (2000), 'Big rhythm and the power of metamorphosis: Some models and precursors for *Histoire(s) du cinéma*', in M. Temple and J. S. Williams (eds), *The Cinema Alone: Essays on the Work of Jean-Luc Godard 1985–2000*, Amsterdam, Amsterdam University Press, 77–95.

Tesson, C. (2001), 'Et l'âge de l'amour', *Cahiers du cinéma*, 557, 38–9.

Williams, J. S. (1999), 'The signs among us: Jean-Luc Godard's *Histoire(s) du cinéma*', *Screen*, 40, 3, 306–15.

Witt, M. (1999), 'The death(s) of cinema according to Jean-Luc Godard', *Screen*, 40, 3, 331–46.

Witt, M. (2000a), 'Montage, my beautiful care, or histories of the cinematograph', in M. Temple and J. S. Williams (eds), *The Cinema Alone: Essays on the Work of Jean-Luc Godard 1985–2000*, Amsterdam, Amsterdam University Press, 33–50.

Witt, M. (2000b), '"Qu'était-ce que le cinéma, Jean-Luc Godard?" An analysis of the cinema(s) at work in and around Godard's *Histoire(s) du cinéma*', in E. Ezra and S. Harris (eds), *France in Focus: Film and National Identity*, Oxford, Berg, 23–41.

Wright, A. (2000), 'Elizabeth Taylor at Auschwitz: JLG and the real object of montage', in M. Temple and J. S. Williams (eds), *The Cinema Alone: Essays on the Work of Jean-Luc Godard 1985–2000*, Amsterdam, Amsterdam University Press, 51–60.

Conclusion

As we suggested in our introduction, Godard's cinema has always shared the concerns of philosophy. This study has demonstrated how the development of Godard's thinking about cinema, as well as his film practice, have constantly mirrored wider trends in continental thought. The phenomenological method of Godard's early films interrogated the relationship between language and the reality perceived through our senses, the director's innovative approach to sound and image repeatedly questioning the nature of representation and its ability to circumscribe the real. By 1968, this had given rise to the giddy deconstructions of *Le Gai Savoir* and the attendant undoing of the ideological implications of cinematic signifiers. Godard's cinema accompanied the renewal of Marxist thought in France, from Debord's critique of spectacle, through Foucault's analysis of power, to the determined unpacking of the harsh realities of postmodernism by the likes of Lyotard. At the same time, Godard followed philosophers such as Bataille and Deleuze, in a tradition of thought inherited from Nietzsche, in denouncing the nihilism of a society that smothers the vitality of life beneath the reifying discourse of truth, and in defending desire against the curmudgeonly categories of psychoanalysis.

But Godard's cinema is not simply cinema *about* philosophy or cinema *with* philosophy, rather it is cinema *as* philosophy. The cinematograph is a machine for thinking, for propelling thought: this conclusion that is most clearly drawn in *Histoire(s) du cinéma* was already implicit in the phenomenological excess of *2 ou 3 choses que je sais d'elle*, in the dialectics of the Dziga Vertov Group, or in the multiple lines of flight sketched by the 1980s films. It is because cinema works with the very stuff of life – because the analytical thought of montage never entirely dispels the preconceptual wonder of the indexical image – that the filmmaker is uniquely placed to scrutinise the structure and complexity of the real without ever surrendering a sense of intoxication before the world. Godard's recurring, and always related, themes of love and work should perhaps ultimately be seen as fundamental to the operation of cinema itself: the cinema is such a remarkable tool for revealing and understanding the world and our place within it because it enables us to look upon that world with love.

Filmography

Opération béton (1954) 20 min., b/w

Production company: Actua-Films
Screenplay: Jean-Luc Godard
Photography: Adrien Porchet

Une femme coquette (1955) 10 min., b/w

Screenplay: Hans Lucas [Jean-Luc Godard]
Photography: Hans Lucas
Principal actors: Marie Lysandre, Roland Tolma

Tous les garçons s'appellent Patrick (Charlotte et Véronique) (1957) 21 min., b/w

Production company: Films de la Péiade
Producer: Pierre Braunberger
Screenplay: Jean-Luc Godard and Eric Rohmer
Photography: Michel Latouche
Editing: Cécile Decugis
Principal actors: Jean-Claude Brialy (Patrick); Anne Colette (Charlotte), Nicole Berger (Véronique)

Une histoire d'eau (1958) 18 min., b/w

Production company: Films de la Pléiade
Producer: Pierre Braunberger
Screenplay: François Truffaut
Photography: Michel Latouche
Editing: Jean-Luc Godard
Sound: Jacques Maumont
Principal actors: Jean-Claude Brialy (him), Carole Dim (her), Jean-Luc Godard (narrator)

Charlotte et son jules (1959) 20 min., b/w

Production company: Films de la Pléiade
Producer: Pierre Braunberger
Screenplay: Jean-Luc Godard
Photography: Michel Latouche
Editing: Cécile Decugis
Sound: Jacques Maumont
Principal actors: Jean-Paul Belmondo (Jean), Anne Colette (Charlotte), Gérard Blain (the guy)

À bout de souffle (1960) 90 min., b/w

Production company: Société Nouvelle de Cinématographie, Productions Georges de Beauregard, Imperia
Producer: Georges de Beauregard
Screenplay: Jean-Luc Godard
Photography: Raoul Coutard
Editing: Cécile Decugis, Lila Herman
Sound: Jacques Maumont
Principal actors: Jean Seberg (Patricia Franchini), Jean-Paul Belmondo (Michel Poiccard), Henri-Jacques Huet (Berruti), Jean-Pierre Melville (Parvulesco), Liliane David (Liliane), Daniel Boulanger (inspector)

Le Petit Soldat (1960) 88 min., b/w

Production company: Société Nouvelle de Cinématographie, Productions Georges de Beauregard
Producer: Georges de Beauregard
Screenplay: Jean-Luc Godard
Photography: Raoul Coutard
Editing: Agnès Guillemot, Lila Herman, Nadine Marquand
Sound: Jacques Maumont
Principal actors: Michel Subor (Bruno Forestier), Anna Karina (Véronica Dreyer), Henri-Jacques Huet (Jacques), Paul Beauvais (Paul), Laszlo Szabo (Laszlo)

Une femme est une femme (1961) 84 min., Eastmancolor

Production company: Rome-Paris-Films
Producer: Georges de Beauregard
Screenplay: Jean-Luc Godard
Photography: Raoul Coutard
Editing: Agnès Guillemot, Lila Herman
Sound: Guy Villette

Principal actors: Anna Karina (Angela Récamier), Jean-Claude Brialy (Émile Récamier), Jean-Paul Belmondo (Alfred Lubitsch), Nicole Paquin (prostitute), Marie Dubois (Suzanne)

La Paresse (1961) 15 min., b/w

Episode of *Les Sept péchés capitaux*
Production company: Films Gibé, Franco-London-Films, Titanus
Screenplay: Jean-Luc Godard
Photography: Henri Decaë
Editing: Jacques Gaillard
Sound: Jean-Claude Marchetti, Jean Labussière
Principal actors: Eddie Constantine (Eddie Constantine), Nicole Mirel (the starlet)

Vivre sa vie (1962) 85 min., b/w

Production company: Films de la Pléiade
Producer: Pierre Braunberger
Screenplay: Jean-Luc Godard
Photography: Raoul Coutard
Editing: Agnès Guillemot, Lila Lakshmanan
Sound: Guy Villette, Jacques Maumont
Principal actors: Anna Karina (Nana), Sady Rebot (Raoul), André S. Labarthe (Paul), Peter Kassovitz (young man), Monique Messine (Élisabeth), Brice Parrain (philosopher)

Le Nouveau Monde (1962) 20 min., b/w

Episode of *RoGoPaG*
Production company: Arco Film, Cineruz, Société Cinématographique Lyre
Screenplay: Jean-Luc Godard
Photography: Jean Rabier
Editing: Agnès Guillemot, Lila Lakshmanan
Sound: André Hervé
Principal actors: Alexandra Stewart, Jean-Marc Bory, Jean-André Fieschi, Michel Delahaye

Les Carabiniers (1963) 80 min., b/w

Production company: Rome-Paris-Films, les Films Marceau, Laetitia
Producer: Georges de Beauregard, Carlo Ponti
Screenplay: Jean-Luc Godard, Roberto Rossellini, Jean Gruault
Photography: Raoul Coutard
Editing: Agnès Guillemot, Lila Lakshmanan

Sound: Jacques Maumont
Principal actors: Marino Masse (Ulysse), Albert Juross (Michel-Ange), Geneviève Galéa (Vénus), Catherine Ribeiro (Cléopâtre)

Le Grand Escroc (1963) 25 min., b/w

Episode of *Les Plus grands escroqueries du monde*
Production company: Ulysse Productions, LUX/CCF, Vides Cinematografica, Toho/Towa, Caesar Film Productie
Screenplay: Jean-Luc Godard
Photography: Raoul Coutard
Editing: Agnès Guillemot, Lila Lakshmanan
Sound:André Hervé
Principal actors: Jean Seberg (Patricia Leacock), Charles Denner (l'escroc), Laszlo Szabo (inspector)

Le Mépris (1963) 105 min., Eastmancolor

Production company: Rome-Paris-Films, Films Concordia, Compagnia Cinematografica Champion
Producer: Carlo Ponti, Georges de Beauregard
Screenplay: Jean-Luc Godard
Photography: Raoul Coutard
Editing: Agnès Guillemot, Lila Lakshmanan
Sound: William Sivel
Principal actors: Brigitte Bardot (Camille Javal), Jack Palance (Jeremiah Prokosch), Fritz Lang (himself), Michel Piccoli (Paul Javal), Georgia Moll (Francesca Vanini), Jean-Luc Godard (assistant director)

Bande à part (1964) 95 min., b/w

Production company: Anouchka Film, Orsay Film
Screenplay: Jean-Luc Godard
Photography: Raoul Coutard
Editing: Agnès Guillemot, Françoise Collin
Sound: René Levert, Antoine Bonfanti
Principal actors: Anna Karina (Odile), Claude Brasseur (Arthur), Sami Frey (Franz), Louisa Colpeyn (Mme Victoria), Danièle Girard (English teacher)

Montparnasse-Levallois (1964) 20 min., Ektachrome

Episode of *Paris vu par...*
Production company: Les Films du Losange, Films du Cyprès
Producer: Barbet Schroeder
Screenplay: Jean-Luc Godard

Photography: Albert Maysles
Editing: Jacqueline Raynal
Sound: René Levert
Principal actors: Johana Shimkus (Monika), Philippe Hiquily (Ivan), Serge Davri (Roger)

Une femme mariée (1964) 98 min., b/w

Production company: Anouchka Films, Orsay Films
Producer: Philippe Dussart
Screenplay: Jean-Luc Godard
Photography: Raoul Coutard
Editing: Agnès Guillemot, Françoise Collin
Sound: Antoine Bonfanti, René Levert, Jacques Maumont
Principal actors: Macha Méril (Charlotte), Bernard Noël (Robert), Philippe Leroy (Pierre), Roger Leenhardt (himself), Rita Maiden (Mme Céline)

Alphaville, une étrange aventure de Lemmy Caution (1965) 98 min., b/w

Production company: Chaumiane Productions, Filmstudio
Producer: André Michelin
Screenplay: Jean-Luc Godard
Photography: Raoul Coutard
Editing: Agnès Guillemot
Sound: René Levert
Principal actors: Eddie Constantine (Lemmy Caution), Anna Karina (Natacha von Braun), Akim Tamiroff (Henri Dickson), Howard Vernon (Professeur Leonard Nosferatu/Professeur von Braun)

Pierrot le fou (1965) 112 min., Eastmancolor

Production company: Rome-Paris-Films, Productions Georges de Beauregard, Dino Laurentiis Cinematografica
Producer: Georges de Beauregard
Screenplay: Jean-Luc Godard
Photography: Raoul Coutard
Editing: Françoise Collin
Sound: René Levert
Principal actors: Jean-Paul Belmondo (Ferdinand), Anna Karina (Marianne), Dirk Sanders (the brother), Raymond Devos (man at the port), Graziella Galvani (Maria)

Masculin féminin (1966) 110 min., b/w

Production company: Anouchka Films, Argos Films, Svensk Filmindustri, Sandrews
Photography: Willy Kurant
Editing: Agnès Guillemot
Sound: René Levert
Principal actors: Jean-Pierre Léaud (Paul), Chantal Goya (Madeleine), Marlène Jobert (Elizabeth), Michel Debord (Robert), Catherine-Isabelle Duport (Catherine-Isabelle)

Made in USA (1966) 90 min., Eastmancolor

Production company: Anouchka Films, Rome-Paris-Film, Sepic
Producer: Georges de Beauregard
Screenplay: Jean-Luc Godard
Photography: Raoul Coutard
Editing: Agnès Guillemot
Sound: René Levert, Jacques Maumont
Principal actors: Anna Karina (Paula Nelson), Laszlo Szabo (Richard Widmark), Jean-Pierre Léaud (Donald Siegel), Yves Afonso (David Goodis), Ernest Menzer (Typhus), Jean-Claude Bouillon (inspector), Kyoko Kosaka (Doris Mizoguchi)

2 ou 3 choses que je sais d'elle (1966) 90 min., Eastmancolor

Production company: Anouchka Films, Argos Films, les Films du Carrosse, Parc Film
Screenplay: Jean-Luc Godard
Photography: Raoul Coutard
Editing: Françoise Collin, Chantal Delattre
Sound: René Levert, Antoine Bonfanti
Principal actors: Marina Vlady (Juliette Janson), Anny Duperey (Marianne), Roger Montsoret (Robert Janson), Raoul Lévy (the American), Jean Narboni (Roger), Christophe Bourseiller (Christophe), Marie Bourseiller (Solange), Joseph Gehrard (M. Gérard)

Anticipation, ou L'Amour en l'an 2000 (1966) 20 min., Eastmancolor

Episode of *Le Plus vieux métier du monde*
Production company: Francoriz Films, Films Gibé, Rialto Films, Rizzoli Films
Producer: Joseph Bergholz
Screenplay: Jean-Luc Godard
Photography: Pierre Lhomme

Editing: Agnès Guillemot
Sound: René Levert
Principal actors: Jacques Charrier (Dick), Anna Karina (Natacha), Marilù Tolo (Marlène)

Caméra-Œil (1967) 15 min., Eastmancolor

Episode of *Loin du Vietnam*
Production company: SLON
Photography: Alain Levent

La Chinoise (1967) 96 min., Eastmancolor

Production company: Anouchka Films, Les Productions de la Guéville, Athos Films, Parc Films, Simar Films
Screenplay: Jean-Luc Godard
Photography: Raoul Coutard
Editing: Agnès Guillemot, Delphine Desfons
Sound: René Levert
Principal actors: Anne Wiazemsky (Véronique), Jean-Pierre Léaud (Guillaume), Michel Semeniako (Henri), Lex de Bruijn (Kirilov), Juliet Berto (Yvonne), Omar Diop (Omar), Francis Jeanson (himself)

Week-end (1967) 95 min., Eastmancolor

Production company: Films Copernic, Comacico, Lira Films, Ascot Cineraïd
Screenplay: Jean-Luc Godard
Photography: Raoul Coutard
Editing: Agnès Guillemot
Sound: René Levert
Principal actors: Mireille Darc (Corinne), Jean Yanne (Roland), Jean-Pierre Kalfon (the chief), Jean-Pierre Léaud (Saint-Just), Yves Afonso (Tom Thumb), Daniel Pomereulle (Joseph Balsamo), Blandine Jeanson (Emily Brontë), Virginie Vignon (Marie-Madeleine)

Le Gai Savoir (1968) 95 min., Eastmancolor

Production company: ORTF, Anouchka Films, Bavaria Atelier
Screenplay: Jean-Luc Godard
Photography: Georges Leclerc
Editing: Germaine Cohen
Principal actors: Juliet Berto (Patricia Lumumba), Jean-Pierre Léaud (Émile Rousseau)

Un film comme les autres (1968) 100 min., Ektachrome

Co-directors: Groupe ARC
Photography: William Lubtchansky
Editing: Christine Aya

One plus one (1968) 99 min., Eastmancolor

Production company: Cupid Productions
Producer: Michael Pearson, lain Quarrier
Screenplay: Jean-Luc Godard
Photography: Tony Richmond
Editing: Ken Rowles
Sound: Arthur Bradburn, Derek Ball
Principal actors: The Rolling Stones, Anne Wiazemsky (Eve Democracy)

One American Movie (1968) 90 min., Ektachrome

Co-directors: Richard Leacock, D. A. Pennebaker
Production company: Leacock- Pennebaker, Inc.
Screenplay: Jean-Luc Godard
Photography: D. A. Pennebaker, Richard Leacock
Editing: D. A. Pennebaker
Sound: Mary Lampson, Robert Leacock, Kate Taylor
Principal actors: Richard Leacock, Eldridge Cleaver, Jean-Luc Godard, Anne Wiazemsky, Rip Torn, The Jefferson Airplane

British Sounds (1969) 99 min., Eastmancolor

Director: Dziga Vertov Group
Production company: Kestrel Productions, London Weekend Television
Producer: Irving Teitelbaum, Kenneth Trodd
Screenplay: Jean-Luc Godard, Jean-Henri Roger
Photography: Charles Stewart
Editing: Elisabeth Koziman
Sound: Fred Sharp

Pravda (1969) 58 min., Agfa-Gevaert col.

Director: Dziga Vertov Group
Production company: CERT
Producer: Claude Nedjar

Vent d'est (1969) 100 min., Eastmancolor

Director: Dziga Vertov Group
Production company: Kunst Films, Poli-Film, Anouchka Films
Producer: Gianni Barcelloni, Ettore Rosboch
Screenplay: Jean-Luc Godard, Daniel Cohn-Bendit, Sergio Bazzini
Photography: Mario Vulpiani
Editing: Christine Aya
Sound: Antonio Ventura, Carlo Diotarelli
Principal actors: Gian Maria Volonte, Anne Wiazemsky, Paolo Pazzesi, Christiana Tullio Altan, Allan Midgette

Lotte in Italia (1969) 76 min., Eastmancolor

Director: Dziga Vertov Group
Production company: Cosmoseion, Anouchka Films
Principal actors: Christiana Tullio Altan, Anne Wiazemsky, Jérôme Hinstin, Paolo Pozzesi

Vladimir et Rosa (1971) 103 min., col.

Director: Dziga Vertov Group
Production company: Munich Tele-Pool, Grove Press
Principal actors: Anne Wiazemsky, Jean-Pierre Gorin, Jean-Luc Godard, Juliet Berto, Ernest Menzer, Yves Afonso, Claude Nedjar

Tout va bien (1972) 95 min., Eastmancolor

95 mins, Eastmancolor
Co-director: Jean-Pierre Gorin
Production company: Anouchka Films, Vicco Films, Empire Film
Producer: J. P. Rassan
Screenplay: Jean-Luc Godard, Jean-Pierre Gorin
Photography: Armand Marco
Editing: Kenout Peltier
Sound: Bernard Orthion, Antoine Bonfanti
Principal actors: Yves Montand. (Jacques), Jane Fonda (Susan), Vittorio Caprioli (the boss), Jean Pipol (CGT delegate), Pierre Oudry (Frédéric), Elisabeth Chauvin (Geneviève), Eric Chartier (Lucien), Yves Gabrielli (Léon)

Letter to Jane (1972) 52 min., b/w and col.

Co-director: Jean-Pierre Gorin
Producer: Jean-Luc Godard, Jean-Pierre Gorin
Screenplay: Jean-Luc Godard, Jean-Pierre Gorin

Ici et ailleurs (1974) 60 min., Eastmancolor

Co-director: Anne-Marie Miéville
Production company: Sonimage, INA
Photography: William Lubtchansky
Editing: Anne-Marie Miéville

Numéro deux (1975) 88 min., Eastmancolor

Production company: Sonimage, Bela, SNC
Producer: Anne-Marie Miéville, Jean-Luc Godard
Screenplay: Jean-Luc Godard, Anne-Marie Miéville
Photography: William Lubtchansky
Sound: Jean-Pierre Ruh
Principal actors: Sandrine Battistella (Sandrine), Pierre Oudry (husband), Alexandre Rignault (grandfather), Rachel Stefanopoli (grandmother)

Comment ça va (1975) 78 min., Eastmancolor

Co-director: Anne-Marie Miéville
Production company: Sonimage, Bela, SNC
Screenplay: Anne-Marie Miéville, Jean-Luc Godard
Photography: William Lubtchansky
Principal actors: M. Marot, Anne-Marie Miéville

Six fois deux (Sur et sous la communication) (1976) Six programmes of 100 min. each, col.

Co-director: Anne-Marie Miéville
Production company: INA, Sonimage
Screenplay: Jean-Luc Godard, Anne-Marie Miéville
Photography: William Lubtchansky

France tour détour deux enfants (1977–78) 12 programmes of 26 min. each, col.

Co-director: Anne-Marie Miéville
Production company: INA, Sonimage
Screenplay: Jean-Luc Godard, Anne-Marie Miéville
Principal actors: Camille Virolleaud, Arnaud Martin, Betty Berr, Albert Dray

Sauve qui peut (la vie) (1979) 87 min., Eastmancolor

Production company: Sara Films, MK2, Saga Production, Sonimage, CNC, ZDF, SSR, Österreichischer Rundfunk-Fernsehen

Producer: Alain Sarde, Jean-Luc Godard
Screenplay: Anne-Marie Miéville, Jean-Claude Carrière, Jean-Luc Godard
Photography: William Lubtchansky, Renato Berta, Jean-Bernard Menoud
Editing: Anne-Marie Miéville, Jean-Luc Godard
Sound: Jacques Maumont, Luc Yersin, Oscar Stellavox
Principal actors: Isabelle Huppert (Isabelle Rivière), Jacques Dutronc (Paul Godard), Nathalie Baye (Denise Rimbaud), Roland Amstutz (client), Anna Baldaccini (Isabelle's sister), Fred Personne (client)

Scénario de Sauve qui peut (la vie) (1979) 20 min., col.

Production company: Sonimage, Télévision Suisse Romande
Screenplay: Jean-Luc Godard

Lettre à Freddy Buache (1981) 11 min., col.

11 mins, colour
Production company: Sonimage, Film et Vidéo Production (Lausanne)
Screenplay: Jean-Luc Godard
Photography: Jean-Bernard Menoud
Editing: Jean-Luc Godard
Sound: François Musy

Passion (1981) 87 min., Eastmancolor

Production company: Sara Films, Sonimage, Films A2, Film et Vidéo Production SA (Lausanne), SSR
Producer: Alain Sarde
Screenplay: Jean-Luc Godard, Anne-Marie Miéville
Photography: Raoul Coutard
Editing: Jean-Luc Godard
Sound: François Musy
Principal actors: Isabelle Huppert (Isabelle), Hanna Schygulla (Hanna), Michel Piccoli (Michel Boulard), Jerzy Radziwilowicz (Jerzy), Laszlo Szabo (the producer)

Scénario du film Passion (1982) 54 min., col.

Production company: JLG Films, Télévision Suisse Romande

Changer d'image (1982) 9 min., col.

Episode in the series *Le Changement a plus d'un titre*
Production company: Sonimage, INA
Principal actors: Jean-Luc Godard

Prénom Carmen (1982) 85 min., Eastmancolor

Production company: Sara Films, Films A2, JLG Films
Producer: Alain Sarde
Screenplay: Anne-Marie Miéville
Photography: Raoul Coutard
Editing: Jean-Luc Godard, Suzanne Lang-Villar
Sound: Frangois Musy
Principal actors: Maruschka Detmers (Carmen), Jacques Bonnaffé (Joseph), Myriem Roussel (Claire), Christophe Odent (the boss), Jean-Luc Godard (uncle Jean), Hyppolite Girardot (Fred)

Je vous salue Marie (1983) 72 min., Eastmancolor

Production company: Pégase Films, SSR, JLG Films, Sara Films, Channel 4, Société Nouvelle des Établissements Gaumont
Screenplay: Jean-Luc Godard
Photography: Jean-Bernard Menoud, Jacques Firmann
Sound: François Musy
Principal actors: Myriem Roussel (Marie), Thierry Rode (Joseph), Philippe Lacoste (the angel Gabriel), Juliette Binoche (Juliette), Johan Meyssen (the professor), Anne Gauthier (Eva)

Petites notes à propos du film Je vous salue Marie (1983) 25 min., col.

Principal actors: Jean-Luc Godard, Myriem Roussel, Thierry Rode, Anne-Marie Miéville

Détective (1984) 95 min., col.

Production company: Sara Films, JLG Films
Producer: Alain Sarde
Screenplay: Alain Sarde, Philippe Setbon, Anne-Marie Miéville, Jean-Luc Godard
Photography: Bruno Nuytten
Editing: Marilyn Dubreuil
Sound: Pierre Garnet, François Musy
Principal actors: Nathalie Baye (Françoise Chenal), Claude Brasseur (Émile Chenal), Johnny Hallyday (Jimmy Fox Warner), Stéphane Ferrara (Tiger Jones), Eugène Berthier (Eugène), Emmanuelle Seigner (Grace Kelly), Laurent Terzieff (William Prospero), Jean-Pierre Léaud (inspector), Alain Cuny (mafioso)

Soft and Hard (A soft conversation between two friends on a hard subject) (1985) 52 min., col.

52 mins, colour
Co-director: Anne-Marie Miéville
Production company: Channel 4, JLG Films
Principal actors: Jean-Luc Godard, Anne-Marie Miéville

Grandeur et décadence d'un petit commerce de cinéma (1986) 52 min., col.

Production company: TF1, Hamster Productions, Télévision Suisse Romande, JLG Films, RTL
Producer: Pierre Grimblat
Screenplay: Jean-Luc Godard
Photography: Caroline Champetier
Editing: Jean-Luc Godard
Sound: François Musy
Principal actors: Jean-Pierre Mocky (Jean Almereyda, dit Jean Vigo), Marie Valéra (Eurydice), Jean-Pierre Léaud (Gaspard Bazin)

Meetin' W. A. (1986) 26 min., col.

Production company: JLG Films
Screenplay: Jean-Luc Godard
Editing: Jean-Luc Godard
Sound: François Musy
Principal actors: Woody Allen, Jean-Luc Godard

Armide (1987) 12 min., col.

Episode of the film *Aria*
Production company: Boyd's Company, RDP Productions, Virgin Vision, Lightyear Entertainment
Producer: Don Boyd
Screenplay: Jean-Luc Godard
Photography: Caroline Champetier
Editing: Jean-Luc Godard
Sound: François Musy
Principal actors: Marion Peterson, Vaérie Alain, Jacques Neuville, Luke Corre, Christian Cauchon, Philippe Pellant, Patrice Linguet, Lionel Sorin, Jean Coffinet, Alexandre des Granges, Gérard Vives, Frédéric Brosse, Pascal Bermot, Jean-Luc Corre, Bernard Gaudray, Dominique Mano, Patrice Tridian

Soigne ta droite (1987) 82 min., Eastmancolor

Production company: Gaumont Productions, JLG Films, Xanadu Films, RTSR
Screenplay: Jean-Luc Godard
Photography: Caroline Champetier, Jacques Loiseleux
Editing: Jean-Luc Godard
Sound: François Musy
Principal actors: Jean-Luc Godard (the Idiot, the Prince), Jacques Villeret (the individual), François Périer (the man), Jane Birkin ('La cigale'), Michel Galabru (the admiral), Dominique Lavanant (the admiral's wife), les Rita Mitsouko

King Lear (1987) 90 min., col.

Production company: Cannon Films International
Producer: Menahem Golan, Yoram Globus
Screenplay: Jean-Luc Godard, Peter Sellars
Photography: Sophie Maintigneux
Editing: Jean-Luc Godard
Sound: François Musy
Principal actors: Burgess Meredith (King Lear), Peter Sellars (William Shakespeare V), Molly Ringwald (Cordelia), Jean-Luc Godard (Professor Pluggy), Woody Allen (Mr Alien), Norman Mailer (himself), Kate Mailer (herself), Leos Carax (Edgar), Julie Delpy (Virginia)

Girbaud advertisements (1988) 10 advertisements of around 15–20 secs each, col.

Producer: Marithé and François Girbaud
Screenplay: Jean-Luc Godard
Photography: Caroline Champetier
Editing: Jean-Luc Godard
Sound: François Musy

On s'est tous défilé (1988) 13 min., col.

Producer: Marithé and François Girbaud
Screenplay: Jean-Luc Godard
Photography: Caroline Champetier
Editing: Jean-Luc Godard
Sound: François Musy

Puissance de la parole (1988) 25 min., col.

Production company: France Télécom, JLG Films, Gaumont
Screenplay: Jean- Luc Godard
Photography: Caroline Champetier, Pierre Binggeli
Editing: Jean-Luc Godard
Sound: François Musy
Principal actors: Jean Bouise (Mr Agathos), Laurence Côte (Mlle Oïnos), Lydia Andréi (Velma), Jean-Michel Iribarren (Franck)

Le Dernier Mot (1988) 13 min., col.

Episode in the series *Les Français vus par...*
Production company: Erato Films
Screenplay: Jean-Luc Godard
Photography: Pierre Binggeli
Editing: Jean-Luc Godard
Sound: Pierre Camus
Principal actors: André Marcon, Hanns Zischler, Catherine Aymerie, Pierre Amoyal, Michel Radio, Luc Briffoch, Laurent Rohrbach, Gilles Laeser, Laurence Nanzer, Damien Nanzer

Le Rapport Darty (1989) 50 min., col.

Co-director: Anne-Marie Miéville
Production company: Gaumont, JLG Films
Screenplay: Jean-Luc Godard, Anne-Marie Miéville
Photography: Hervé Duhamel
Sound: François Musy
Cast: Anne-Marie Miéville, Jean-Luc Godard

Nouvelle Vague (1990) 89 min., col.

Production company: Sara Films, Peripheria, Canal Plus, Vega Film, Télévision Romande, Films A2, CNC, SOFICA Investimage, SOFICA Créations
Producer: Alain Sarde
Screenplay: Jean-Luc Godard
Photography: William Lubtchansky
Editing: Jean-Luc Godard
Sound: Henri Morelle, François Musy
Principal actors: Alain Delon (Roger/Richard Lennox), Domiziana Giordano (Elena Torlato-Favrini), Roland Amstutz (gardener), Laurence Côte (governess), Jacques Dacqmine (C.E.O.), Christophe Odent (lawyer), Laurence Guerre (secretary), Joseph Lisbona (doctor), Laure Killing (doctor's wife), Cécile Reigher (waitress)

L'Enfance de l'art (1990) 8 min., col.

Episode of the film *Comment vont les enfants*
Co-director: Anne-Marie Miéville
Production company: UNICEF
Screenplay: Jean-Luc Godard, Anne-Marie Miéville
Photography: Sophie Maintigneux
Editing: Jean-Luc Godard
Sound: Pierre-Alain Besse
Principal actors: Antoine Reyes, Nathalie Kadem

Pour Thomas Wainggai (1991) 3 min., col.

Episode in the television programme *Contre l'oubli*
Co-director: Anne-Marie Miéville
Production company: Amnesty International
Screenplay: Jean-Luc Godard, Anne-Marie Miéville
Photography: Jean-Marc Fabre
Editing: Jean-Luc Godard
Principal actors: André Rousselet

Allemagne neuf zéro (1991) 62 min., col.

Production company: Antenne 2, Brainstorm Productions
Producer: Nicole Ruelle
Screenplay: Jean-Luc Godard
Photography: Christophe Pollock
Editing: Jean-Luc Godard
Sound: Pierre-Alain Besse
Principal actors: Eddie Constantine (Lemmy Caution), Hanns Zischler (Comte Zelten), Claudia Michelson (Charlotte/Dora), André S. Labarthe (narrator), Nathalie Kadern (Delphine de Staël), Robert Wittmers (Don Quixote), Kim Kashkashian (violinist)

Les Enfants jouent à la Russie (1993) 60 min., col.

Production company: Worldvision, Cecco Films, RTR
Producer: Alessandro Cecconi, Ira Barmak, Ruth Waldburger
Screenplay: Jean-Luc Godard
Photography: Caroline Champetier
Editing: Jean-Luc Godard
Sound: Stéphane Thiébaud
Principal actors: Laszlo Szabo (Jack Valenti), Jean-Luc Godard (the Idiot, Prince Mychkine), Bernard Eisenschitz (Harry Blount), André S. Labarthe (Alcide Jolivet)

Hélas pour moi (1993) 84 min., col.

Production company: Les Films Alain Sarde, Vega Films, Peripheria, Télévision Suisse Romande, Département Fédéral de l'Intérieur, Cofimage 4, Investimage 4
Producer: Ruth Waldburger
Screenplay: Jean-Luc Godard
Photography: Caroline Champetier
Editing: Jean-Luc Godard
Sound: Frangois Musy
Principal actors: Gérard Depardieu (Simon Donnadieu), Laurence Masliah (Rachel Donnadieu), Bernard Verney (Abraham Klimt), Jean-Louis Loca (Max Mercure), François Germond (the pastor), Anny Romand (Aude), Marc Betton (doctor)

Je vous salue Sarajevo (1994)

JLG/JLG: Autoportrait de décembre (1994) 62 min., col.

Production company: Peripheria, Gaumont
Screenplay: Jean-Luc Godard
Photography: Yves Pouliguen
Editing: Jean-Luc Godard
Sound: Pierre-Alain Besse
Principal actors: Jean-Luc Godard, Geneviève Pasquier, Denis Jadot, Brigitte Bastien, Elizabeth Kaza, André S. Labarthe, Louis Séguin, Bernard Eisenschitz, Nathalie Aguillar

2 x 50 ans de cinéma français (1995) 50 min., col.

Co-director: Anne-Marie Miéville
Production company: British Film Institute, Peripheria
Screenplay: Jean-Luc Godard, Anne-Marie Miéville
Photography: Isabelle Czajka
Editing: Jean-Luc Godard
Sound: Stéphane Thiébaud
Principal actors: Jean-Luc Godard, Michel Piccoli, Cécile Reigher, Estelle Grynspan, Dominique Jacquet, Patrick Gillieron, Xavier Jougleux, Fabrice Dierx-Bemard

For Ever Mozart (1996) 84 min., col.

Production company: Avventura Films, Peripheria, CEC Rhône Alpes, France 2 Cinéma, Canal Plus, CNC, Vega Film, TSR, Eurimages, DFI, ECM Records
Producer: Alain Sarde

Screenplay: Jean-Luc Godard
Photography: Christophe Pollock
Editing: Jean-Luc Godard
Sound: François Musy
Principal actors: Madeleine Assas (Camille), Ghalya Lacroix (Rosette), Bérangère Allaux (actress), Vicky Messica (director), Frédéric Pierrot (Jérôme), Michel Francini (Baron), Euryale Wynter (Mozart)

Histoire(s) du cinéma (1988–98) 8 episodes of varying lengths, total time 265 min., b/w and col.

Production company: Gaumont, CNC, Fémis, Peripheria, la Sept, FR3, JLG Films, RTSR, Vega Films
Screenplay: Jean-Luc Godard
Editing: Jean-Luc Godard
Principal actors: Alain Cuny, Juliette Binoche, Sabine Azéma, Serge Daney, Julie Delpy, Jean-Luc Godard

The Old Place (1998) 50 min., col.

Co-director: Anne-Marie Miéville
Production company: Museum of Modem Art, New York
Screenplay: Jean-Luc Godard, Anne-Marie Miéville
Editing: Jean-Luc Godard

De l'origine du XXIe siècle (2000) 15 min., col.

Production company: Canal Plus, Vega Films
Screenplay: Jean-Luc Godard
Editing: Jean-Luc Godard
Sound: François Musy

Éloge de l'amour (2001) 98 min., b/w and col.

Production company: Avventura Films, Peripheria, Canal Plus, France Arte Cinéma, Vega Films, TSR, Studio Image 6
Screenplay: Jean-Luc Godard
Photography: Christophe Pollock, Julien Hirsch
Editing: Raphaële Urtin
Principal actors: Bruno Putzulu (Edgar), Cécile Camp (Berthe), Claude Baignères (Mr Rosenthal), Remo Forlani (Mayor Forlani), Philippe Loyrette (Philippe), Audrey Klebaner (Églantine), Mark Hunter (himself), Jérémy Lippmann (Perceval), Bruno Mesrine (magician), Jean Davy (grandfather), Françoise Verny (grandmother), William Doherty (US official), Jean Lacouture (himself)

Dans le noir du temps (2002) Episode of the film *Ten Minutes Older: The Cello*

Producer: Ulrich Felsberg, Nicolas McClintock, Nigel Thomas
Screenplay: Anne-Marie Miéville
Photography: Julien Hirsch
Sound: François Musy

Liberté et patrie (2002) 16 mins, b/w and col.

Co-director: Anne-Marie Miéville

Select bibliography

The available literature on Godard is simply vast and readers seeking references on particular films are encouraged to consult the relevant chapters of this book. This (extremely) select bibliography lists only the most useful of the many general books on Godard.

Books by Godard

Jean-Luc Godard par Jean-Luc Godard, 2 vols, ed. by Alain Bergala, Paris, Cahiers du cinéma, 1998. This invaluable and beautifully illustrated source book contains all of Godard's film criticism and numerous interviews and texts related to his films. It also includes a complete filmography and a useful index of proper names and film titles, handy for tracing some of Godard's cultural references.

Books on Godard

Bellour, Raymond and Bandy, Mary Lea (eds), *Jean-Luc Godard: Son + Image 1974–1991*, New York, Museum of Modern Art, 1992. A large and generally very useful collection of articles, although some texts are rather awkwardly translated from the French. The book gathers together a number of key texts by feminist critics (Bergstrom, Lyon, Mulvey, Penley) that are available elsewhere.

Bergala, Alain, *Nul mieux que Godard*, Paris, Cahiers du cinéma, 1999. A collection of reviews and articles covering Godard's work from the late 1970s to the late 199s. Beautifully written and full of breathtaking insights, this is by some distance the finest work available on Godard's cinema of the 1980s.

MacCabe, Colin, *Godard: Images, Sounds, Politics*, London, Macmillan,

1980. The dialectical–materialist rhetoric is beginning to look a little dated, but this remains a good introduction to Godard's political work of the late 1960s and early 1970s.

MacCabe, Colin, *Godard: A Portrait of the Artist at 70*, London, Bloomsbury, 2003. A long-overdue biography of the director, MacCabe's book does an excellent job of contextualising Godard's life and work, although, for anyone who has followed Godard's career with interest, the amount of new information presented here proves rather disappointing.

Silverman, Kaja and Farocki, Harun, *Speaking about Godard*, New York, New York University Press, 1998. The format of this study – a dialogue between film theorist Silverman and film maker Farocki – takes a little getting used to, but the book seems to improve with age. Relatively few films are discussed (eight), but the quality of analysis is consistently high and Farocki's filmmaker's eye offers a refreshingly new perspective on Godard's work.

Sterritt, David, *The Films of Jean-Luc Godard: Seeing the Invisible*, Cambridge, Cambridge University Press, 1999. A well-written, if rather pedestrian, plod through the usual suspects (*À bout de souffle*, *Vivre sa vie*, *Week-end*, *Numéro deux*, *Je vous salue Marie* and *Nouvelle Vague*), Sterritt's book is nonetheless a useful general introduction to Godard's cinema.

Temple, Michael and Williams, James S. (eds), *The Cinema Alone: Essays on the Work of Jean-Luc Godard 1985–2000*, Amsterdam, Amsterdam University Press, 2000. An important work in shifting the focus of Godard studies towards the later films – six of the ten chapters included here are devoted to *Histoire(s) du cinéma*. Quality is inevitably varied, with a number of contributors rather beholden to theoretical jargon, but the essays by Temple, Williams and Witt are particularly fine.

Index

Note: 'n.' after a page reference indicates the number of a note on that page.